All that glitters...

Even the stars

All things precious...

Even your life

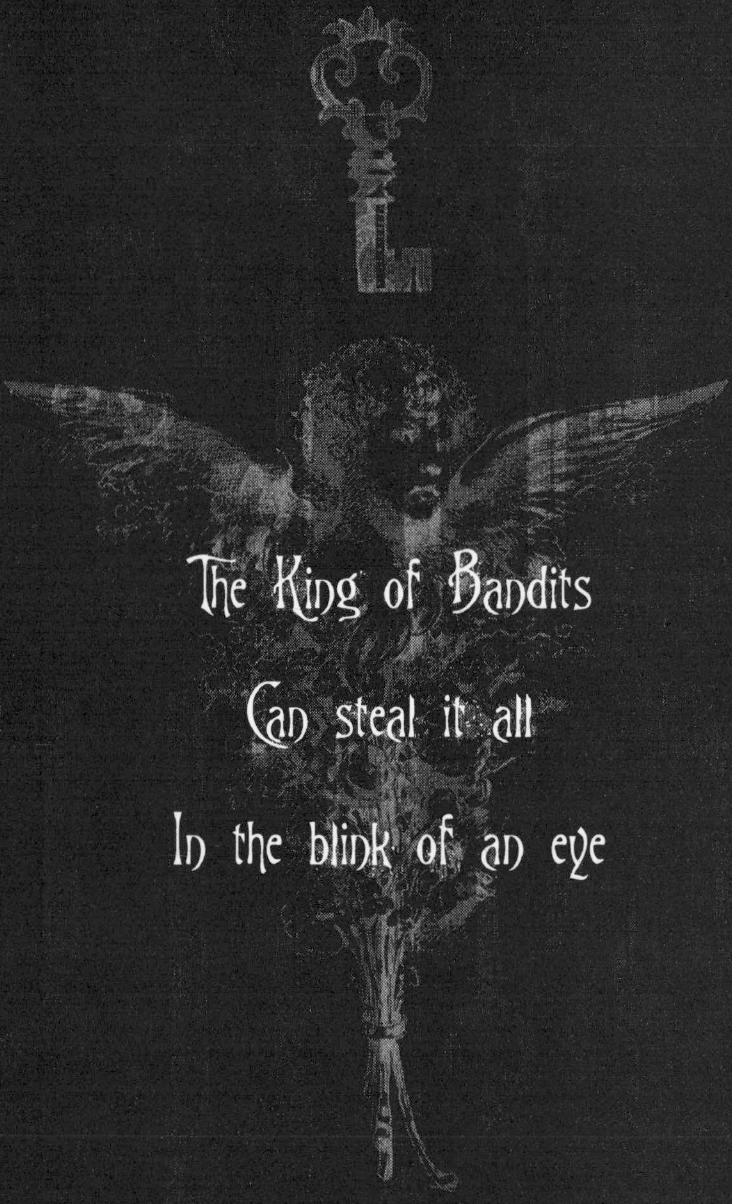
The King of Bandits
Can steal it all
In the blink of an eye

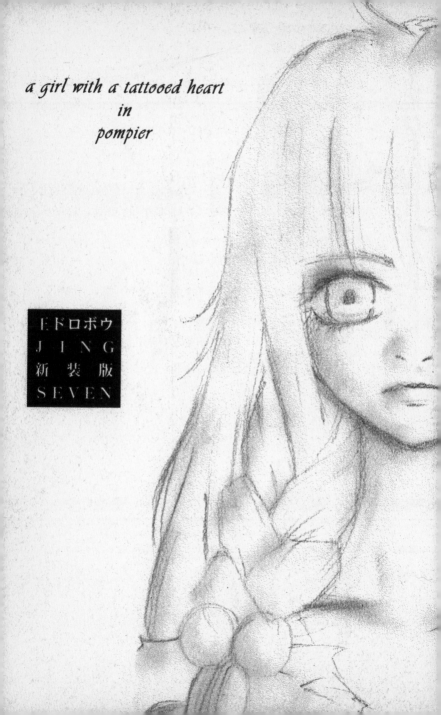

a girl with a tattooed heart
in
pompier

王ドロボウ
J I N G
新 装 版
S E V E N

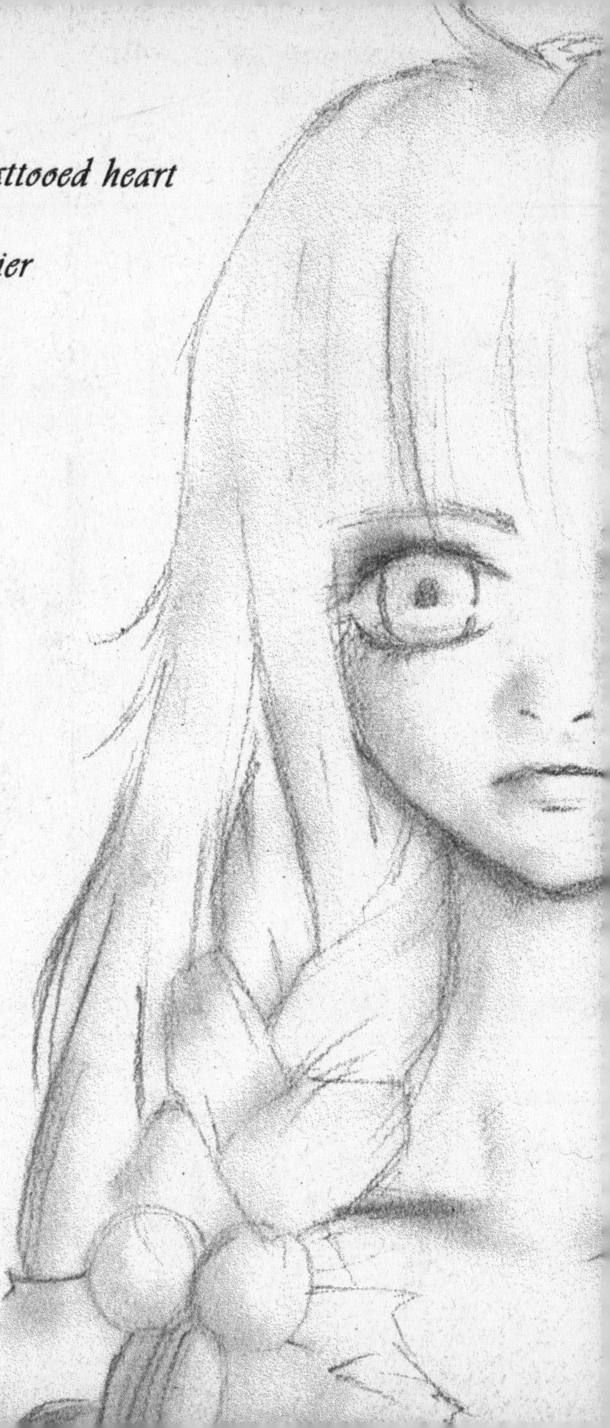

Translator - Kong Chang
English Adaptation - Carol Fox
Copy Editors - Troy Lewter and Alexis Kirsch
Retouch and Lettering - Vicente Rivera, Jr
Cover Layout - Gary Shum
Graphic Designer - James Dashiell

Editor - Paul Morrissey
Digital Imaging Manager - Chris Buford
Pre-Press Manager - Antonio DePietro
Production Managers - Jennifer Miller and Mutsumi Miyazaki
Art Director - Matt Alford
Managing Editor - Jill Freshney
VP of Production - Ron Klamert
President & C.O.O. - John Parker
Publisher & C.E.O. - Stuart Levy

E-mail: info@TOKYOPOP.com
Come visit us online at www.TOKYOPOP.com

A  Manga

TOKYOPOP Inc.
5900 Wilshire Blvd. Suite 2000
Los Angeles, CA 90036

Jing: King of Bandits Vol. 7

ISBN: 1-59182-468-0

First TOKYOPOP printing: July 2004

10 9 8 7 6 5 4 3 2 1

Printed in the USA

KING OF BANDITS

王ドロボウ JING

VOLUME 7 OF 7

STORY AND ART BY
YUICHI KUMAKURA

Los Angeles • Tokyo • London • Hamburg

Once upon a midnight dreary, a thief named Jing was weak and weary,
Many strange and forgotten lands he did traverse and explore.
His companion was a bird named Kir, his black wings a-flapping,
While Jing nodded, nearly napping, Kir saw booty galore.
"Wake up, Jing," Kir muttered, "all around us is loot galore."
Treasure from ceiling to floor!

Thus, this ebony bird's wiling, sent Jing's sad face into smiling,
For Jing could steal the stars from the sky, thievery he truly did adore.
The albatross sat proudly on Jing's placid bust, his beady eyes did implore,
One more thing Kir did utter, his feathers all a greedy flutter, his voice a roar,
Quoth the albatross, "Let's steal some more!"

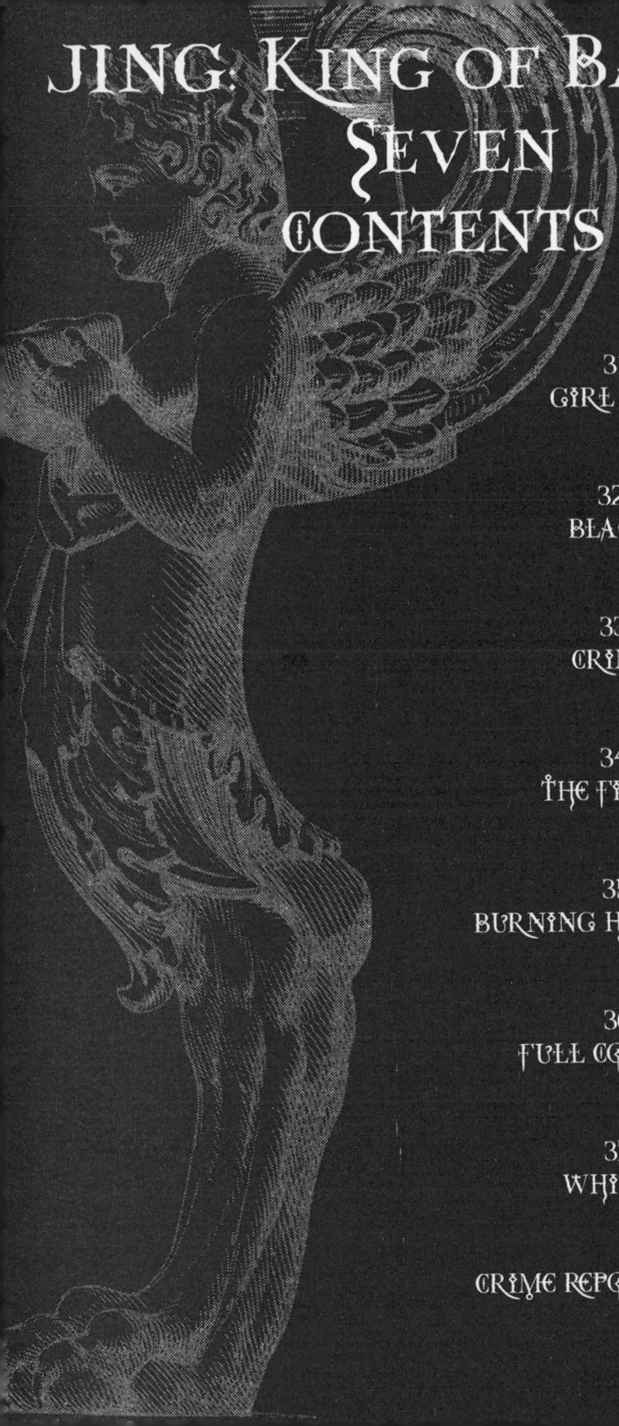

JING: KING OF BANDITS
SEVEN
CONTENTS

merry X'mas !!

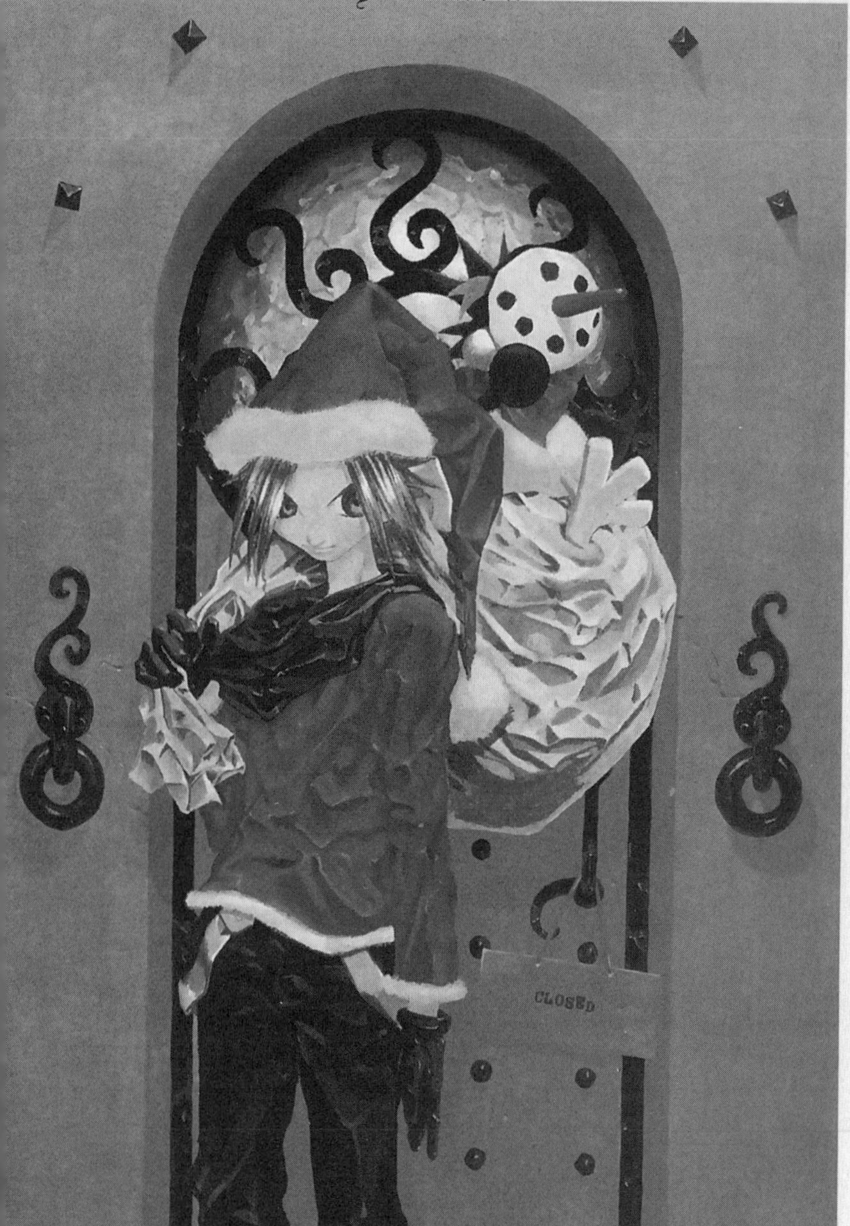
CLOSED

let's have a break !!

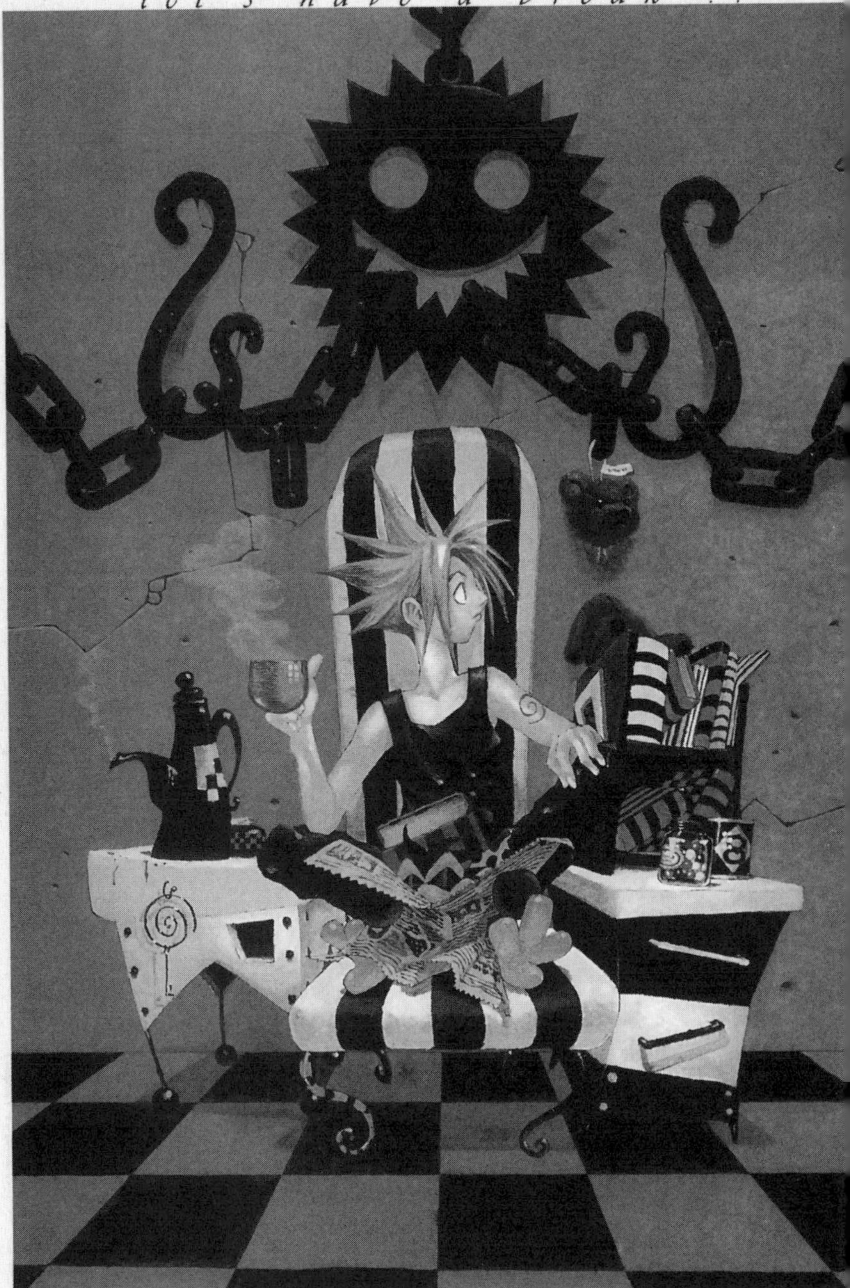

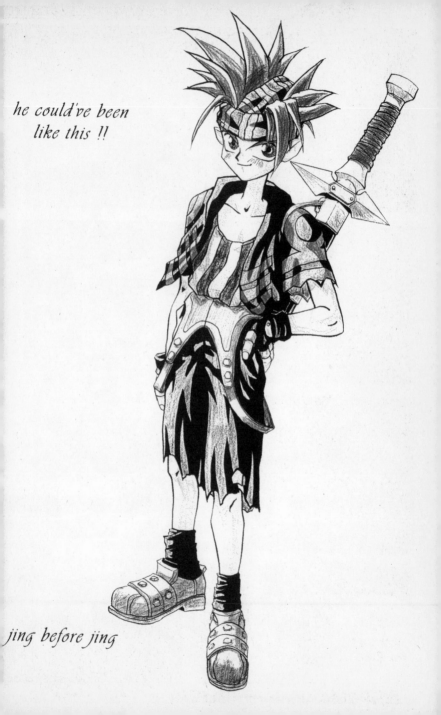

he could've been
like this !!

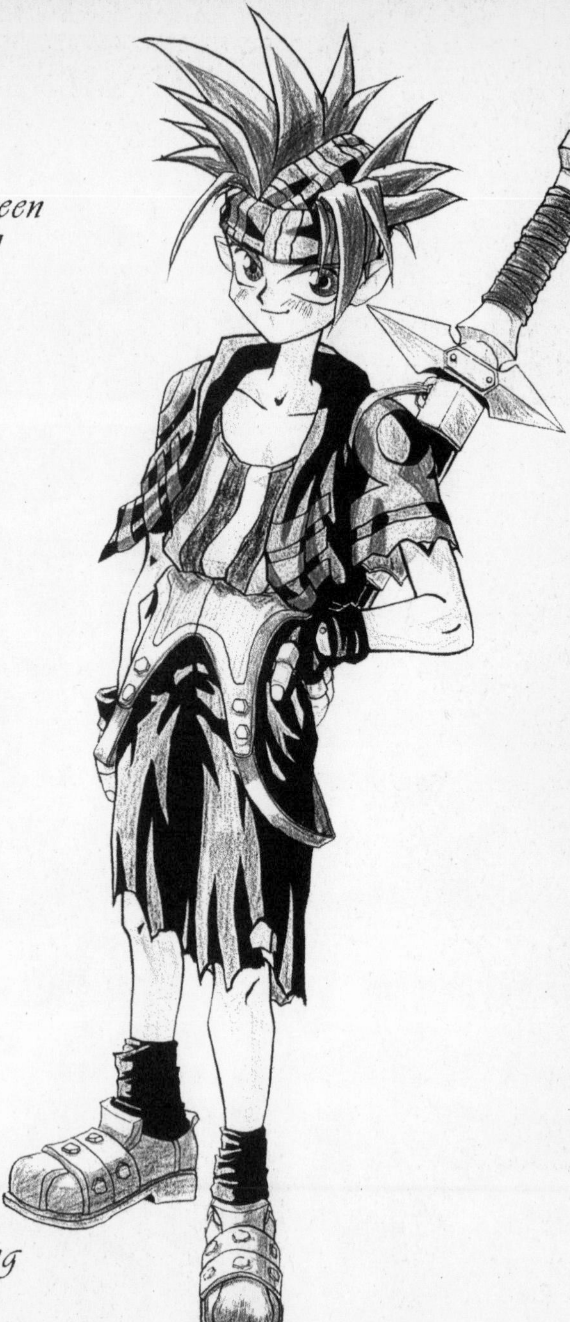

jing before jing

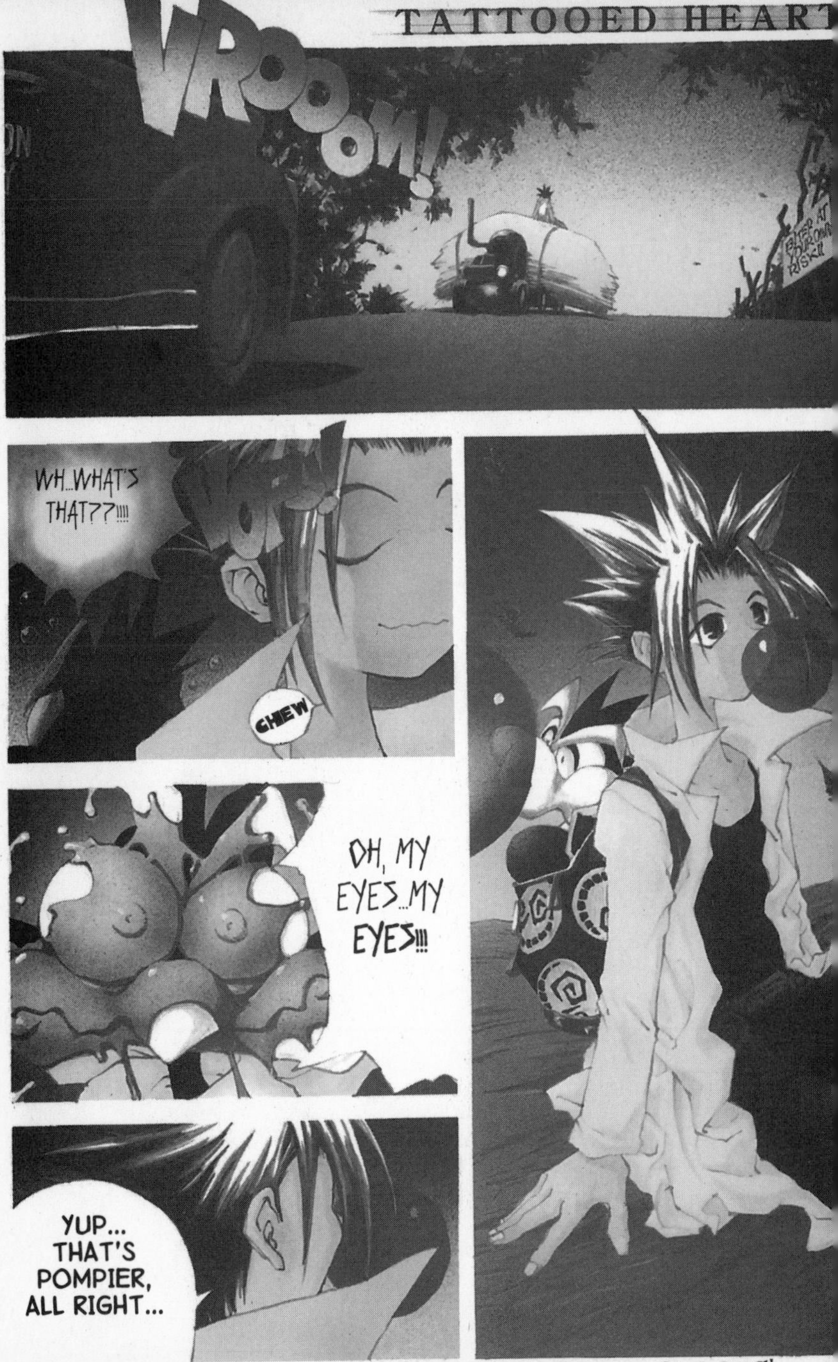
VROOOOM!!
ENTER AT YOUR OWN RISK!!
WH...WHAT'S THAT??!!!!
CHEW
OH, MY EYES...MY EYES!!!
YUP... THAT'S POMPIER, ALL RIGHT...

色彩都市の少女編

THE GIRL OF COLOR TOWN

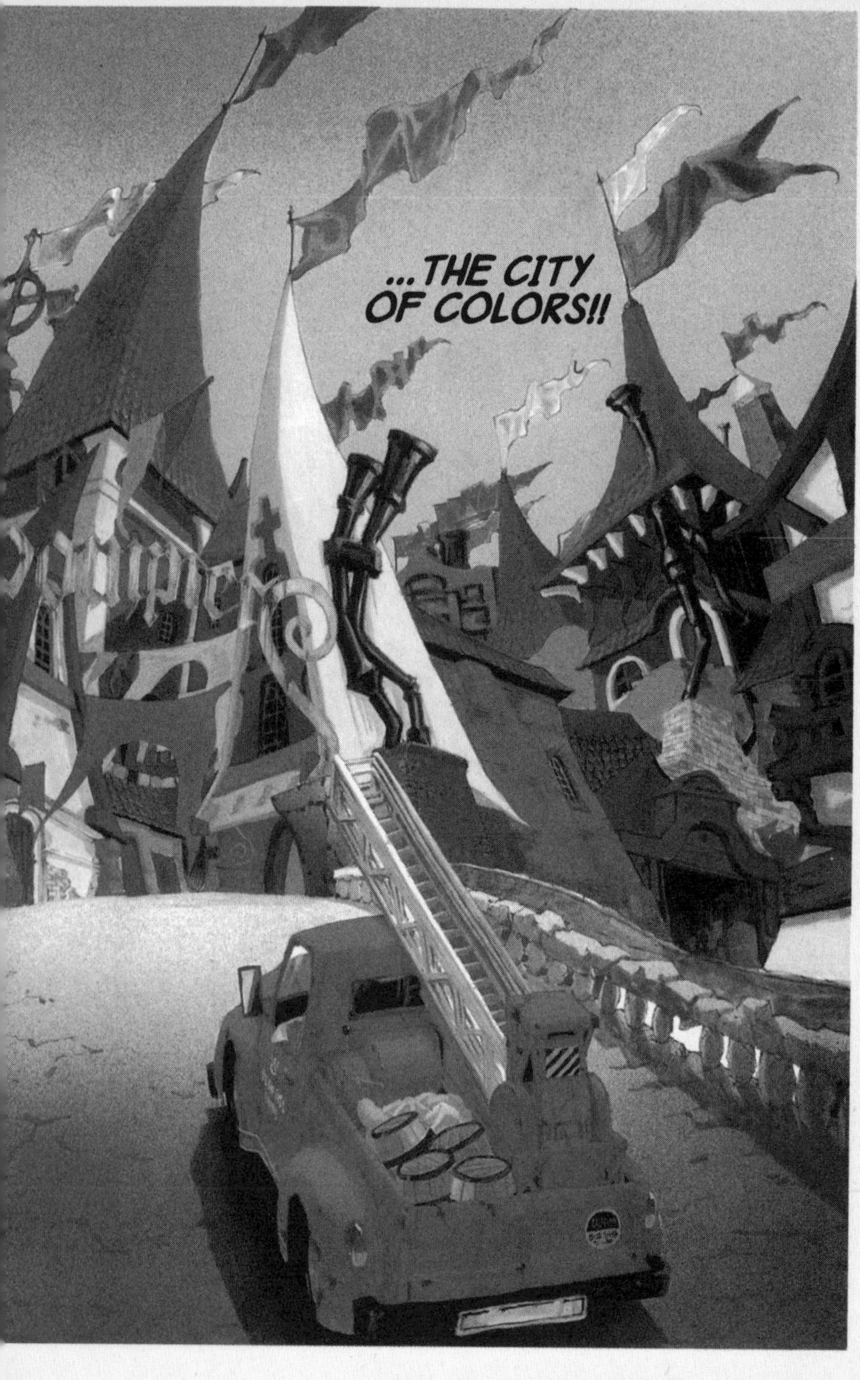
...THE CITY OF COLORS!!

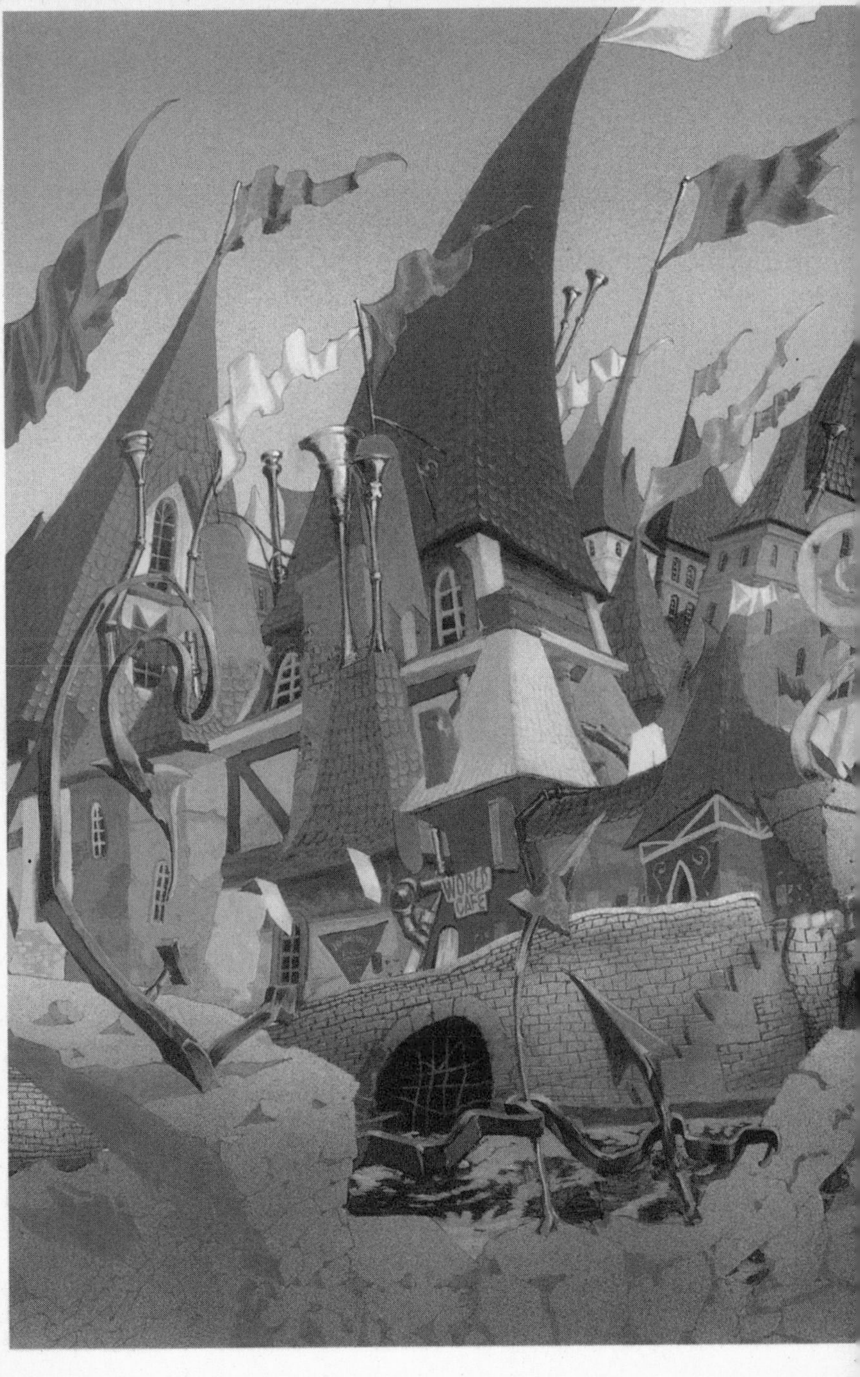
WORLD
CAFE

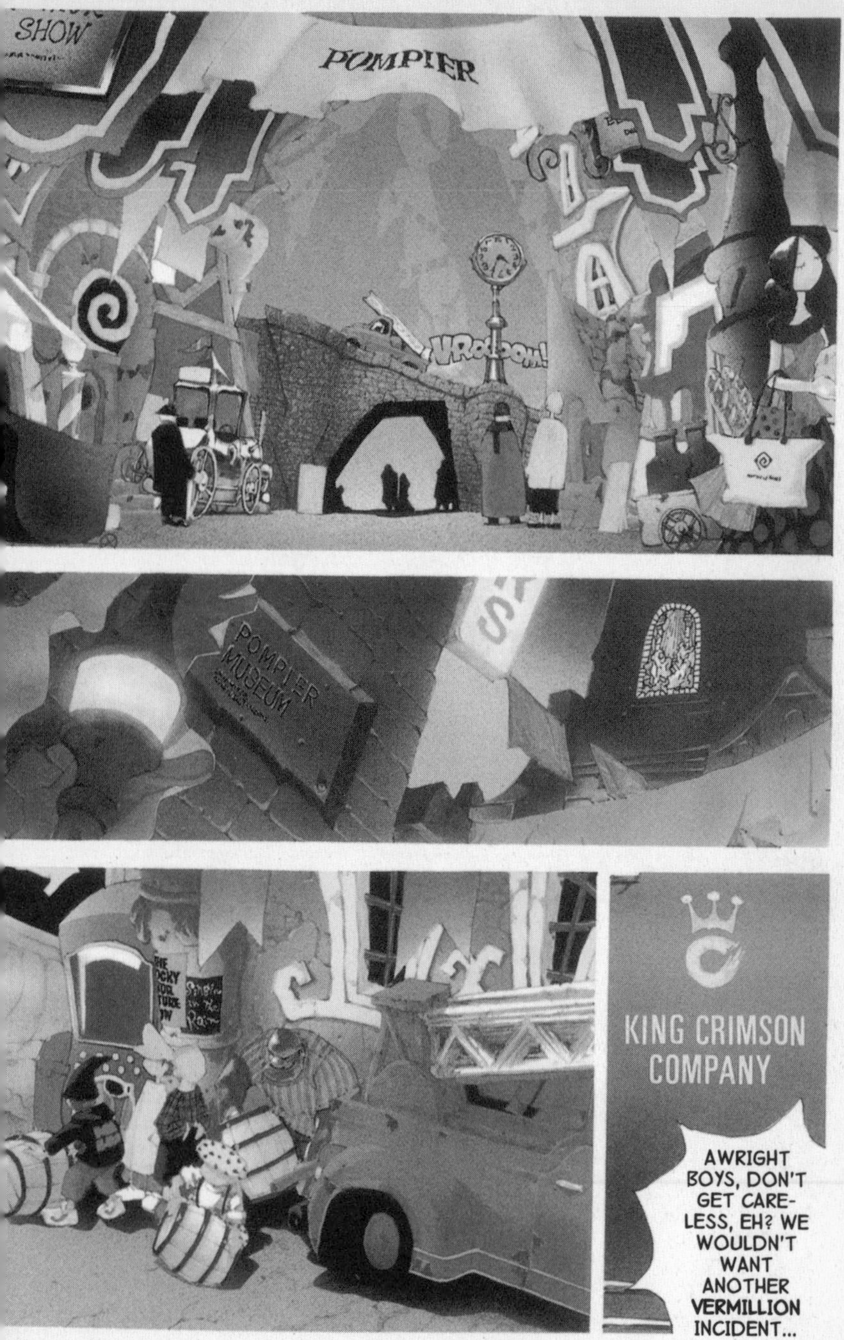
SHOW
POMPIER
VROOOOM!
POMPIER MUSEUM
KING CRIMSON COMPANY
AWRIGHT BOYS, DON'T GET CARE-LESS, EH? WE WOULDN'T WANT ANOTHER VERMILLION INCIDENT...

TIME ENOUGH FOR RESTIN' AFTER WE FINISH.

BAR

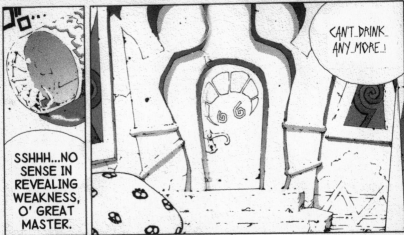

CAN'T...DRINK... ANY...MORE...♪

SSHHH...NO SENSE IN REVEALING WEAKNESS, O' GREAT MASTER.

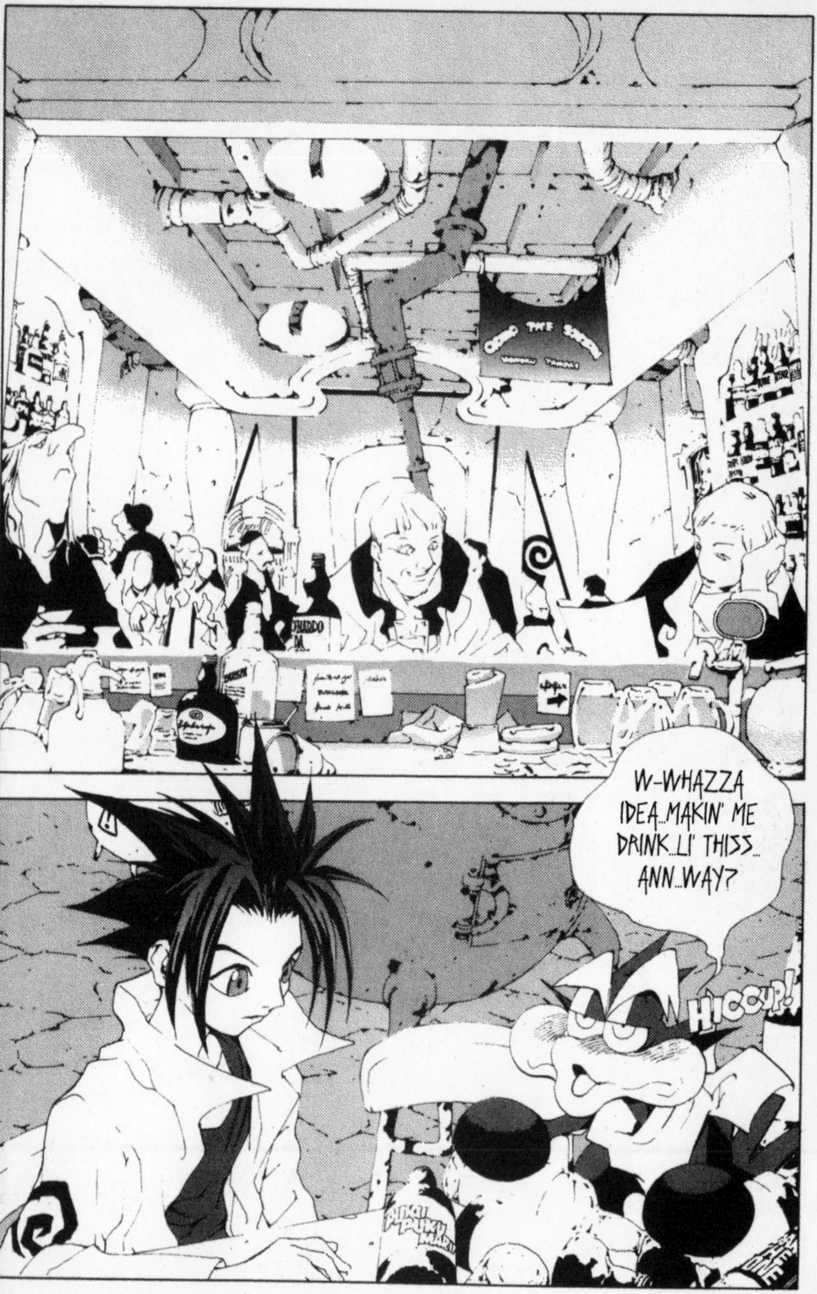
W-WHAZZA IDEA...MAKIN' ME DRINK...LI' THISS... ANN...WAY?
HICCUP!

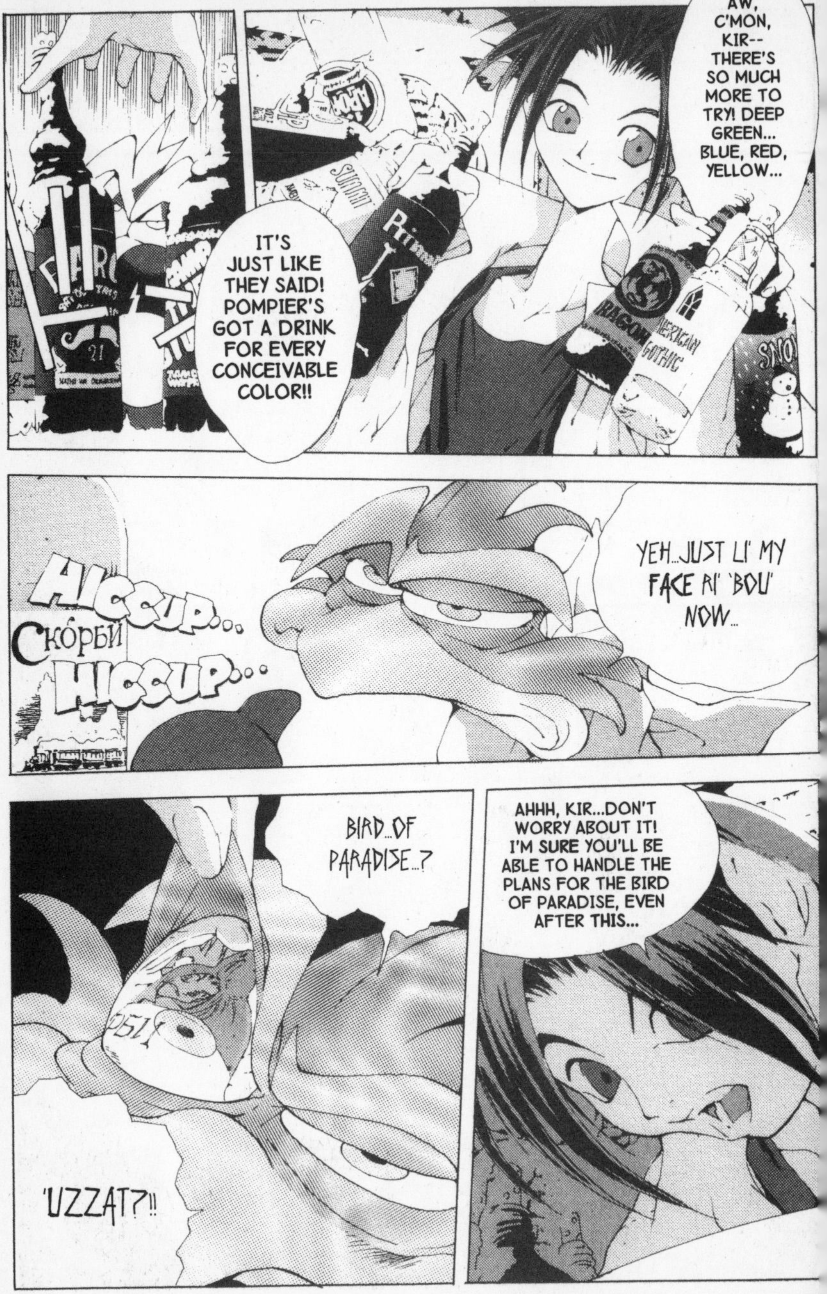
AW, C'MON, KIR-- THERE'S SO MUCH MORE TO TRY! DEEP GREEN... BLUE, RED, YELLOW...
IT'S JUST LIKE THEY SAID! POMPIER'S GOT A DRINK FOR EVERY CONCEIVABLE COLOR!!
YEH...JUST LI' MY FACE RI' 'BOU' NOW...
HICCUP...
Скорби
HICCUP...
AHHH, KIR...DON'T WORRY ABOUT IT! I'M SURE YOU'LL BE ABLE TO HANDLE THE PLANS FOR THE BIRD OF PARADISE, EVEN AFTER THIS...
BIRD...OF PARADISE...?
'UZZAT?!!

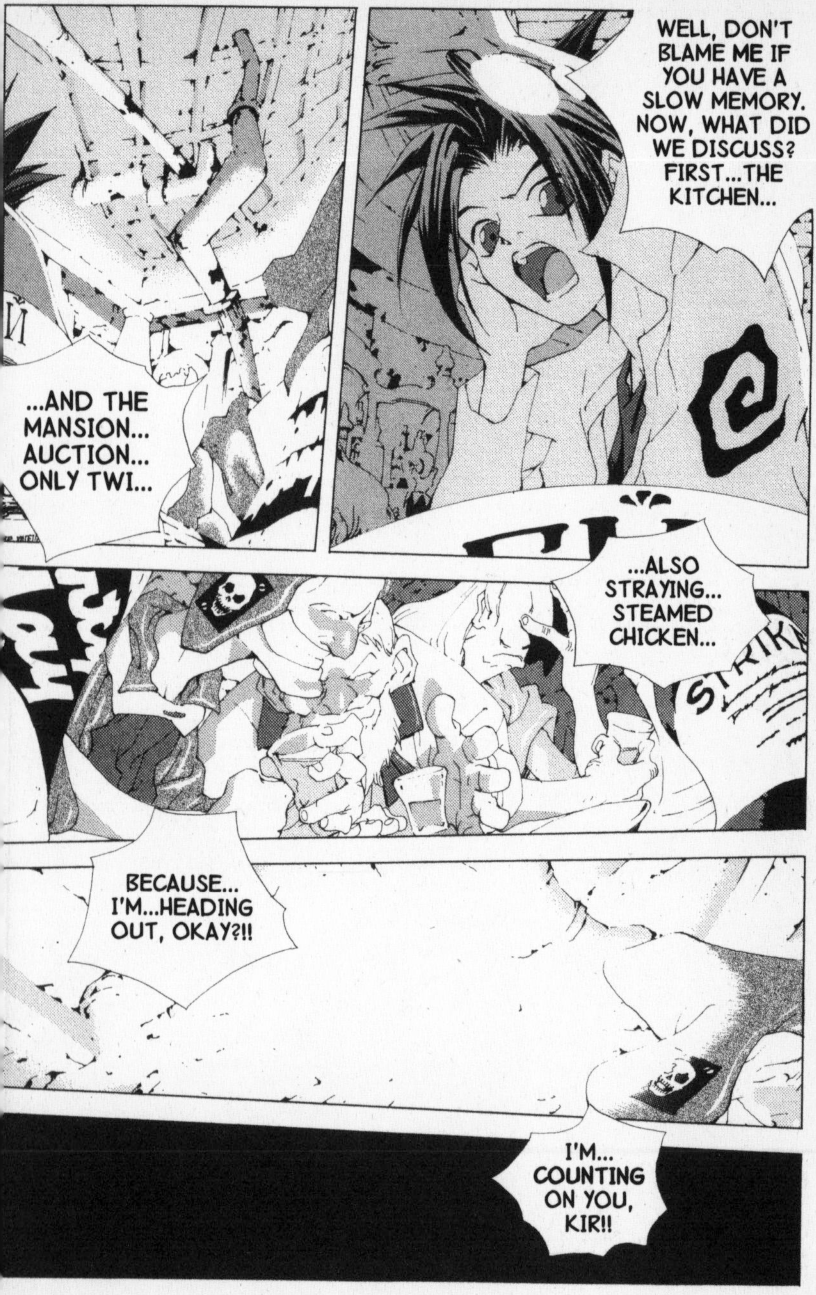
WELL, DON'T BLAME ME IF YOU HAVE A SLOW MEMORY. NOW, WHAT DID WE DISCUSS? FIRST...THE KITCHEN...
...AND THE MANSION... AUCTION... ONLY TWI...
...ALSO STRAYING... STEAMED CHICKEN...
BECAUSE... I'M...HEADING OUT, OKAY?!!
I'M... COUNTING ON YOU, KIR!!

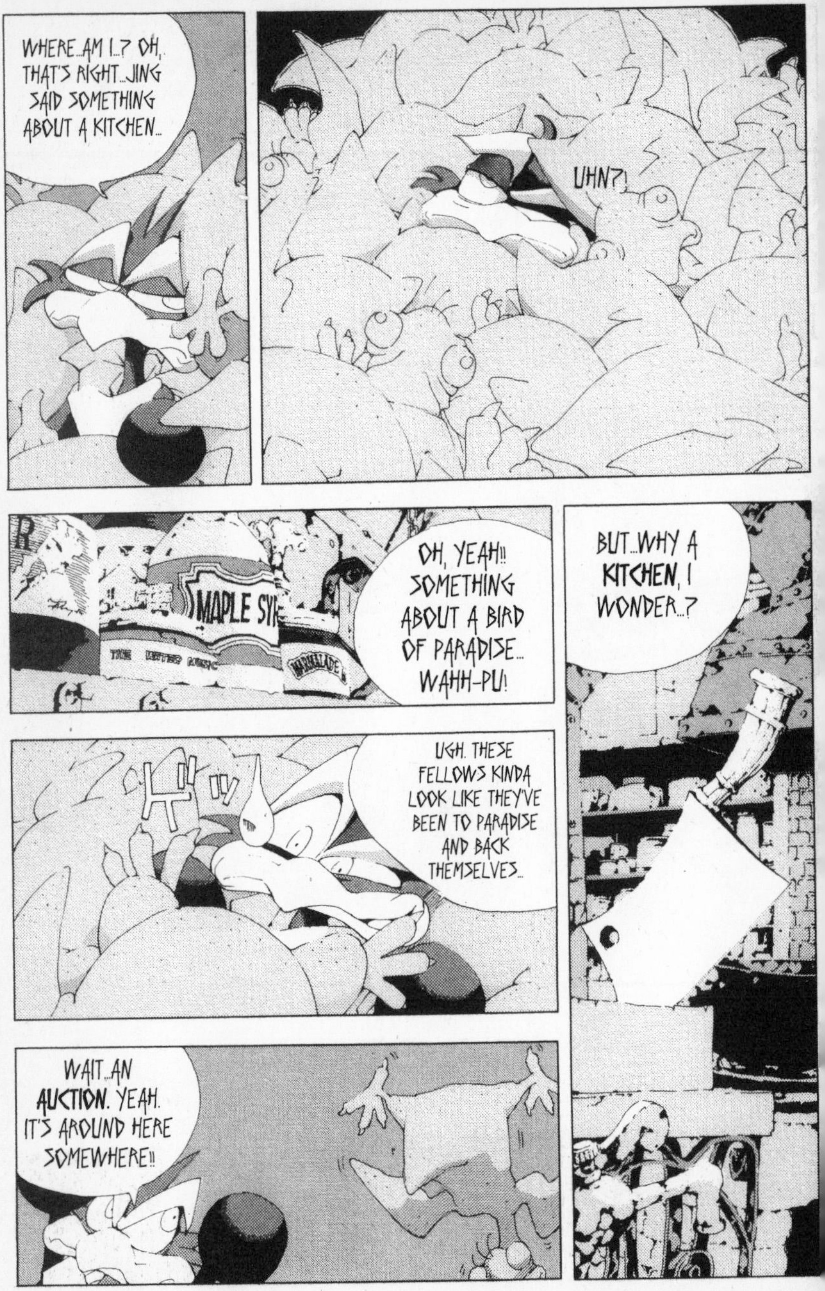
UHN?!
WHERE...AM I...? OH, THAT'S RIGHT...JING SAID SOMETHING ABOUT A KITCHEN...
BUT...WHY A **KITCHEN**, I WONDER...?
MAPLE SYR
OH, YEAH!! SOMETHING ABOUT A BIRD OF PARADISE... WAHH-PU!
UGH. THESE FELLOWS KINDA LOOK LIKE THEY'VE BEEN TO PARADISE AND BACK THEMSELVES...
WAIT...AN **AUCTION**. YEAH. IT'S AROUND HERE SOMEWHERE!!

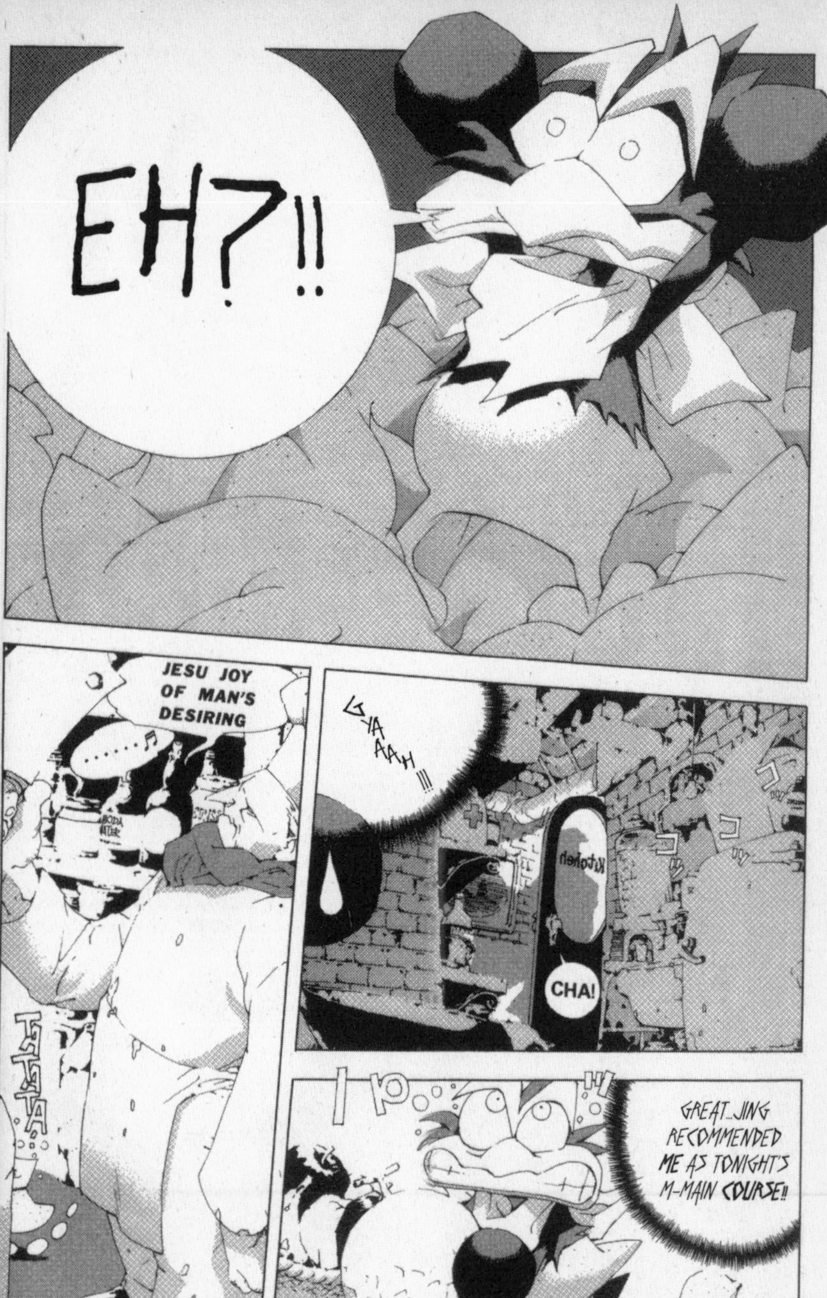
EH?!!
GYAAAH!!!
CHA!
GREAT...JING RECOMMENDED ME AS TONIGHT'S M-MAIN COURSE!!
JESU JOY OF MAN'S DESIRING
......♪
TATATA

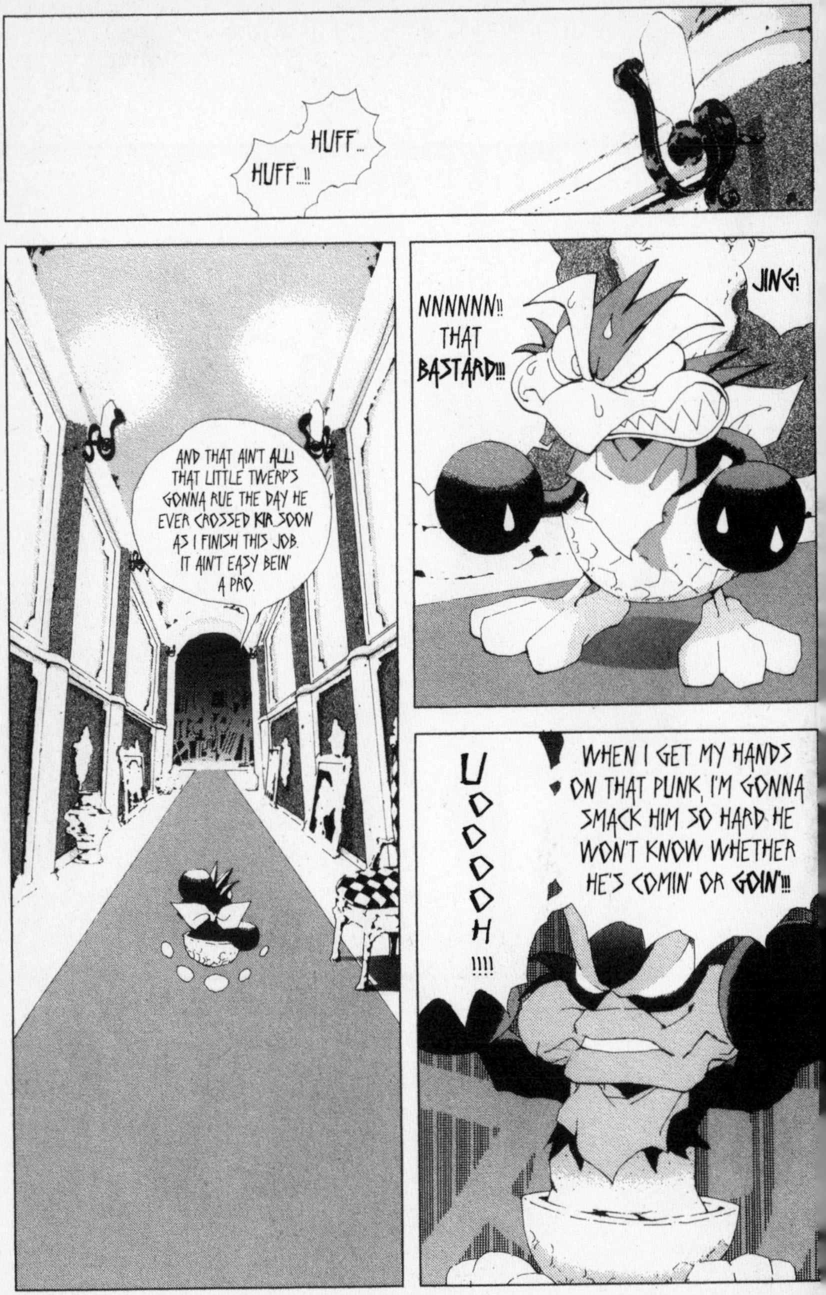
HUFF...
HUFF...!!
JING!
NNNNNN!! THAT BASTARD!!!
WHEN I GET MY HANDS ON THAT PUNK, I'M GONNA SMACK HIM SO HARD HE WON'T KNOW WHETHER HE'S COMIN' OR GOIN'!!!
UOOOOOH !!!!
AND THAT AIN'T ALL! THAT LITTLE TWERP'S GONNA RUE THE DAY HE EVER CROSSED KIR SOON AS I FINISH THIS JOB. IT AIN'T EASY BEIN' A PRO.

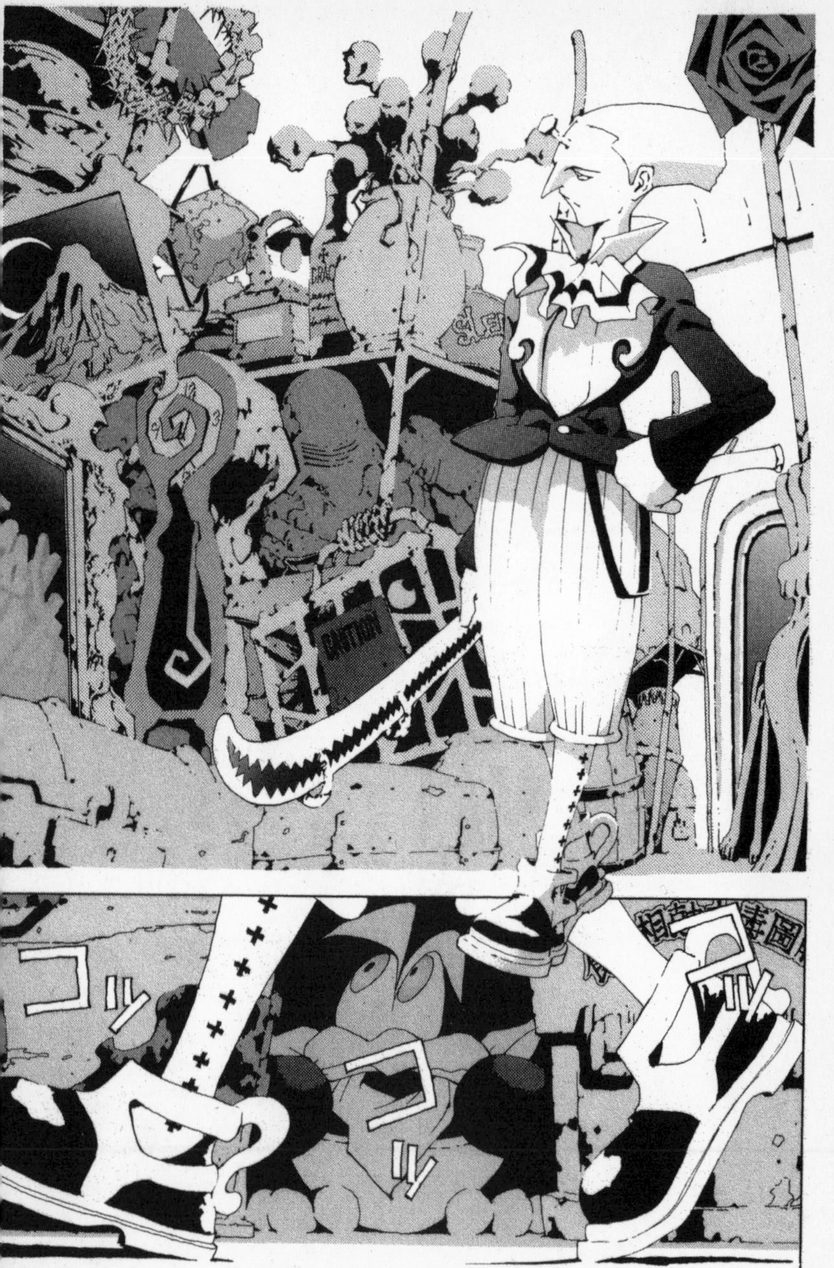
CAUTION
コッ
コッ
コッ

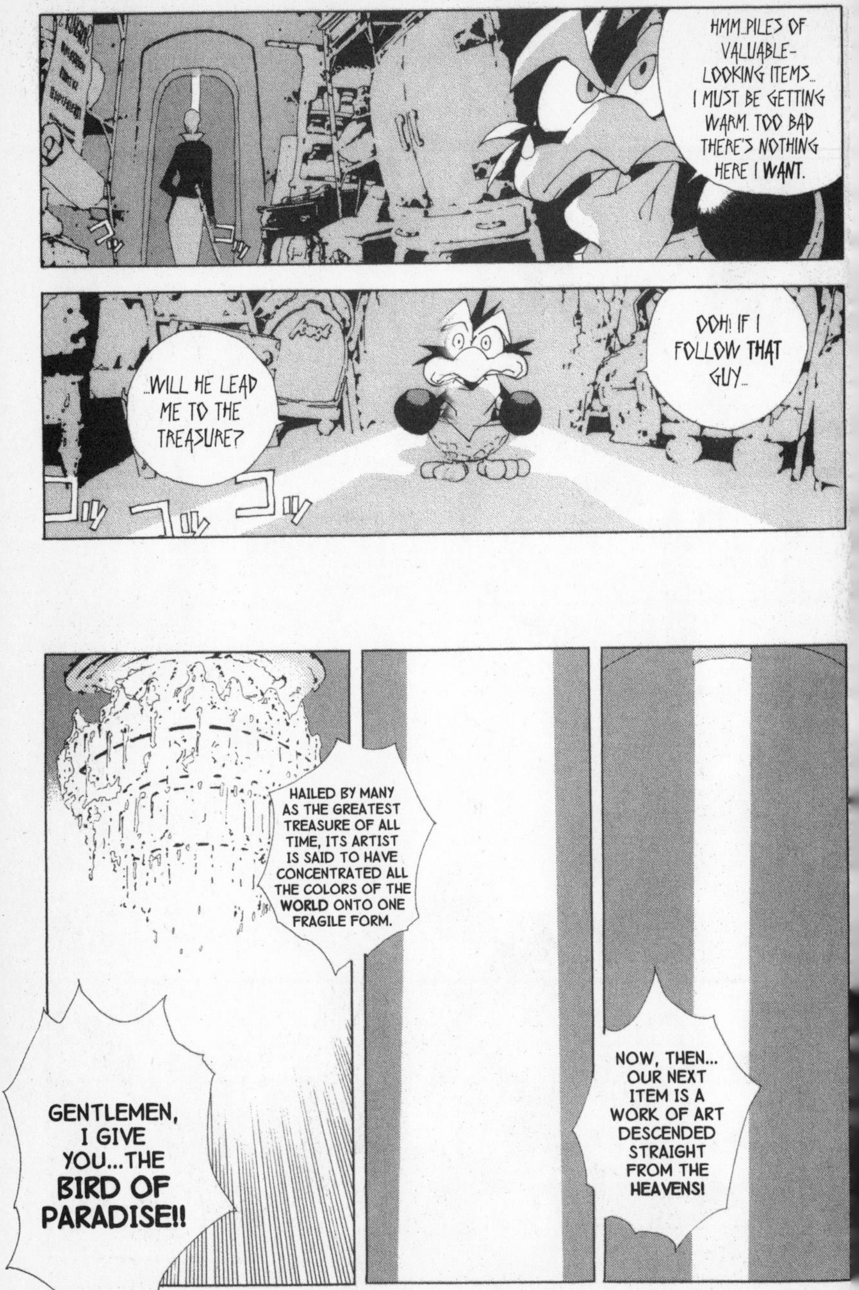
HMM...PILES OF VALUABLE-LOOKING ITEMS... I MUST BE GETTING WARM. TOO BAD THERE'S NOTHING HERE I WANT.
OOH! IF I FOLLOW THAT GUY...
...WILL HE LEAD ME TO THE TREASURE?
NOW, THEN... OUR NEXT ITEM IS A WORK OF ART DESCENDED STRAIGHT FROM THE HEAVENS!
HAILED BY MANY AS THE GREATEST TREASURE OF ALL TIME, ITS ARTIST IS SAID TO HAVE CONCENTRATED ALL THE COLORS OF THE WORLD ONTO ONE FRAGILE FORM.
GENTLEMEN, I GIVE YOU...THE BIRD OF PARADISE!!

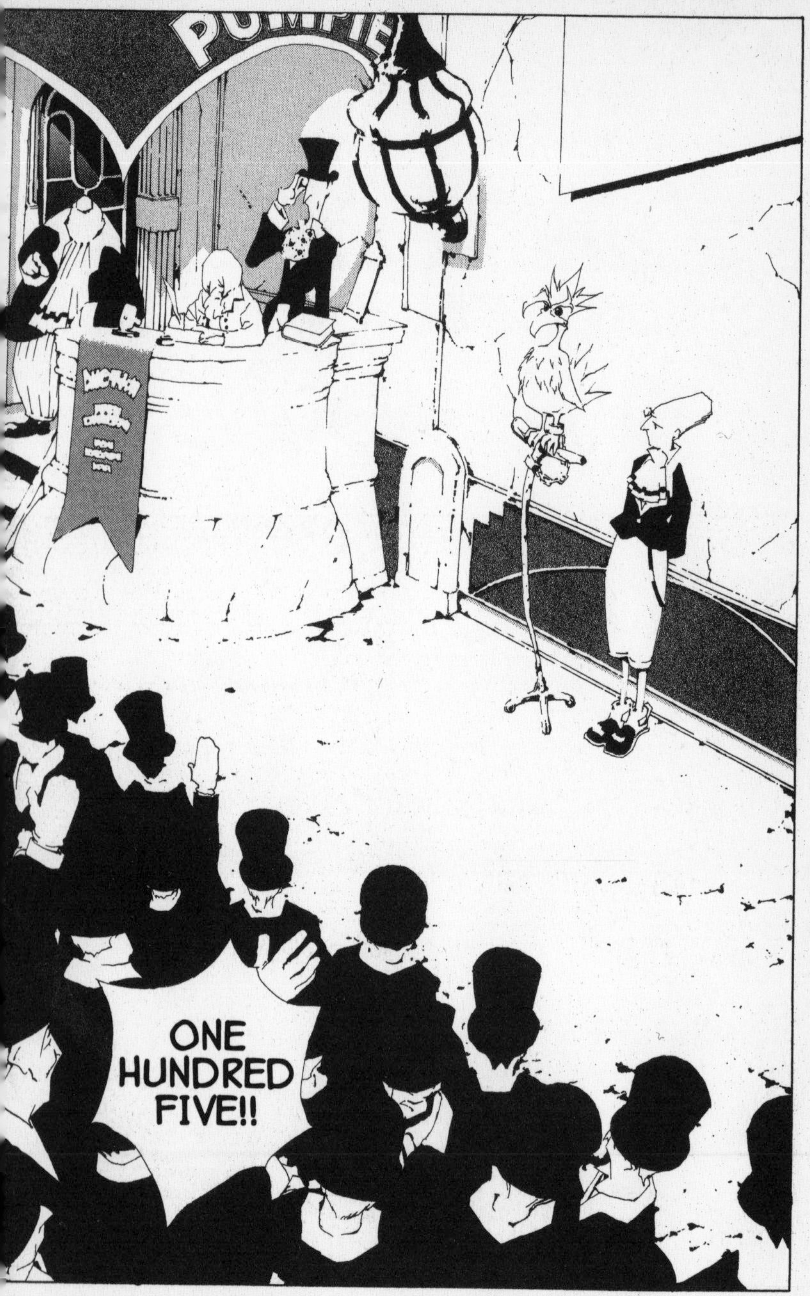
POMPIE
ONE HUNDRED FIVE!!

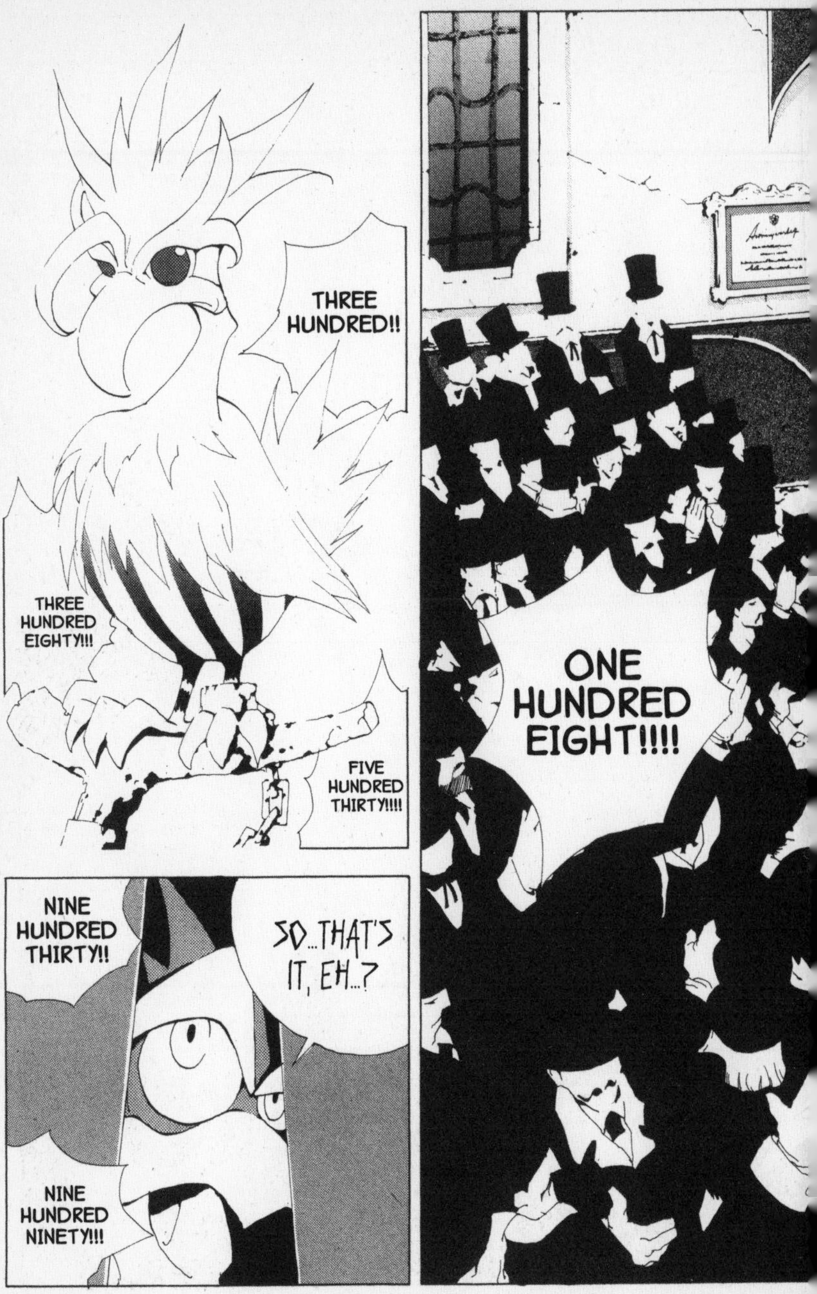
ONE HUNDRED EIGHT!!!!
THREE HUNDRED!!
THREE HUNDRED EIGHTY!!!
FIVE HUNDRED THIRTY!!!!
SO...THAT'S IT, EH...?
NINE HUNDRED THIRTY!!
NINE HUNDRED NINETY!!!

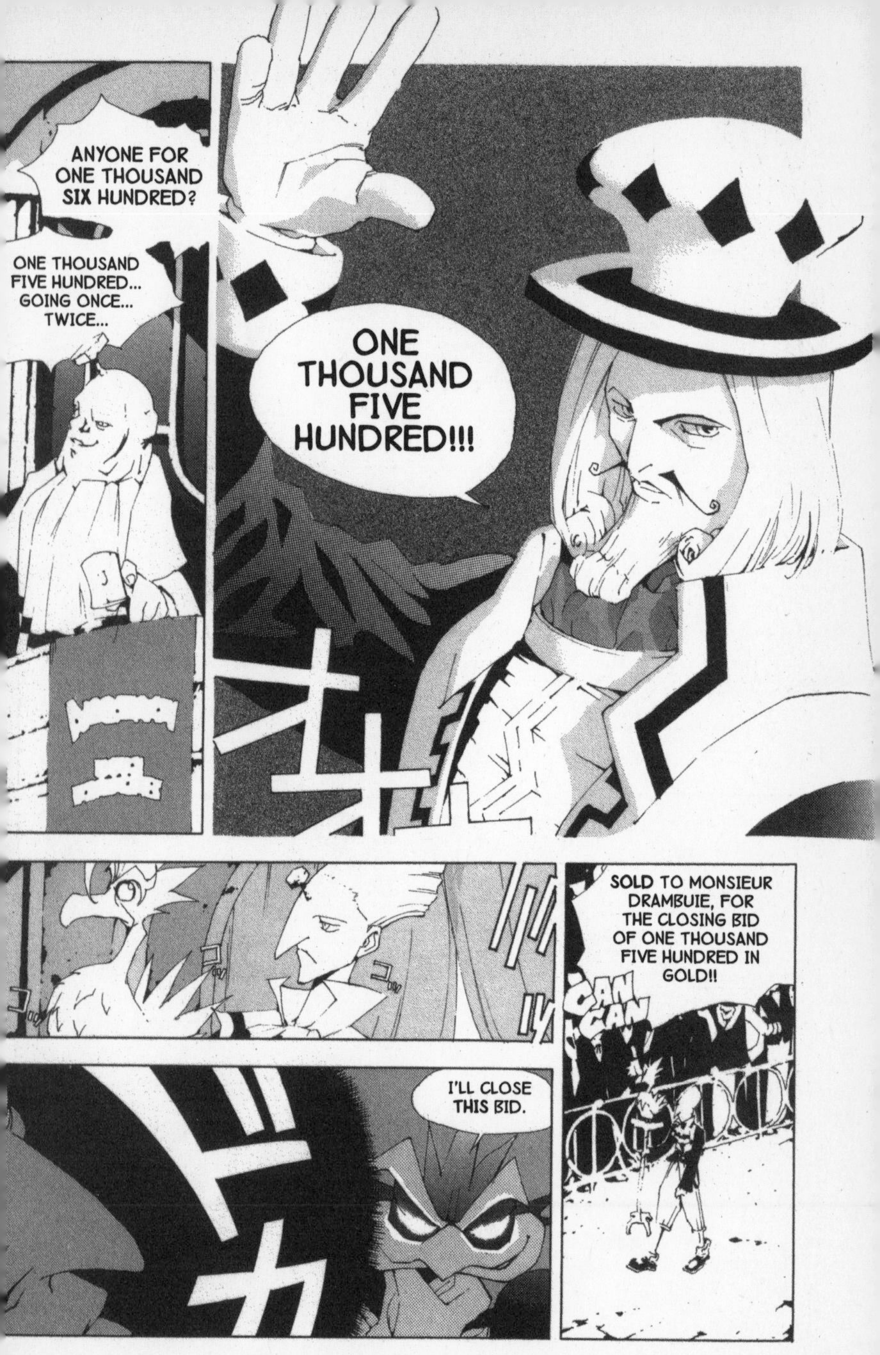
ONE THOUSAND FIVE HUNDRED!!!
ANYONE FOR ONE THOUSAND SIX HUNDRED?
ONE THOUSAND FIVE HUNDRED... GOING ONCE... TWICE...
SOLD TO MONSIEUR DRAMBUIE, FOR THE CLOSING BID OF ONE THOUSAND FIVE HUNDRED IN GOLD!!
CAN CAN
I'LL CLOSE THIS BID.

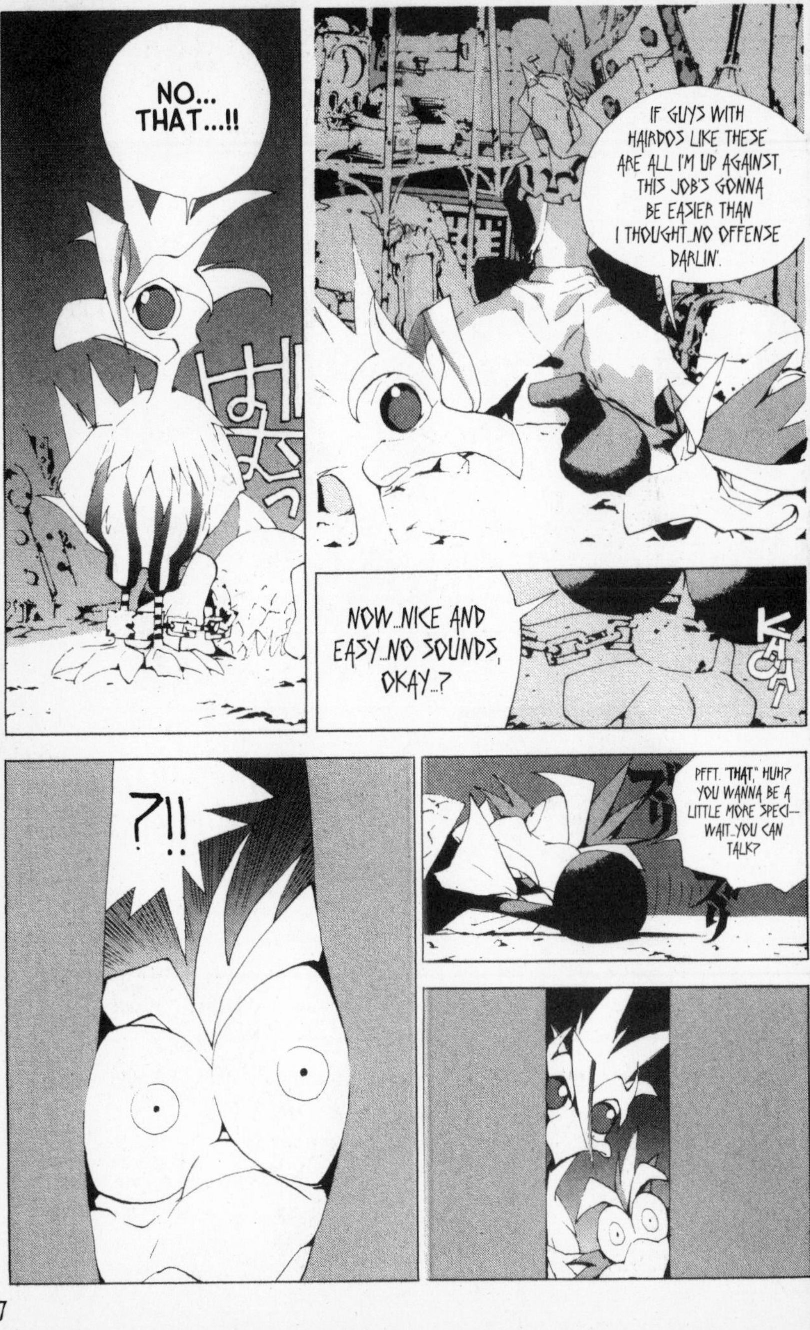

IF GUYS WITH HAIRDOS LIKE THESE ARE ALL I'M UP AGAINST, THIS JOB'S GONNA BE EASIER THAN I THOUGHT...NO OFFENSE DARLIN'.
NOW...NICE AND EASY...NO SOUNDS, OKAY...?
KACHA!
NO... THAT...!!
PFFT. "THAT," HUH? YOU WANNA BE A LITTLE MORE SPECI-- WAIT...YOU CAN TALK?
?!!

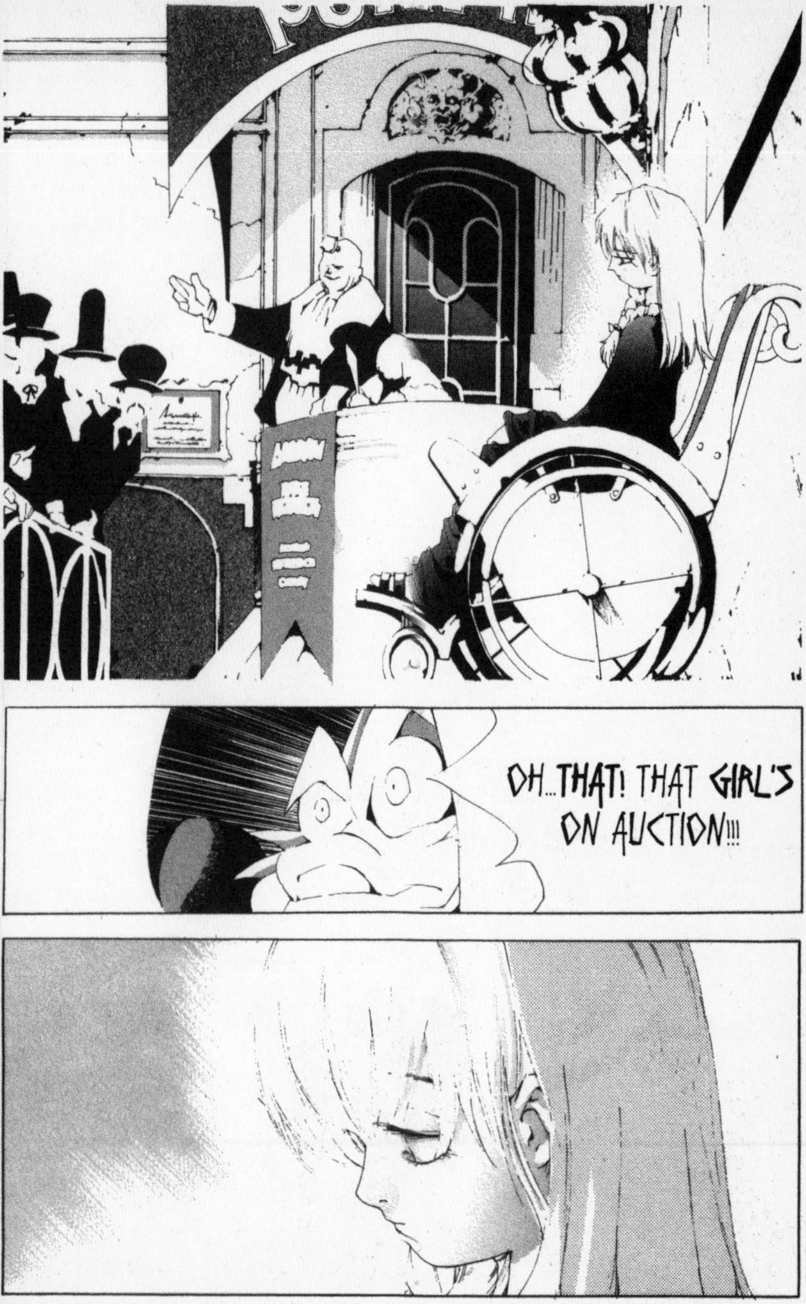
OH...THAT! THAT GIRL'S ON AUCTION!!!

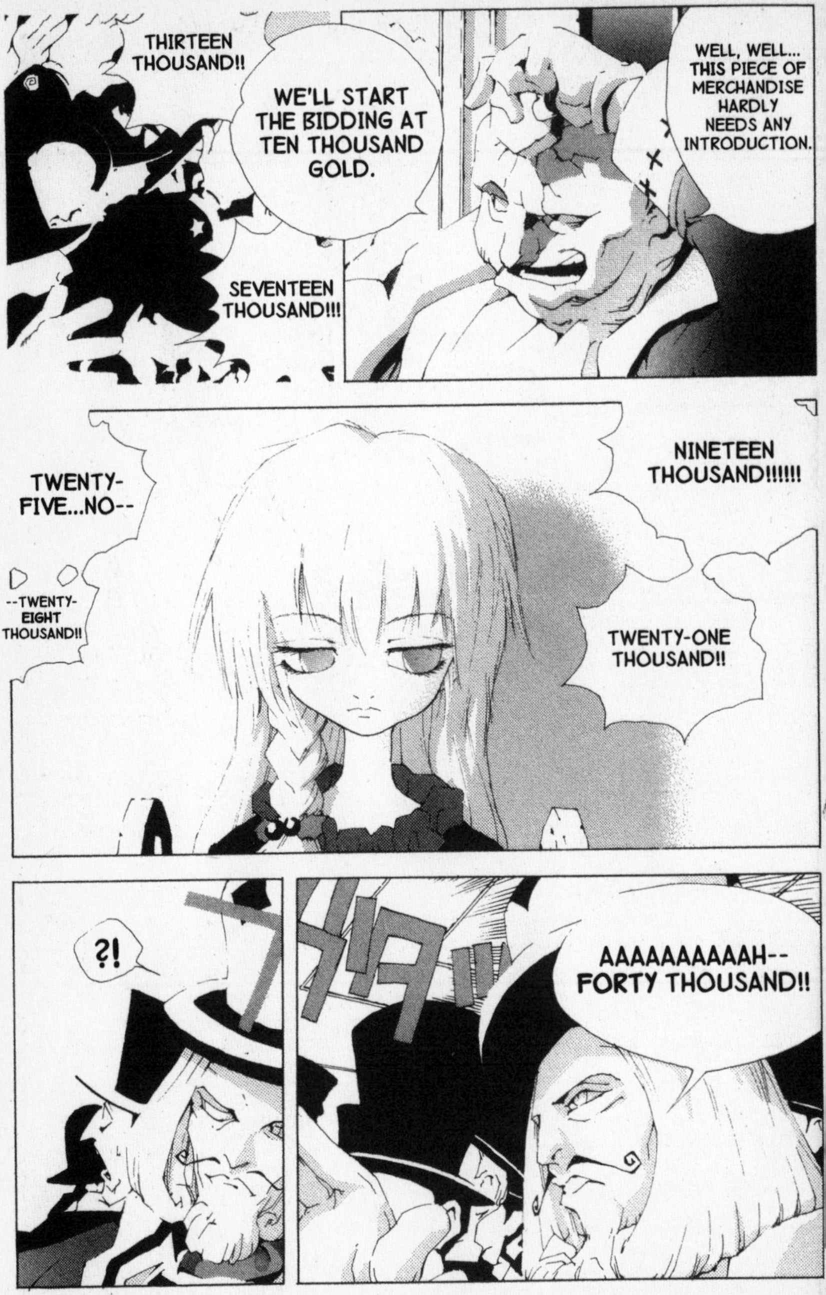
WELL, WELL... THIS PIECE OF MERCHANDISE HARDLY NEEDS ANY INTRODUCTION.
WE'LL START THE BIDDING AT TEN THOUSAND GOLD.
THIRTEEN THOUSAND!!
SEVENTEEN THOUSAND!!!
NINETEEN THOUSAND!!!!!!
TWENTY-ONE THOUSAND!!
TWENTY-FIVE...NO--
--TWENTY-EIGHT THOUSAND!!
AAAAAAAAAAH--FORTY THOUSAND!!
?!

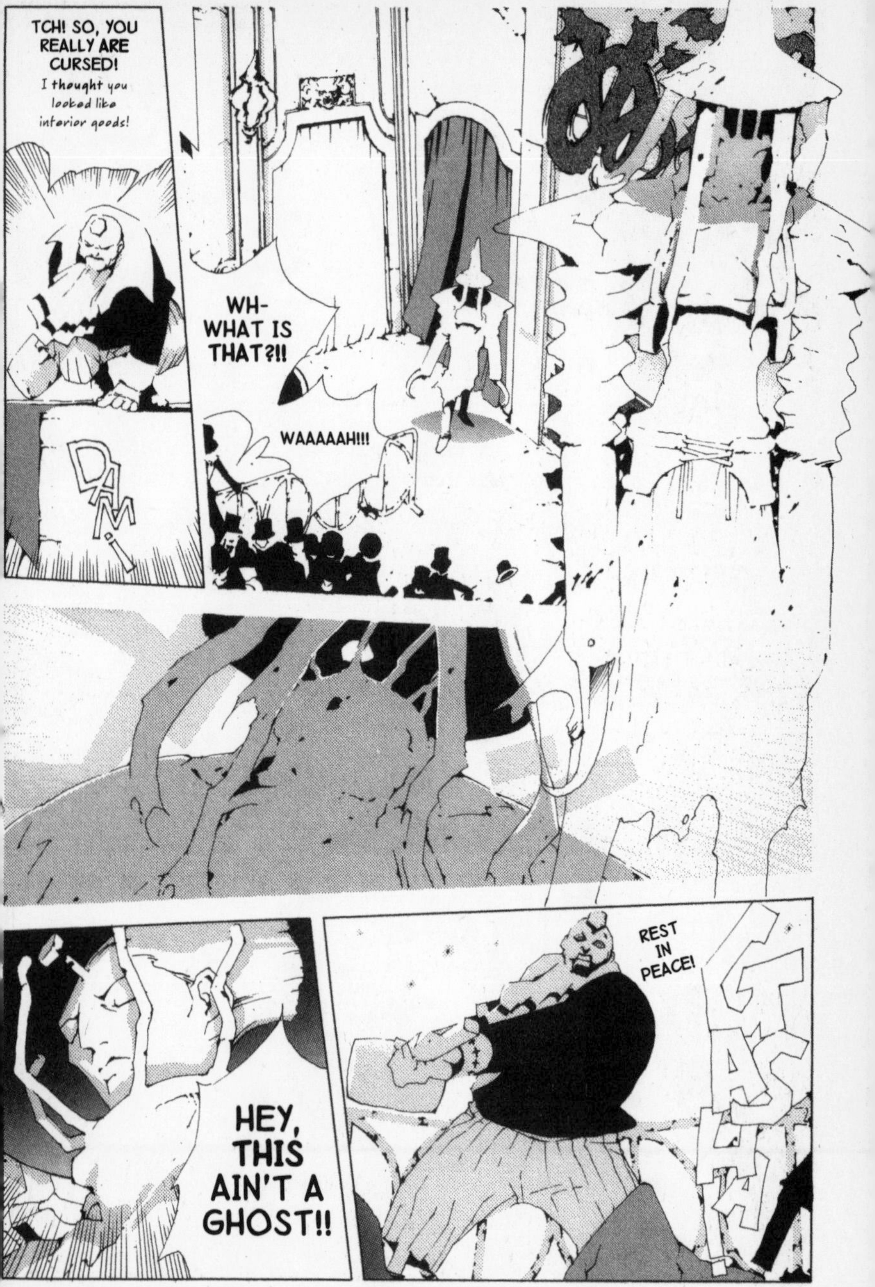
WH- WHAT IS THAT?!!
WAAAAAH!!!
TCH! SO, YOU REALLY ARE CURSED!
I thought you looked like interior goods!
DAM
REST IN PEACE!
HEY, THIS AIN'T A GHOST!!

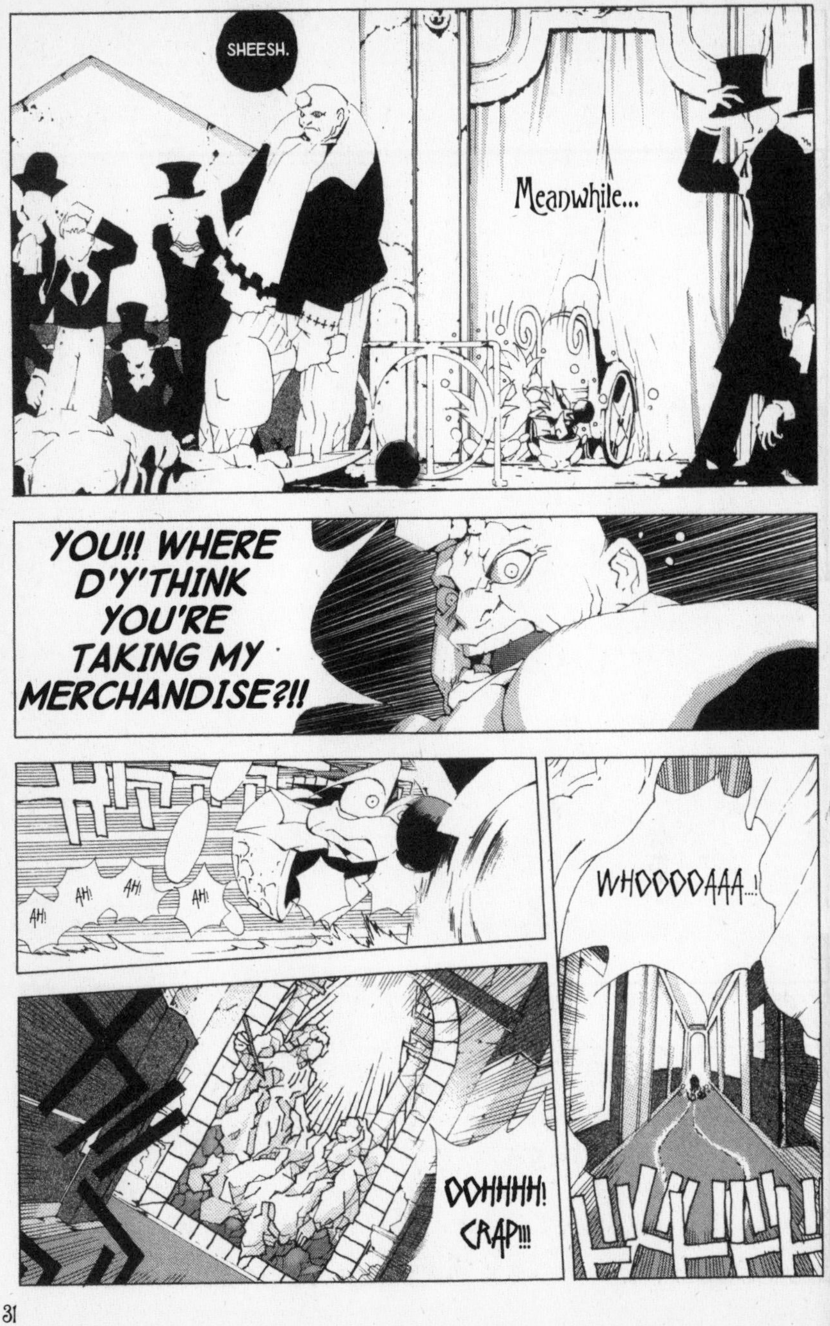
Meanwhile...
SHEESH.
YOU!! WHERE D'Y'THINK YOU'RE TAKING MY MERCHANDISE?!!
WHOOOOAAA...!
AH! AH! AH! AH!
OOHHHH! CRAP!!!

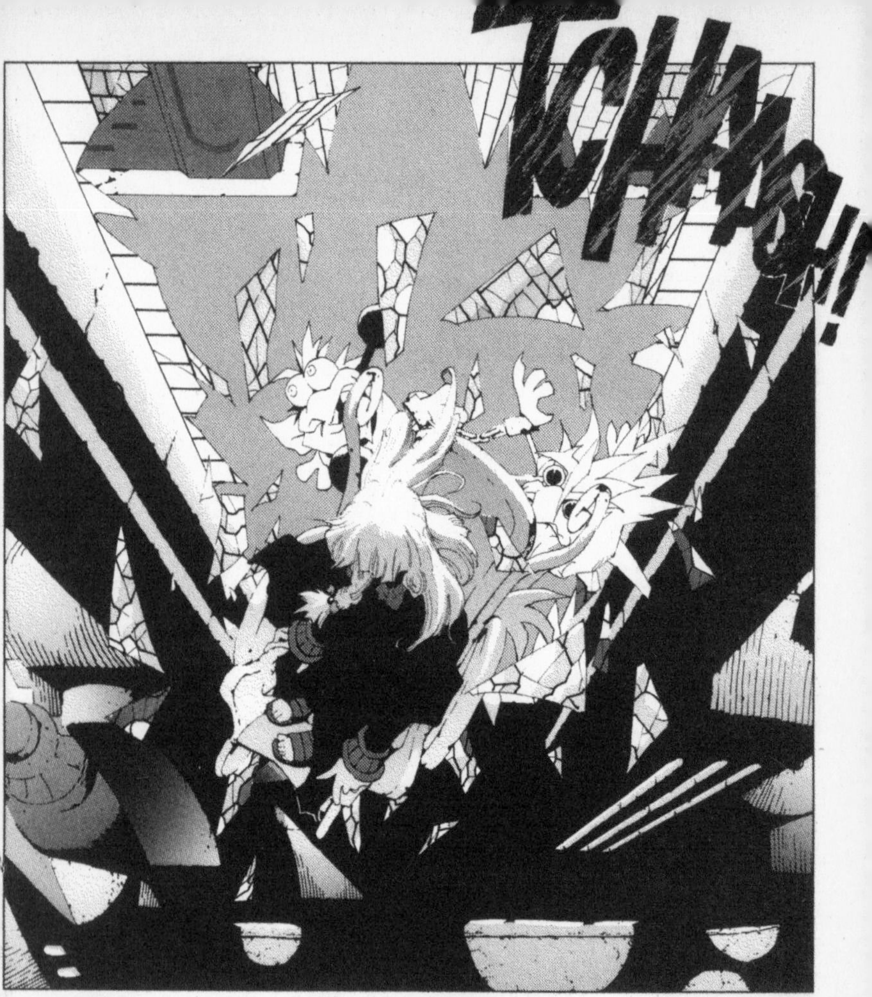
TCHAASH!!
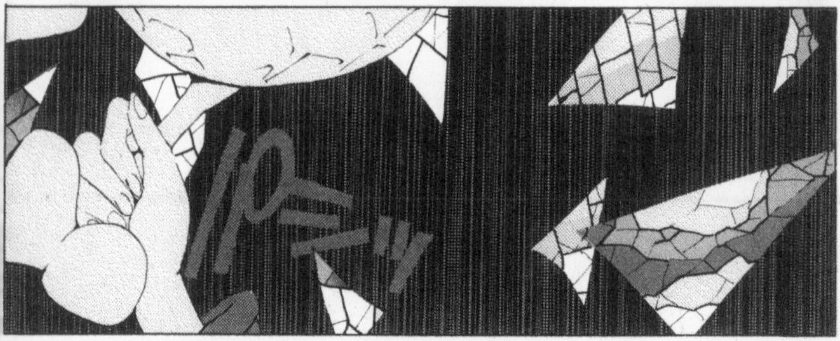

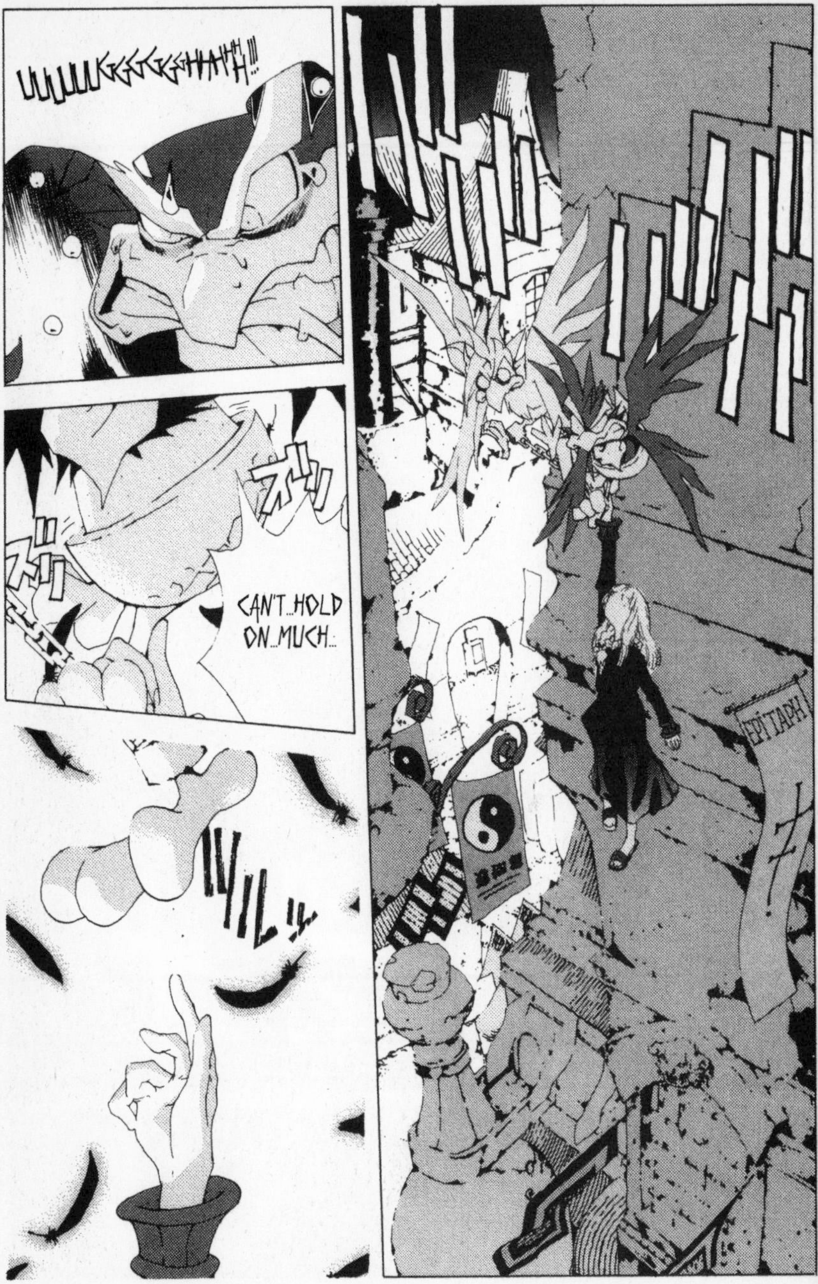
EPITAPH
UUUUUUKGGGGGHHAHHH!!!
CAN'T...HOLD ON...MUCH...

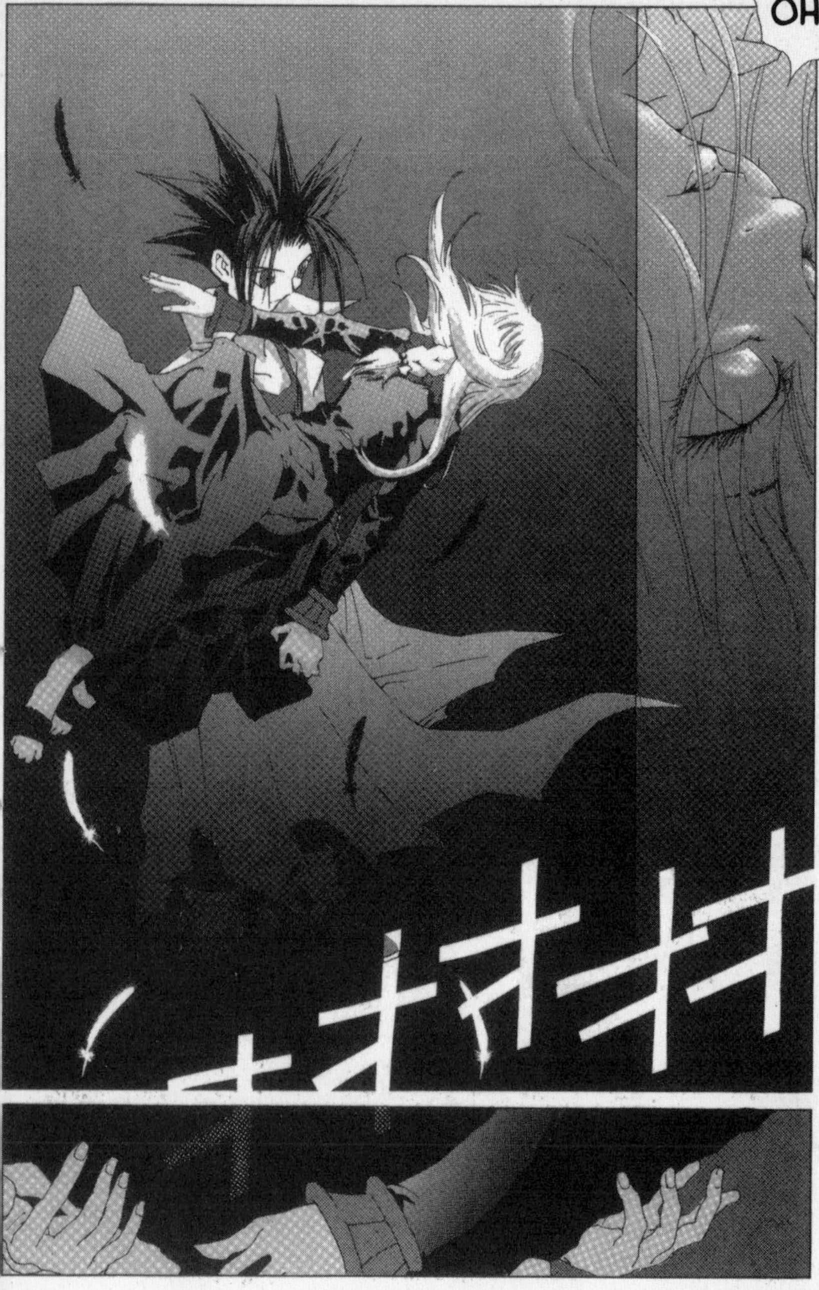
OH!
オオオオ

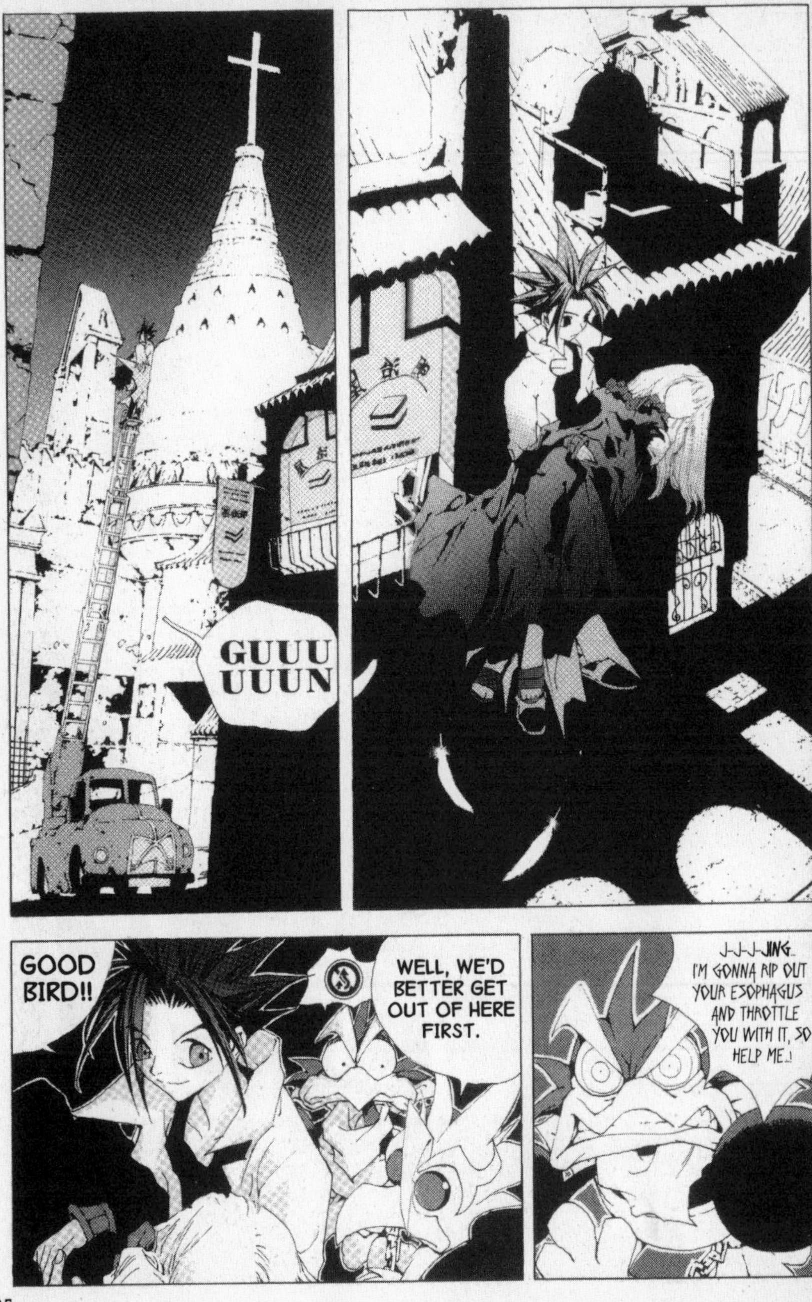
GUUU UUUN
J-J-J-JING... I'M GONNA RIP OUT YOUR ESOPHAGUS AND THROTTLE YOU WITH IT, SO HELP ME...!
WELL, WE'D BETTER GET OUT OF HERE FIRST.
GOOD BIRD!!

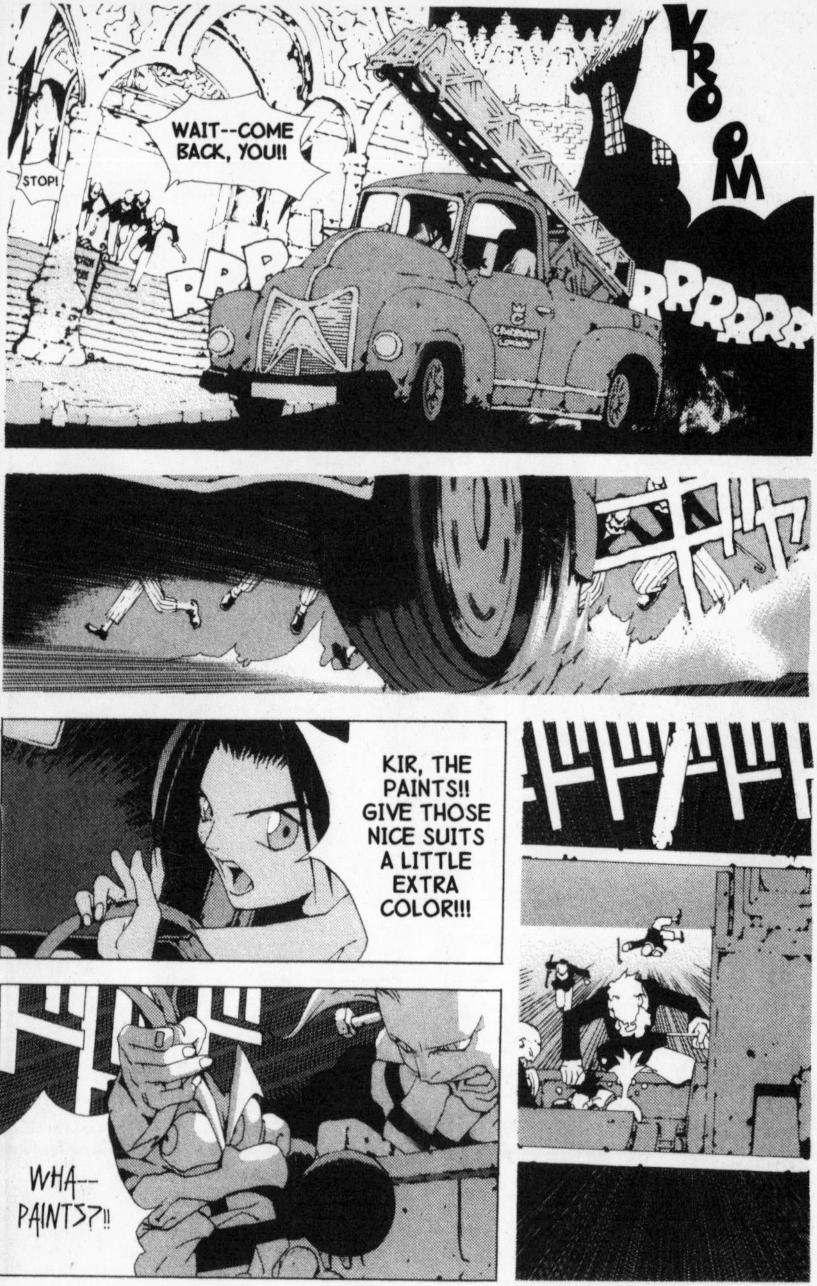
VROOM
RRRRRR
WAIT--COME BACK, YOU!!
STOP!
RRR
KIR, THE PAINTS!! GIVE THOSE NICE SUITS A LITTLE EXTRA COLOR!!!
WHA-- PAINTS?!!

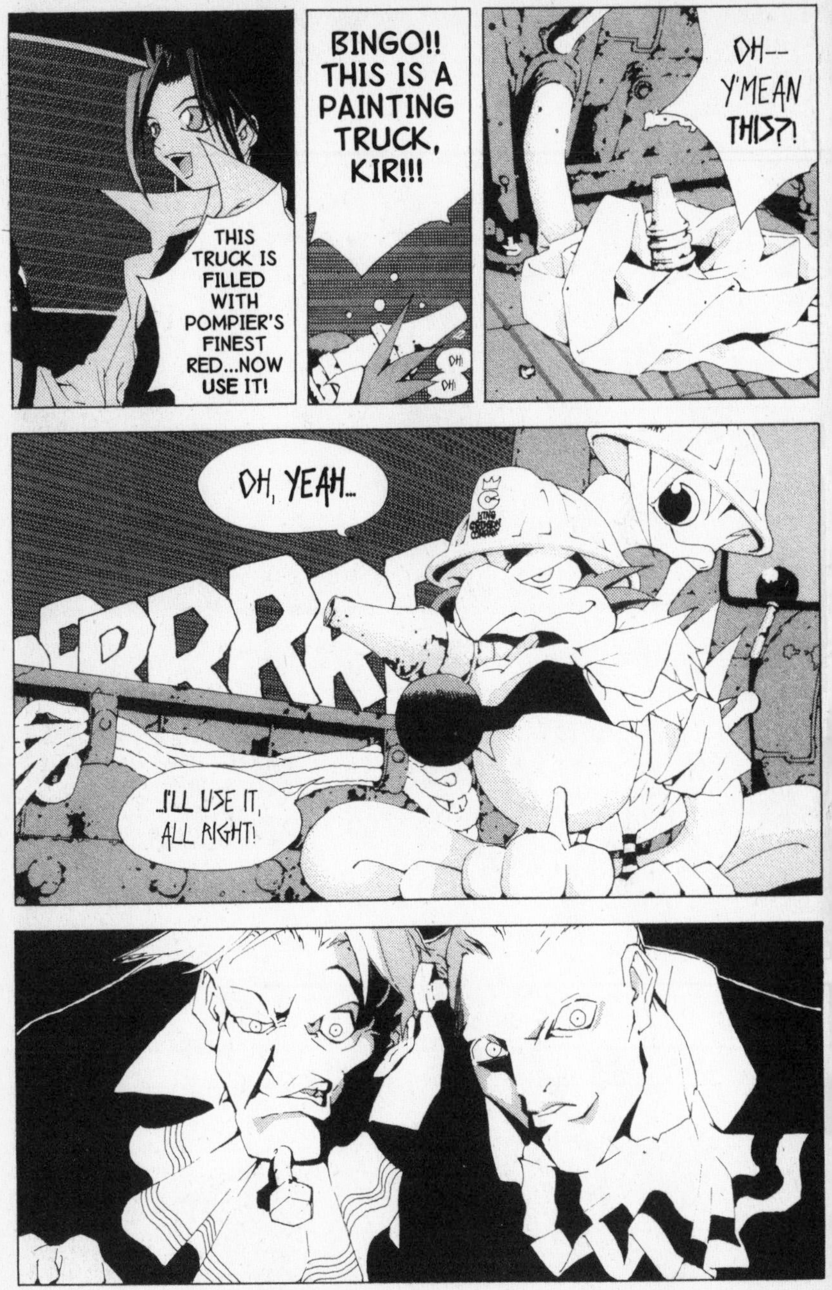
OH-- Y'MEAN THIS?!
BINGO!! THIS IS A PAINTING TRUCK, KIR!!!
OH!
OH!
THIS TRUCK IS FILLED WITH POMPIER'S FINEST RED...NOW USE IT!
OH, YEAH...
...I'LL USE IT, ALL RIGHT!

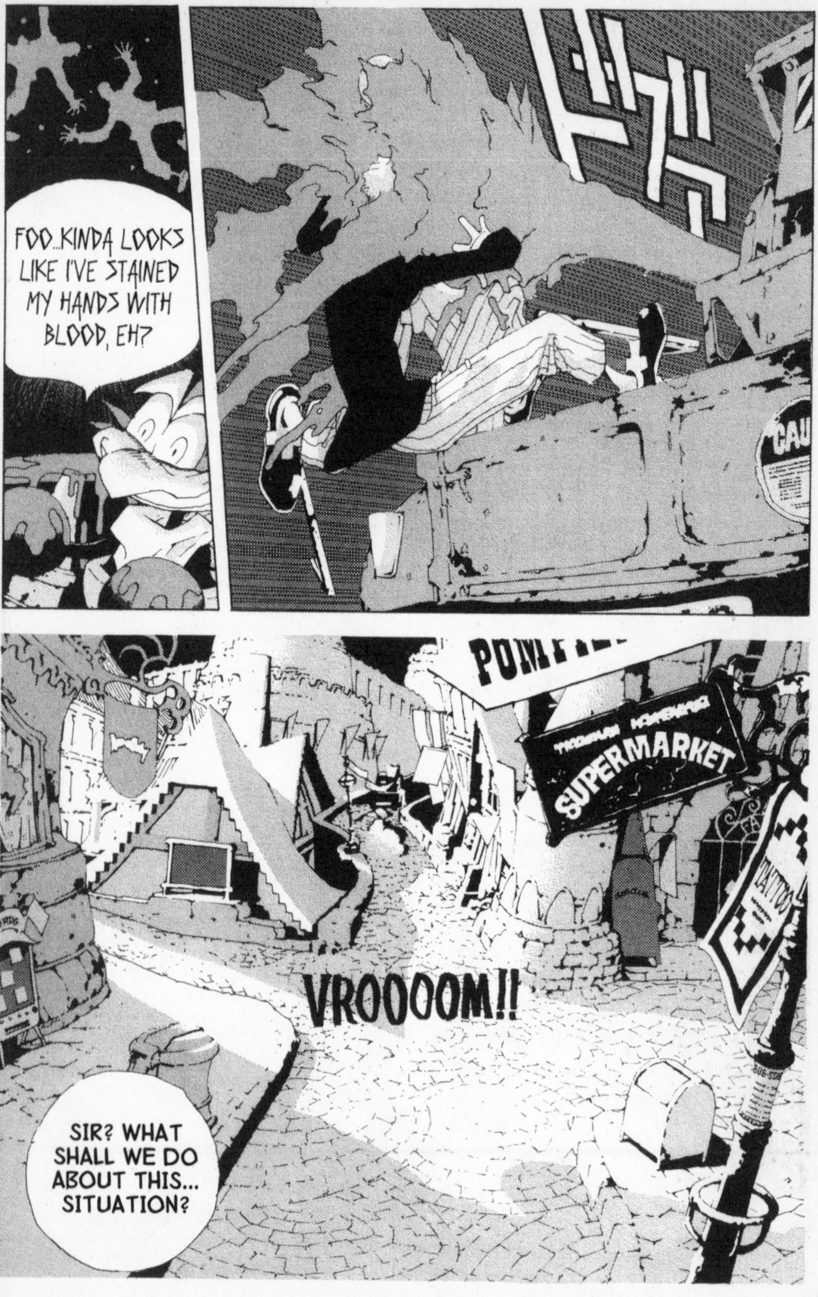
FOO...KINDA LOOKS LIKE I'VE STAINED MY HANDS WITH BLOOD, EH?
SUPERMARKET
TATTOO
VROOOOM!!
SIR? WHAT SHALL WE DO ABOUT THIS... SITUATION?

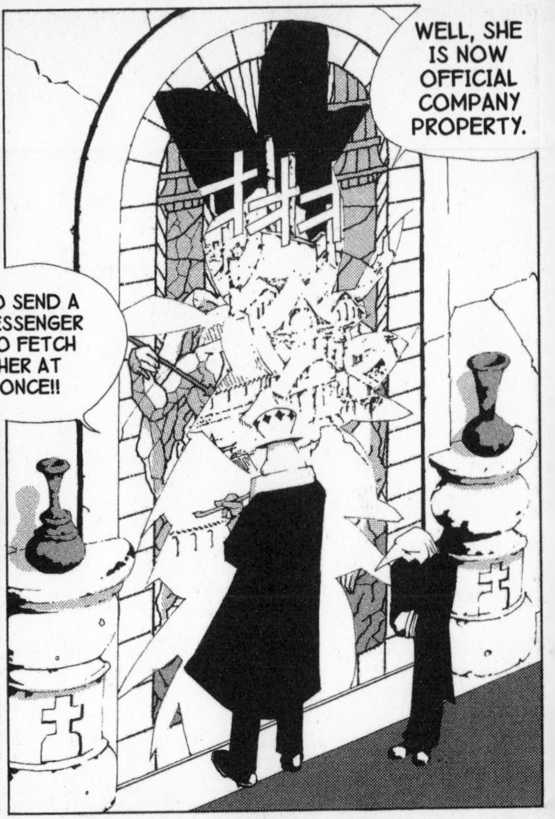
WELL, SHE IS NOW OFFICIAL COMPANY PROPERTY.
SO SEND A MESSENGER TO FETCH HER AT ONCE!!

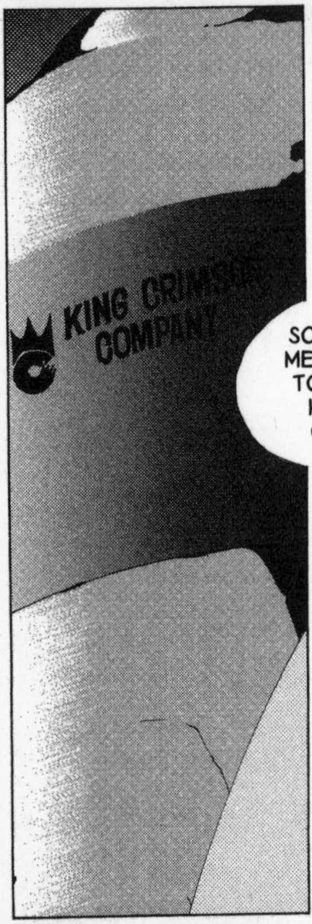
KING CRIMSO
COMPANY

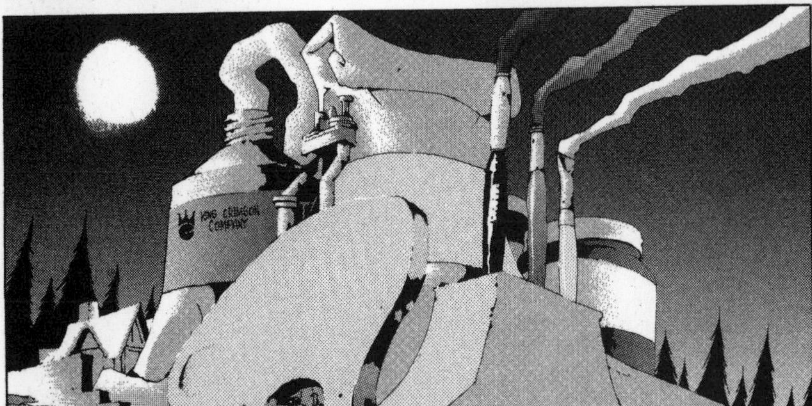
KING CRIMSON COMPANY

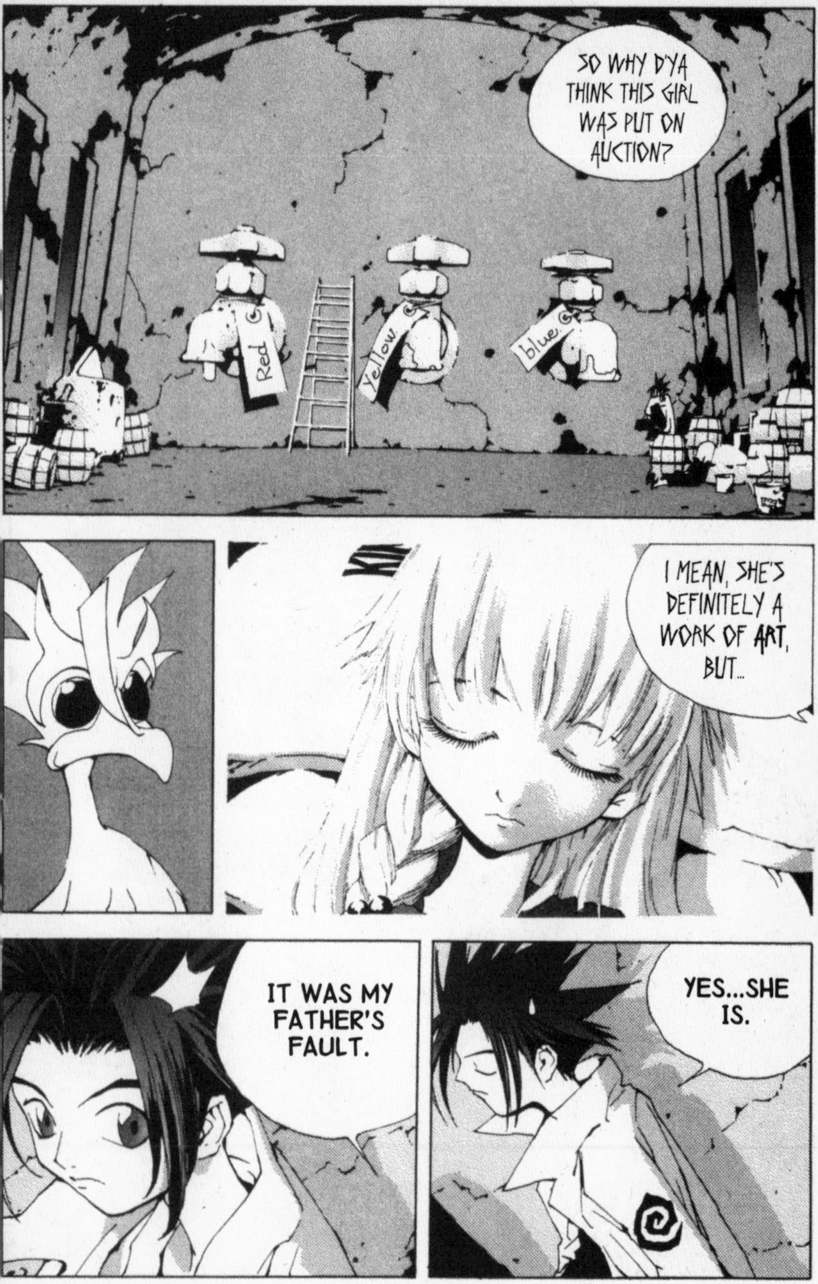
SO WHY D'YA THINK THIS GIRL WAS PUT ON AUCTION?
blue.
yellow.
Red
I MEAN, SHE'S DEFINITELY A WORK OF ART, BUT...
YES...SHE IS.
IT WAS MY FATHER'S FAULT.

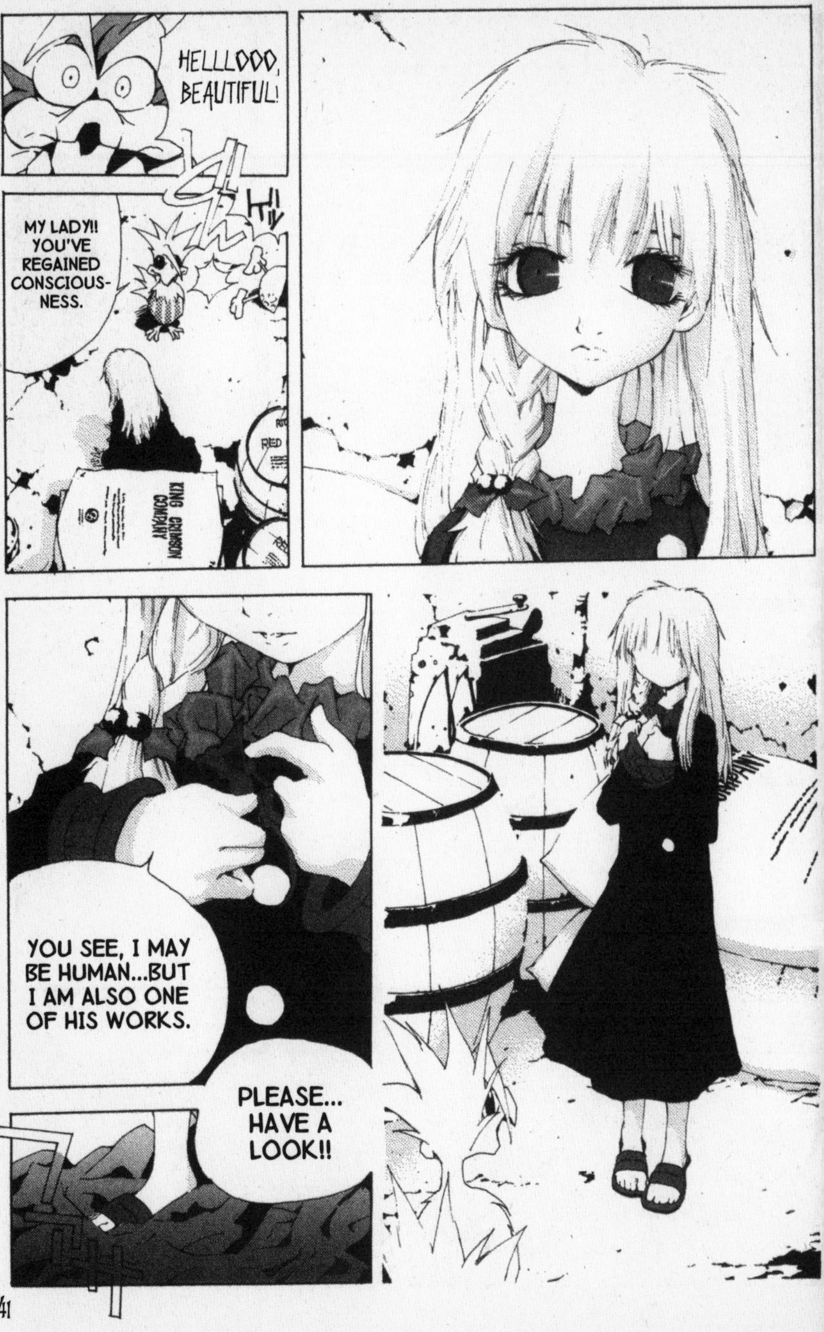
HELLLOOO, BEAUTIFUL!
MY LADY!! YOU'VE REGAINED CONSCIOUS-NESS.
KING CRIMSON COMPANY
RED
YOU SEE, I MAY BE HUMAN...BUT I AM ALSO ONE OF HIS WORKS.
PLEASE... HAVE A LOOK!!

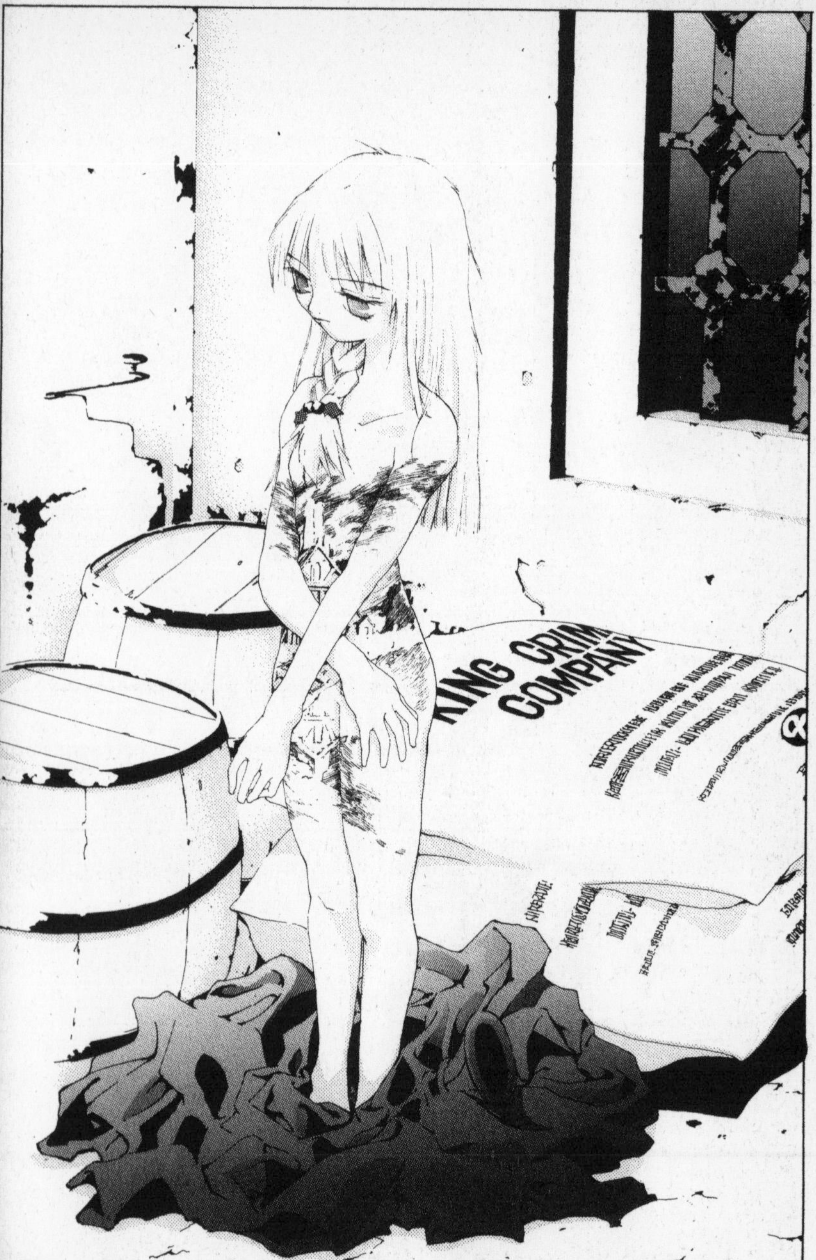
KING CRIM
COMPANY

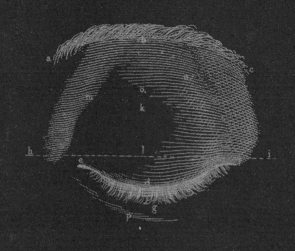

If perchance I were to ask
The one almighty, perfect God,
I am sure I'd be rewarded
With a simple "It is so..."
But for me, in all my tears
It is not beauty, but its extracts
That defeat my wounded, rebel eyes.
For within such nuance,
All colors live
In brilliant harmony...

...Then again,
It could all be colorless
For all I know.

(From the epitaph series,
"The Analects of Vin Quart")

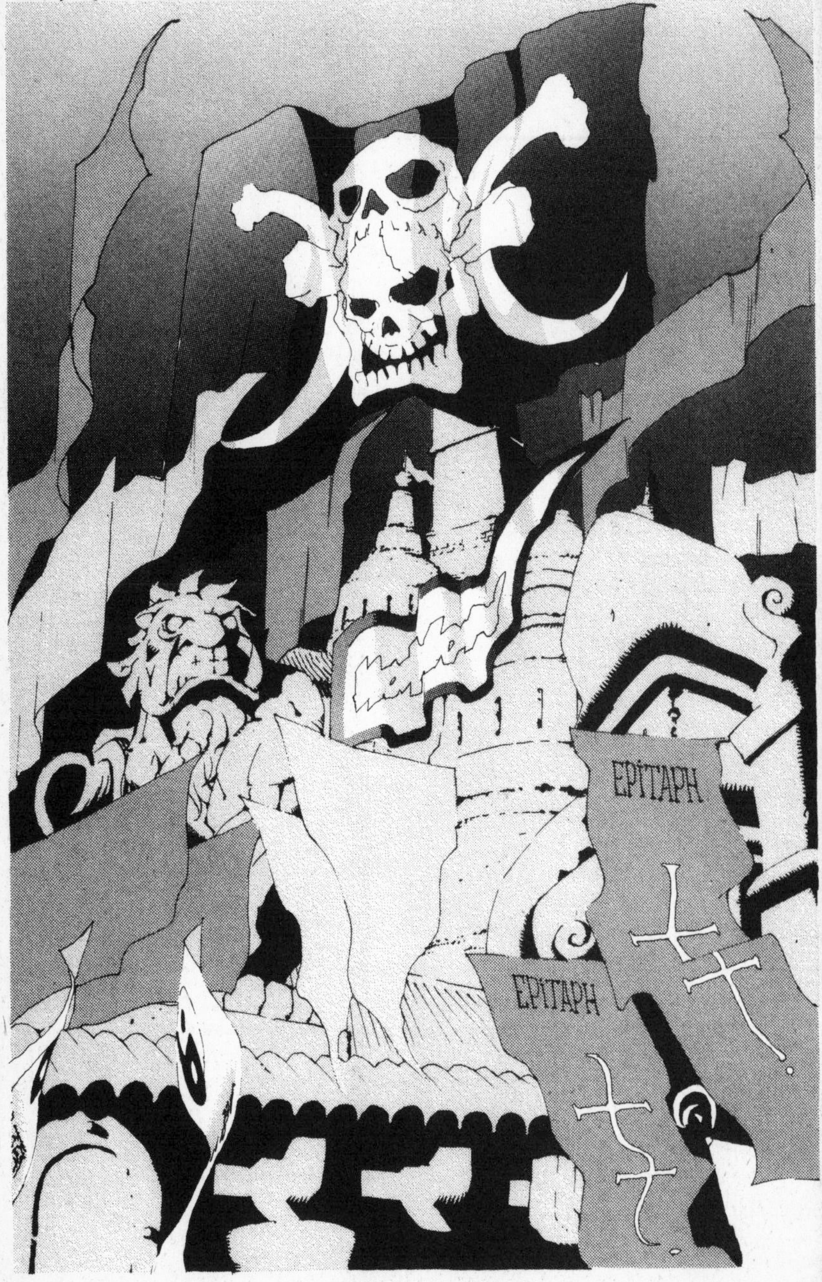
EPITAPH
EPITAPH

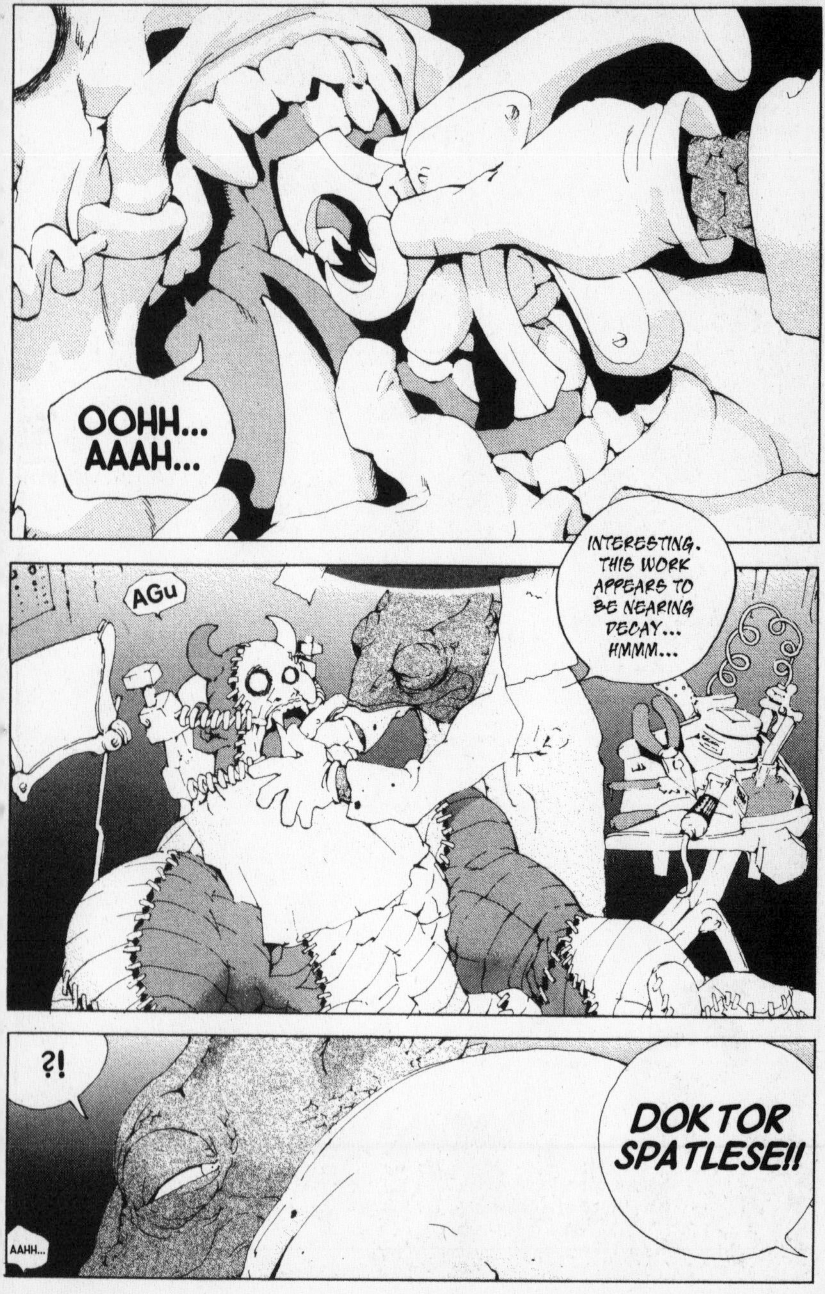
OOHH... AAAH...
INTERESTING. THIS WORK APPEARS TO BE NEARING DECAY... HMMM...
AGu
DOKTOR SPATLESE!!
?!
AAHH...

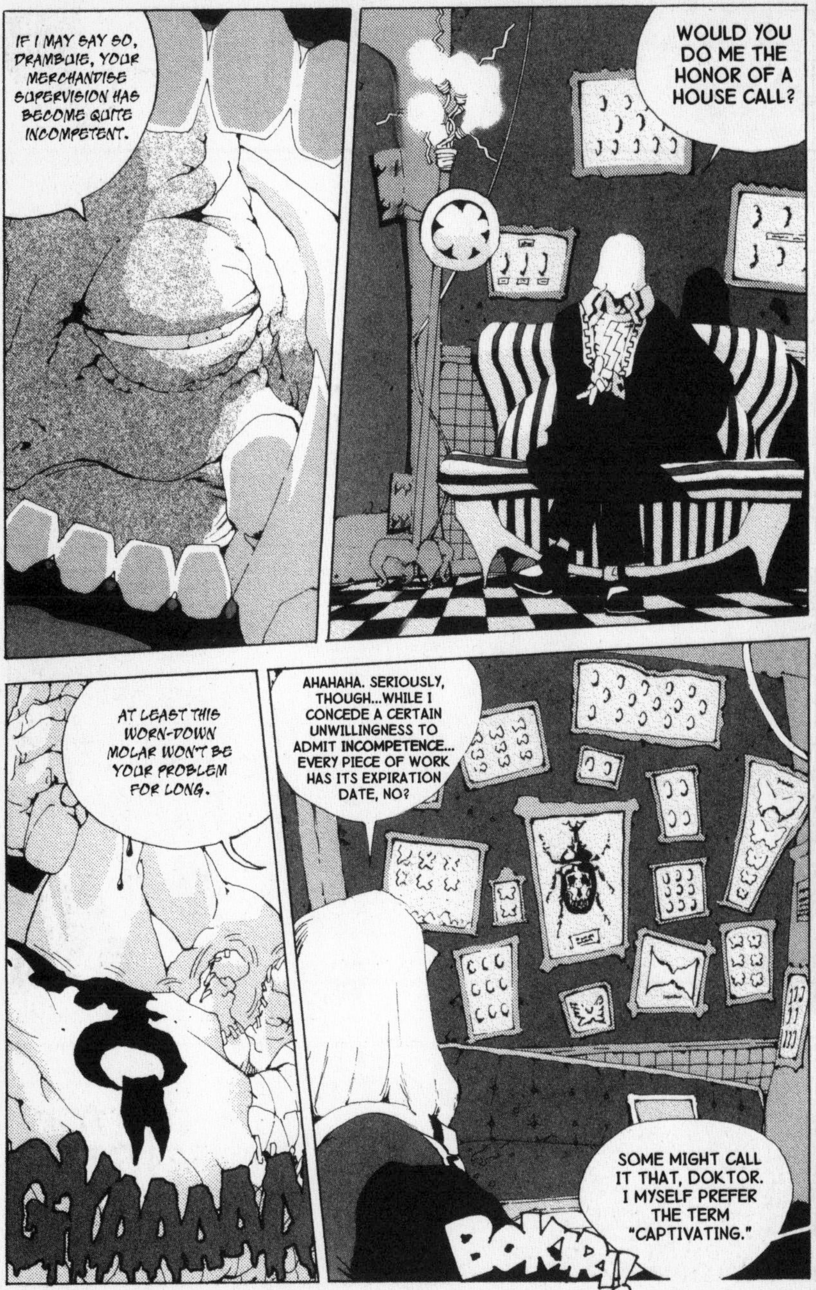
WOULD YOU DO ME THE HONOR OF A HOUSE CALL?
IF I MAY SAY SO, DRAMBUIE, YOUR MERCHANDISE SUPERVISION HAS BECOME QUITE INCOMPETENT.
AHAHAHA. SERIOUSLY, THOUGH...WHILE I CONCEDE A CERTAIN UNWILLINGNESS TO ADMIT INCOMPETENCE... EVERY PIECE OF WORK HAS ITS EXPIRATION DATE, NO?
SOME MIGHT CALL IT THAT, DOKTOR. I MYSELF PREFER THE TERM "CAPTIVATING."
BOKIRI!
AT LEAST THIS WORN-DOWN MOLAR WON'T BE YOUR PROBLEM FOR LONG.
GYAAAAA

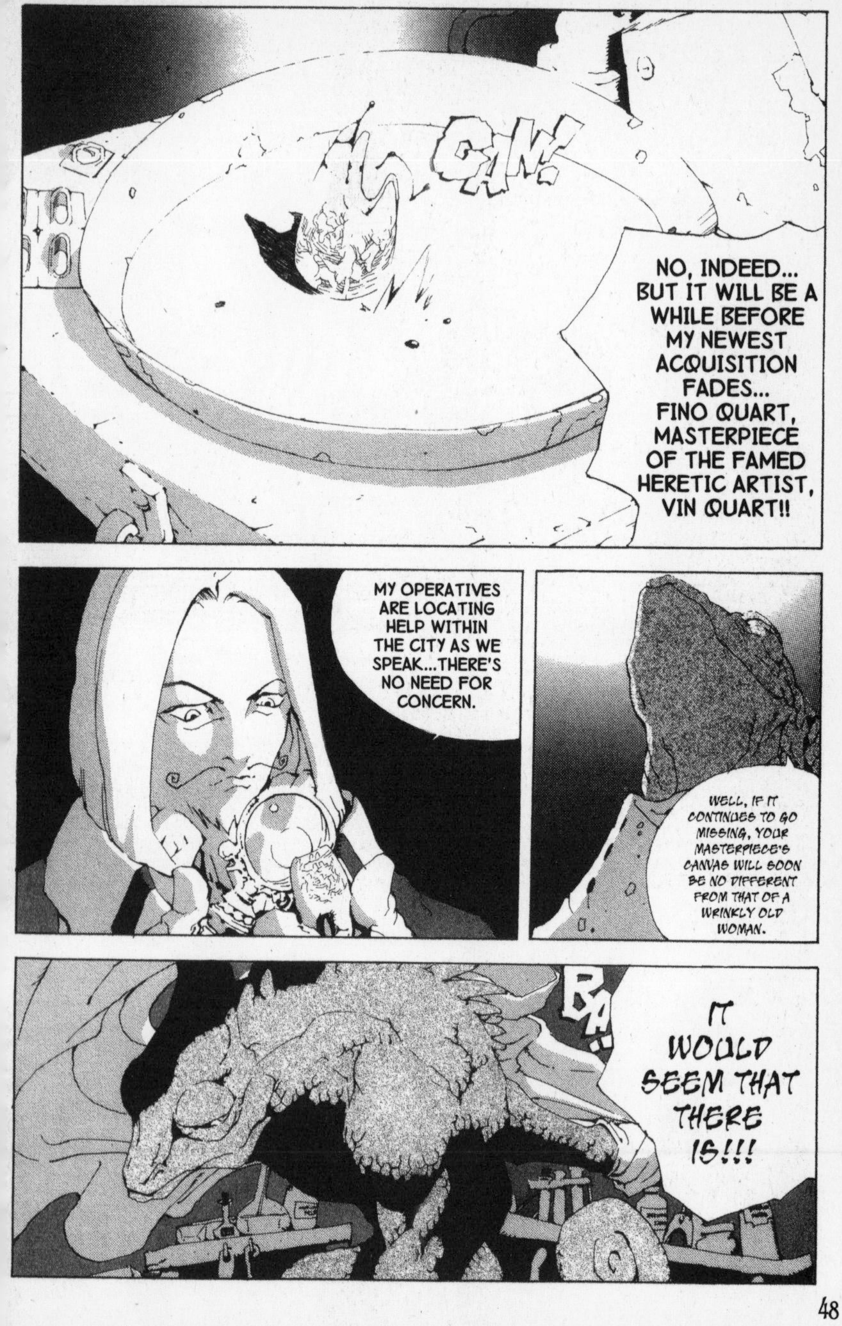
GAN!
NO, INDEED... BUT IT WILL BE A WHILE BEFORE MY NEWEST ACQUISITION FADES... FINO QUART, MASTERPIECE OF THE FAMED HERETIC ARTIST, VIN QUART!!
WELL, IF IT CONTINUES TO GO MISSING, YOUR MASTERPIECE'S CANVAS WILL SOON BE NO DIFFERENT FROM THAT OF A WRINKLY OLD WOMAN.
MY OPERATIVES ARE LOCATING HELP WITHIN THE CITY AS WE SPEAK...THERE'S NO NEED FOR CONCERN.
IT WOULD SEEM THAT THERE IS!!!

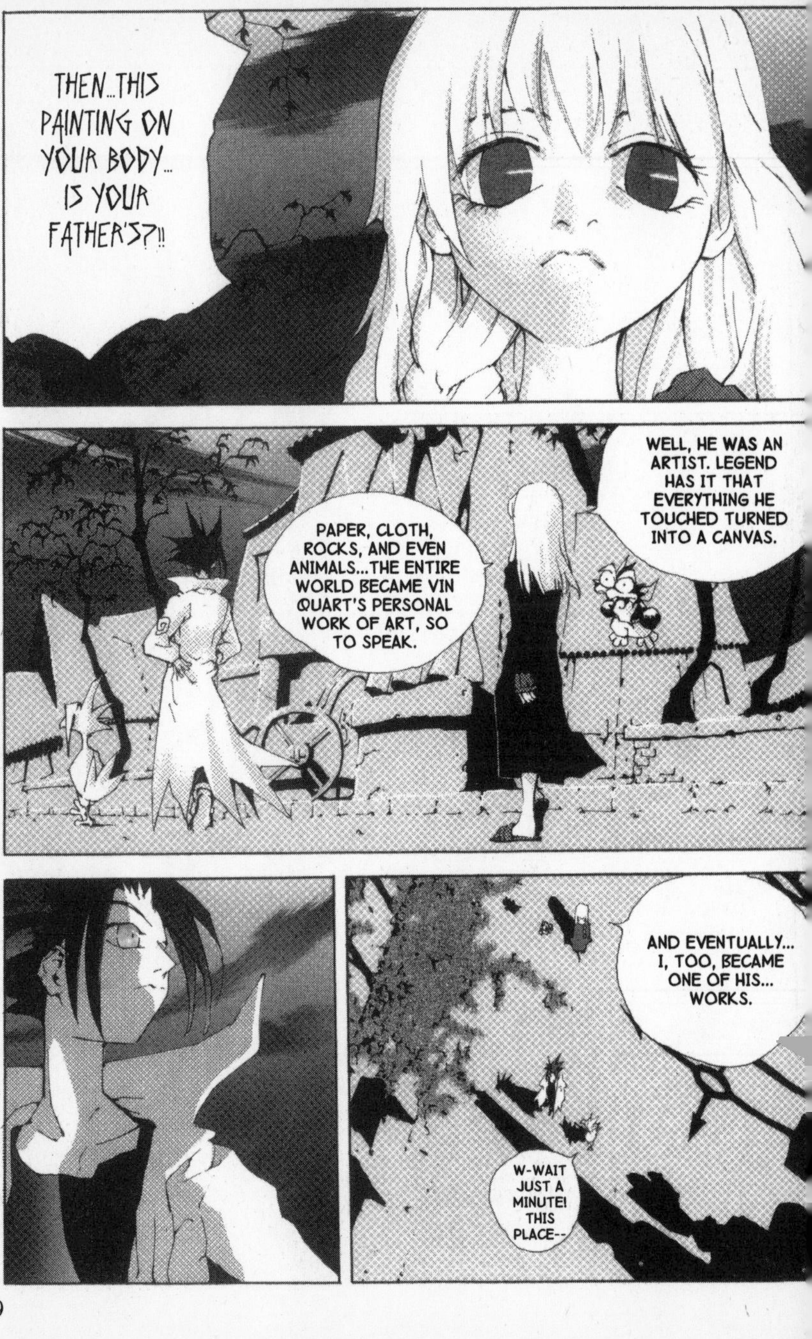
THEN...THIS PAINTING ON YOUR BODY... IS YOUR FATHER'S?!!
WELL, HE WAS AN ARTIST. LEGEND HAS IT THAT EVERYTHING HE TOUCHED TURNED INTO A CANVAS.
PAPER, CLOTH, ROCKS, AND EVEN ANIMALS...THE ENTIRE WORLD BECAME VIN QUART'S PERSONAL WORK OF ART, SO TO SPEAK.
AND EVENTUALLY... I, TOO, BECAME ONE OF HIS... WORKS.
W-WAIT JUST A MINUTE! THIS PLACE--

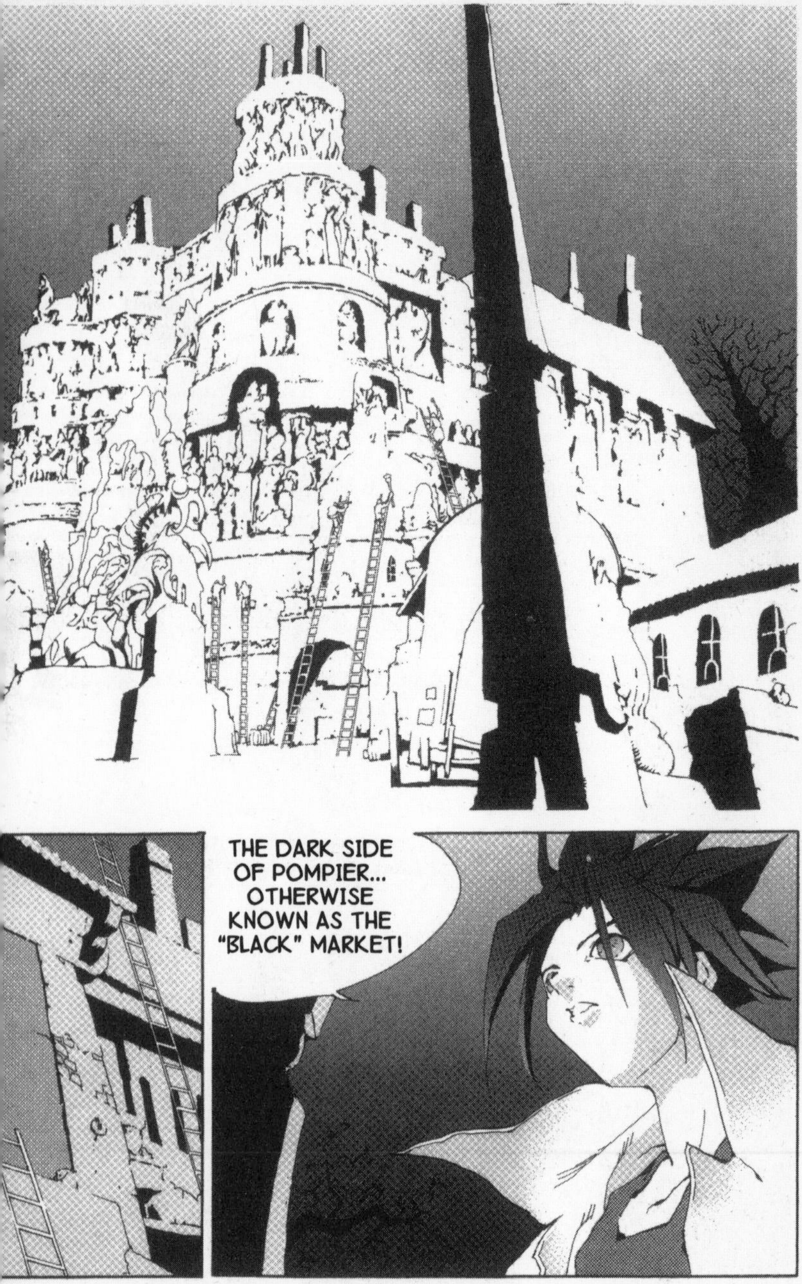
THE DARK SIDE OF POMPIER... OTHERWISE KNOWN AS THE "BLACK" MARKET!

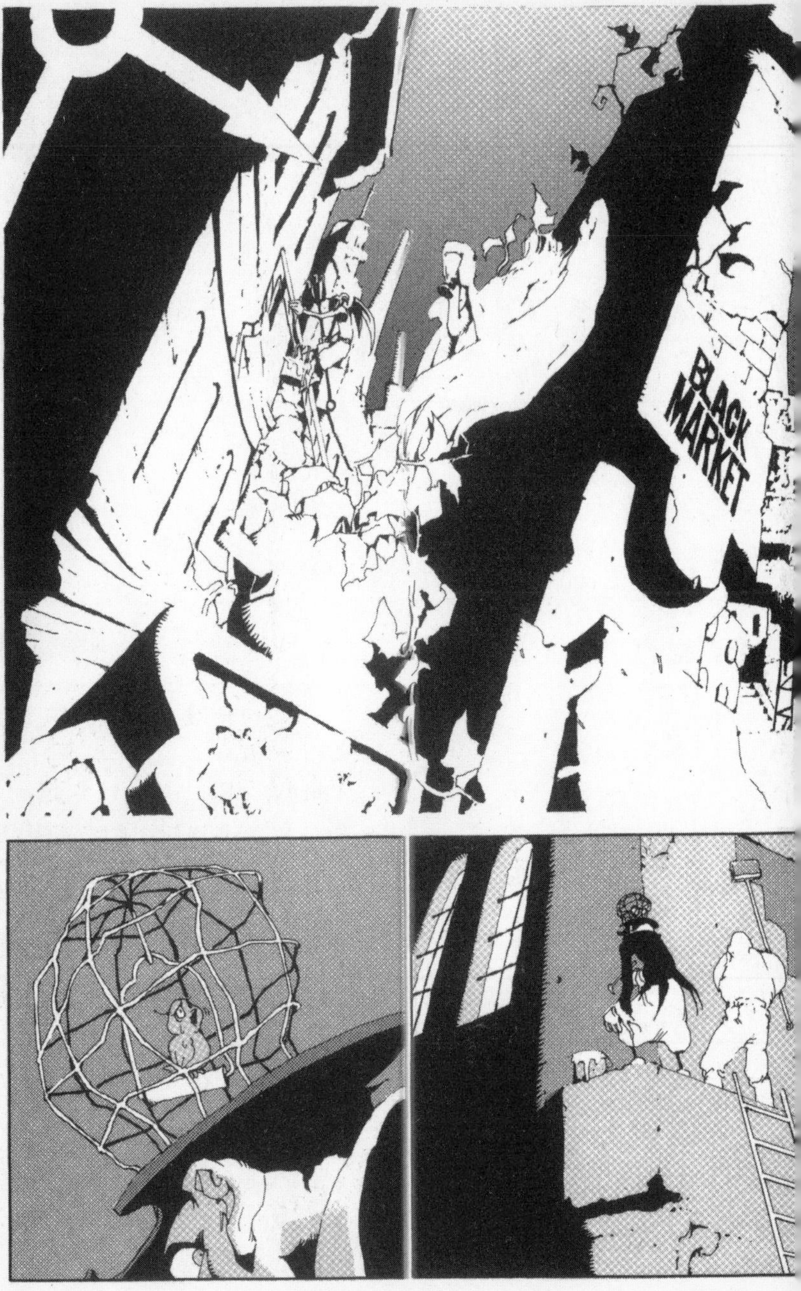
BLACK MARKET

SPLASH!

SO A FATHER'S LOVE TRANSFORMED HIS OWN DAUGHTER INTO A PIECE OF ART...

NOT BAD, IF I DO SAY SO MYSELF!!

JING!! OH NO, YOU PROBABLY COULDN'T APPRECIATE THIS DAZZLING BEAUTY'S PRESENTATION...

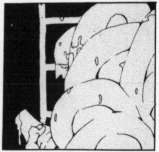

NOPE... GUESS NOT.

K-KIR... WAIT A MINUTE...!

I EXPECT YOUR FATHER WOULD FIND SOMETHING TO ADMIRE IN *MY* MATCHLESS BEAUTY, TOO, FINO!!

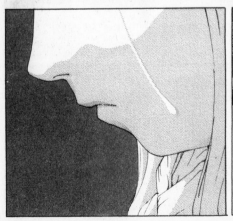

COME NOW! INTRODUCE ME TO THIS FATHER OF YOURS...AS YOUR FIANCÉ!!

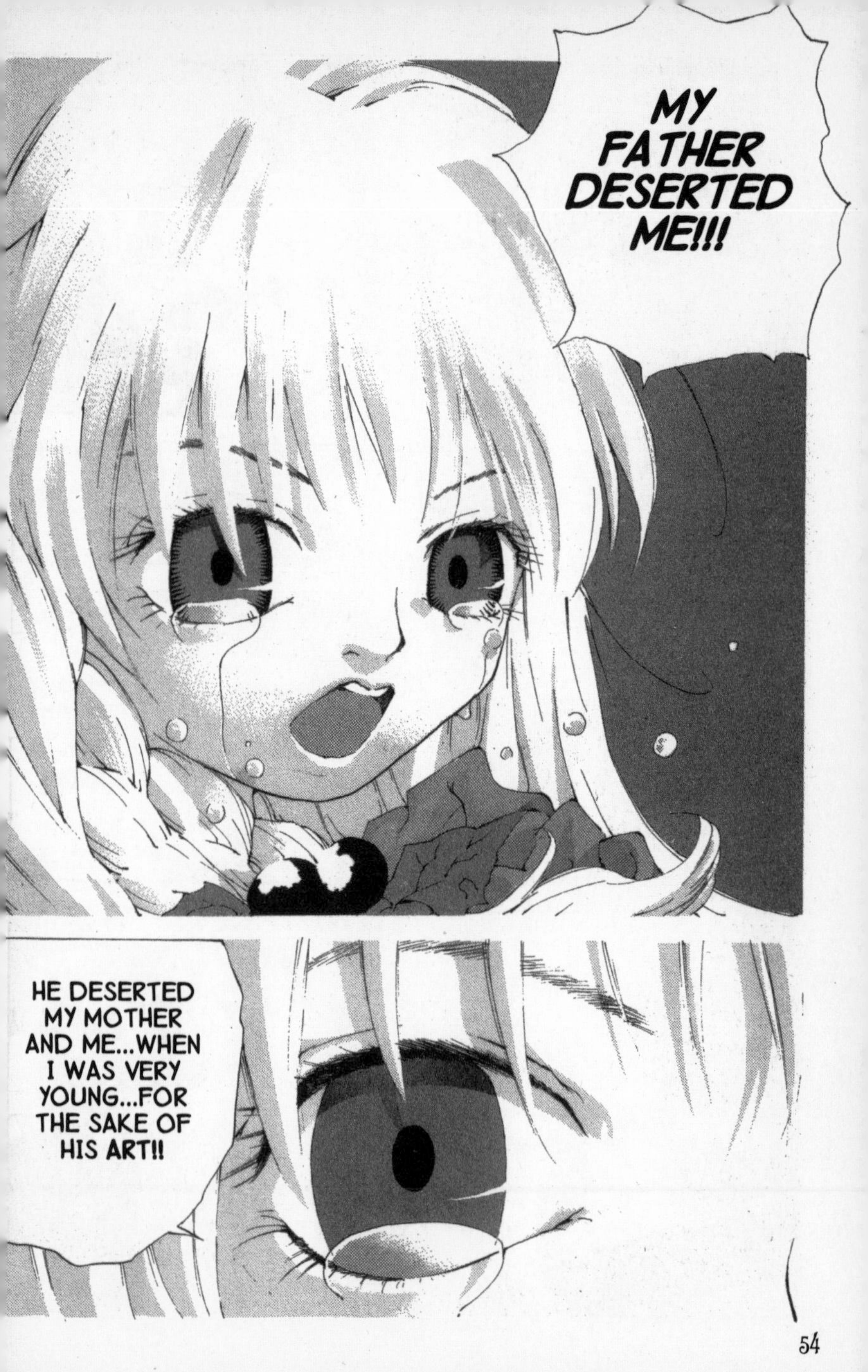
MY FATHER DESERTED ME!!!
HE DESERTED MY MOTHER AND ME...WHEN I WAS VERY YOUNG...FOR THE SAKE OF HIS ART!!

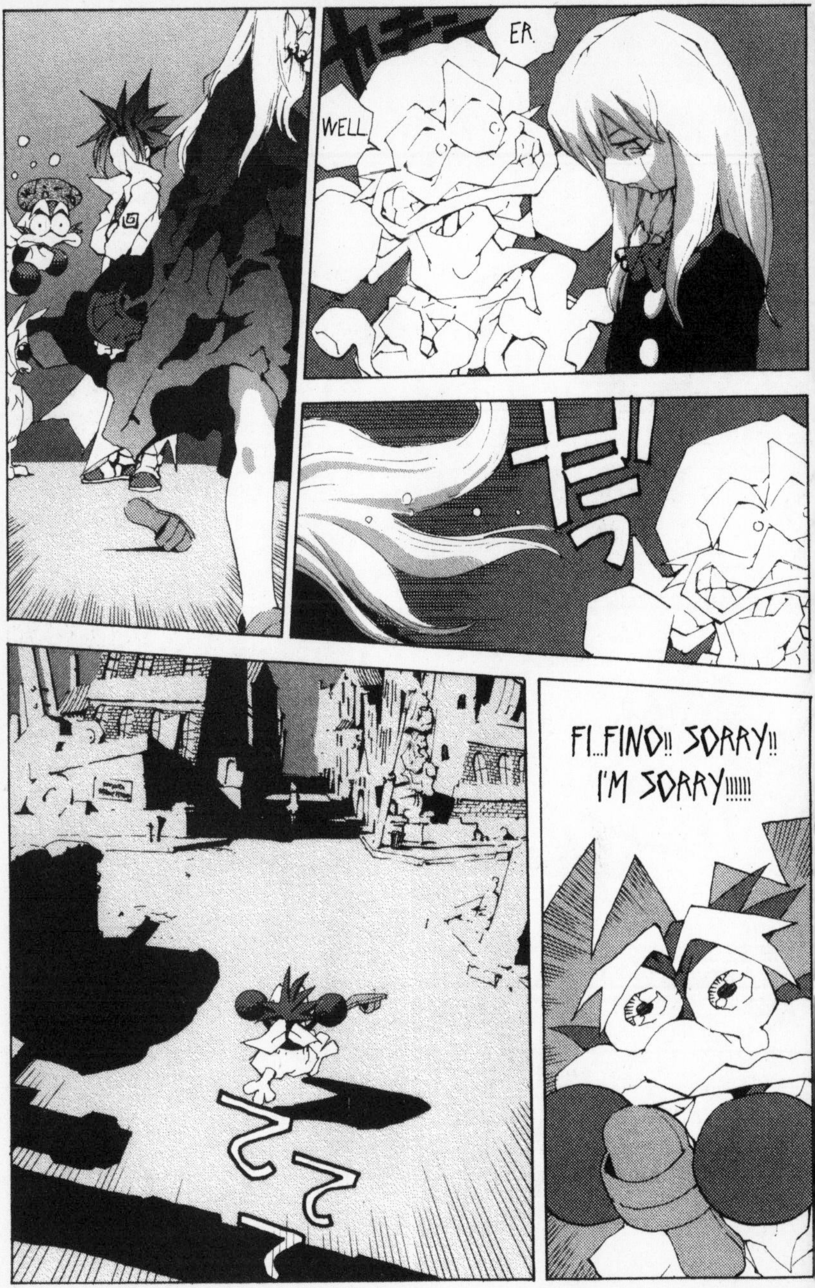
ER.
WELL.
FI...FINO!! SORRY!! I'M SORRY!!!!!!

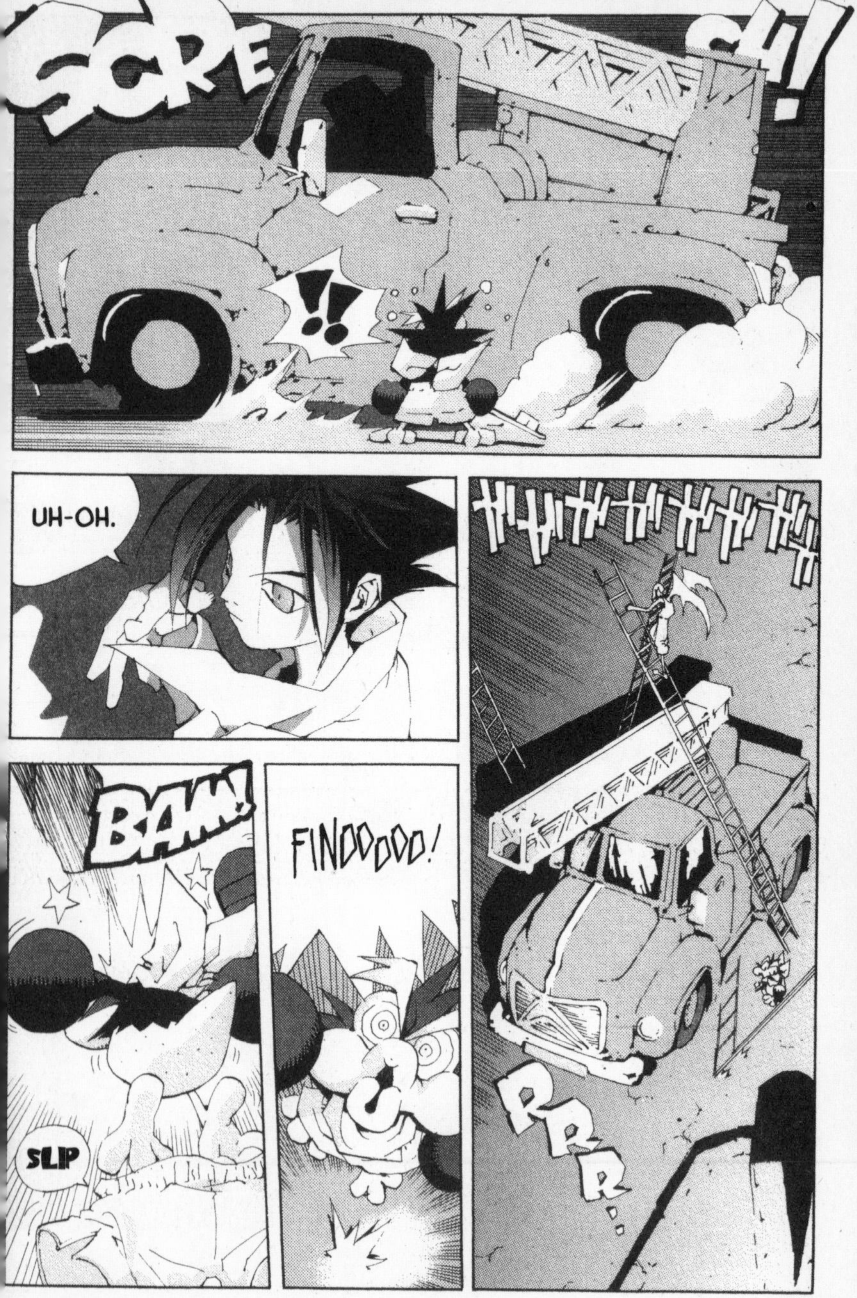
SCRE
CH!
!!
RRR..
UH-OH.
FINOOOOO!
BAM!
SLIP

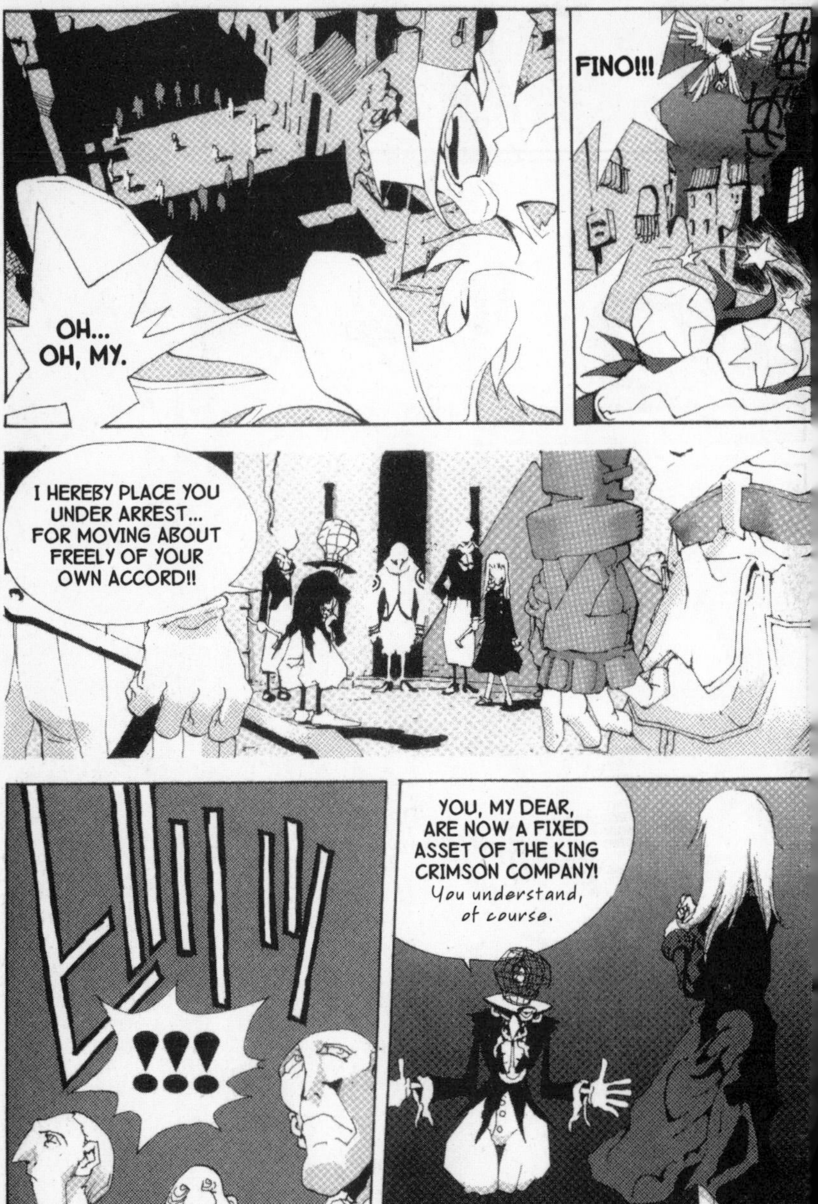
FINO!!!
OH...
OH, MY.
I HEREBY PLACE YOU UNDER ARREST... FOR MOVING ABOUT FREELY OF YOUR OWN ACCORD!!
YOU, MY DEAR, ARE NOW A FIXED ASSET OF THE KING CRIMSON COMPANY! You understand, of course.
!!!

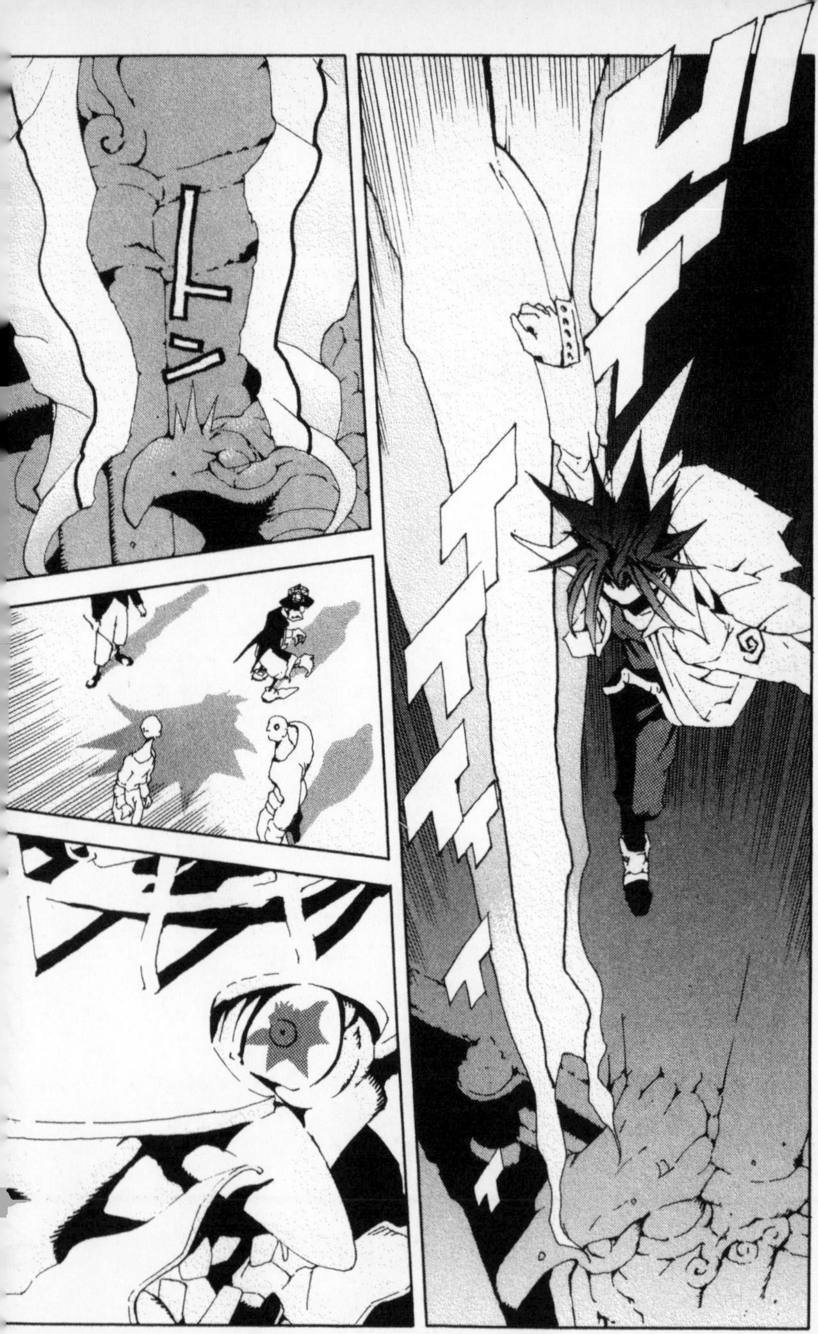
トン

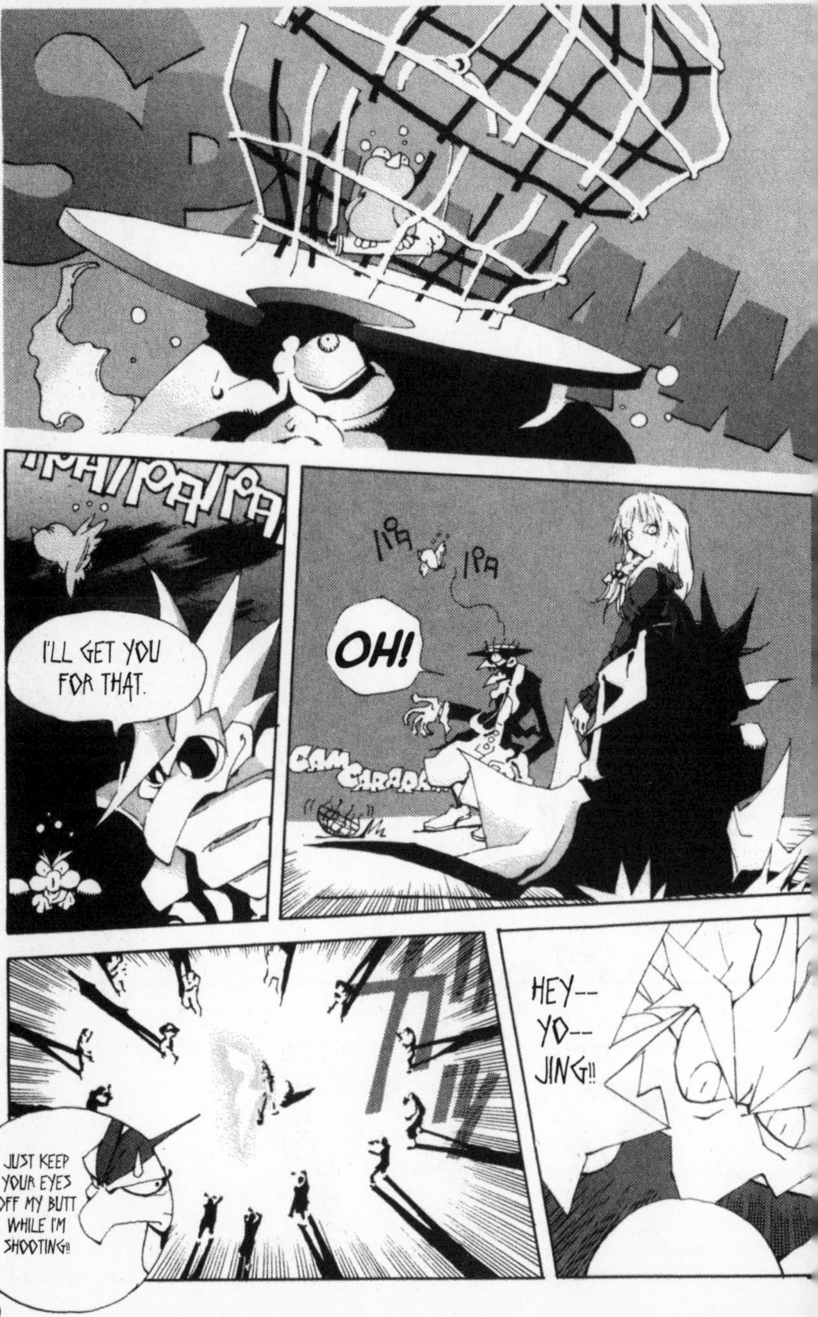
OH!
I'LL GET YOU FOR THAT.
HEY-- YO-- JING!!
JUST KEEP YOUR EYES OFF MY BUTT WHILE I'M SHOOTING!!

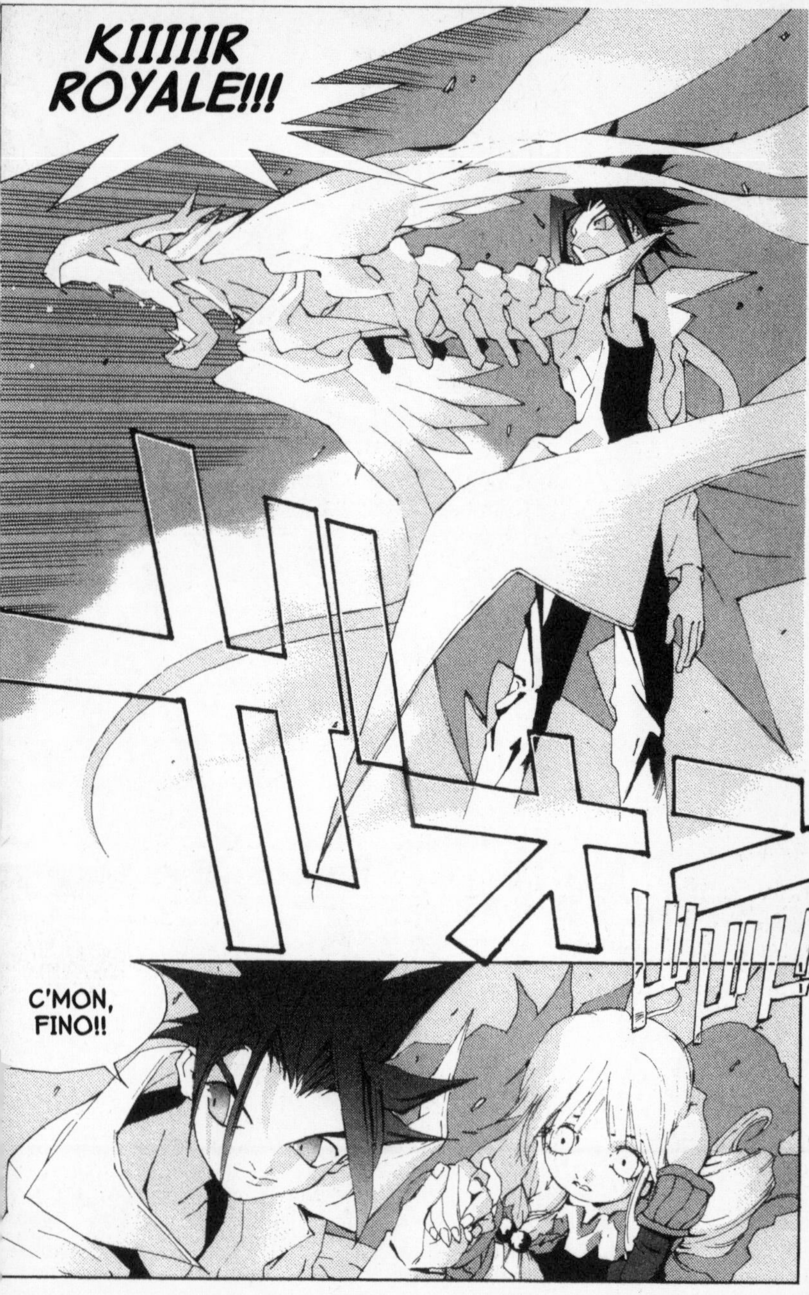
KIIIIIR ROYALE!!!
C'MON, FINO!!

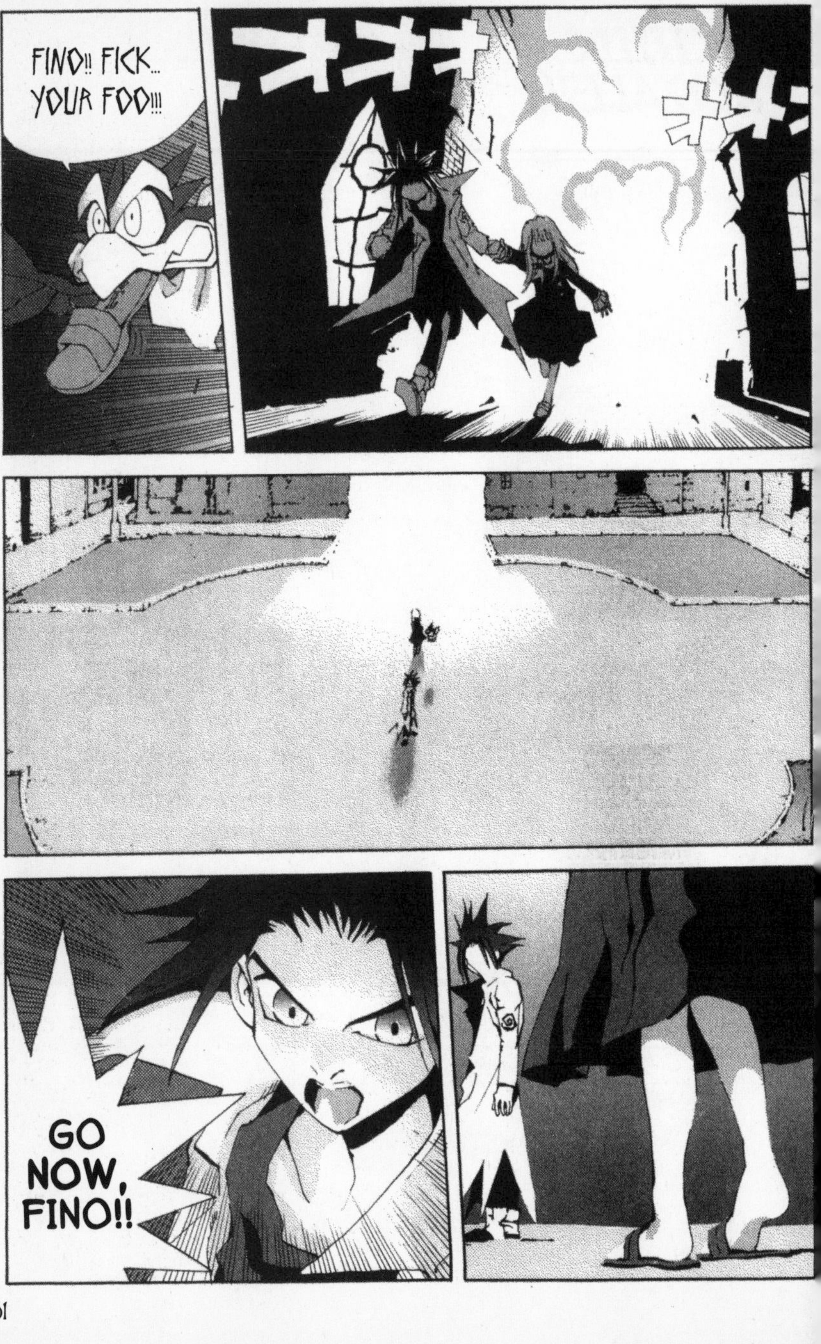
FINO!! FICK... YOUR FOO!!!
GO NOW, FINO!!

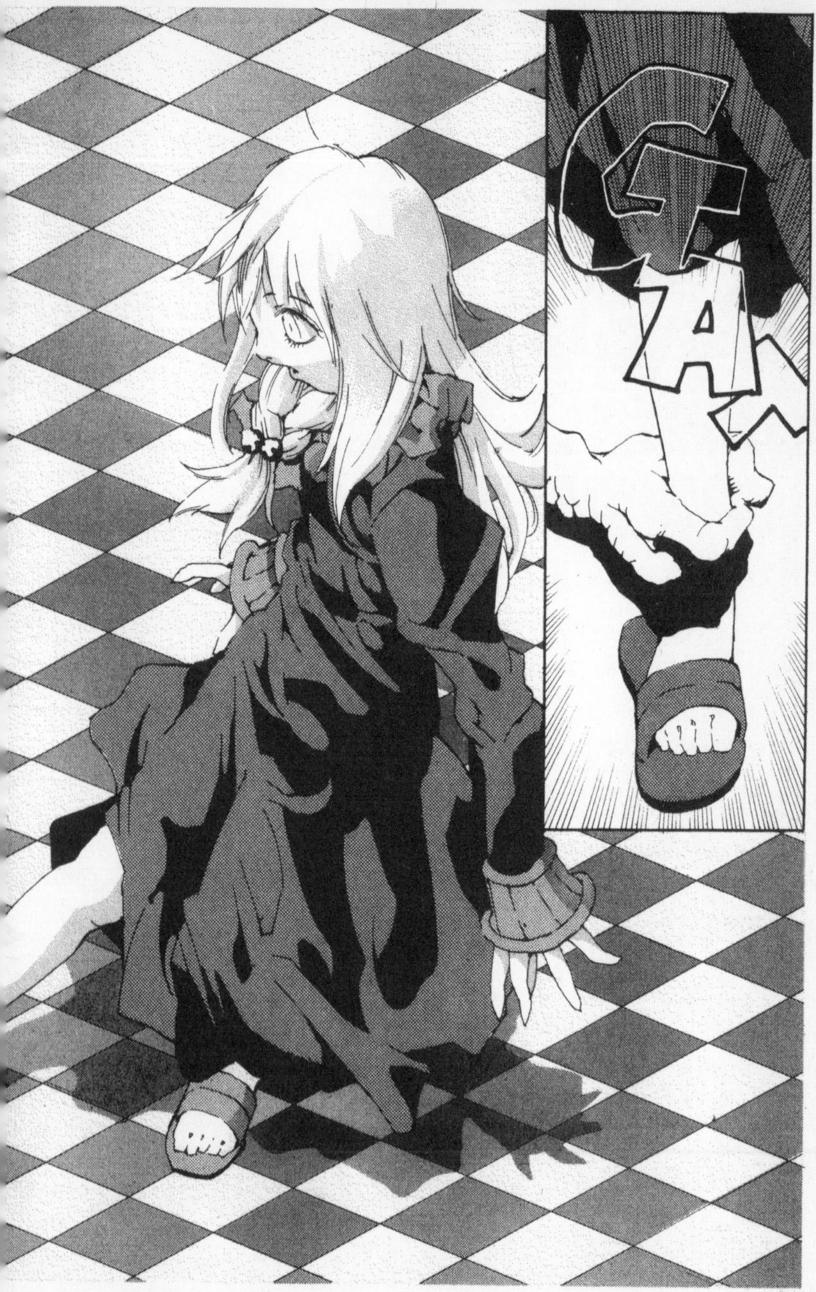
GA

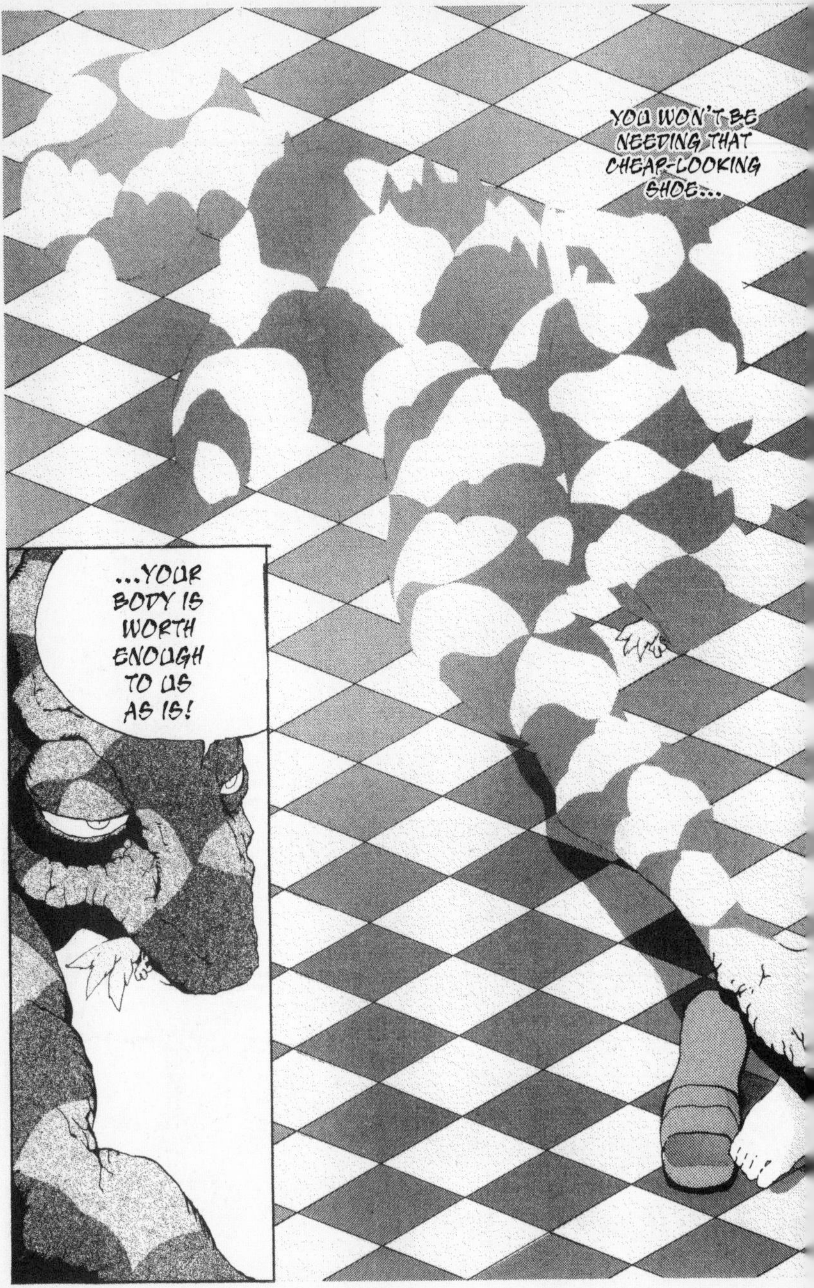
YOU WON'T BE NEEDING THAT CHEAP-LOOKING SHOE...
...YOUR BODY IS WORTH ENOUGH TO US AS IS!

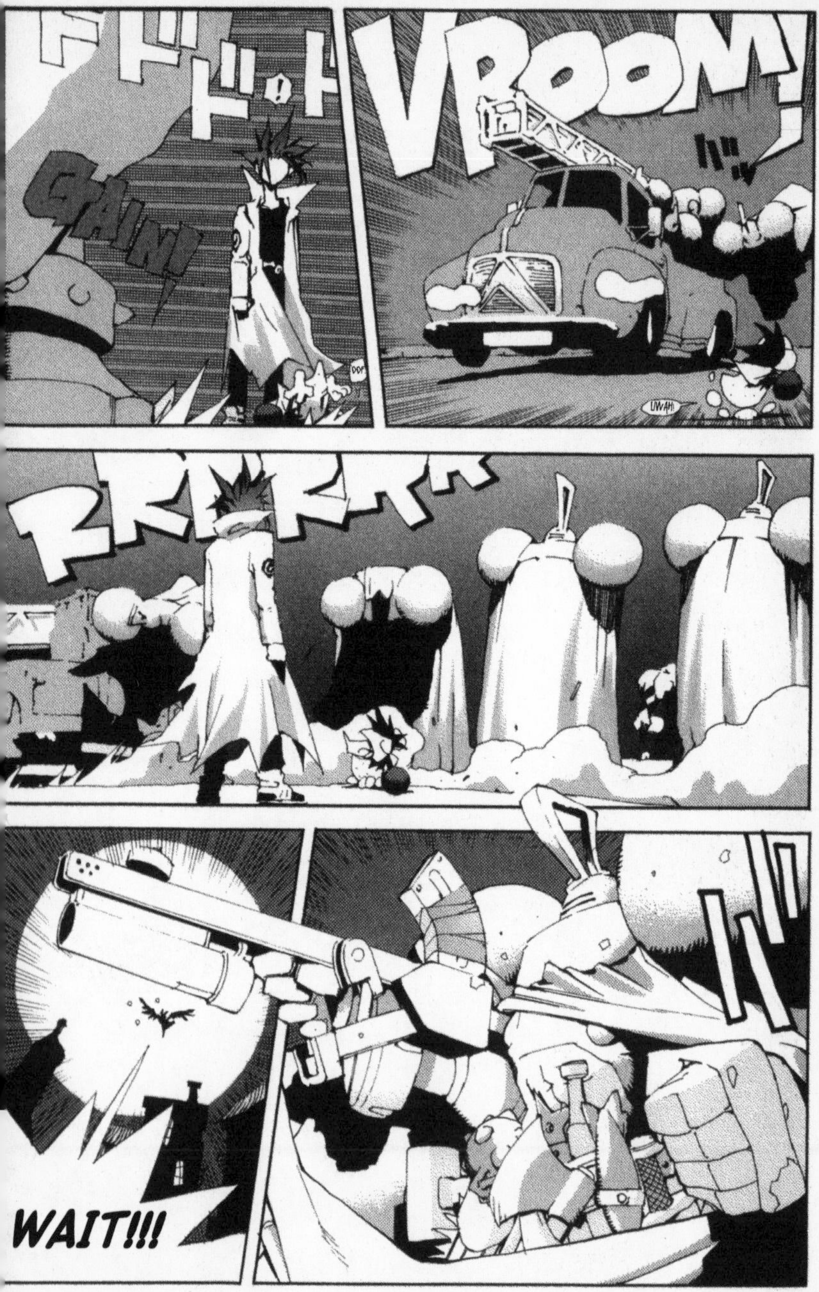
VROOM!
UWAH!
GAIN!
WAIT!!!

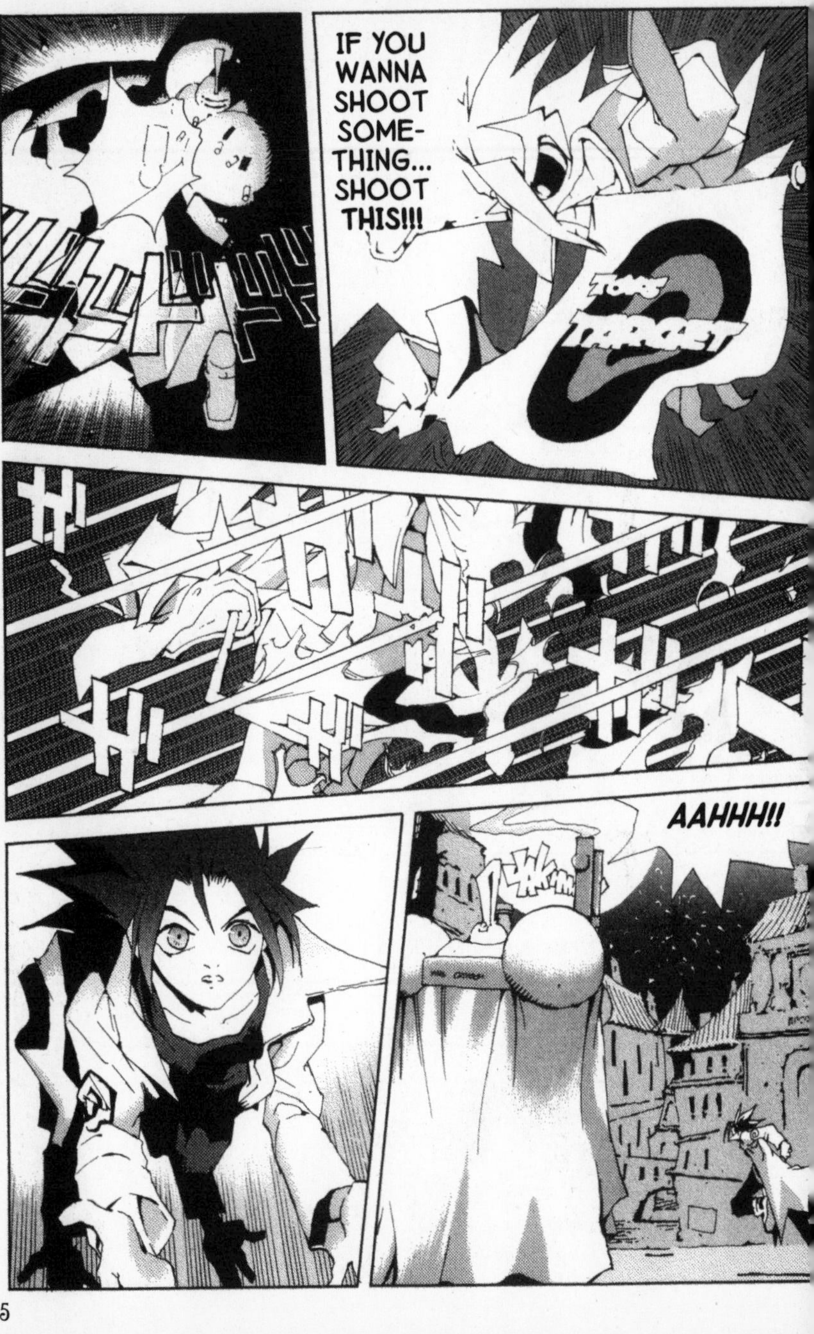
IF YOU WANNA SHOOT SOME-THING... SHOOT THIS!!!
TOM'S TARGET
AAHHH!!

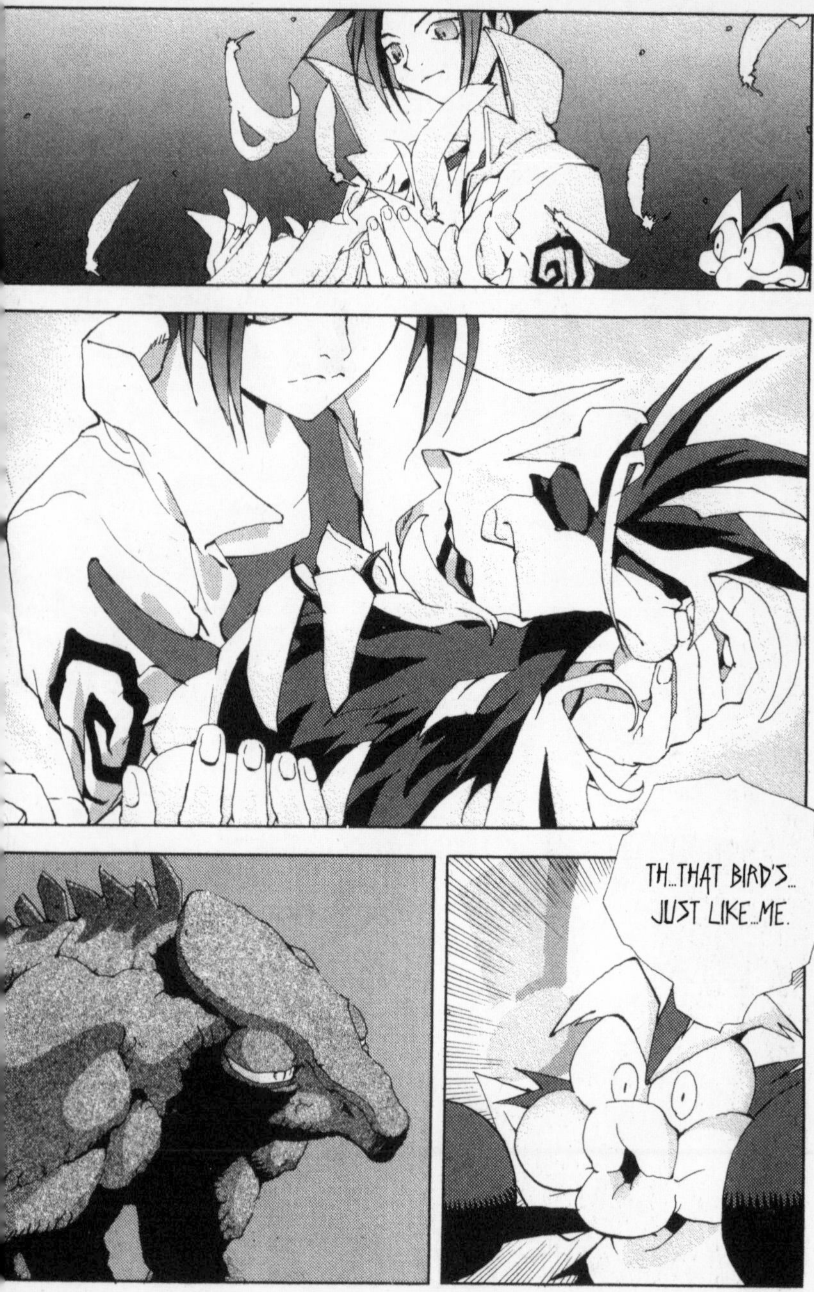
TH...THAT BIRD'S... JUST LIKE...ME.

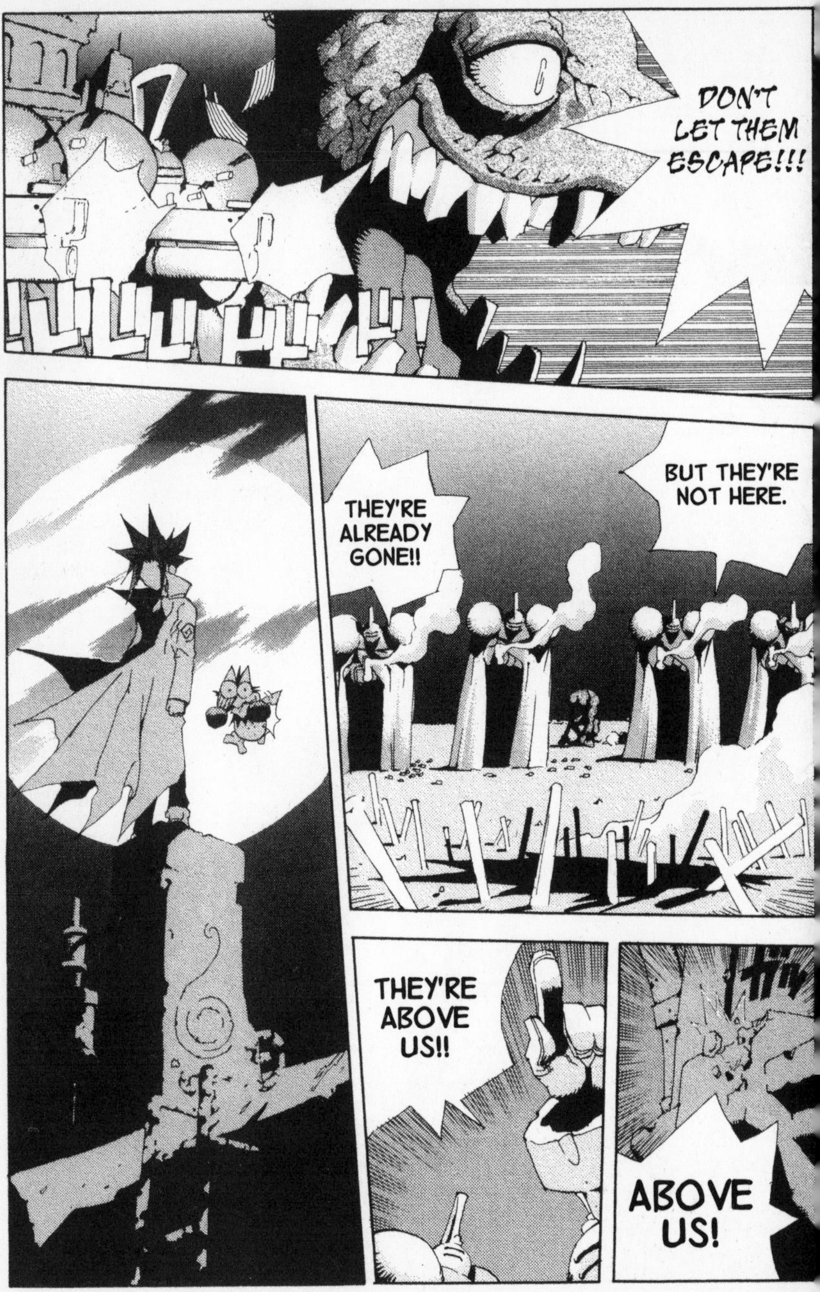
DON'T LET THEM ESCAPE!!!
BUT THEY'RE NOT HERE.
THEY'RE ALREADY GONE!!
ABOVE US!
THEY'RE ABOVE US!!

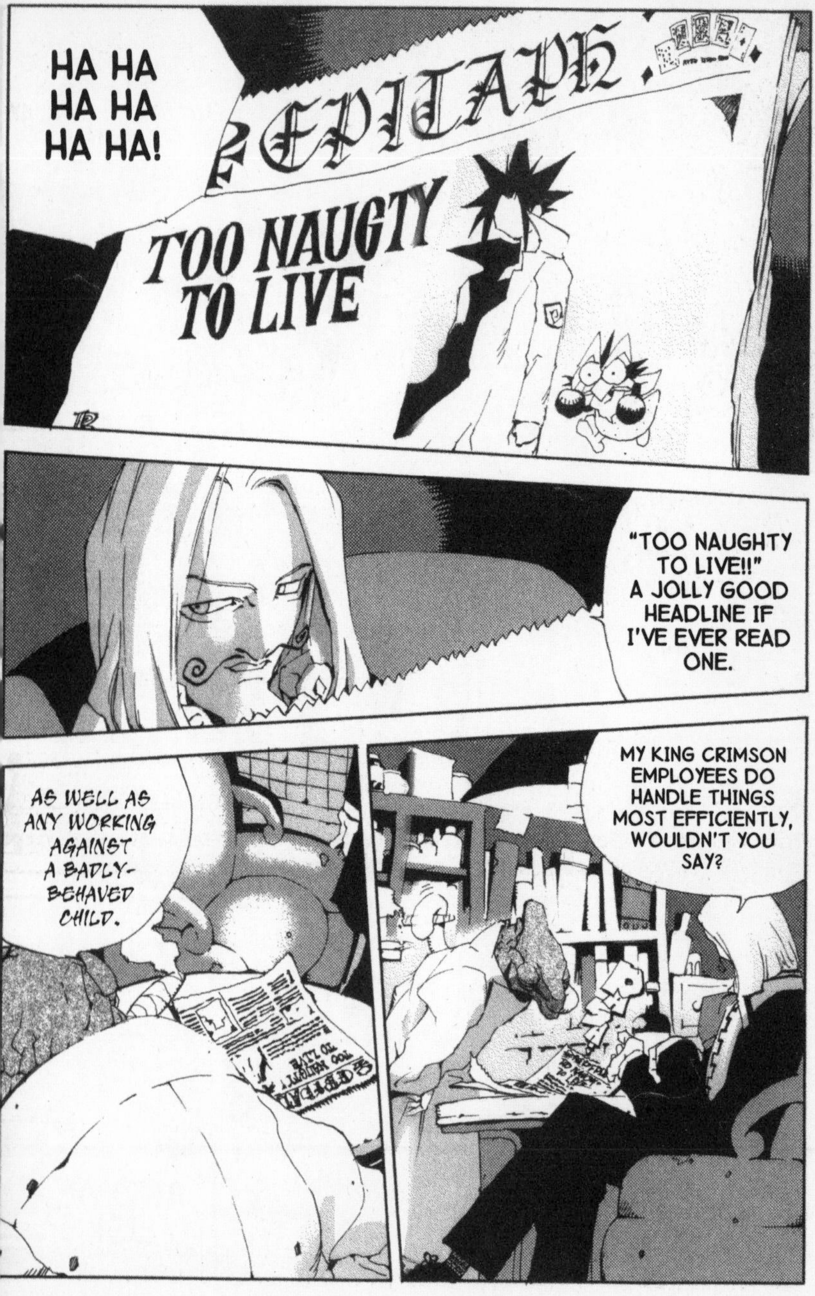
EPITAPH
HA HA HA HA HA HA!
TOO NAUGTY TO LIVE
"TOO NAUGHTY TO LIVE!!" A JOLLY GOOD HEADLINE IF I'VE EVER READ ONE.
MY KING CRIMSON EMPLOYEES DO HANDLE THINGS MOST EFFICIENTLY, WOULDN'T YOU SAY?
AS WELL AS ANY WORKING AGAINST A BADLY-BEHAVED CHILD.

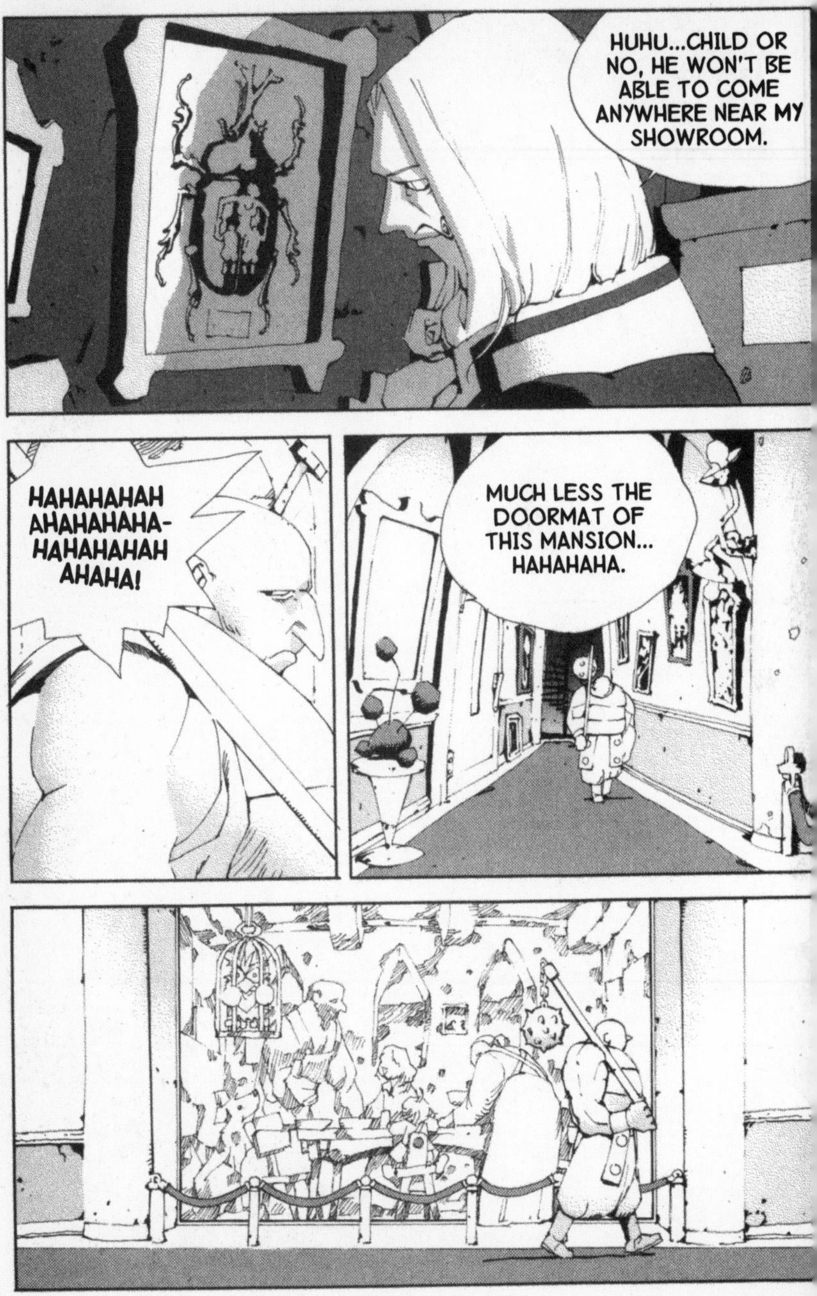
HUHU...CHILD OR NO, HE WON'T BE ABLE TO COME ANYWHERE NEAR MY SHOWROOM.
MUCH LESS THE DOORMAT OF THIS MANSION... HAHAHAHA.
HAHAHAHAH AHAHAHAHA-HAHAHAHAH AHAHA!

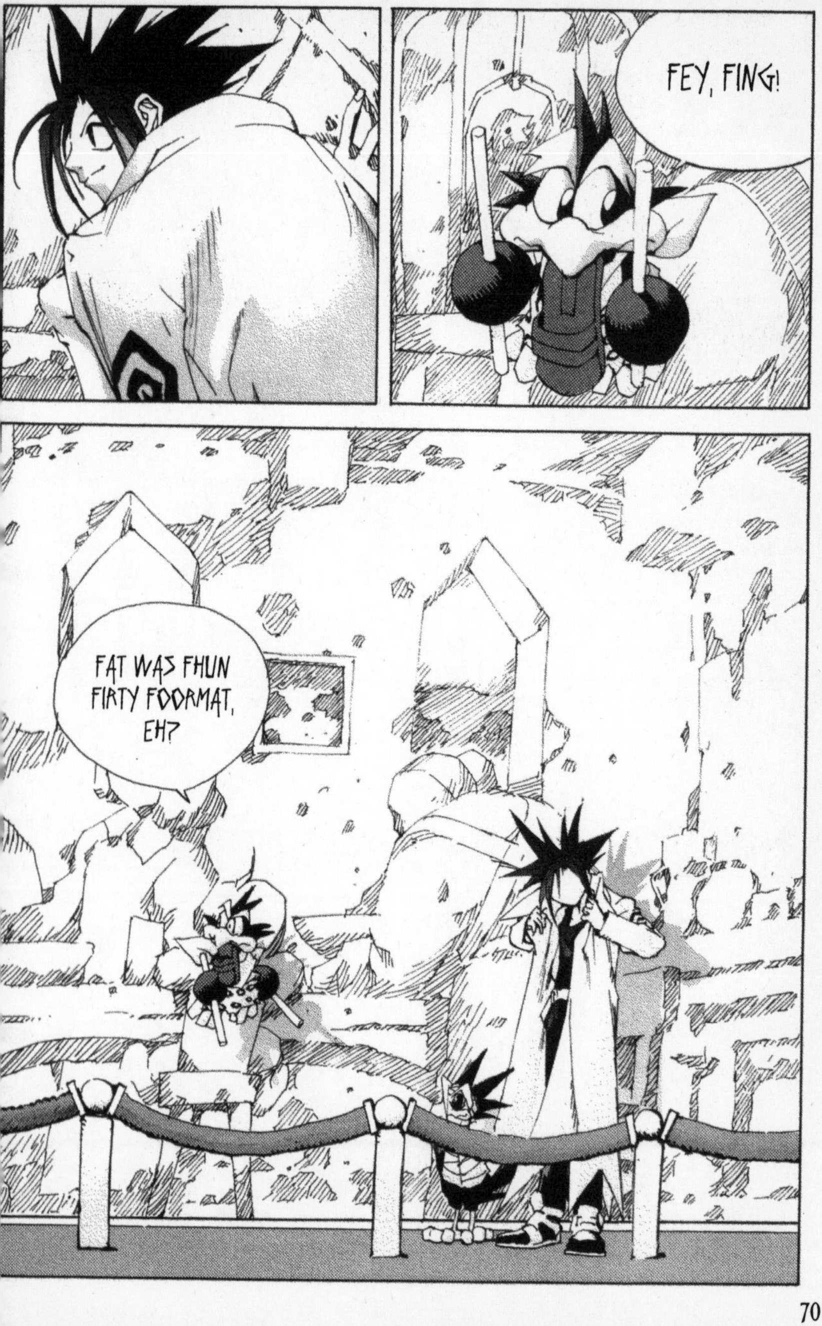
FEY, FING!
FAT WAS FHUN FIRTY FOORMAT, EH?

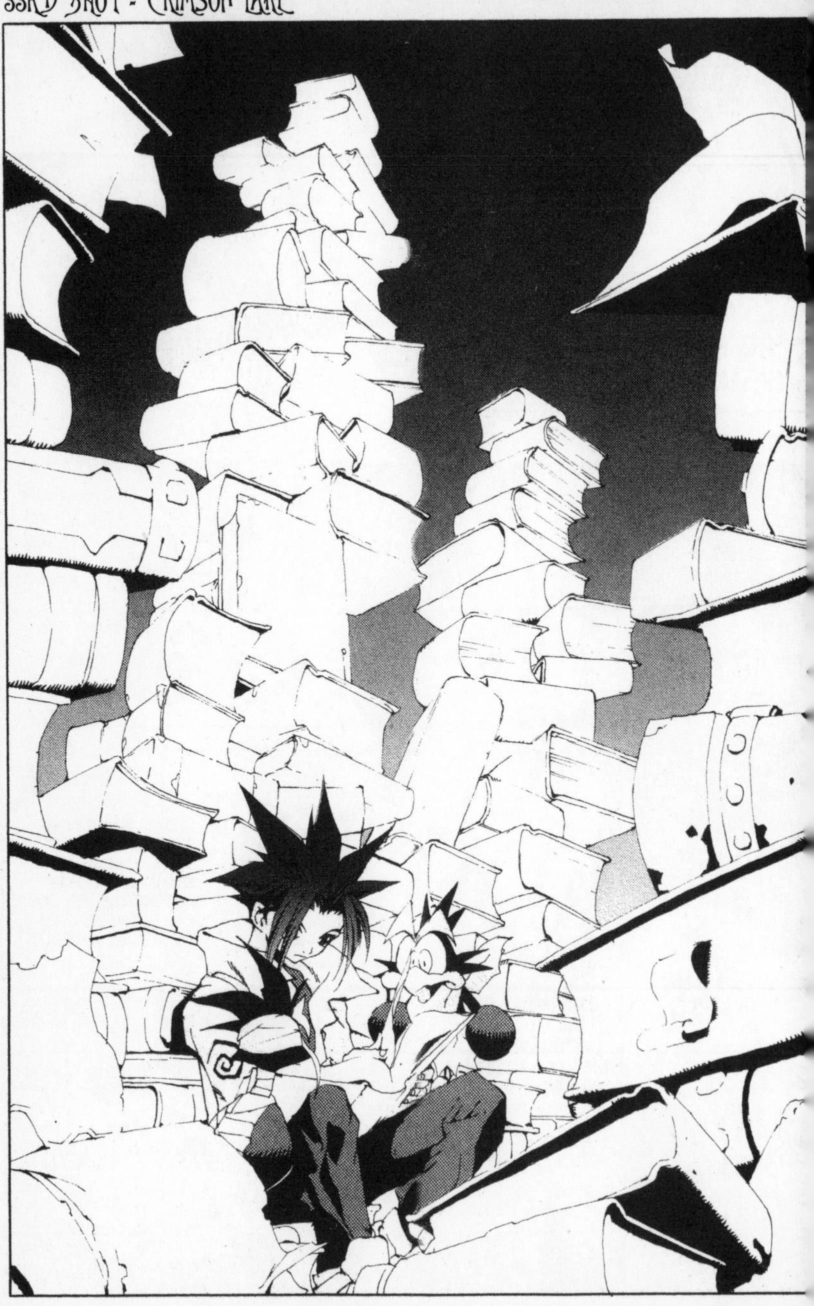

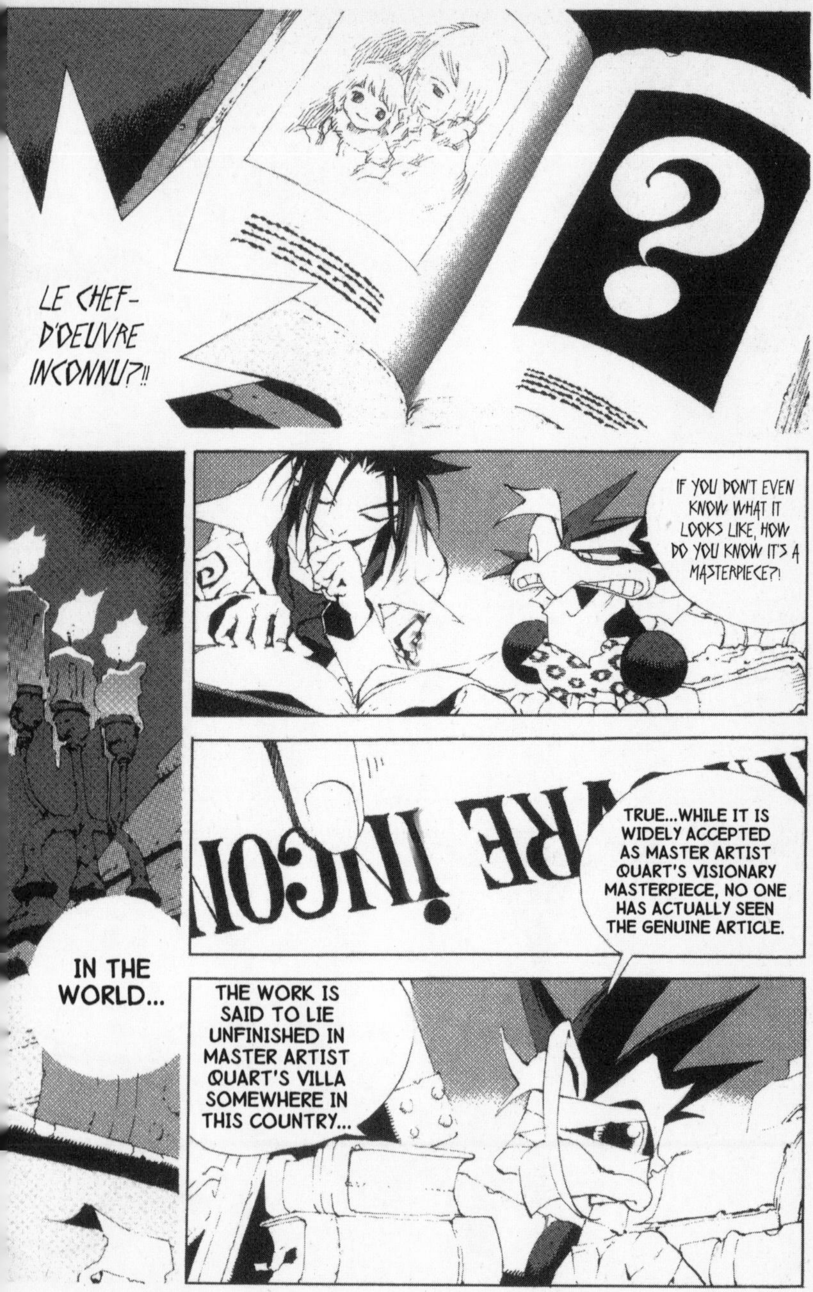
LE CHEF-D'OEUVRE INCONNU?!!
IF YOU DON'T EVEN KNOW WHAT IT LOOKS LIKE, HOW DO YOU KNOW IT'S A MASTERPIECE?!
TRUE...WHILE IT IS WIDELY ACCEPTED AS MASTER ARTIST QUART'S VISIONARY MASTERPIECE, NO ONE HAS ACTUALLY SEEN THE GENUINE ARTICLE.
IN THE WORLD...
THE WORK IS SAID TO LIE UNFINISHED IN MASTER ARTIST QUART'S VILLA SOMEWHERE IN THIS COUNTRY...

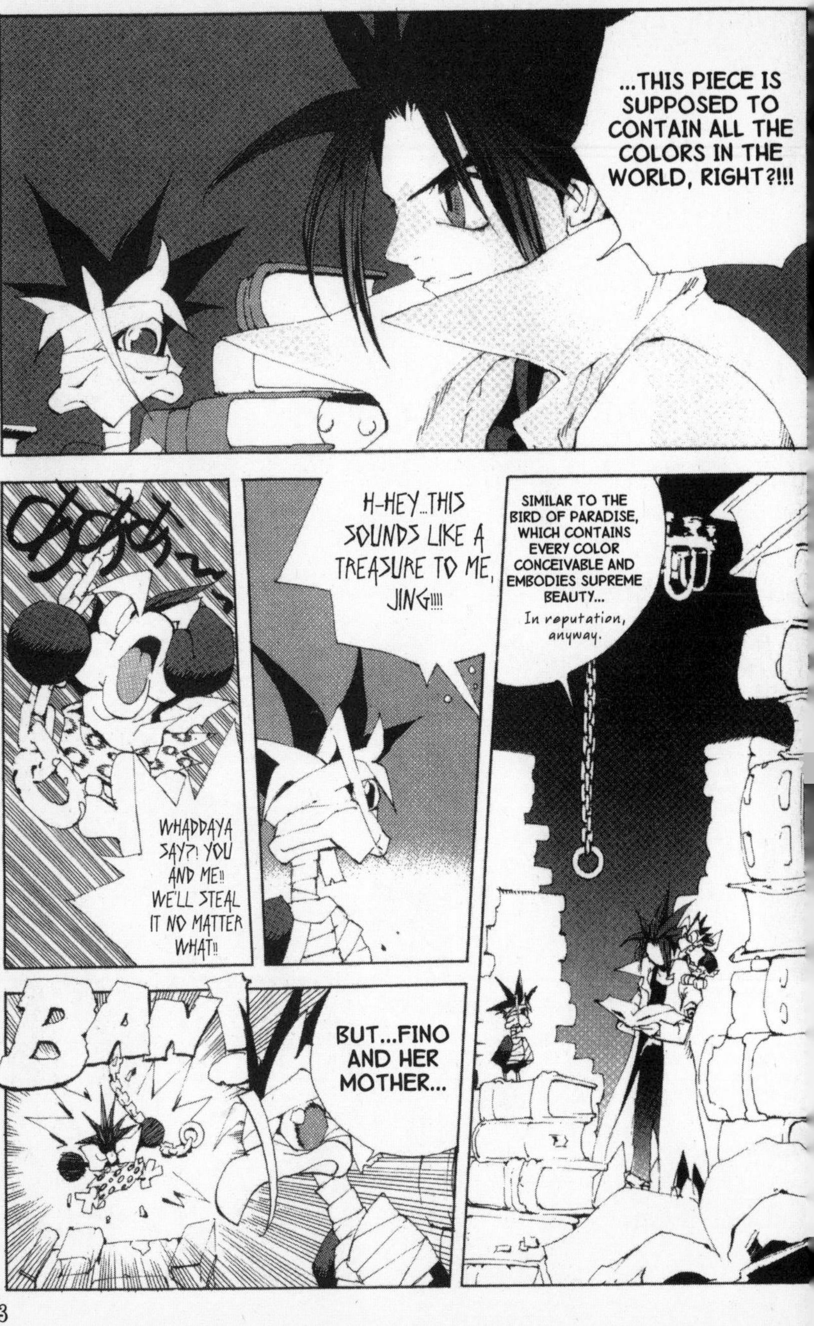
...THIS PIECE IS SUPPOSED TO CONTAIN ALL THE COLORS IN THE WORLD, RIGHT?!!!
SIMILAR TO THE BIRD OF PARADISE, WHICH CONTAINS EVERY COLOR CONCEIVABLE AND EMBODIES SUPREME BEAUTY...
In reputation, anyway.
H-HEY...THIS SOUNDS LIKE A TREASURE TO ME, JING!!!!
WHADDAYA SAY?! YOU AND ME!! WE'LL STEAL IT NO MATTER WHAT!!
BUT...FINO AND HER MOTHER...
BAM!

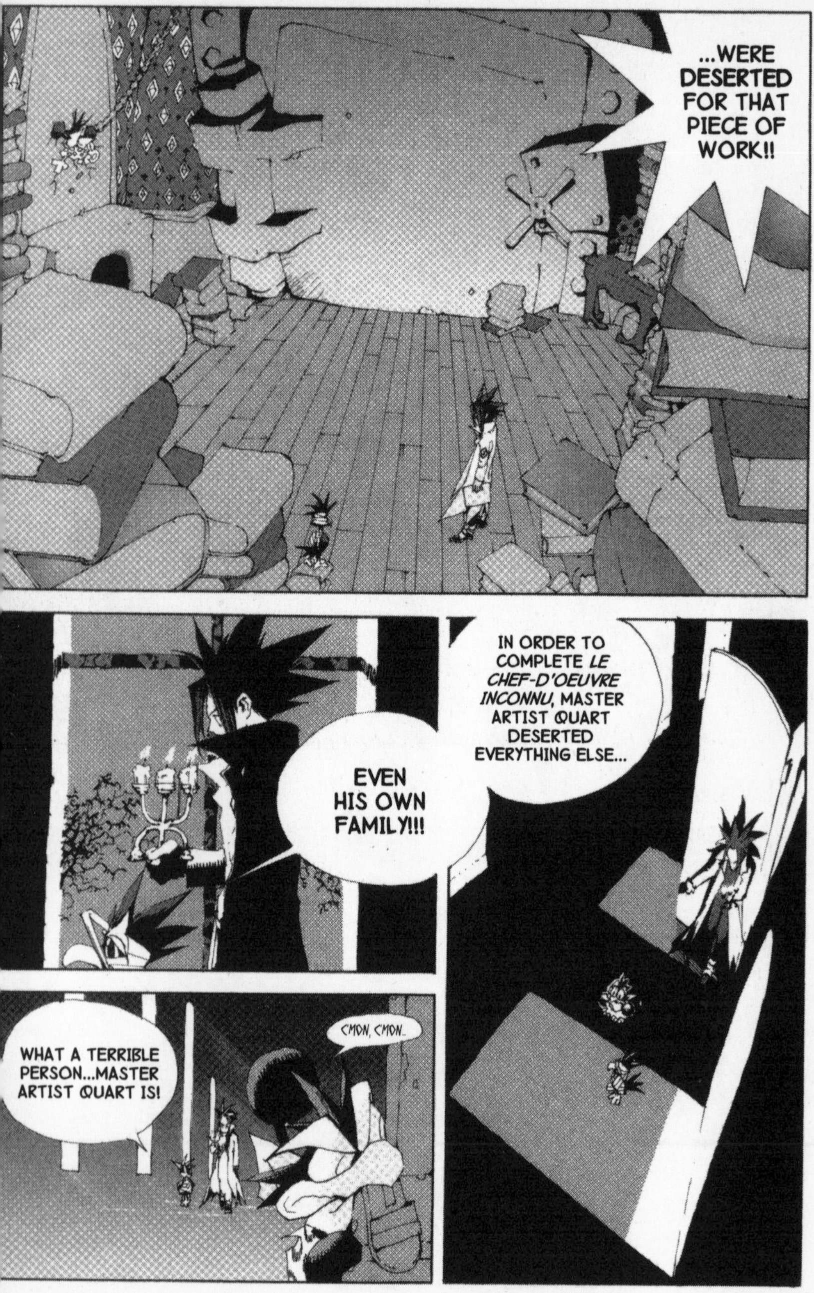
...WERE DESERTED FOR THAT PIECE OF WORK!!
IN ORDER TO COMPLETE *LE CHEF-D'OEUVRE INCONNU*, MASTER ARTIST QUART DESERTED EVERYTHING ELSE...
EVEN HIS OWN FAMILY!!!
CMON, CMON..
WHAT A TERRIBLE PERSON...MASTER ARTIST QUART IS!

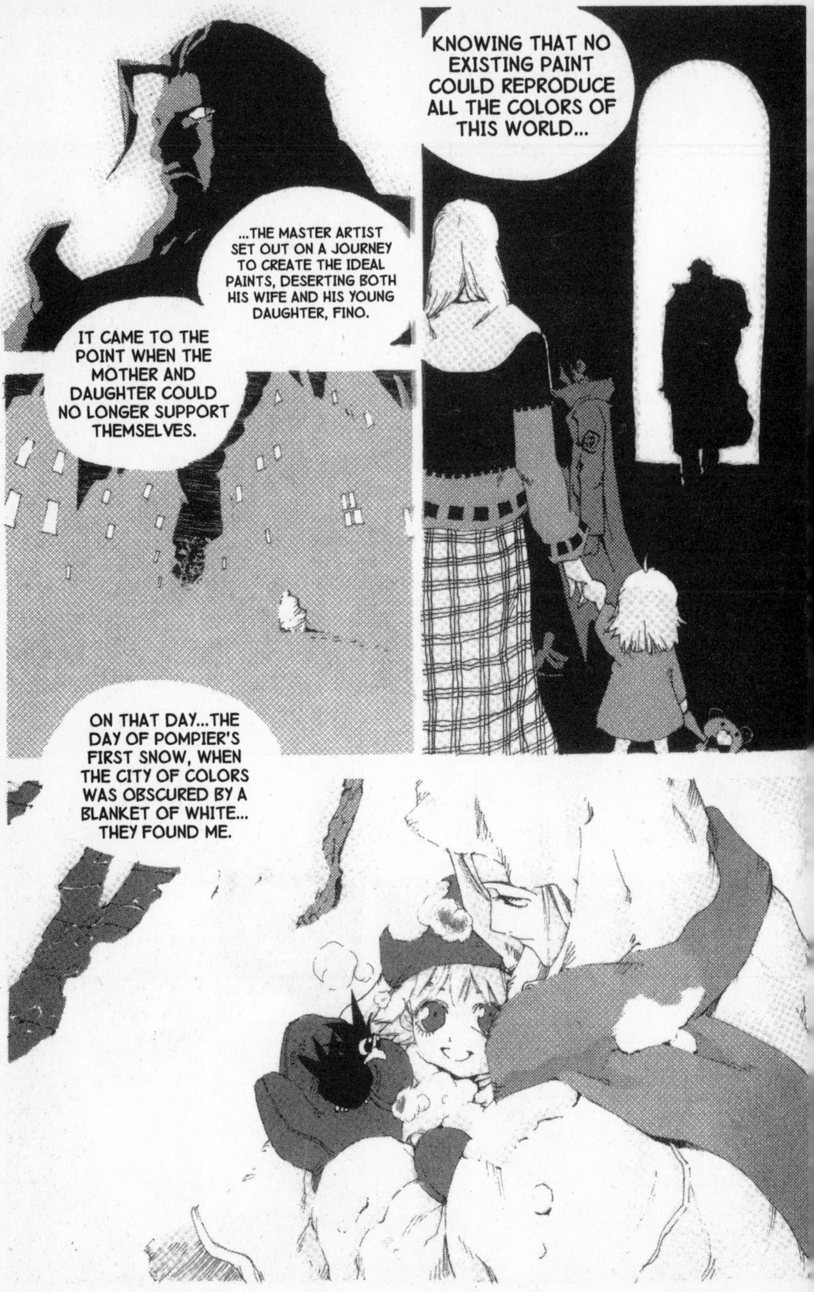
KNOWING THAT NO EXISTING PAINT COULD REPRODUCE ALL THE COLORS OF THIS WORLD...
...THE MASTER ARTIST SET OUT ON A JOURNEY TO CREATE THE IDEAL PAINTS, DESERTING BOTH HIS WIFE AND HIS YOUNG DAUGHTER, FINO.
IT CAME TO THE POINT WHEN THE MOTHER AND DAUGHTER COULD NO LONGER SUPPORT THEMSELVES.
ON THAT DAY...THE DAY OF POMPIER'S FIRST SNOW, WHEN THE CITY OF COLORS WAS OBSCURED BY A BLANKET OF WHITE... THEY FOUND ME.

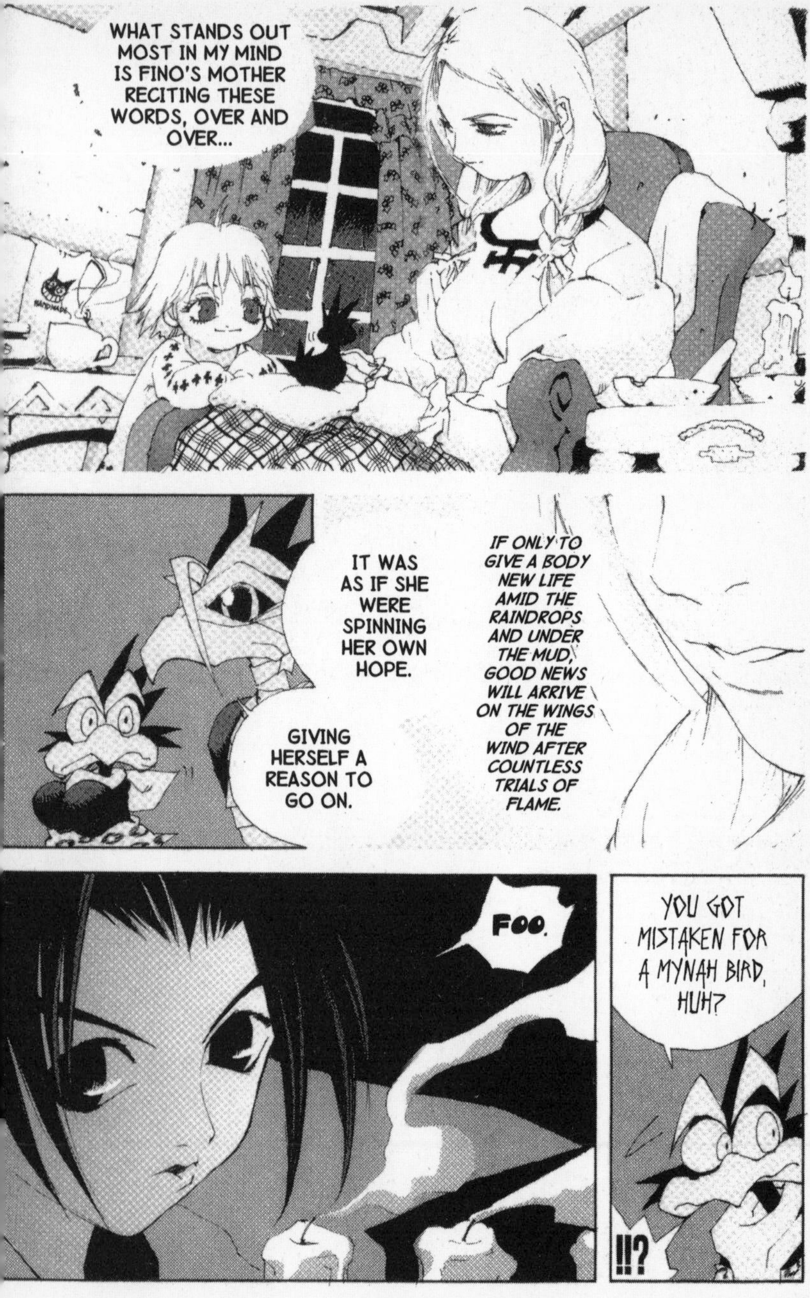
WHAT STANDS OUT MOST IN MY MIND IS FINO'S MOTHER RECITING THESE WORDS, OVER AND OVER...
IF ONLY TO GIVE A BODY NEW LIFE AMID THE RAINDROPS AND UNDER THE MUD, GOOD NEWS WILL ARRIVE ON THE WINGS OF THE WIND AFTER COUNTLESS TRIALS OF FLAME.
IT WAS AS IF SHE WERE SPINNING HER OWN HOPE.
GIVING HERSELF A REASON TO GO ON.
YOU GOT MISTAKEN FOR A MYNAH BIRD, HUH?
!!?
FOO.

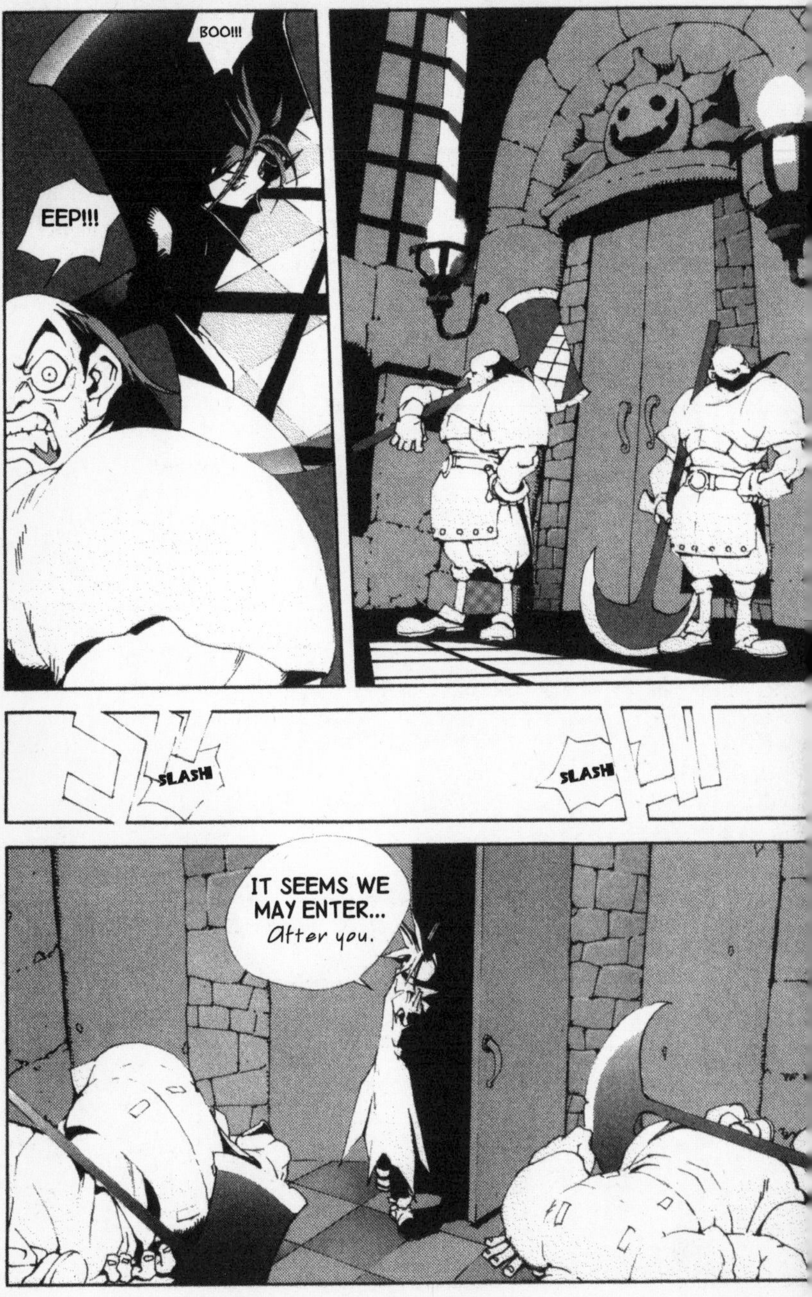
BOO!!!
EEP!!!
SLASH!
SLASH!
IT SEEMS WE MAY ENTER... After you.

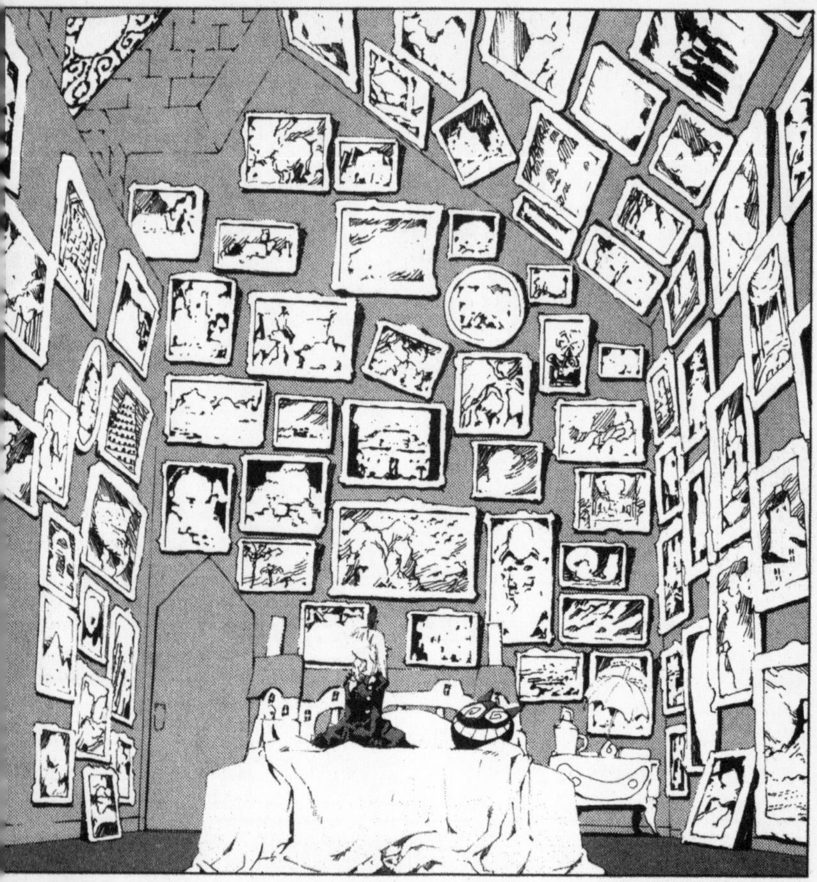
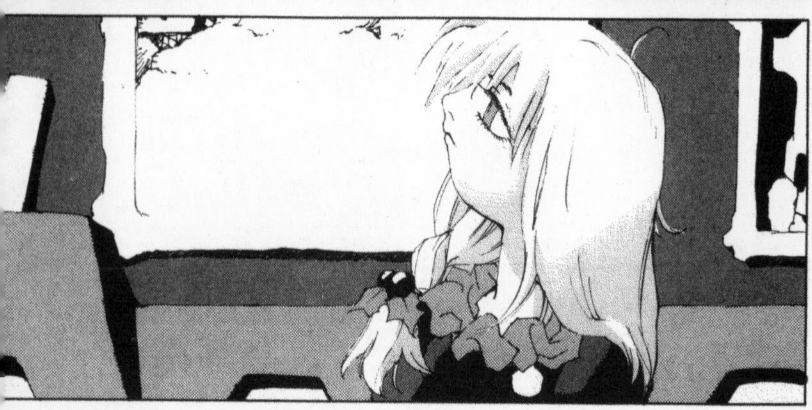

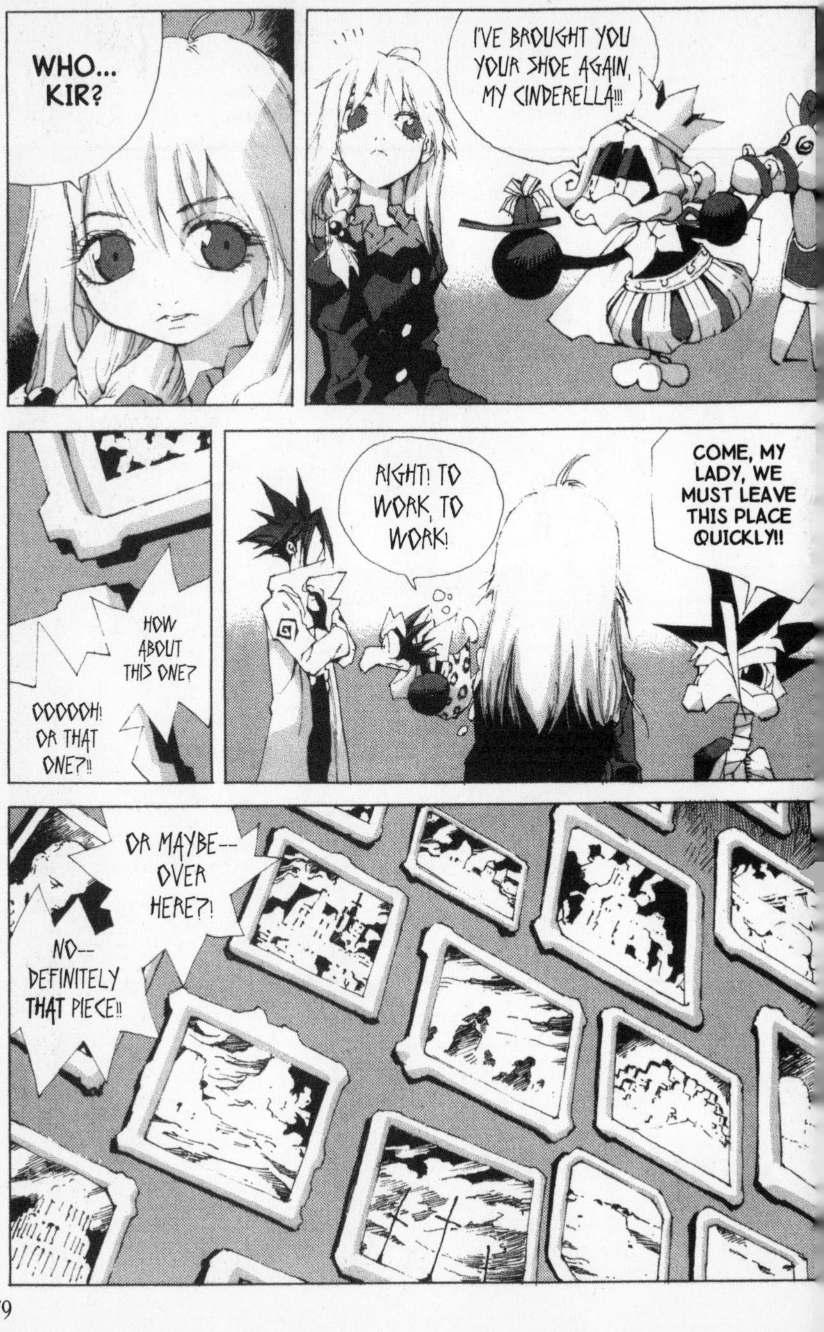
I'VE BROUGHT YOU YOUR SHOE AGAIN, MY CINDERELLA!!!
WHO... KIR?
COME, MY LADY, WE MUST LEAVE THIS PLACE QUICKLY!!
RIGHT! TO WORK, TO WORK!
HOW ABOUT THIS ONE?
OOOOOH! OR THAT ONE?!!
OR MAYBE-- OVER HERE?!
NO-- DEFINITELY THAT PIECE!!

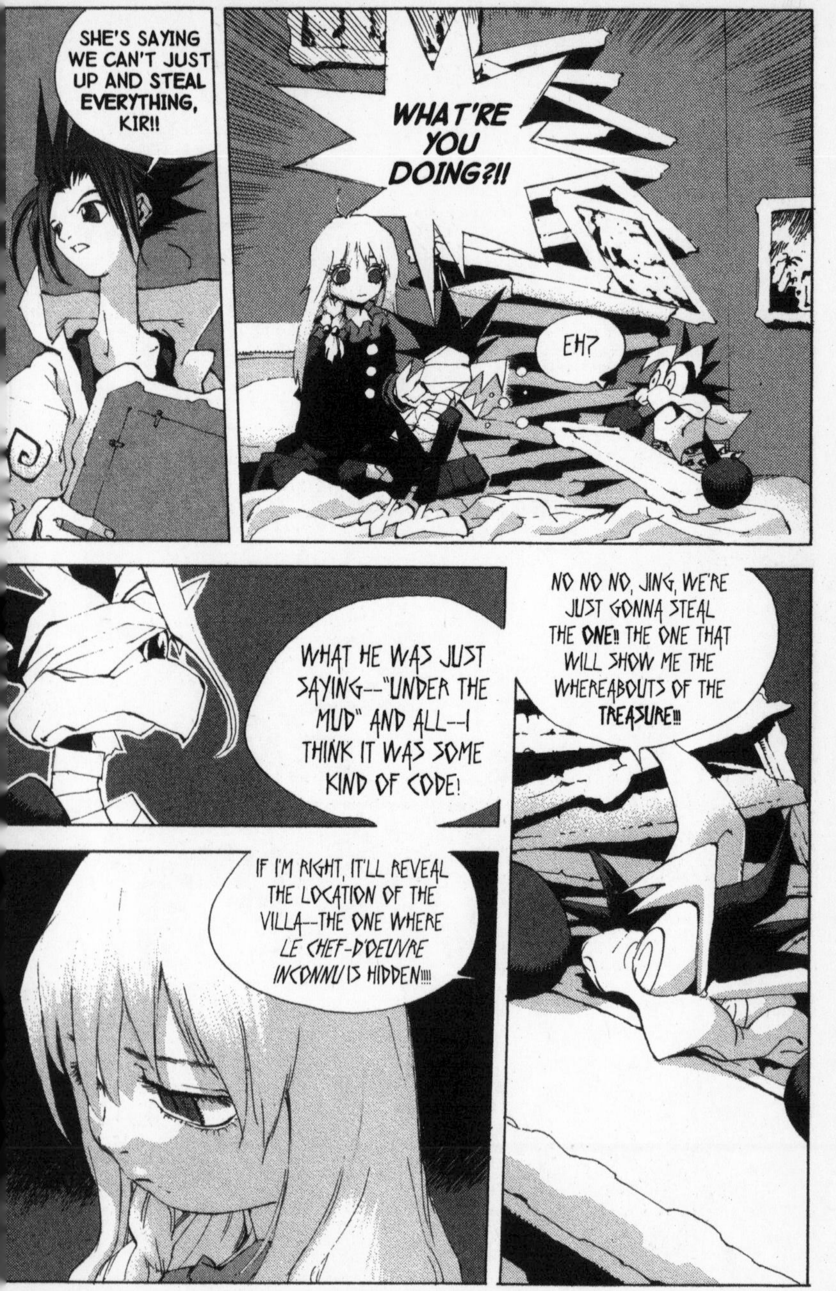
WHAT'RE YOU DOING?!!
EH?
SHE'S SAYING WE CAN'T JUST UP AND STEAL EVERYTHING, KIR!!
NO NO NO, JING, WE'RE JUST GONNA STEAL THE ONE!! THE ONE THAT WILL SHOW ME THE WHEREABOUTS OF THE TREASURE!!!
WHAT HE WAS JUST SAYING--"UNDER THE MUD" AND ALL--I THINK IT WAS SOME KIND OF CODE!
IF I'M RIGHT, IT'LL REVEAL THE LOCATION OF THE VILLA--THE ONE WHERE *LE CHEF-D'OEUVRE INCONNU* IS HIDDEN!!!!

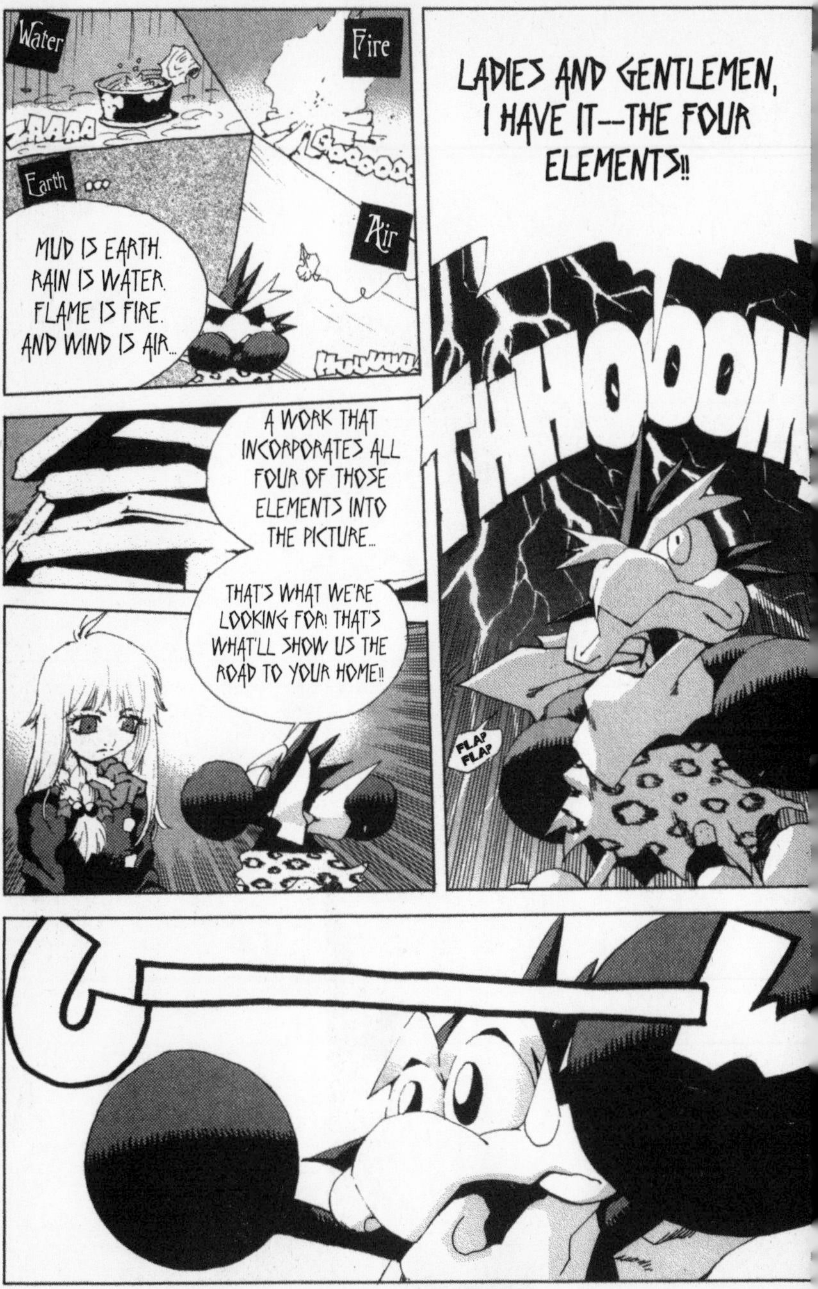
LADIES AND GENTLEMEN, I HAVE IT--THE FOUR ELEMENTS!!
THHOOOM
FLAP FLAP
Fire
Water
ZAAAA
GOOOOOO
Air
Earth
...
MUD IS EARTH. RAIN IS WATER. FLAME IS FIRE. AND WIND IS AIR...
HUUUUU
A WORK THAT INCORPORATES ALL FOUR OF THOSE ELEMENTS INTO THE PICTURE...
THAT'S WHAT WE'RE LOOKING FOR! THAT'S WHAT'LL SHOW US THE ROAD TO YOUR HOME!!

*SILENCE

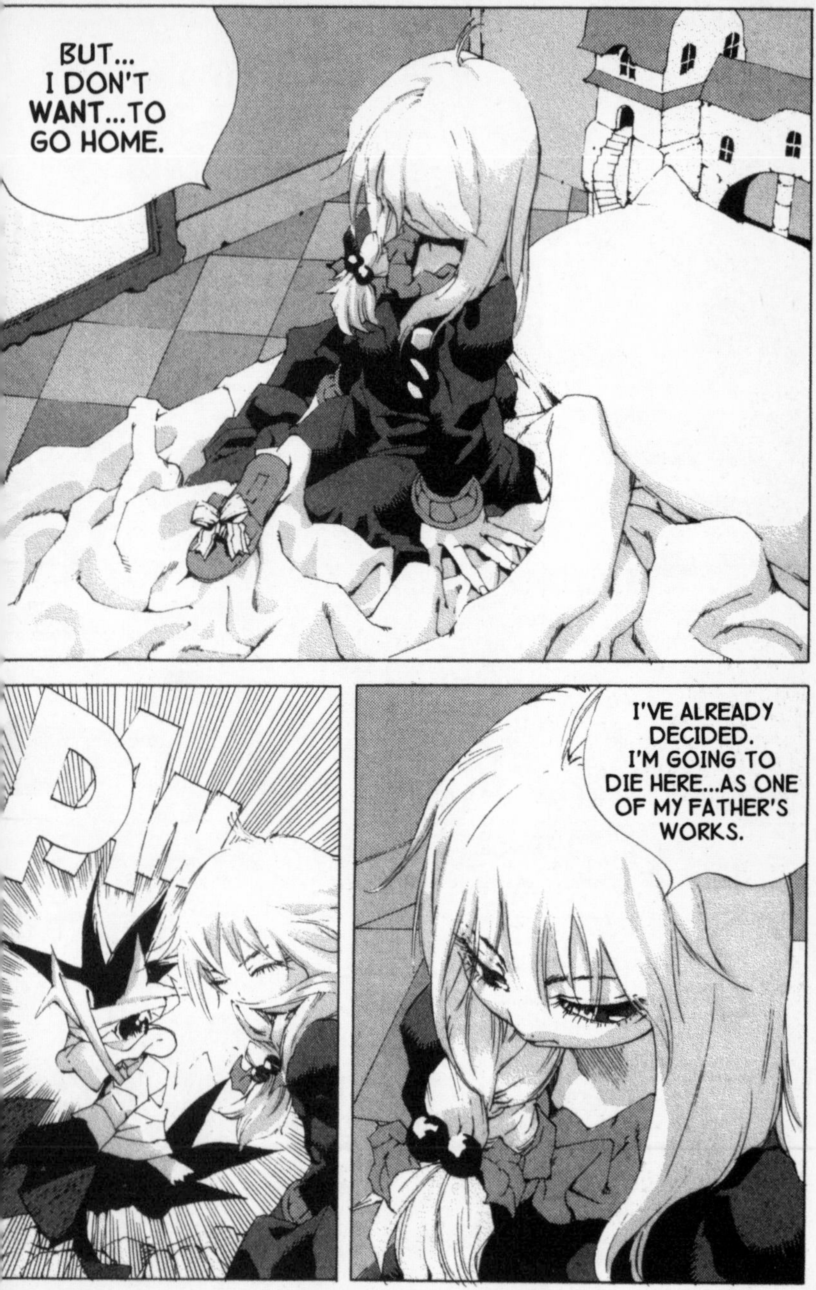
BUT...
I DON'T
WANT...TO
GO HOME.
I'VE ALREADY
DECIDED.
I'M GOING TO
DIE HERE...AS ONE
OF MY FATHER'S
WORKS.

IDIOT!!!

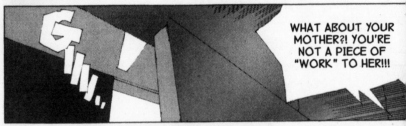

WHAT ABOUT YOUR MOTHER?! YOU'RE NOT A PIECE OF "WORK" TO HER!!!

RUN!!

UH-OH!! THEY'RE ON TO US!!

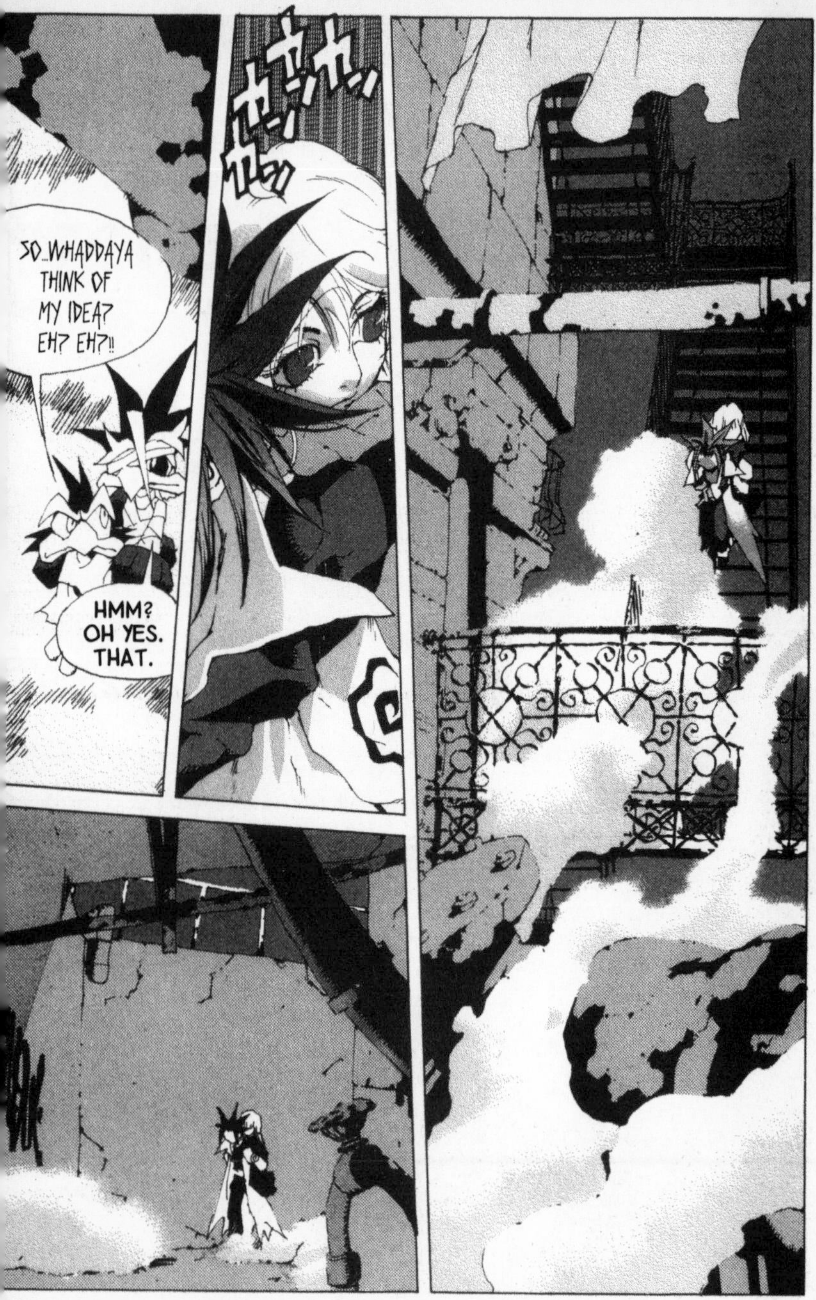
SO...WHADDAYA THINK OF MY IDEA? EH? EH?!!
HMM? OH YES. THAT.

OF COURSE. UNDERNEATH THE MANSION... THAT'S WHERE HIS FACTORY IS!

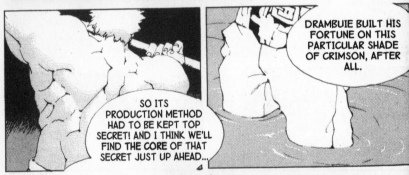

DRAMBUIE BUILT HIS FORTUNE ON THIS PARTICULAR SHADE OF CRIMSON, AFTER ALL.

SO ITS PRODUCTION METHOD HAD TO BE KEPT TOP SECRET! AND I THINK WE'LL FIND THE CORE OF THAT SECRET JUST UP AHEAD...

IN AN UNDERGROUND WELL, SO TO SPEAK.

TATA!

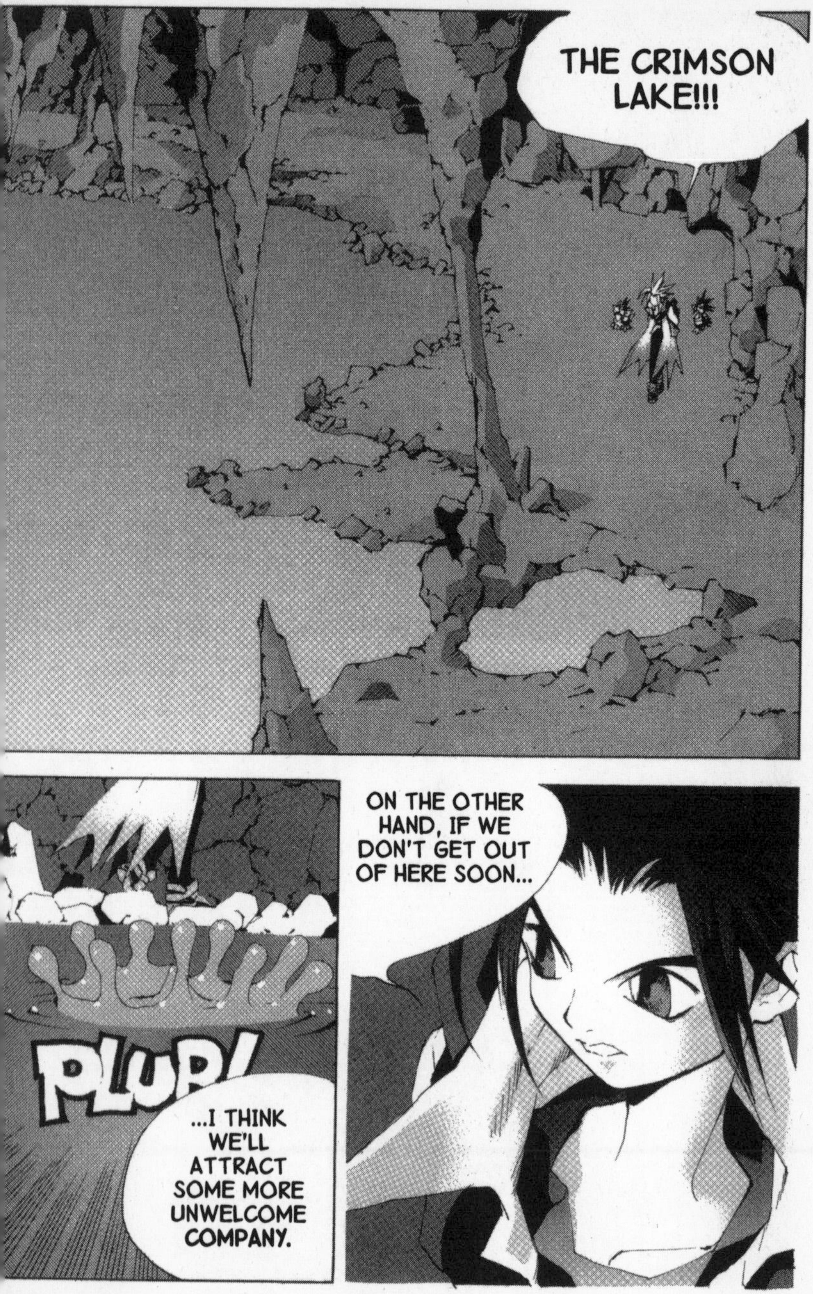
THE CRIMSON LAKE!!!
ON THE OTHER HAND, IF WE DON'T GET OUT OF HERE SOON...
PLUP!
...I THINK WE'LL ATTRACT SOME MORE UNWELCOME COMPANY.

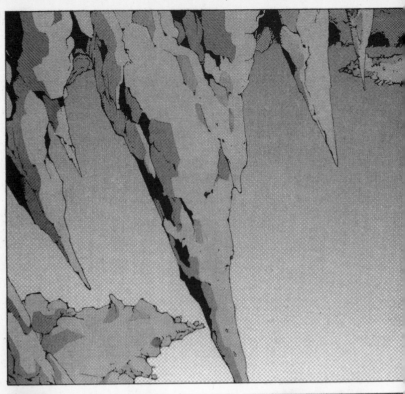

LOOK!!! THERE!!!

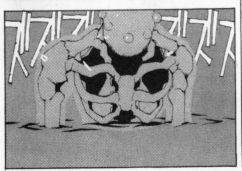

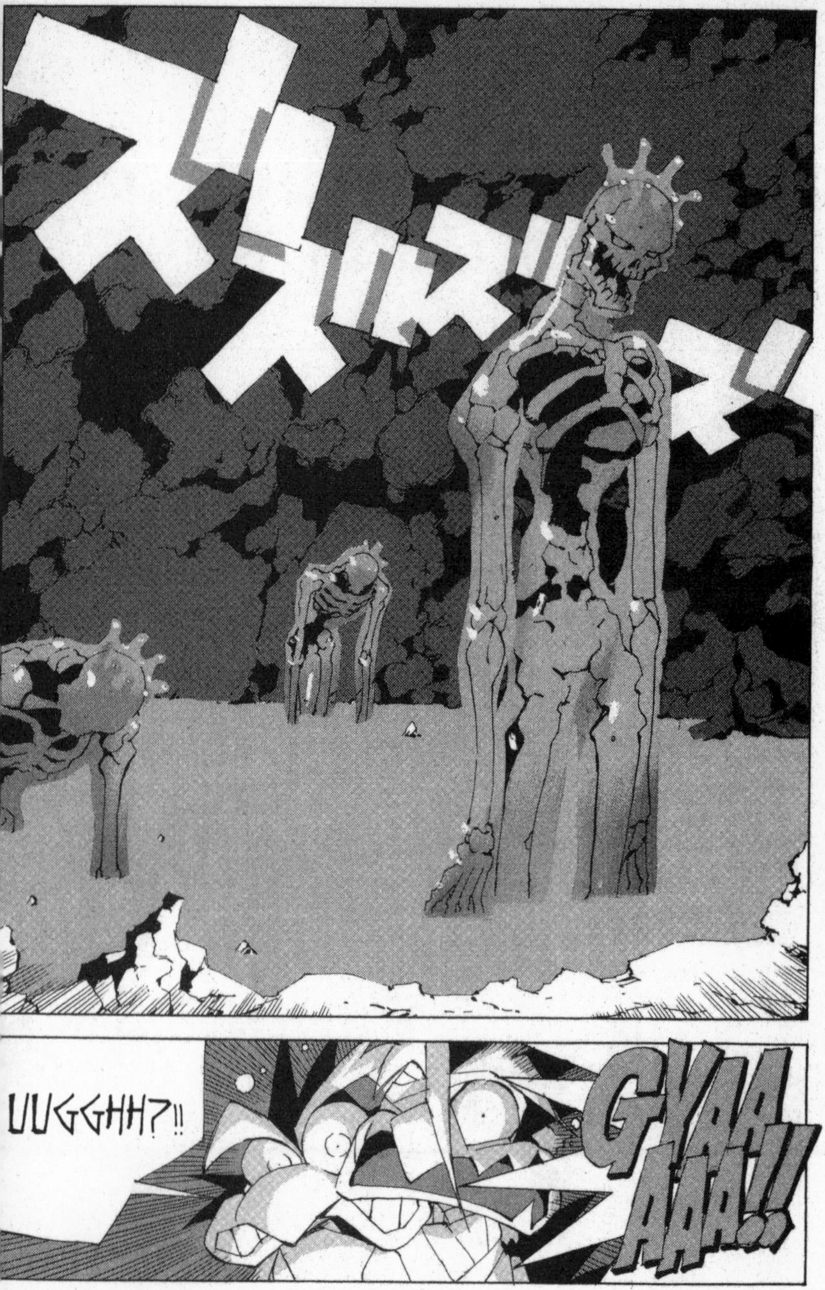
ズズズズズ
GYAAAAA!!
UUGGHH?!!

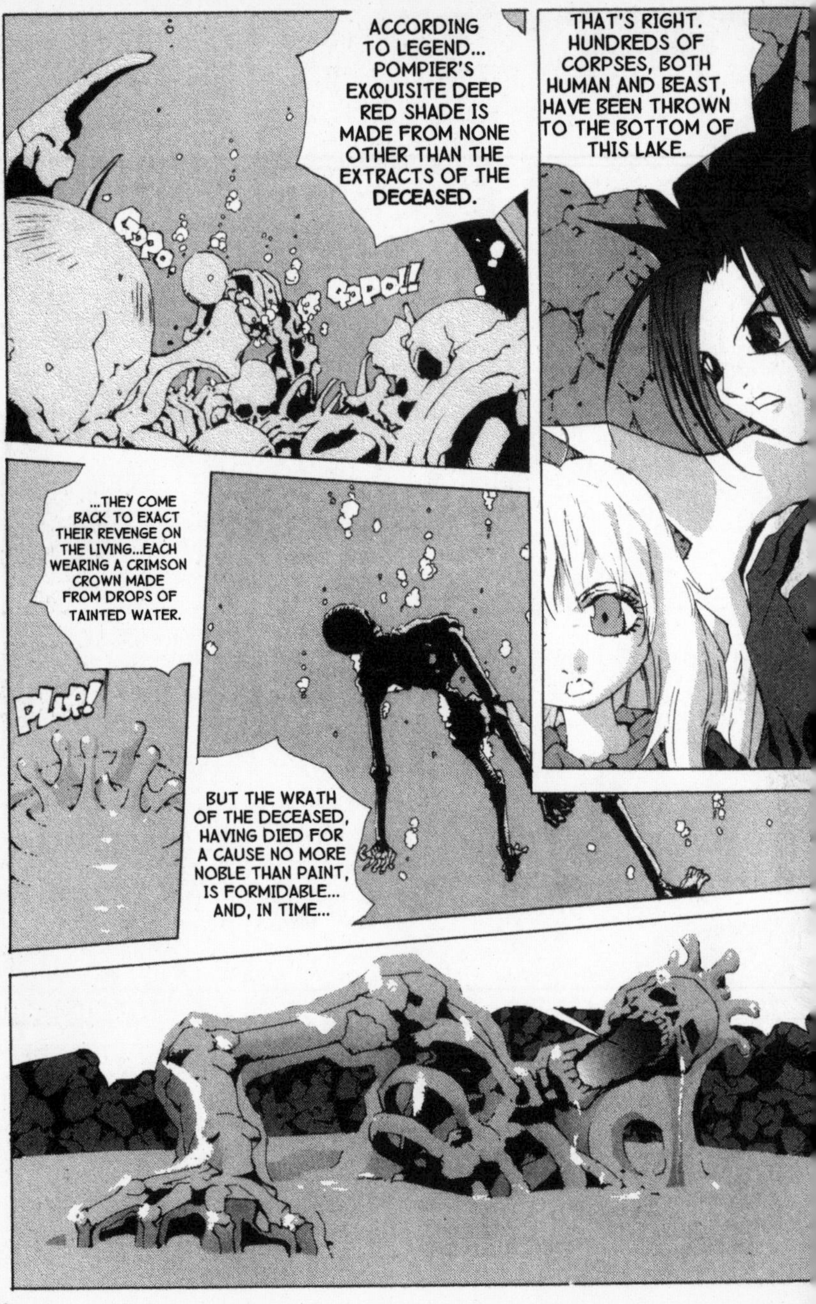
THAT'S RIGHT. HUNDREDS OF CORPSES, BOTH HUMAN AND BEAST, HAVE BEEN THROWN TO THE BOTTOM OF THIS LAKE.
ACCORDING TO LEGEND... POMPIER'S EXQUISITE DEEP RED SHADE IS MADE FROM NONE OTHER THAN THE EXTRACTS OF THE DECEASED.
GOPO!!
GOPO.
BUT THE WRATH OF THE DECEASED, HAVING DIED FOR A CAUSE NO MORE NOBLE THAN PAINT, IS FORMIDABLE... AND, IN TIME...
...THEY COME BACK TO EXACT THEIR REVENGE ON THE LIVING...EACH WEARING A CRIMSON CROWN MADE FROM DROPS OF TAINTED WATER.
PLUP!

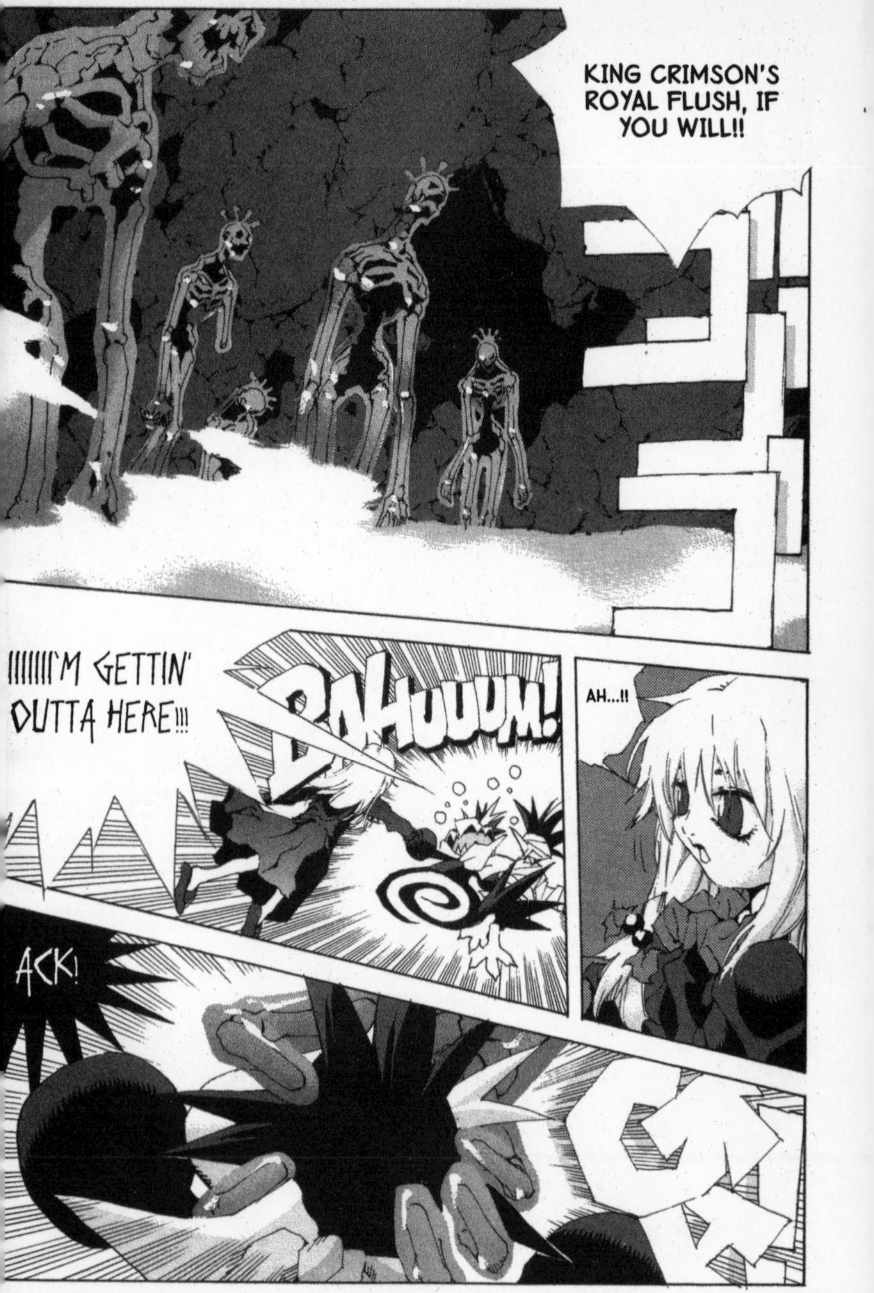
KING CRIMSON'S ROYAL FLUSH, IF YOU WILL!!
AH...!!
IIIIIII'M GETTIN' OUTTA HERE!!!
BAHUUUM!
ACK!

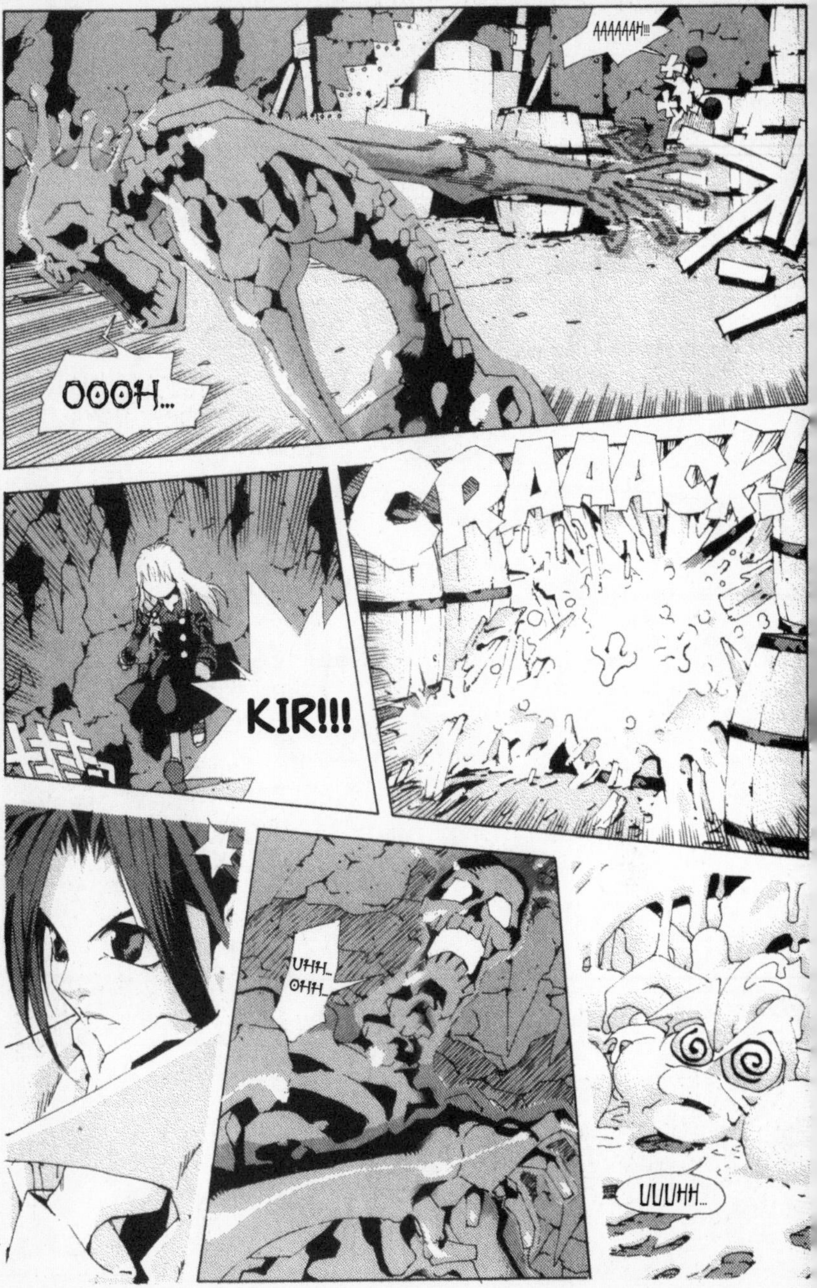
AAAAAAH!!!
OOOH...
CRAAACK!
KIR!!!
UUUHH...
UHH... OHH...

HEH?!

DROP ALL THE BARRELS INTO THE LAKE!! DON'T LEAVE ANY BEHIND!!!!

WHITE!! THEY SAY THE KING CRIMSONS ARE AFRAID OF THE COLOR WHITE... IT SULLIES THEIR CROWNS.

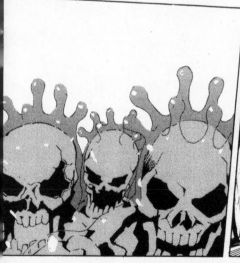

QUICKLY!! QUICKLY!!!

WH..WHICH WAY..?

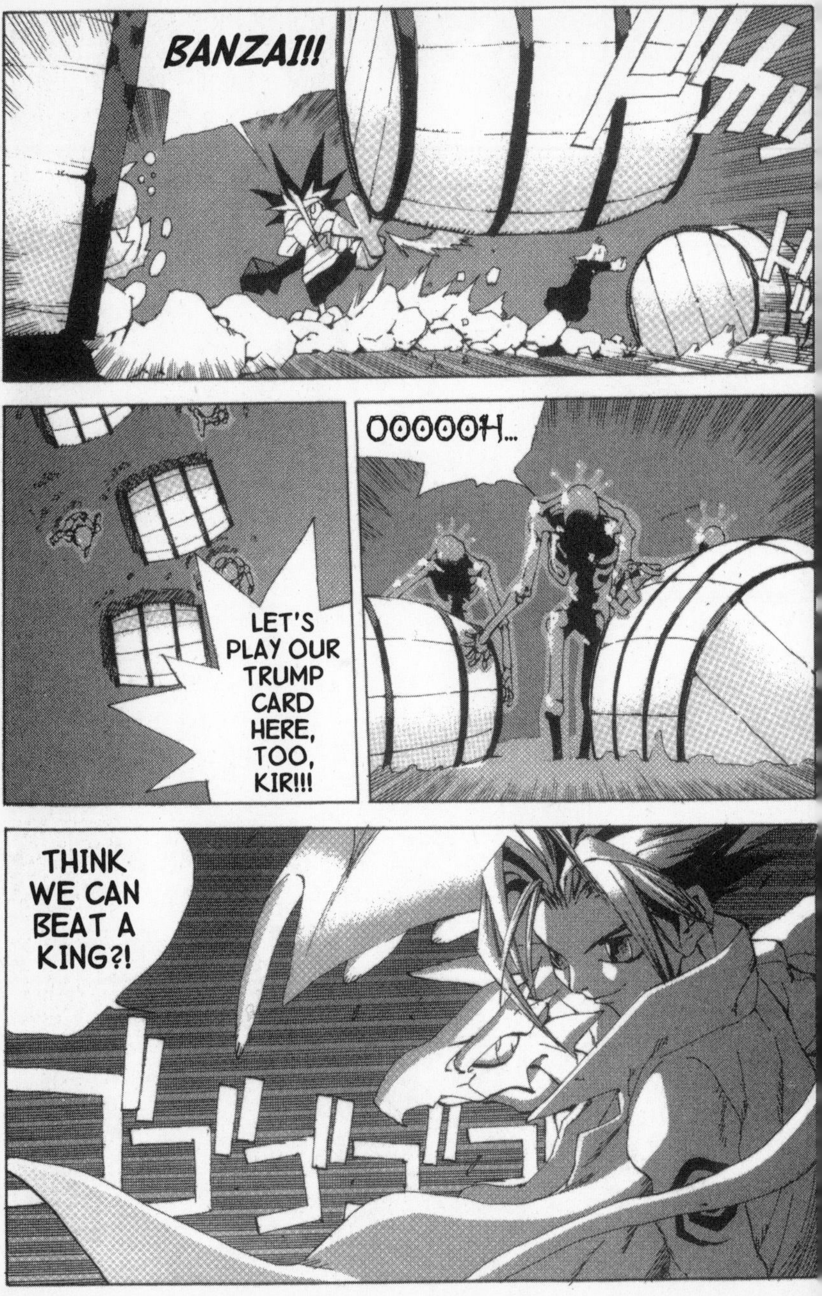
BANZAI!!
OOOOOH...
LET'S PLAY OUR TRUMP CARD HERE, TOO, KIR!!!
THINK WE CAN BEAT A KING?!

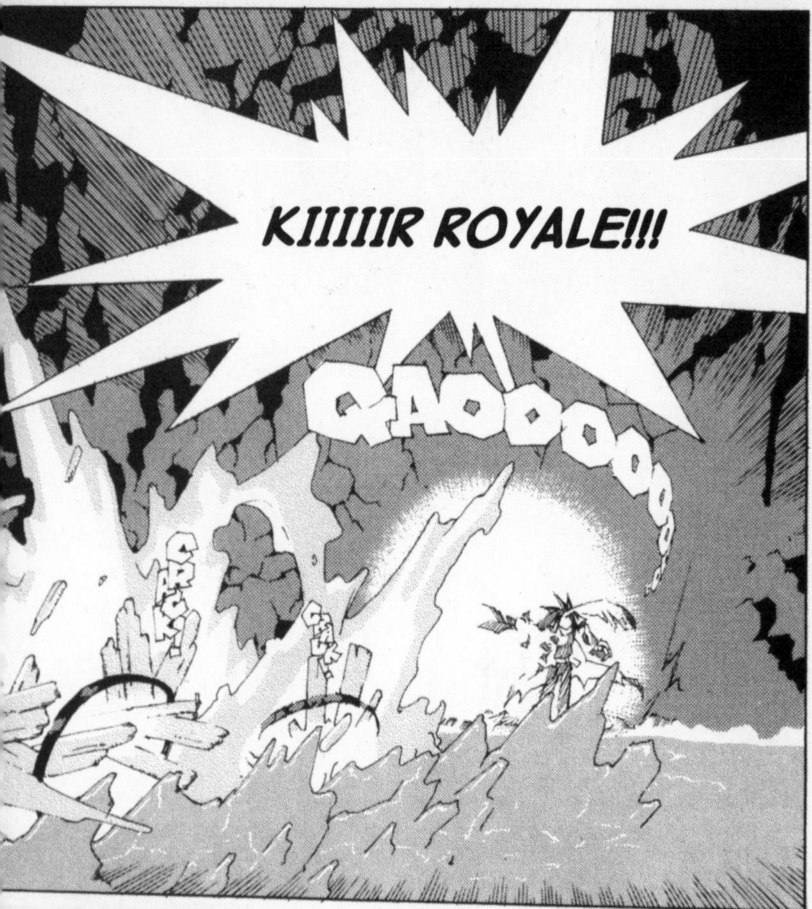
KIIIIIR ROYALE!!!
GAOOOOOOO
CRACK!
CRACK!

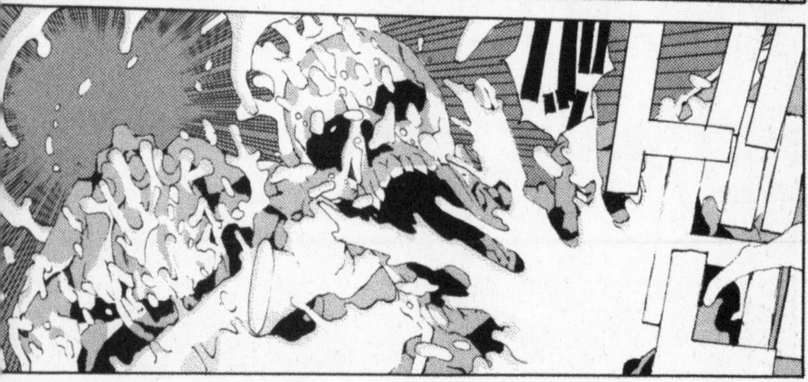

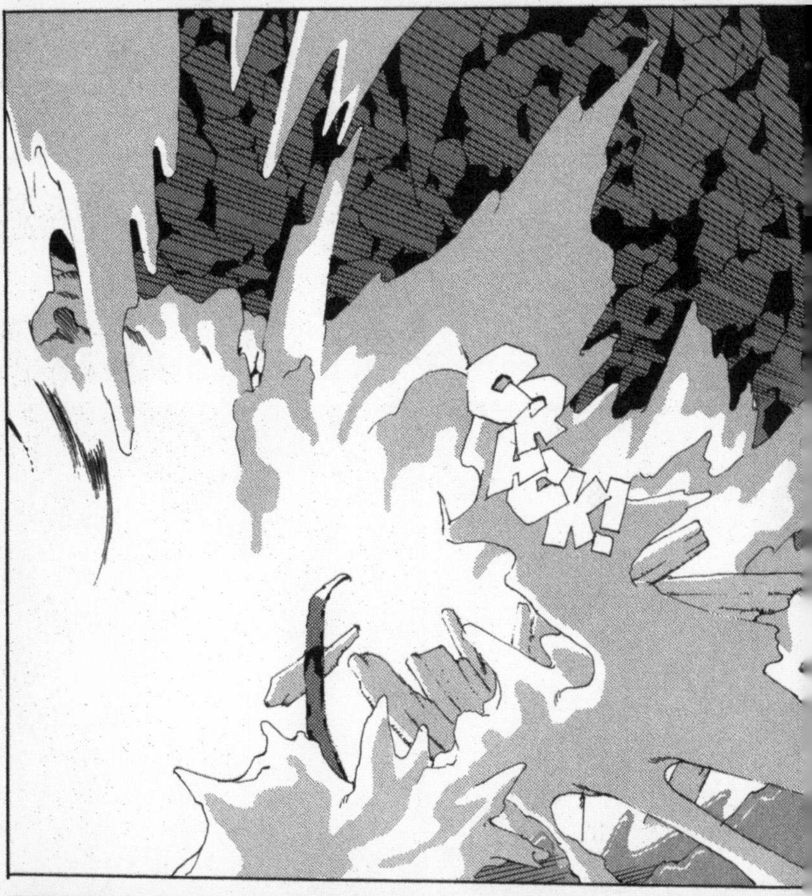
CRACK!
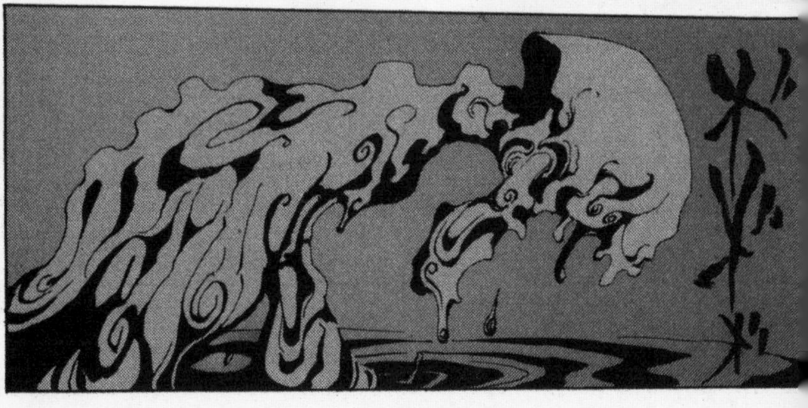

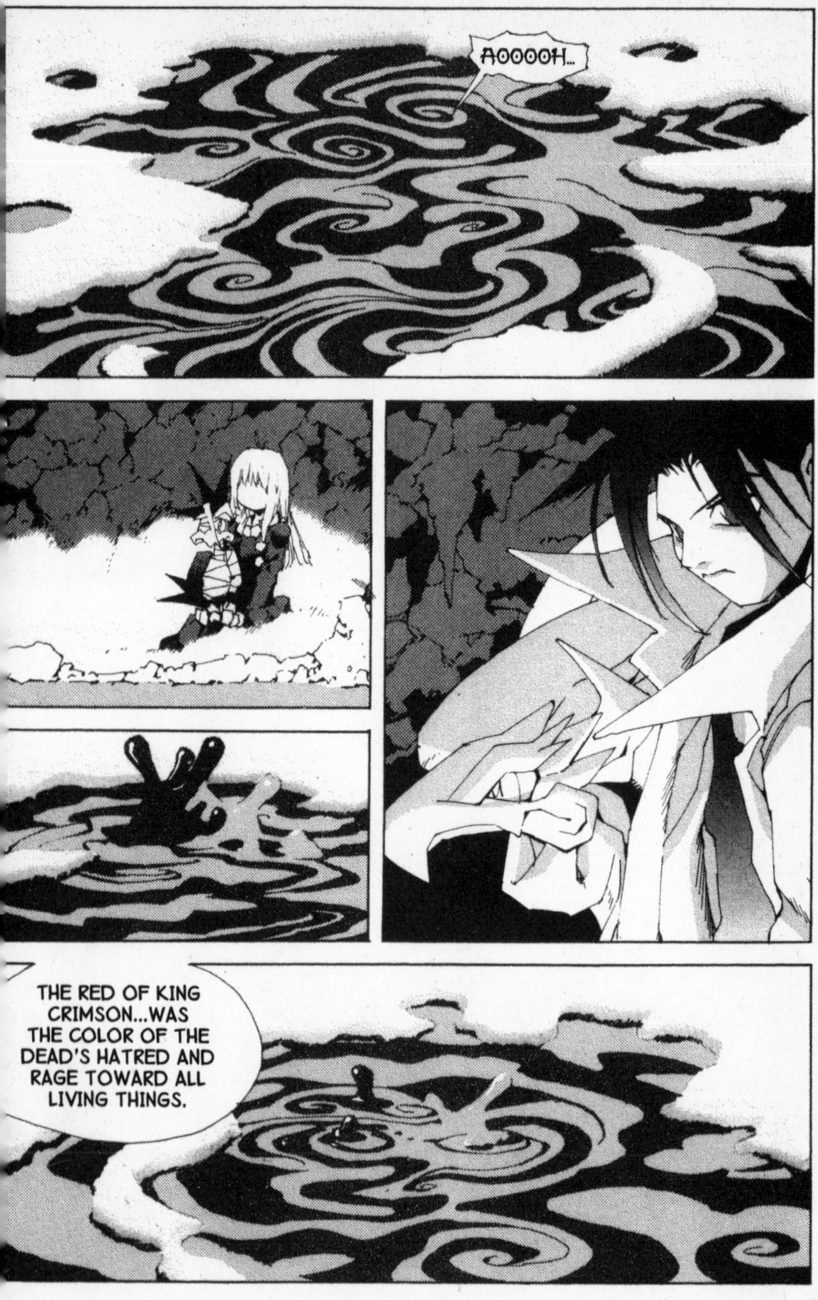
AOOOOH...
THE RED OF KING CRIMSON...WAS THE COLOR OF THE DEAD'S HATRED AND RAGE TOWARD ALL LIVING THINGS.

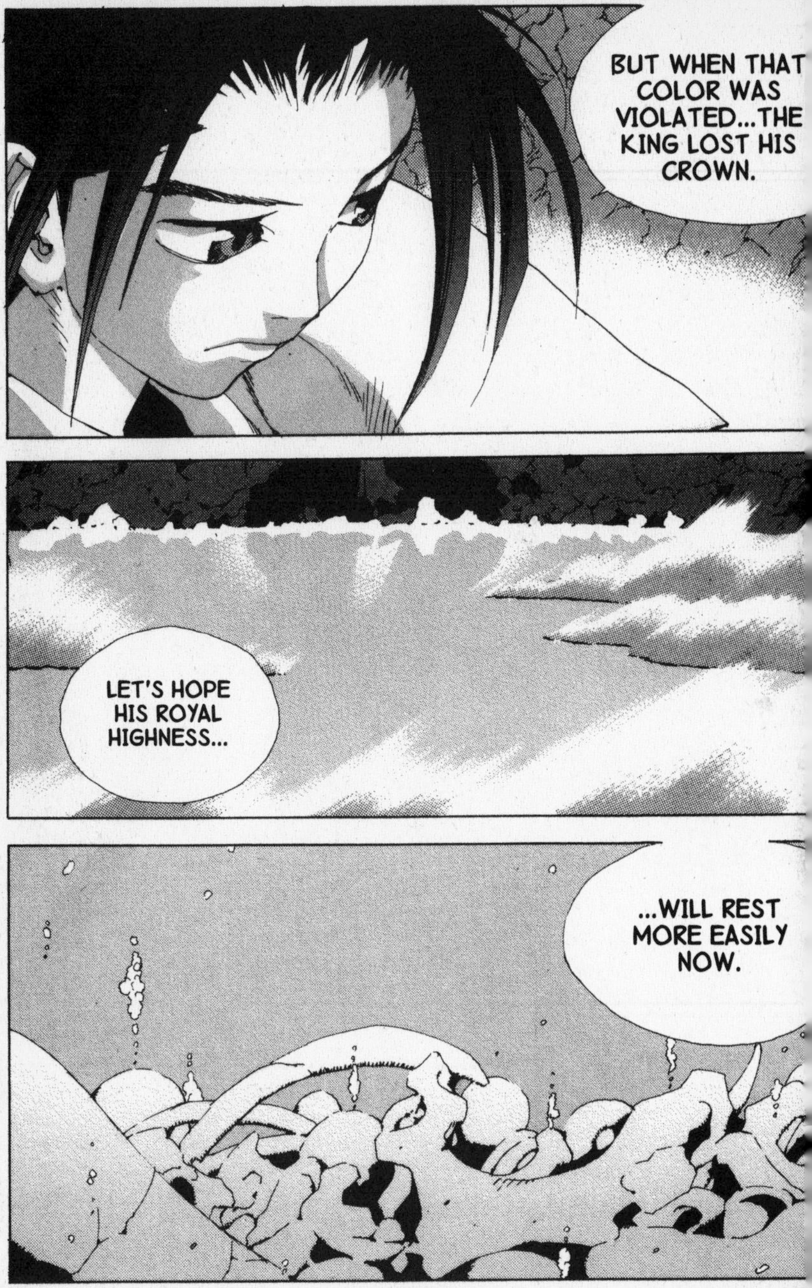
BUT WHEN THAT COLOR WAS VIOLATED...THE KING LOST HIS CROWN.
LET'S HOPE HIS ROYAL HIGHNESS...
...WILL REST MORE EASILY NOW.

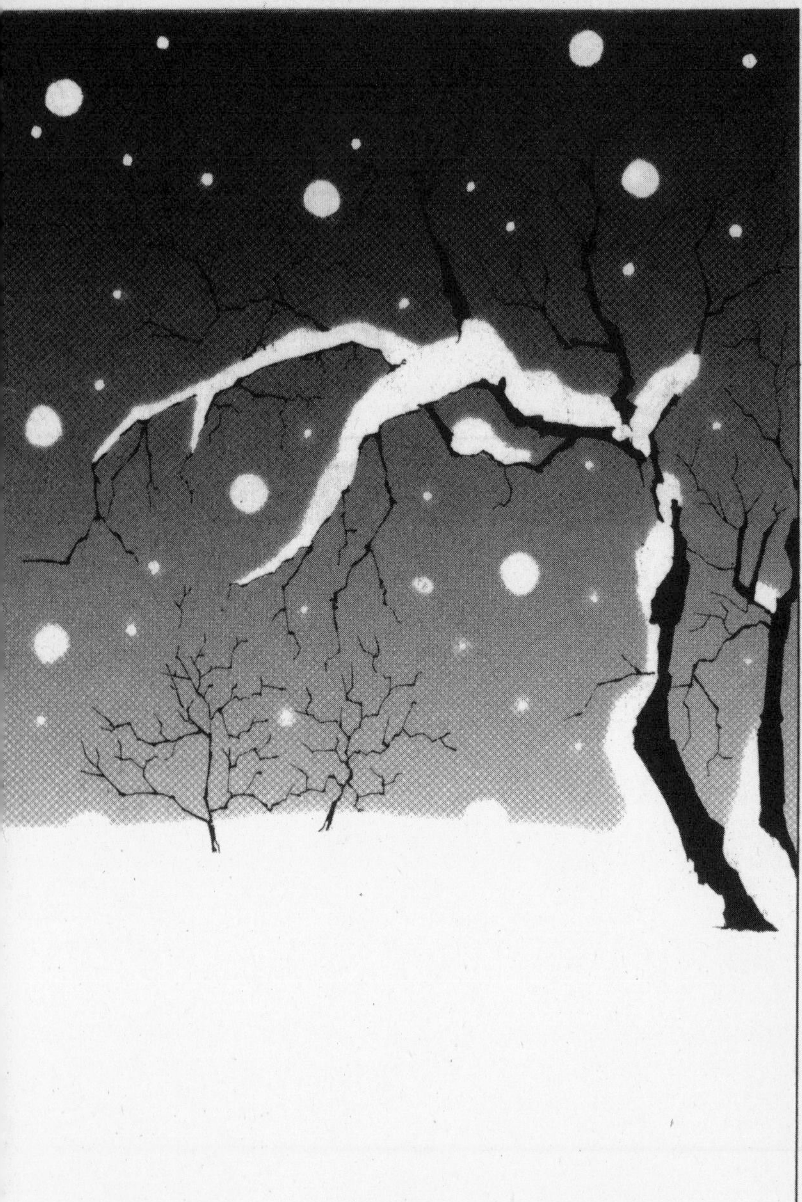
34th SHOT - THE FIFTH ELEMENT

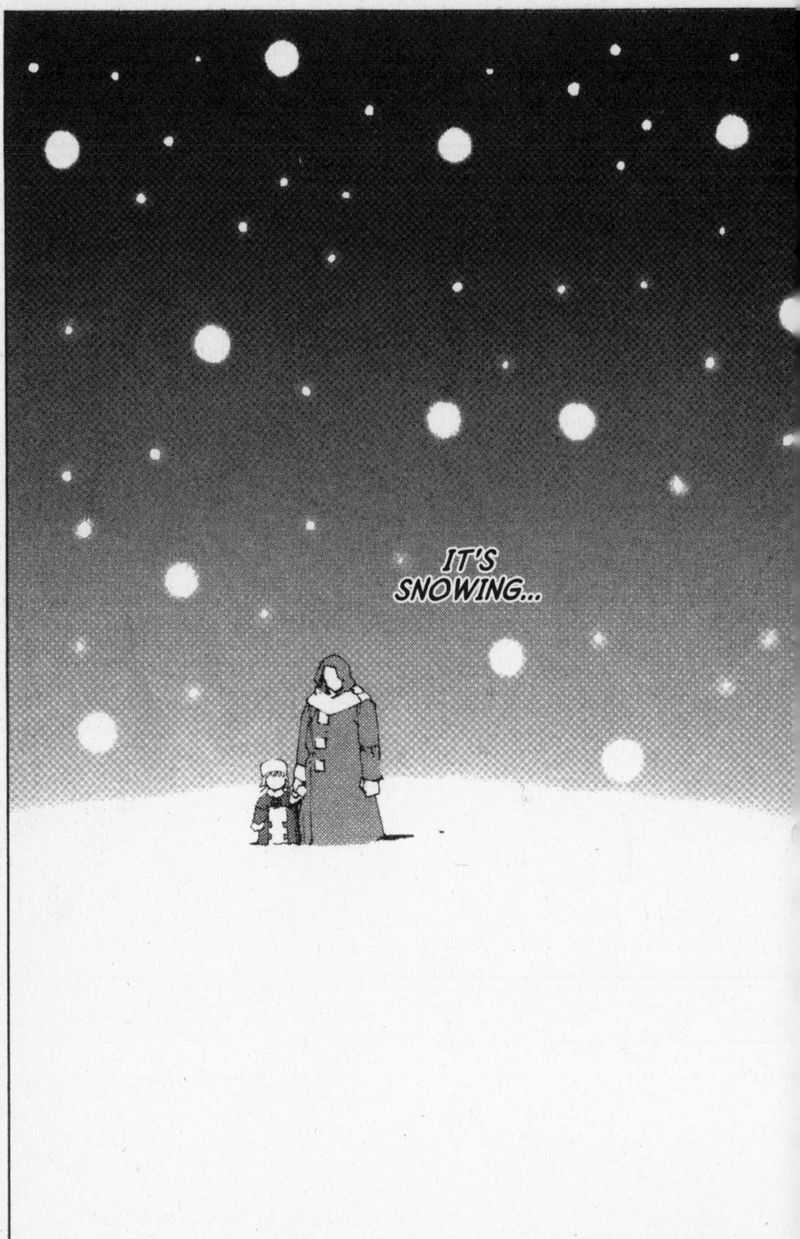
IT'S SNOWING...

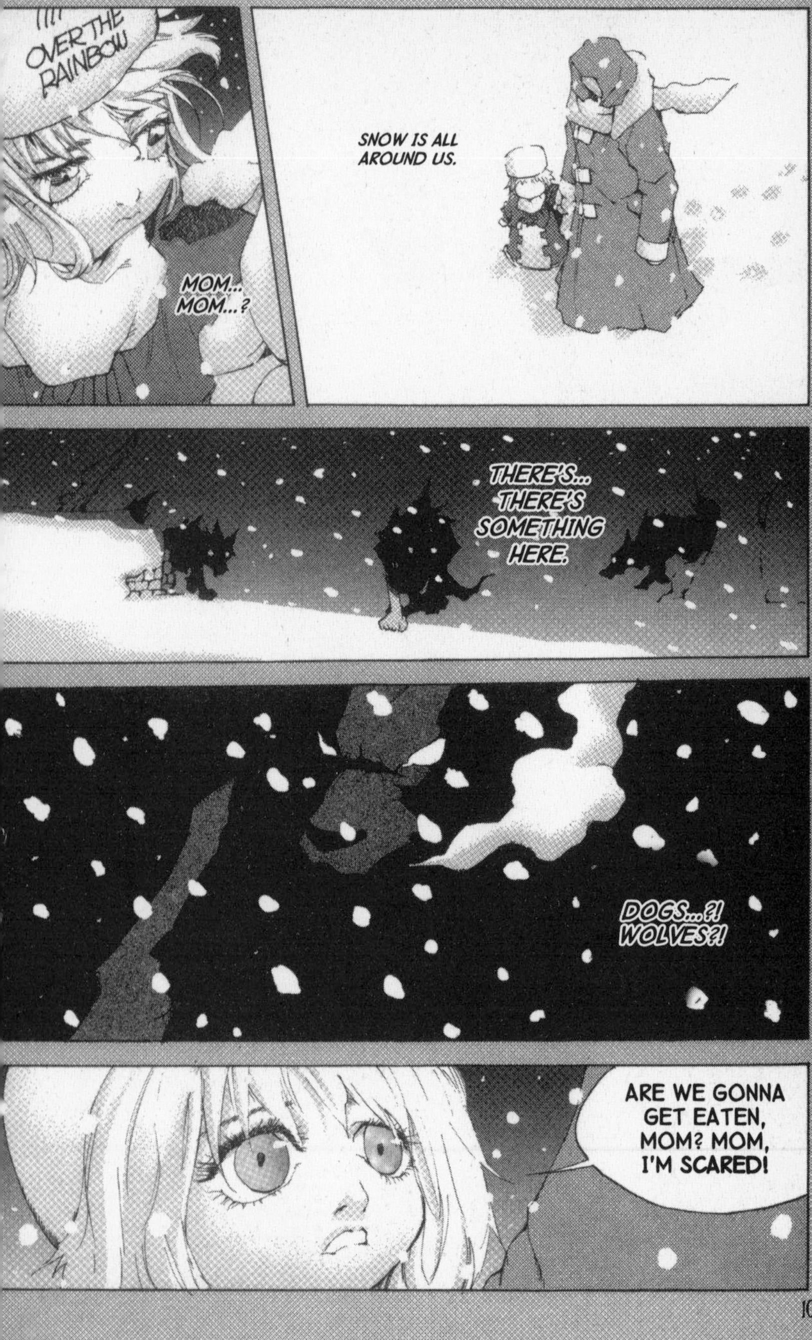
SNOW IS ALL AROUND US.
OVER THE RAINBOW
MOM... MOM...?
THERE'S... THERE'S SOMETHING HERE.
DOGS...?! WOLVES?!
ARE WE GONNA GET EATEN, MOM? MOM, I'M SCARED!

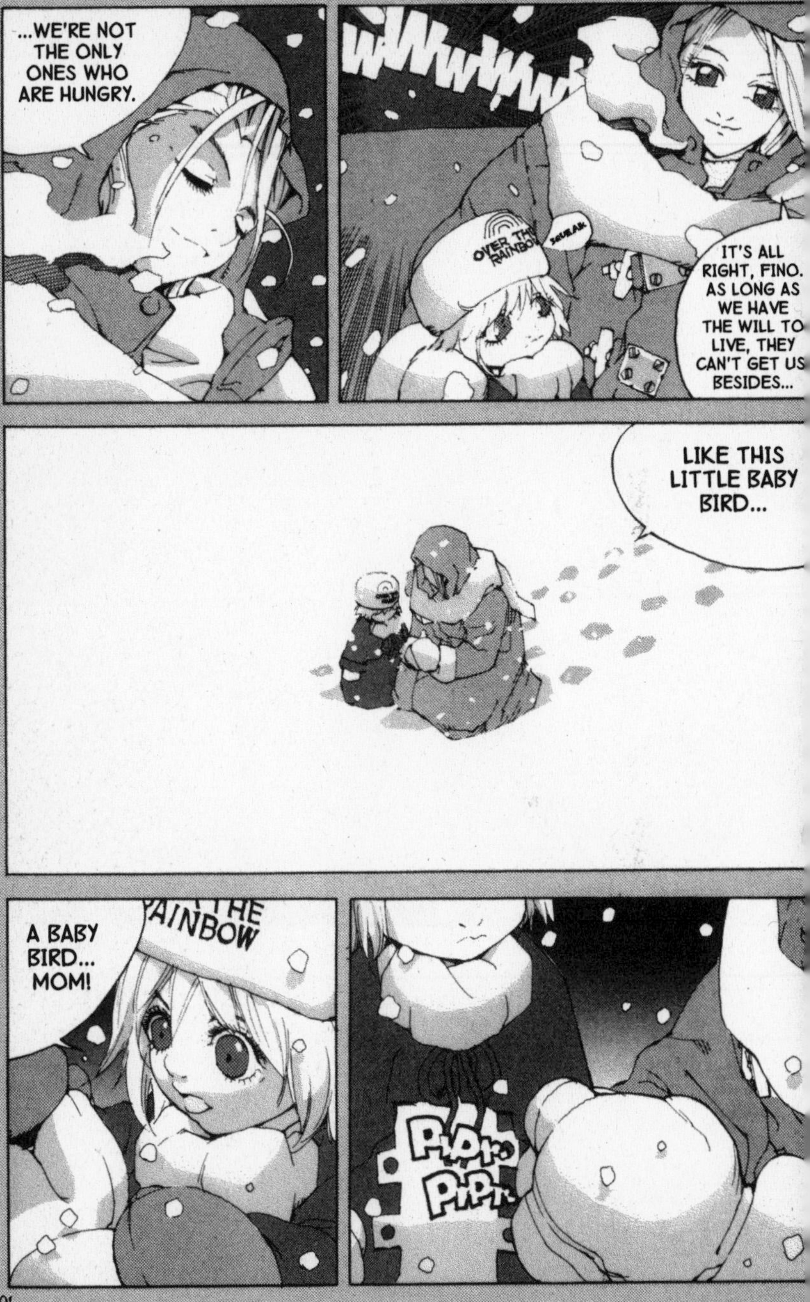
SQUEAK
IT'S ALL RIGHT, FINO. AS LONG AS WE HAVE THE WILL TO LIVE, THEY CAN'T GET US. BESIDES...
...WE'RE NOT THE ONLY ONES WHO ARE HUNGRY.
LIKE THIS LITTLE BABY BIRD...
A BABY BIRD... MOM!

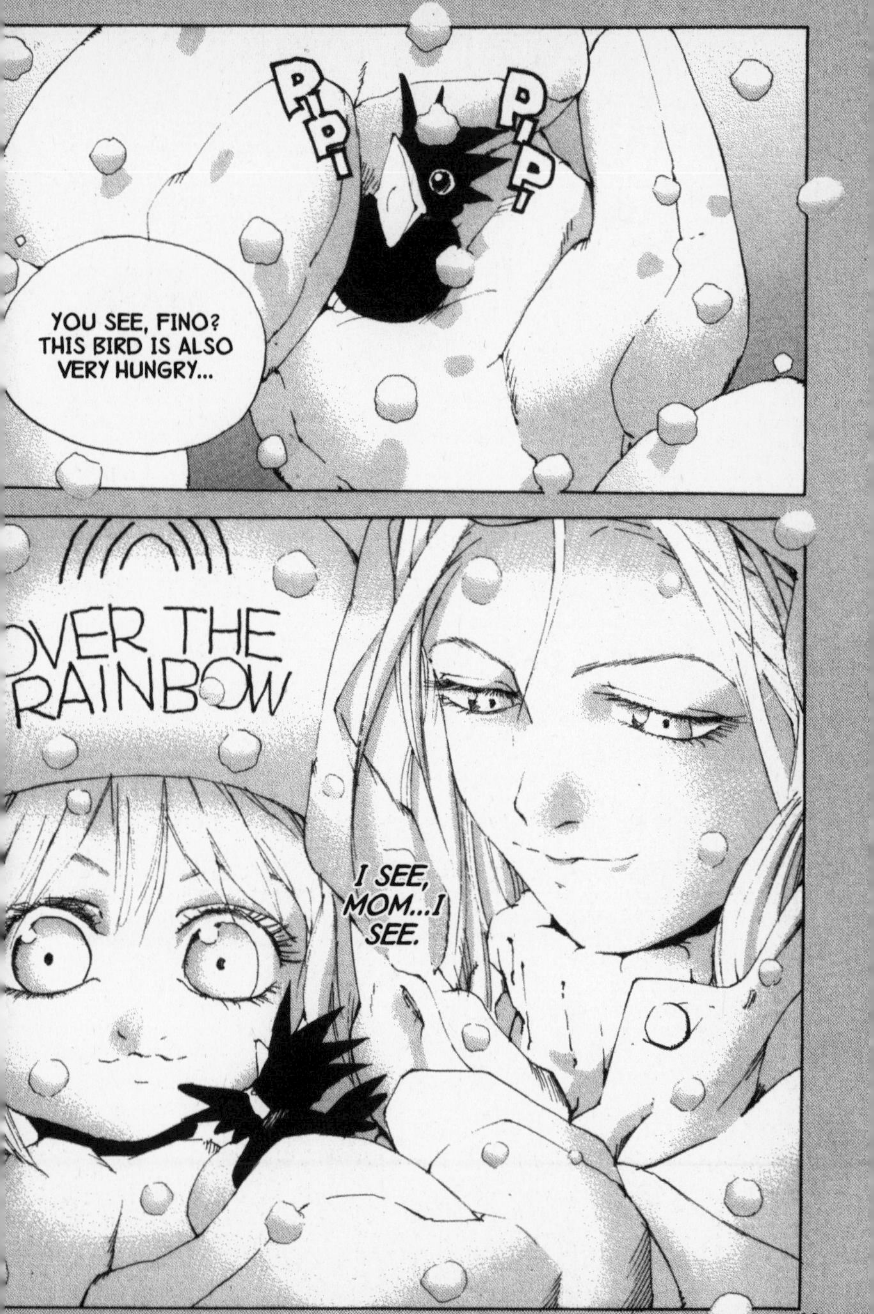
PIPI
PIPI
YOU SEE, FINO? THIS BIRD IS ALSO VERY HUNGRY...
OVER THE RAINBOW
I SEE, MOM...I SEE.

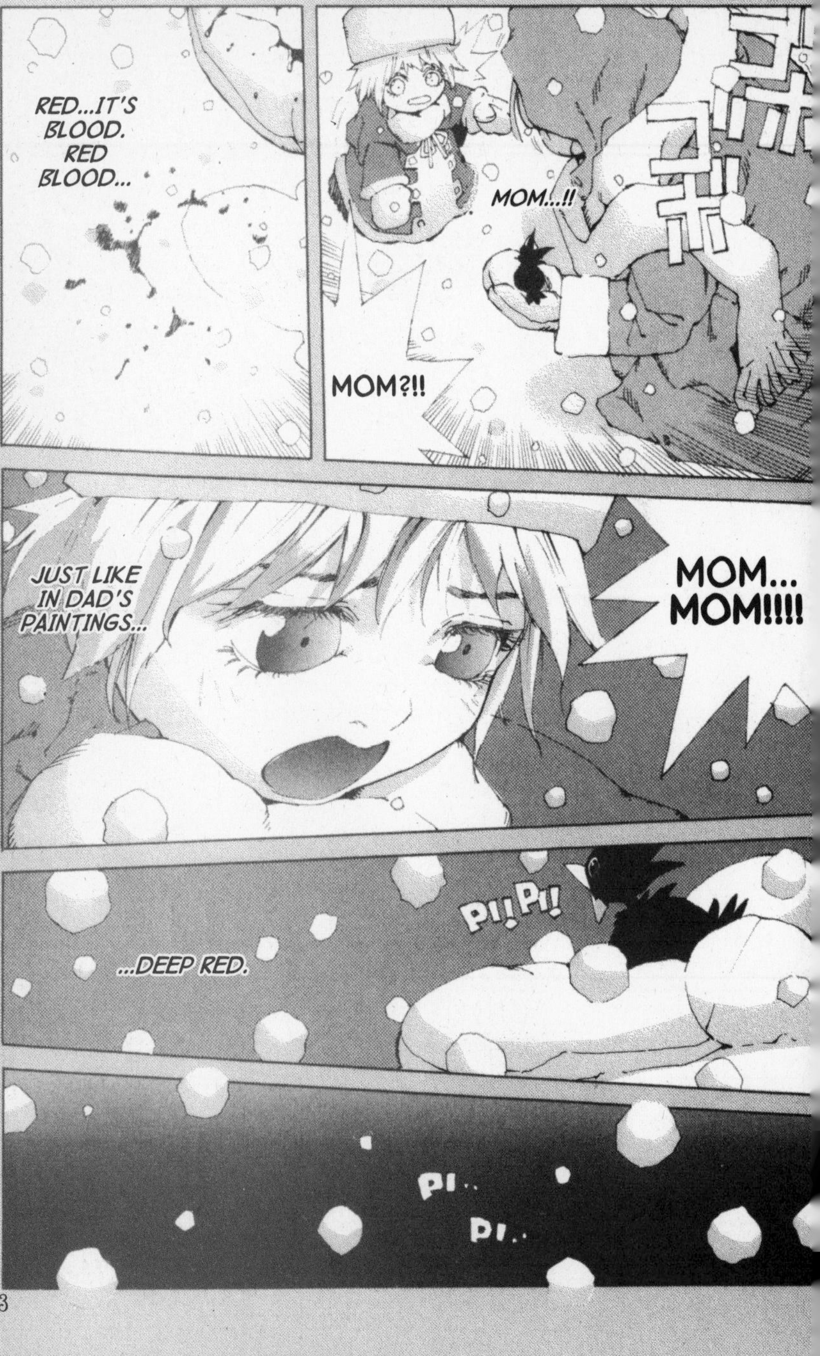
MOM...!!
MOM?!!
RED...IT'S BLOOD. RED BLOOD...
MOM... MOM!!!!
JUST LIKE IN DAD'S PAINTINGS...
PI! PI!
...DEEP RED.
PI..
PI..

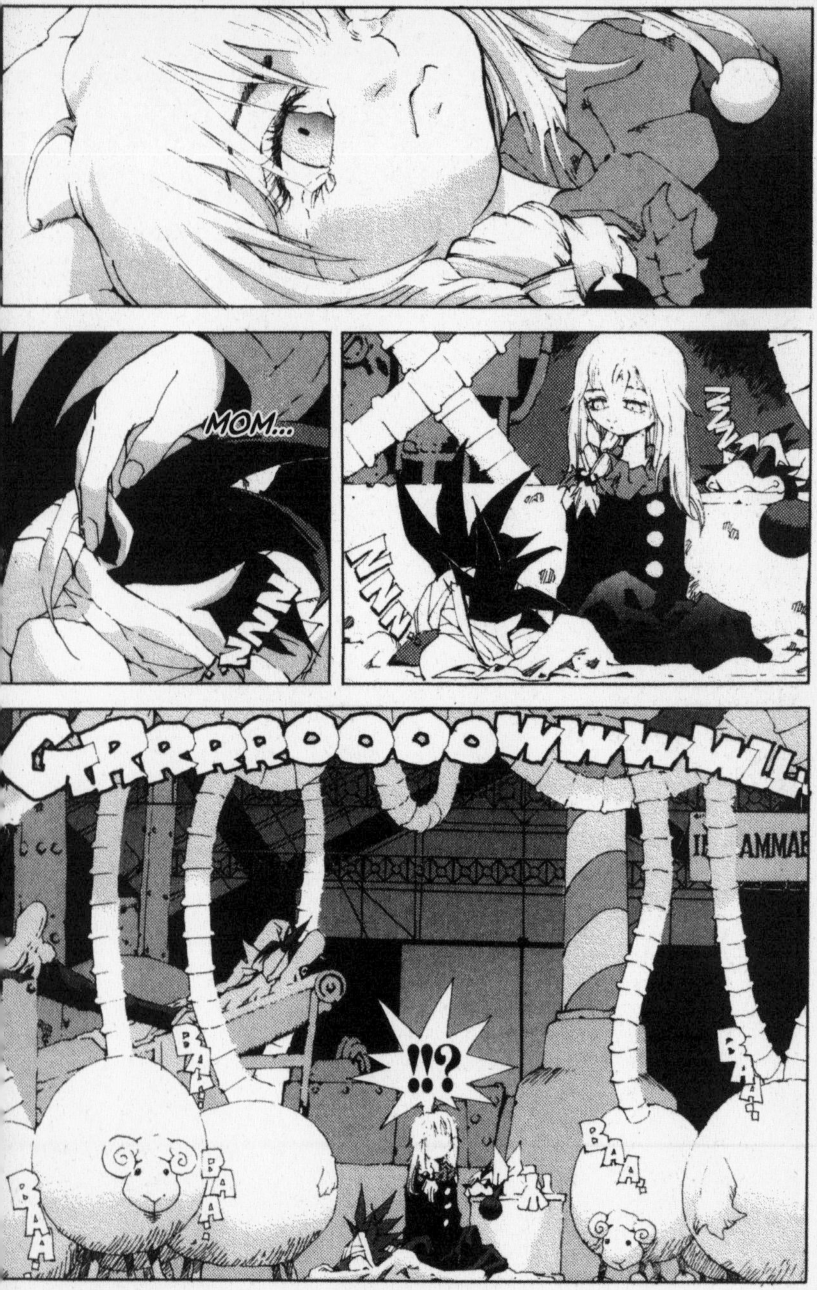
NNN...
NNN...
MOM...
NNN...
GRRRROOOOOWWWWLL...
BAA...
BAA...
!!?
BAA...
BAA...
BAA...

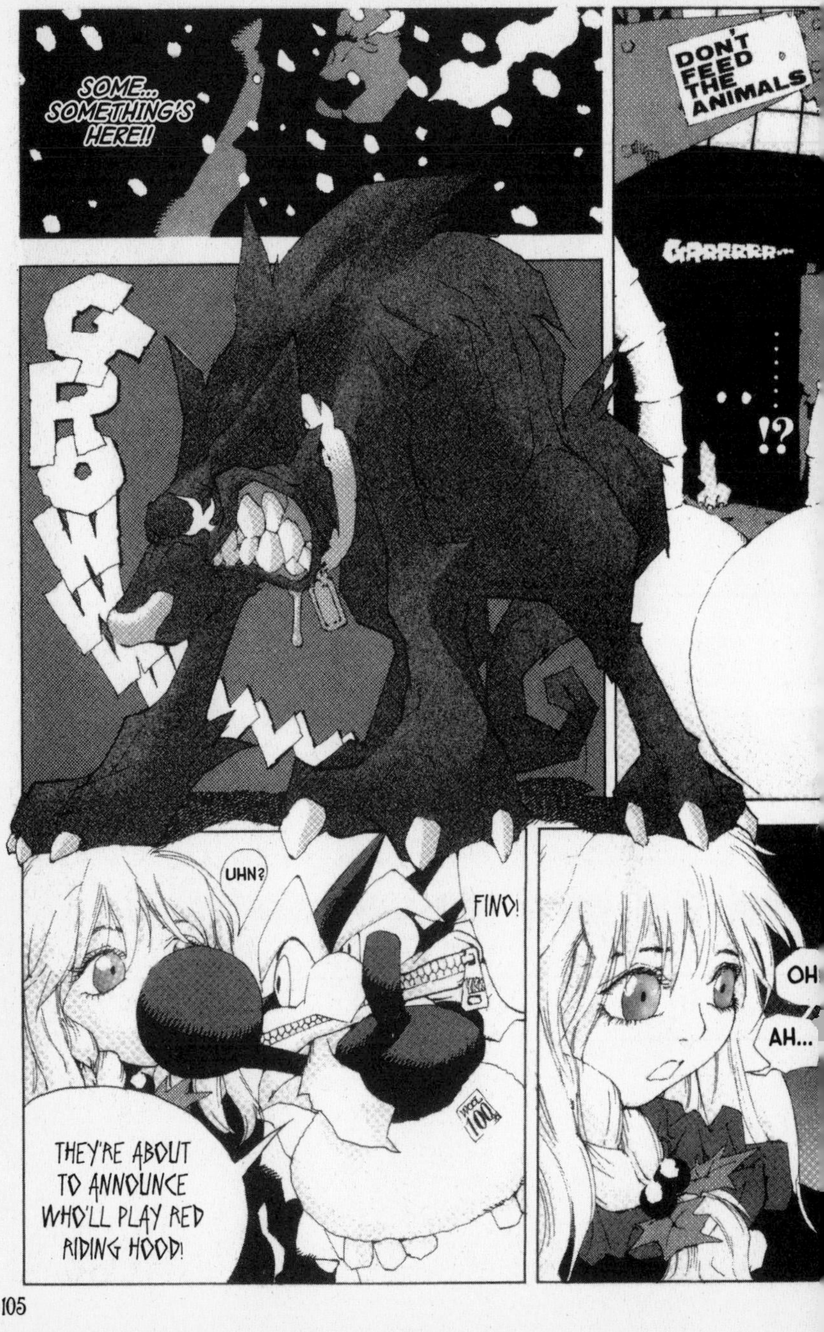
DON'T FEED THE ANIMALS
GRRRRRR...
......
!?
SOME... SOMETHING'S HERE!!
GROWWWLLL
OH
AH...
UHN?
FINO!
THEY'RE ABOUT TO ANNOUNCE WHO'LL PLAY RED RIDING HOOD!

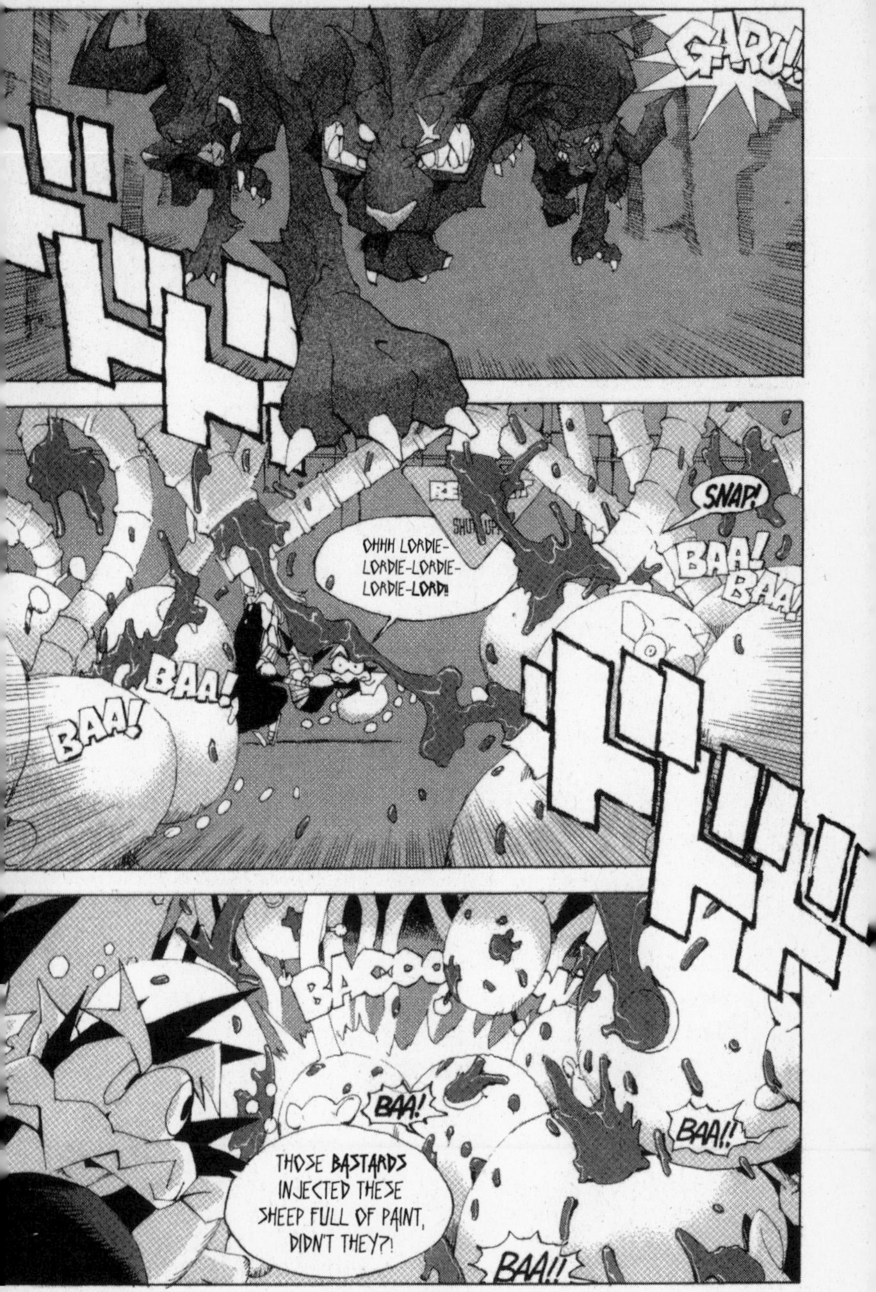
GARU!!
SNAP!
BAA!
BAA!
OHHH LORDIE-LORDIE-LORDIE-LORDIE-LORD!!
BAA!
BAA!
BAA!!
BAA!
THOSE BASTARDS INJECTED THESE SHEEP FULL OF PAINT, DIDN'T THEY?!
BAA!!

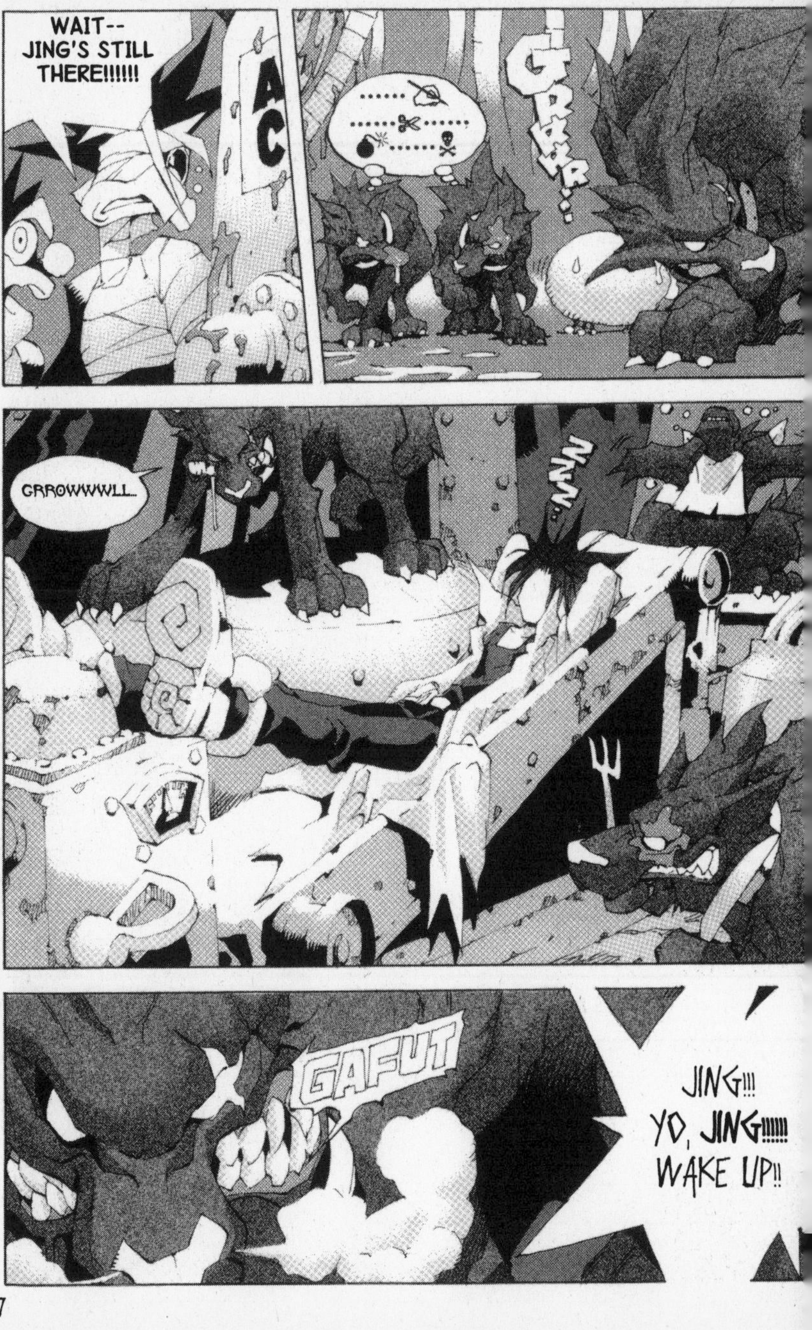
GRRRR...
WAIT-- JING'S STILL THERE!!!!!!
NNN..
GRROWWWLL...
JING!!! YO, JING!!!!!! WAKE UP!!
GAFUT

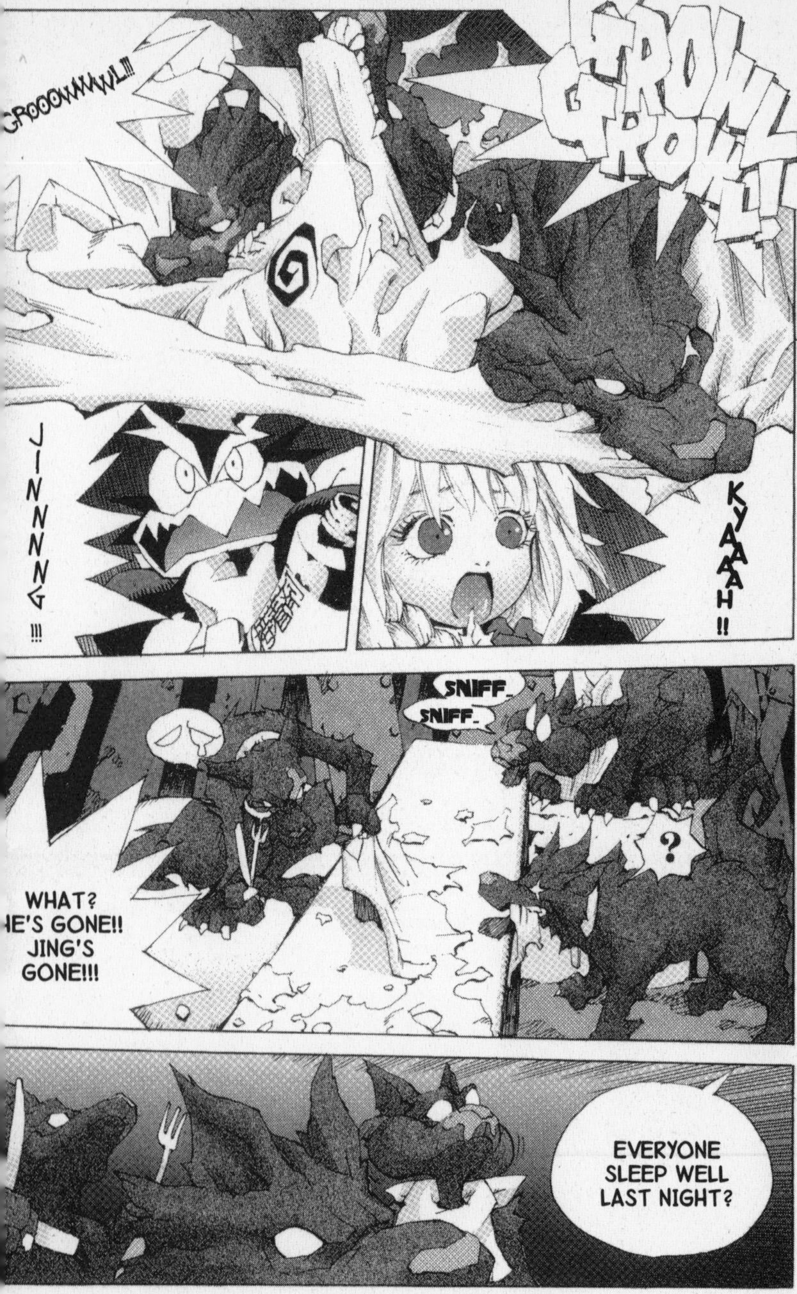
GROWL GROWL!!
GROOOWWWL!!!
KYAAAAH!!
JINNNNG!!!
SNIFF_
SNIFF_
?
WHAT? HE'S GONE!! JING'S GONE!!!
EVERYONE SLEEP WELL LAST NIGHT?

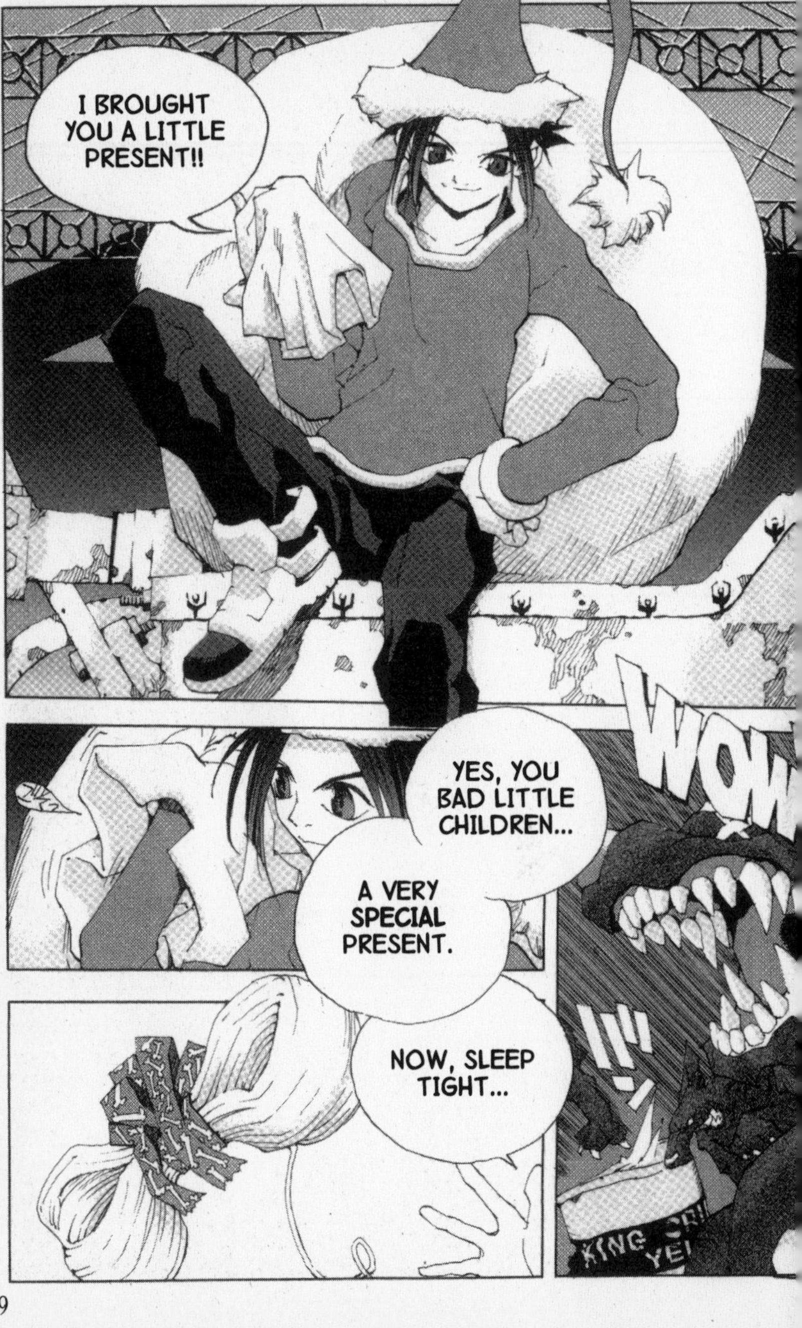
I BROUGHT YOU A LITTLE PRESENT!!
YES, YOU BAD LITTLE CHILDREN...
A VERY SPECIAL PRESENT.
NOW, SLEEP TIGHT...
WOW
!!

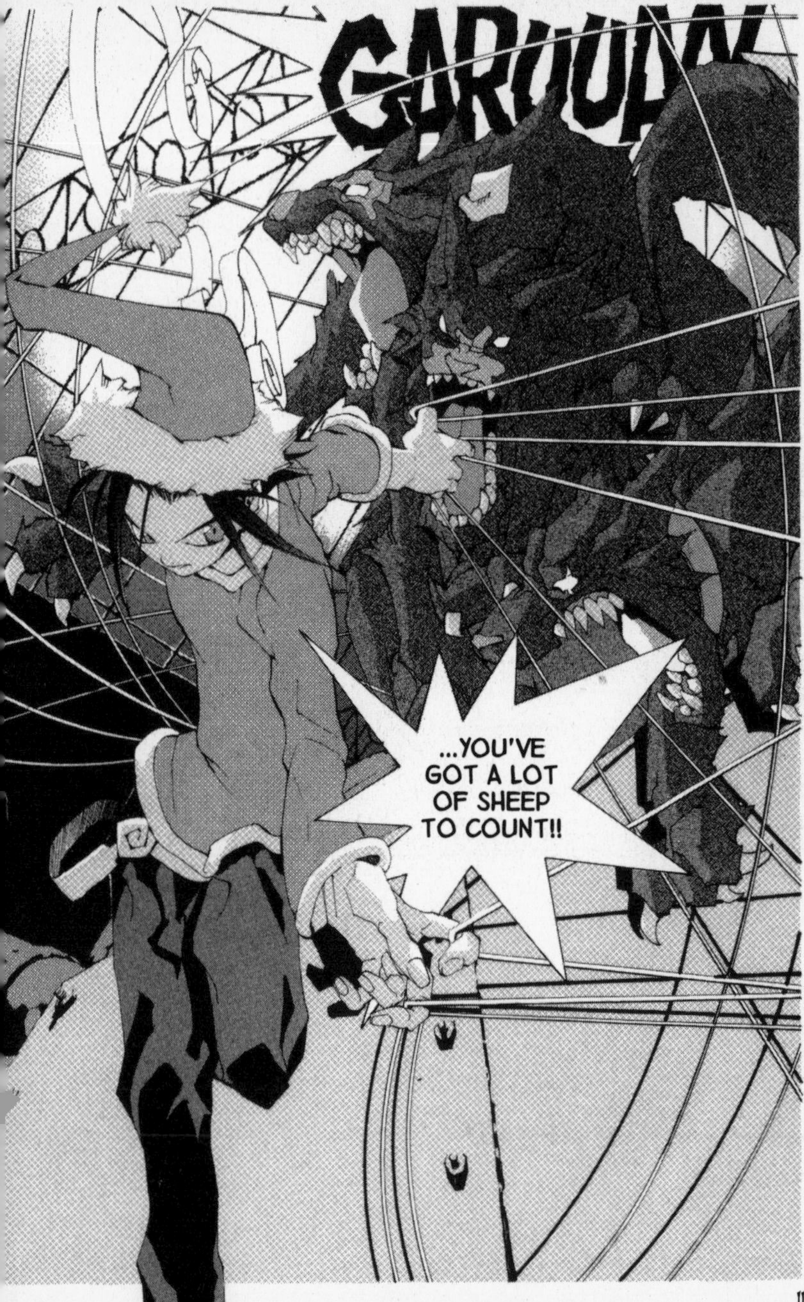
GAROOAW
...YOU'VE GOT A LOT OF SHEEP TO COUNT!!

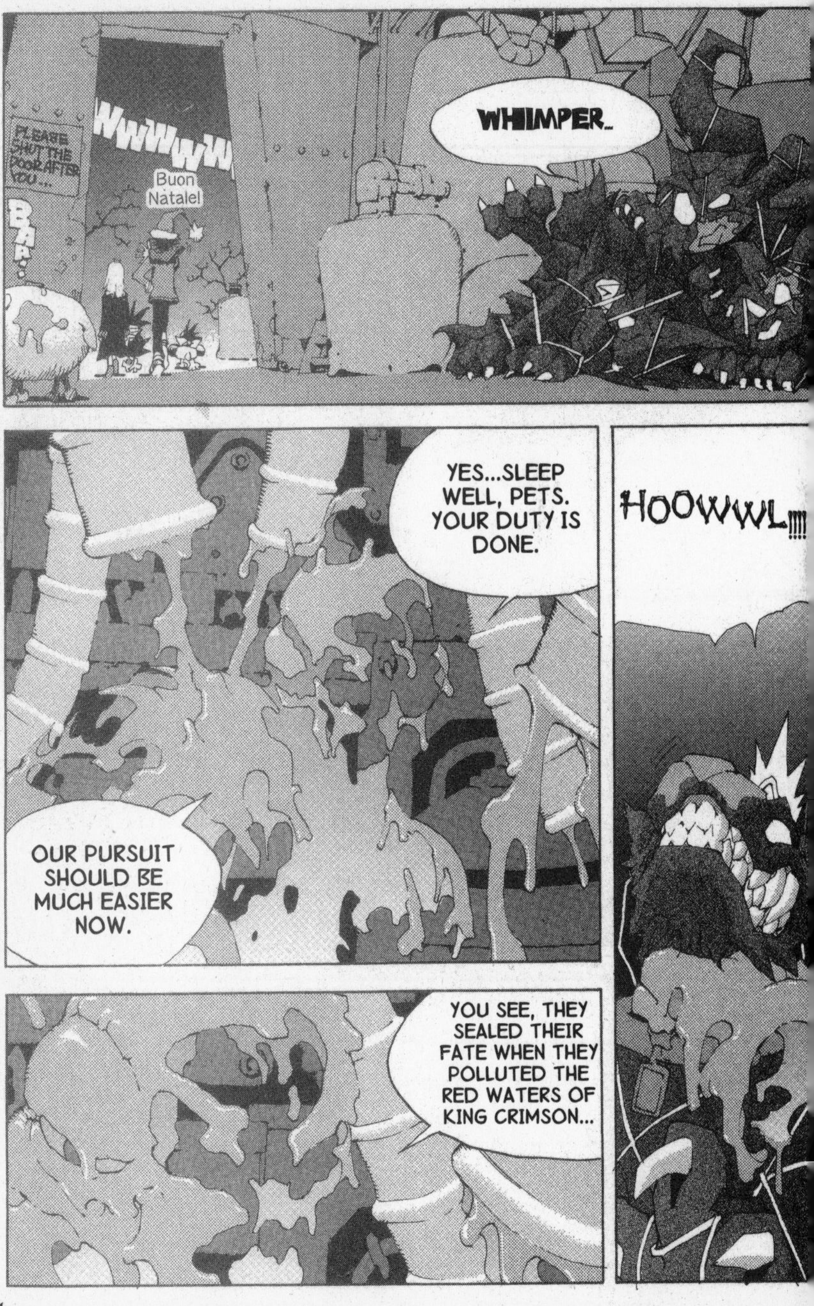

WHIMPER...
WWWWWW
Buon Natale!
PLEASE SHUT THE DOOR AFTER YOU...
BAA..
HOOWWL!!!!
YES...SLEEP WELL, PETS. YOUR DUTY IS DONE.
OUR PURSUIT SHOULD BE MUCH EASIER NOW.
YOU SEE, THEY SEALED THEIR FATE WHEN THEY POLLUTED THE RED WATERS OF KING CRIMSON...

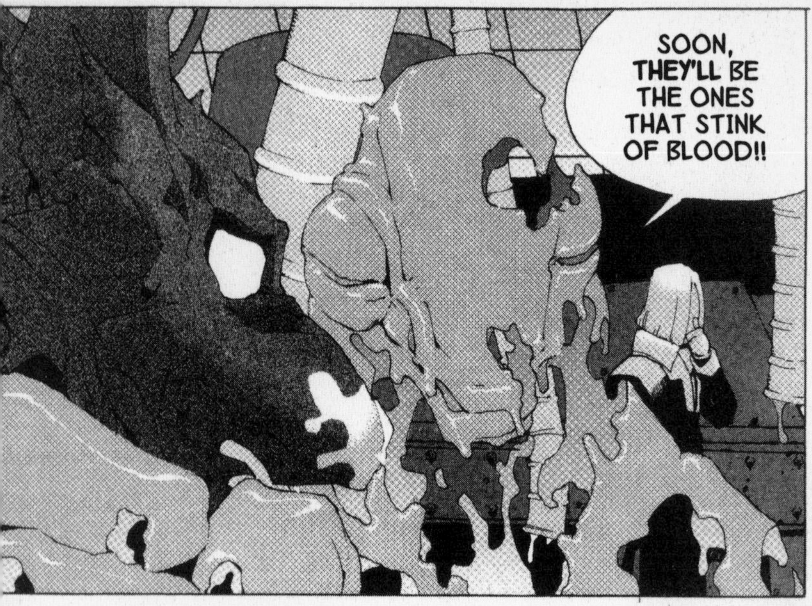
SOON, THEY'LL BE THE ONES THAT STINK OF BLOOD!!

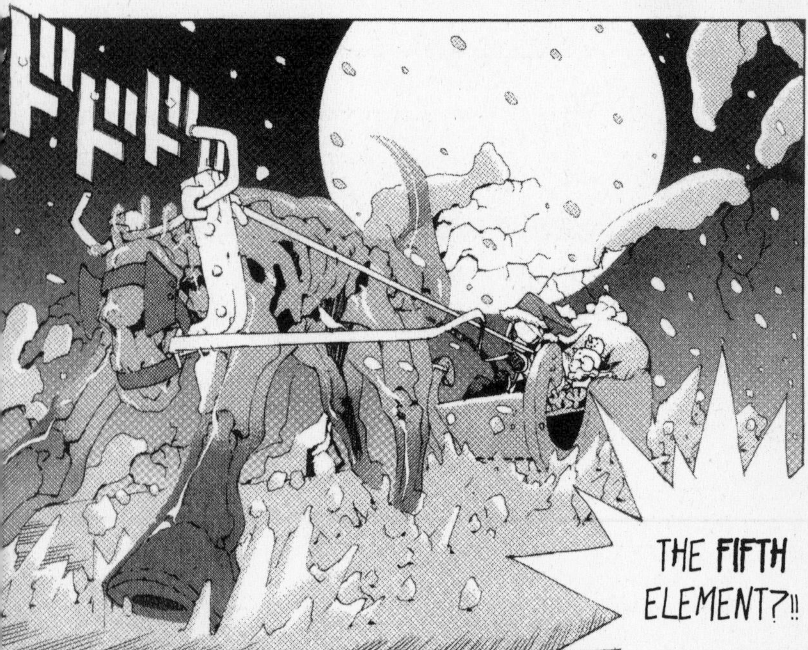
ドドド
THE FIFTH ELEMENT?!!

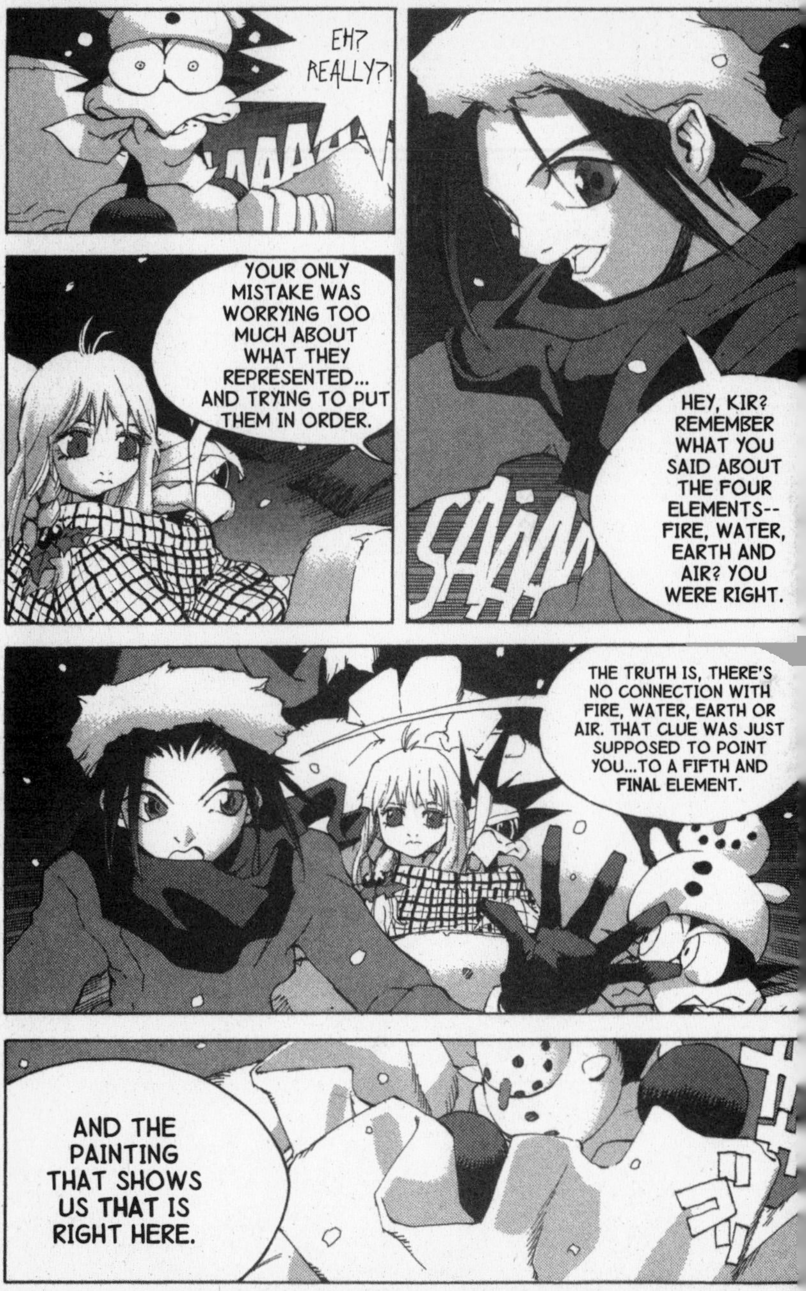
HEY, KIR? REMEMBER WHAT YOU SAID ABOUT THE FOUR ELEMENTS-- FIRE, WATER, EARTH AND AIR? YOU WERE RIGHT.
EH? REALLY?!
YOUR ONLY MISTAKE WAS WORRYING TOO MUCH ABOUT WHAT THEY REPRESENTED... AND TRYING TO PUT THEM IN ORDER.
THE TRUTH IS, THERE'S NO CONNECTION WITH FIRE, WATER, EARTH OR AIR. THAT CLUE WAS JUST SUPPOSED TO POINT YOU...TO A FIFTH AND FINAL ELEMENT.
AND THE PAINTING THAT SHOWS US THAT IS RIGHT HERE.

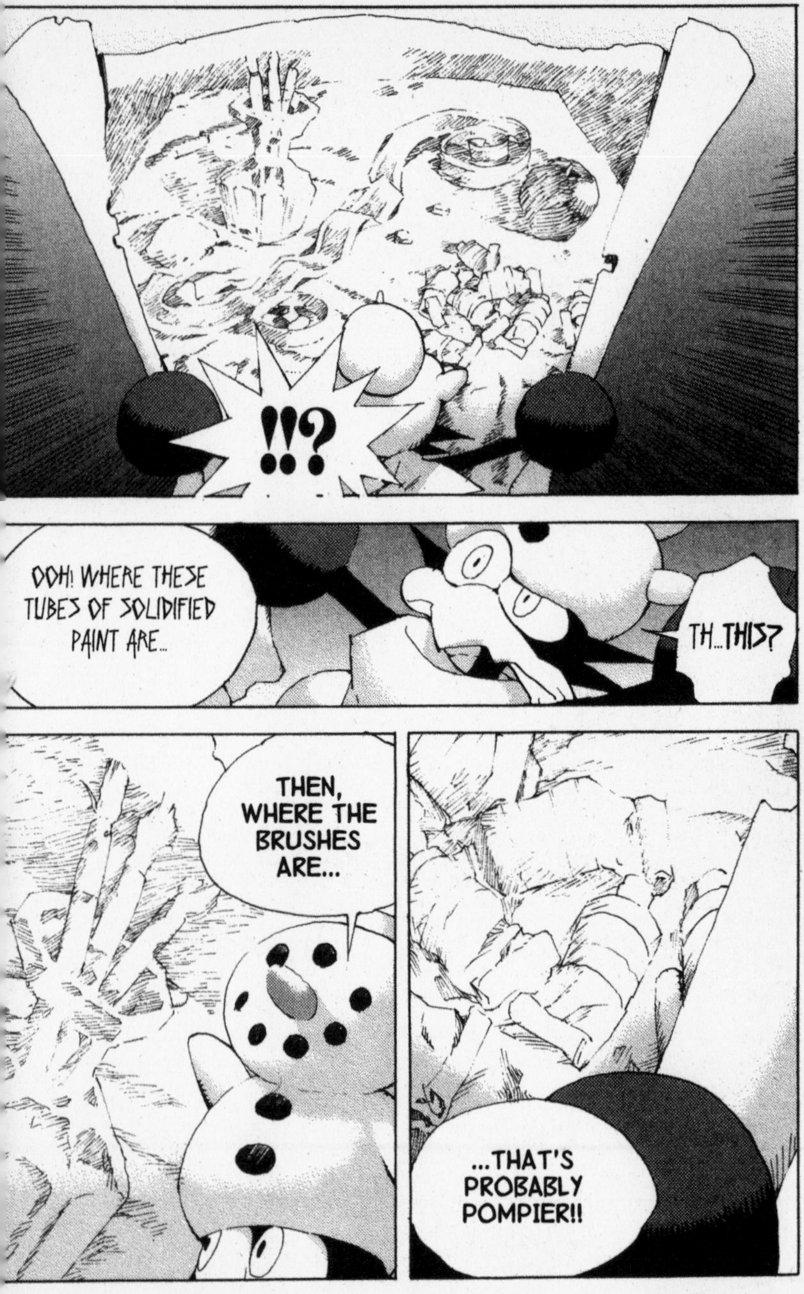
!!?
OOH! WHERE THESE TUBES OF SOLIDIFIED PAINT ARE...
TH...THIS?
THEN, WHERE THE BRUSHES ARE...
...THAT'S PROBABLY POMPIER!!

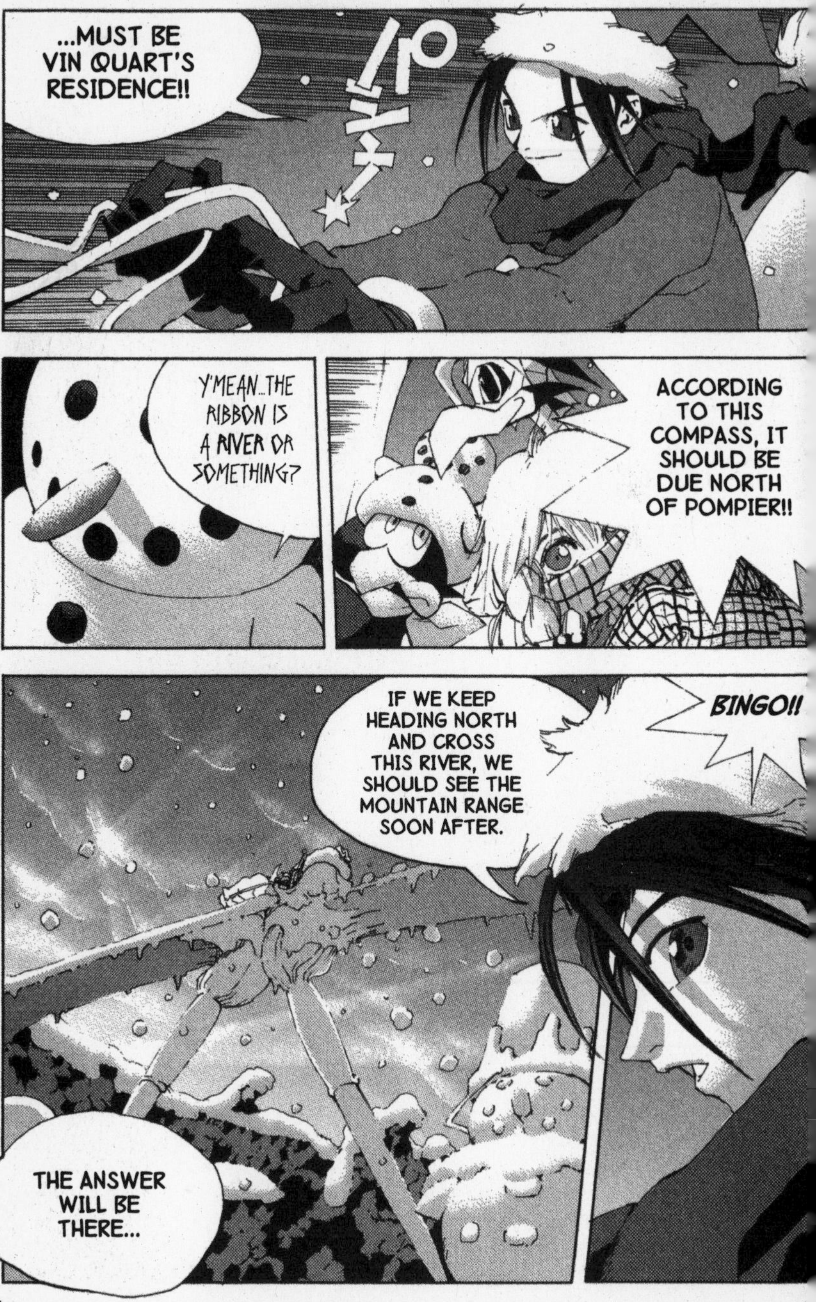
...MUST BE VIN QUART'S RESIDENCE!!
ACCORDING TO THIS COMPASS, IT SHOULD BE DUE NORTH OF POMPIER!!
Y'MEAN...THE RIBBON IS A RIVER OR SOMETHING?
BINGO!!
IF WE KEEP HEADING NORTH AND CROSS THIS RIVER, WE SHOULD SEE THE MOUNTAIN RANGE SOON AFTER.
THE ANSWER WILL BE THERE...

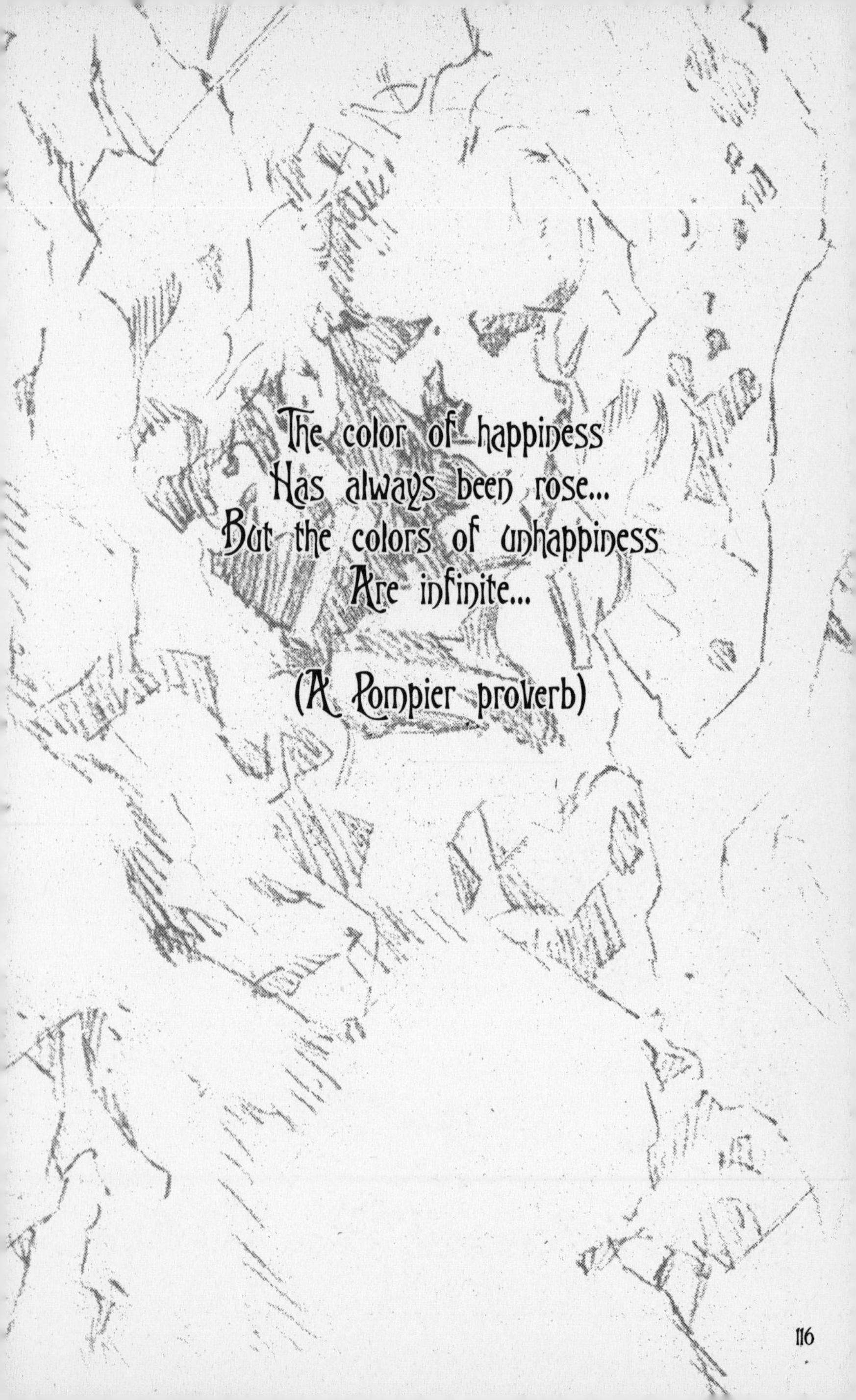

The color of happiness
Has always been rose...
But the colors of unhappiness
Are infinite...

(A Pompier proverb)

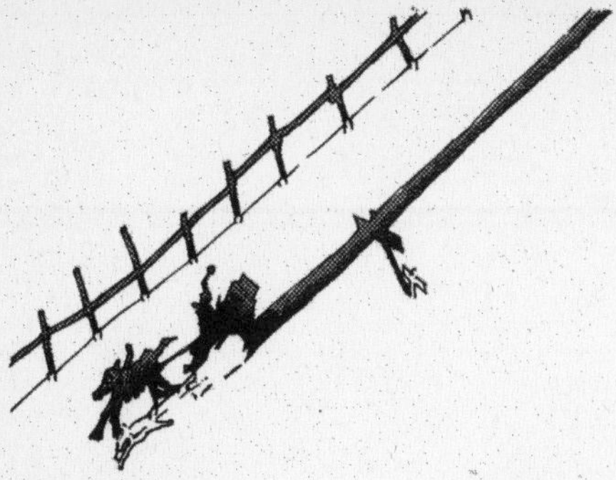

KING OF BANDIT JING

TATTOOED HEART

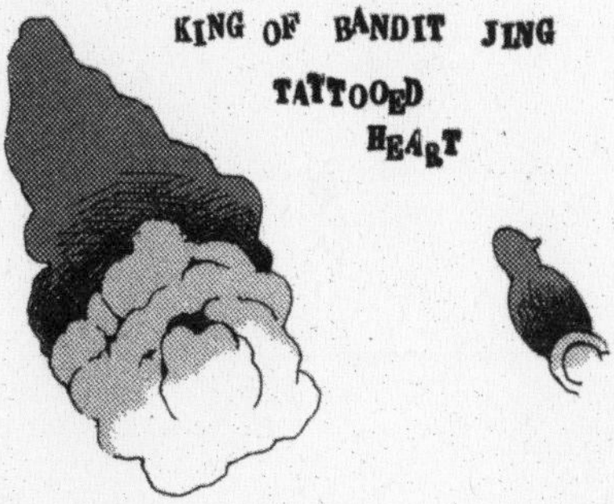

35TH SHOT - BURNING HOUSE OF ICE RIVER

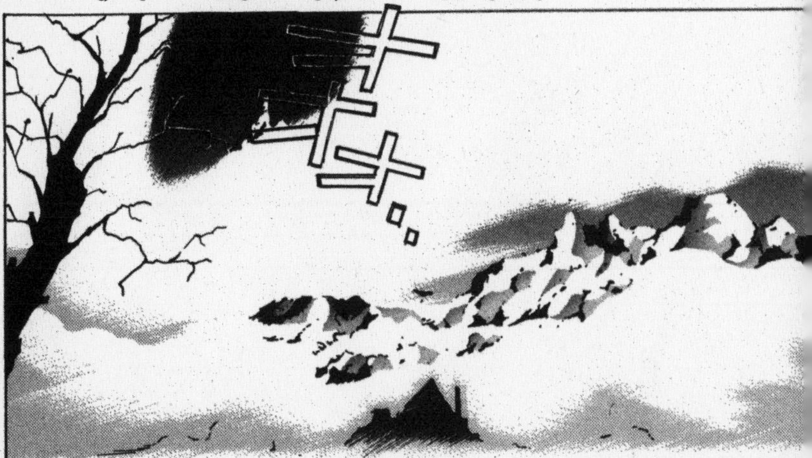

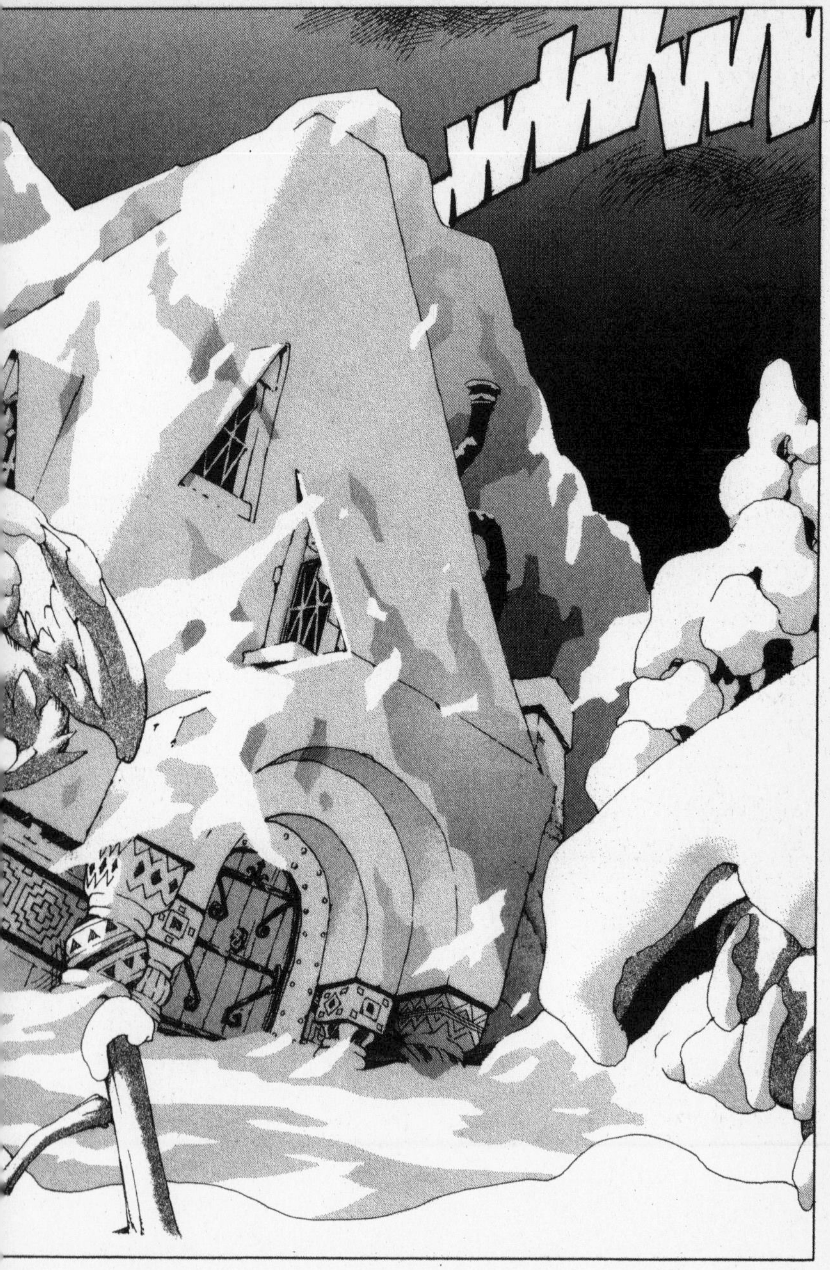

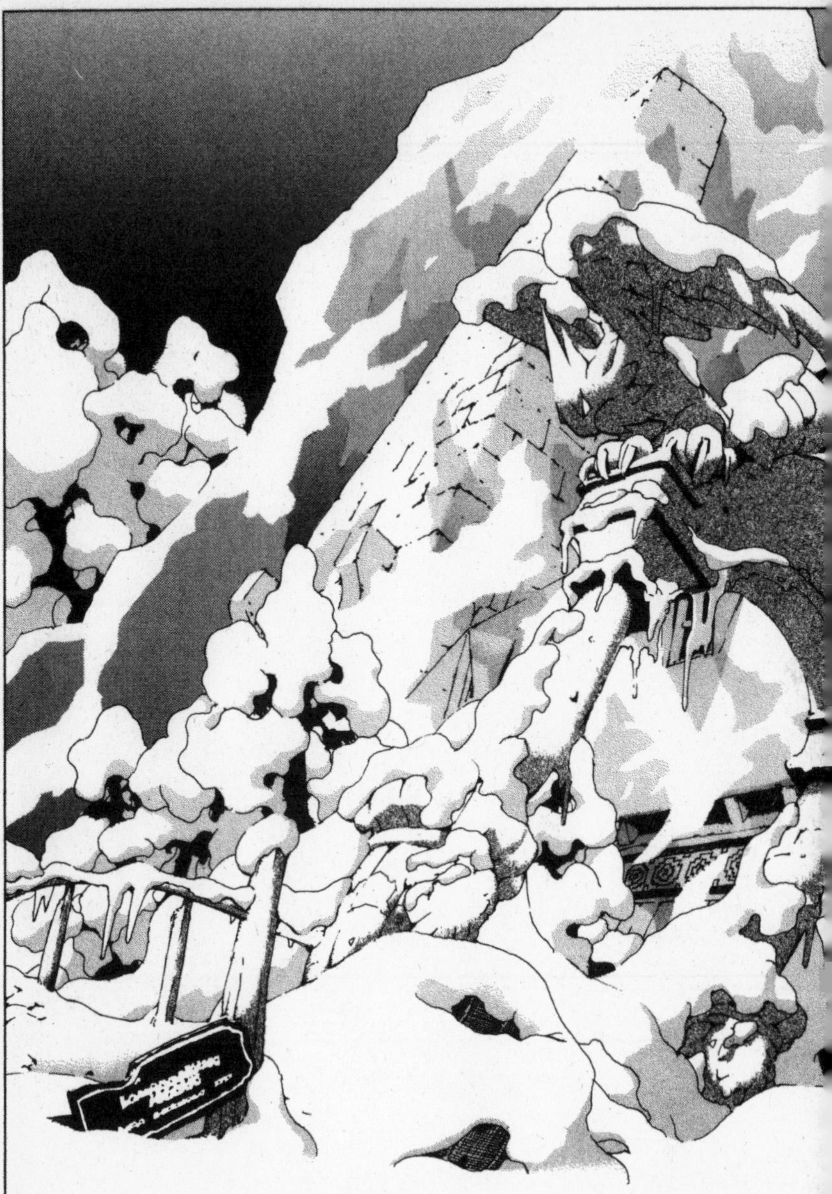

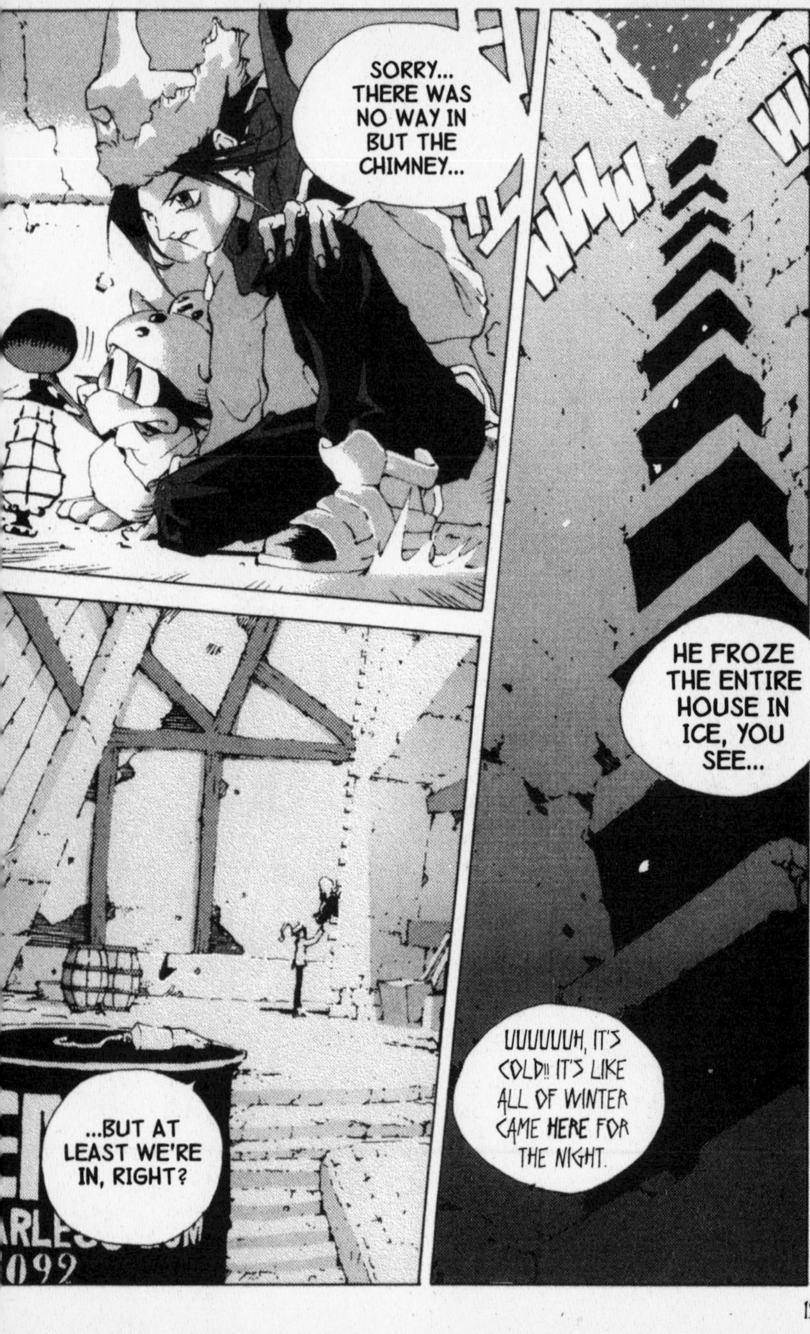
HE FROZE THE ENTIRE HOUSE IN ICE, YOU SEE...
UUUUUUH, IT'S COLD!! IT'S LIKE ALL OF WINTER CAME HERE FOR THE NIGHT.
SORRY... THERE WAS NO WAY IN BUT THE CHIMNEY...
...BUT AT LEAST WE'RE IN, RIGHT?

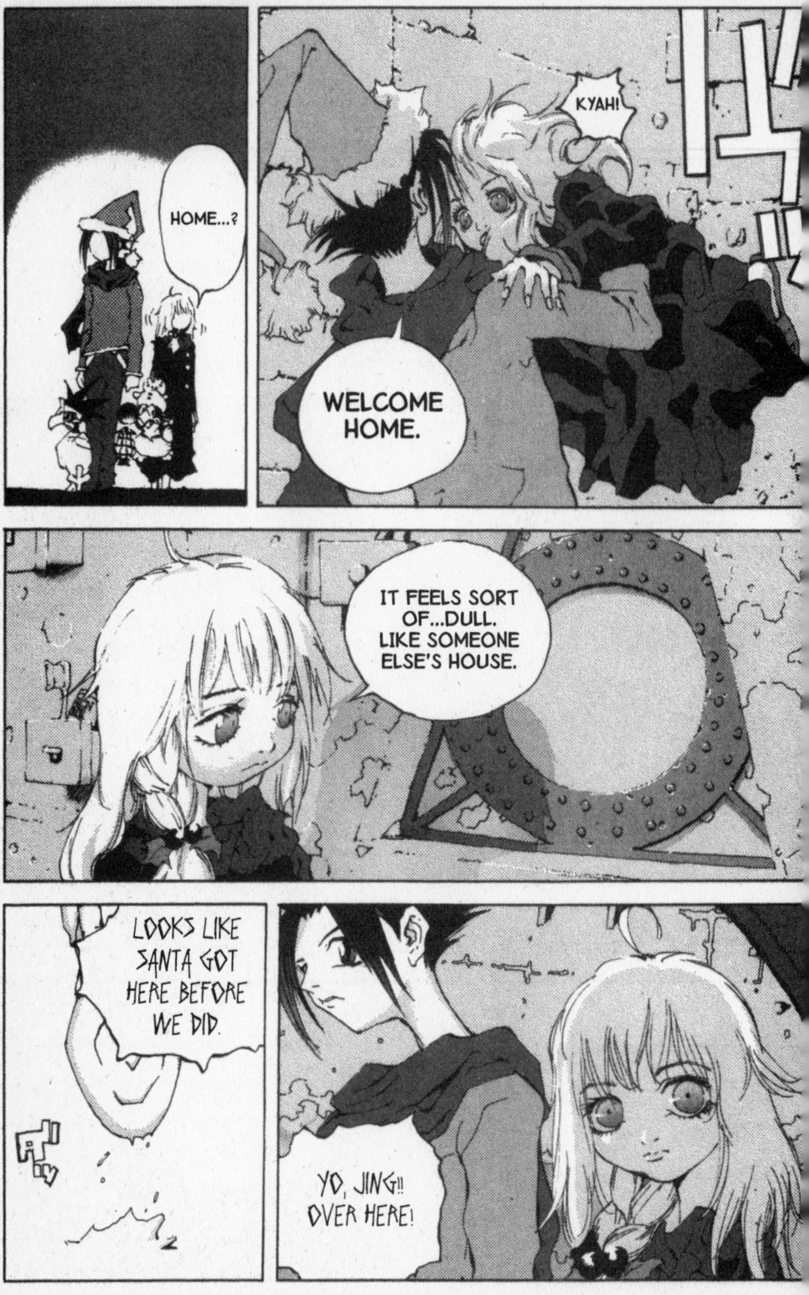
KYAH!
WELCOME HOME.
HOME...?
IT FEELS SORT OF...DULL. LIKE SOMEONE ELSE'S HOUSE.
YO, JING!! OVER HERE!
LOOKS LIKE SANTA GOT HERE BEFORE WE DID.

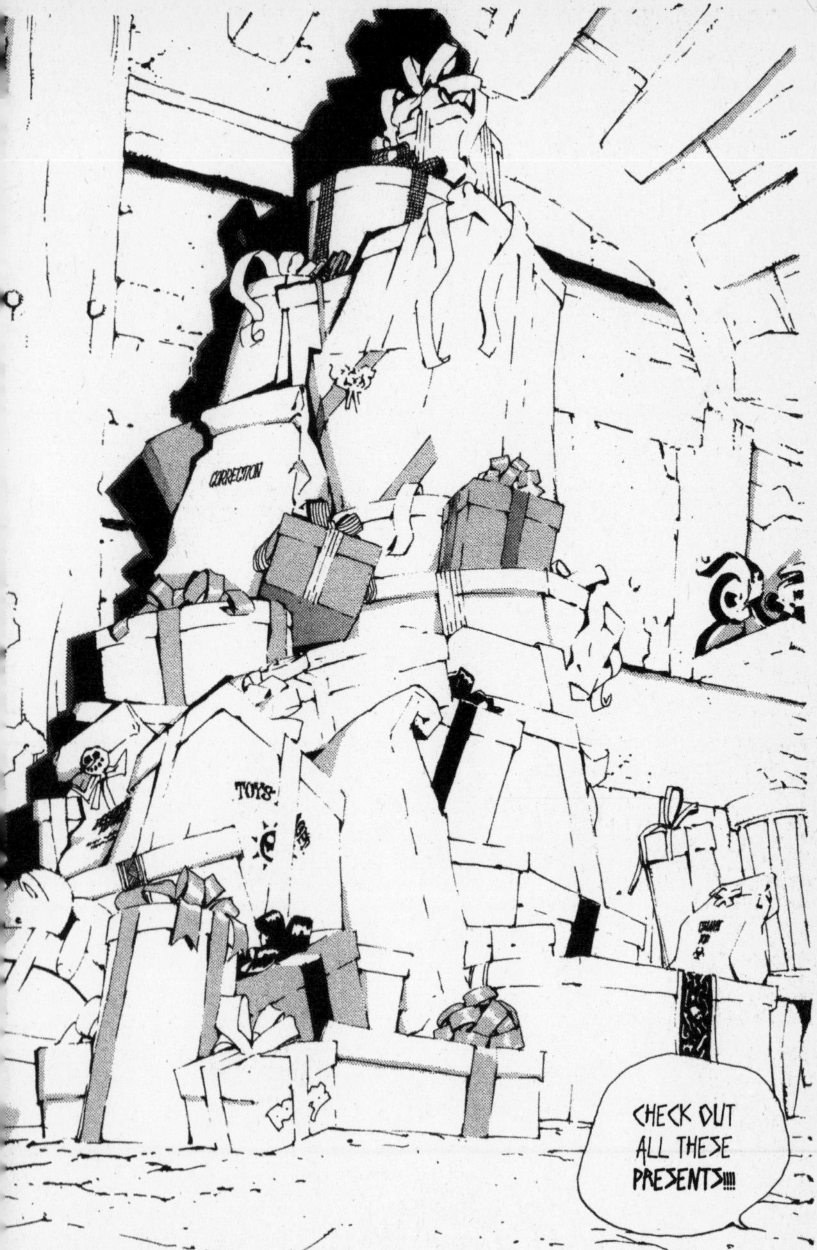
CORRECTION
TOYS
CHECK OUT ALL THESE PRESENTS!!!!

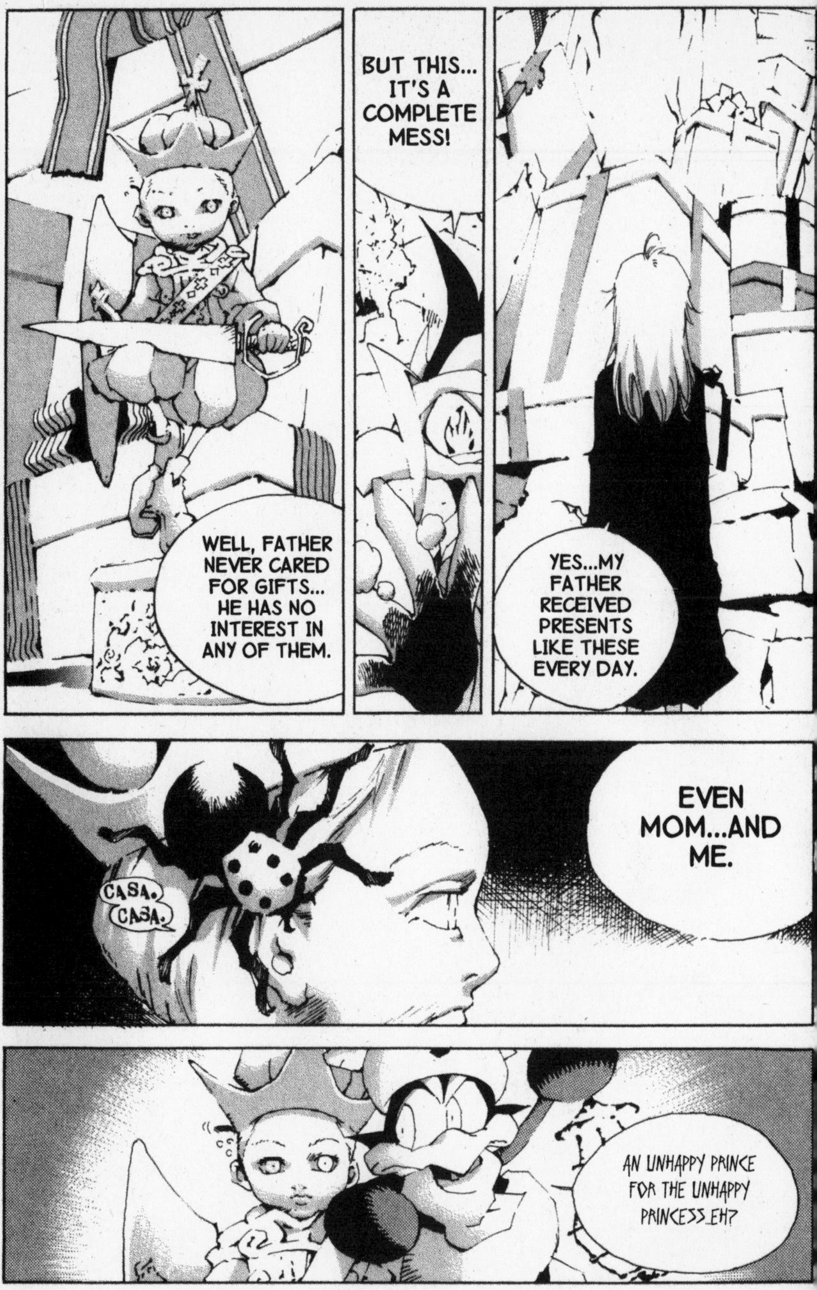
YES...MY FATHER RECEIVED PRESENTS LIKE THESE EVERY DAY.
BUT THIS... IT'S A COMPLETE MESS!
WELL, FATHER NEVER CARED FOR GIFTS... HE HAS NO INTEREST IN ANY OF THEM.
EVEN MOM...AND ME.
CASA. CASA.
AN UNHAPPY PRINCE FOR THE UNHAPPY PRINCESS..EH?

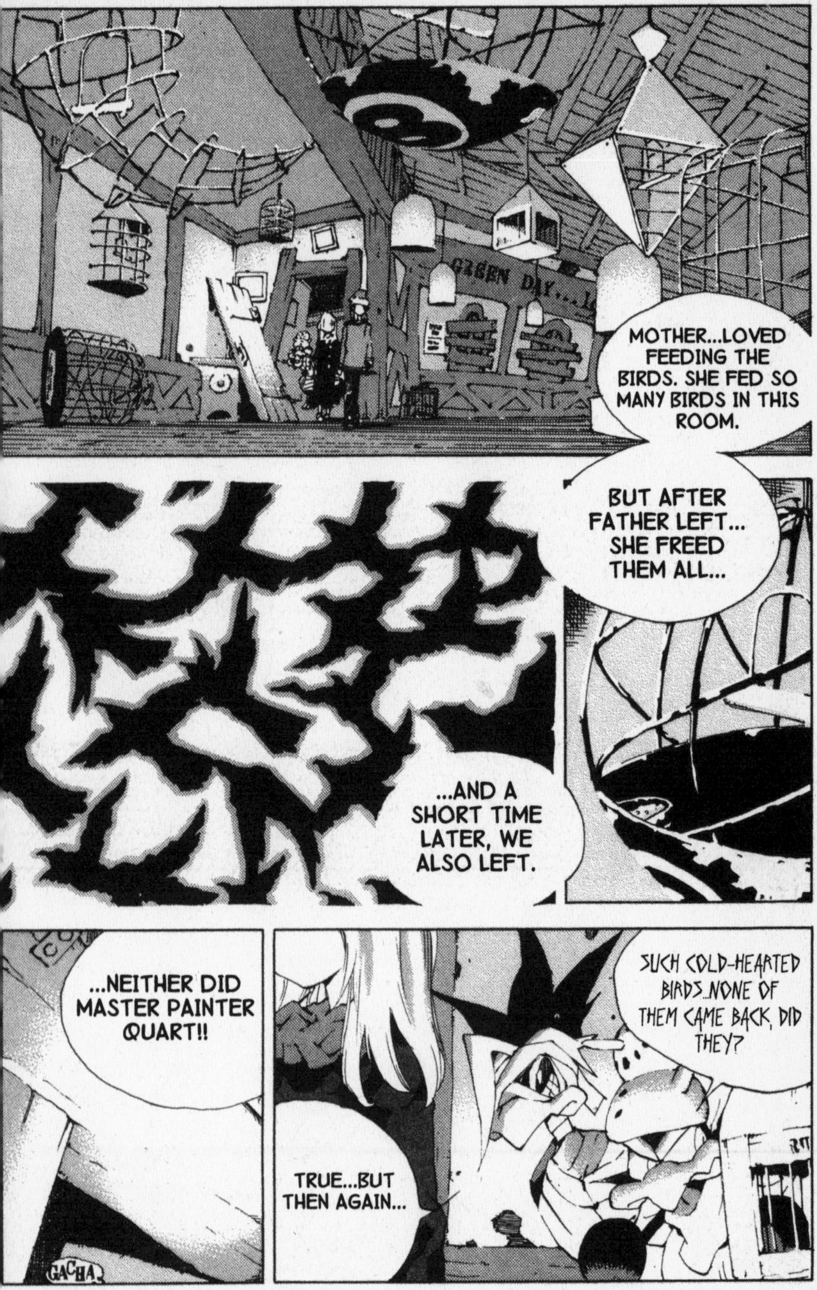
MOTHER...LOVED FEEDING THE BIRDS. SHE FED SO MANY BIRDS IN THIS ROOM.
BUT AFTER FATHER LEFT... SHE FREED THEM ALL...
...AND A SHORT TIME LATER, WE ALSO LEFT.
SUCH COLD-HEARTED BIRDS...NONE OF THEM CAME BACK, DID THEY?
TRUE...BUT THEN AGAIN...
...NEITHER DID MASTER PAINTER QUART!!
GACHA

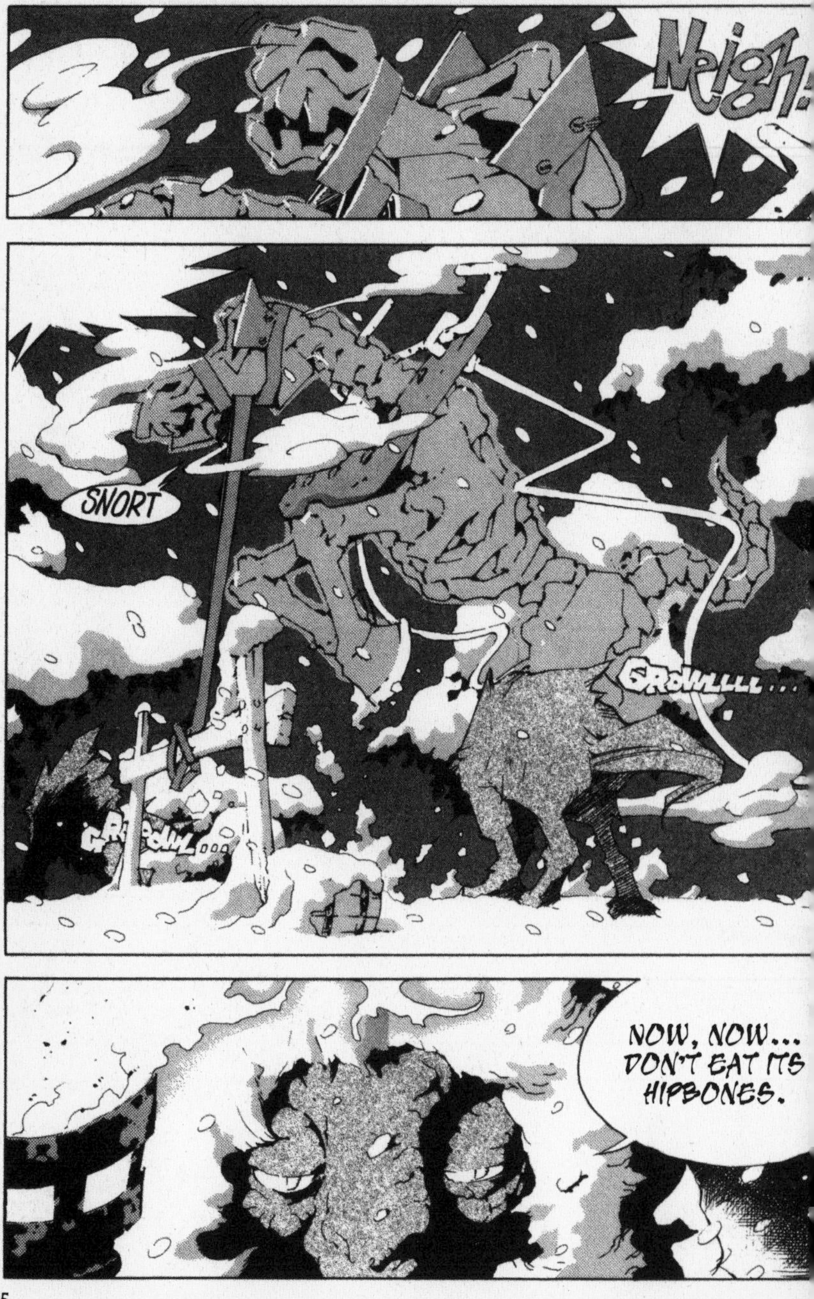
Neigh!
SNORT
GROWLLLL...
NOW, NOW... DON'T EAT ITS HIPBONES.

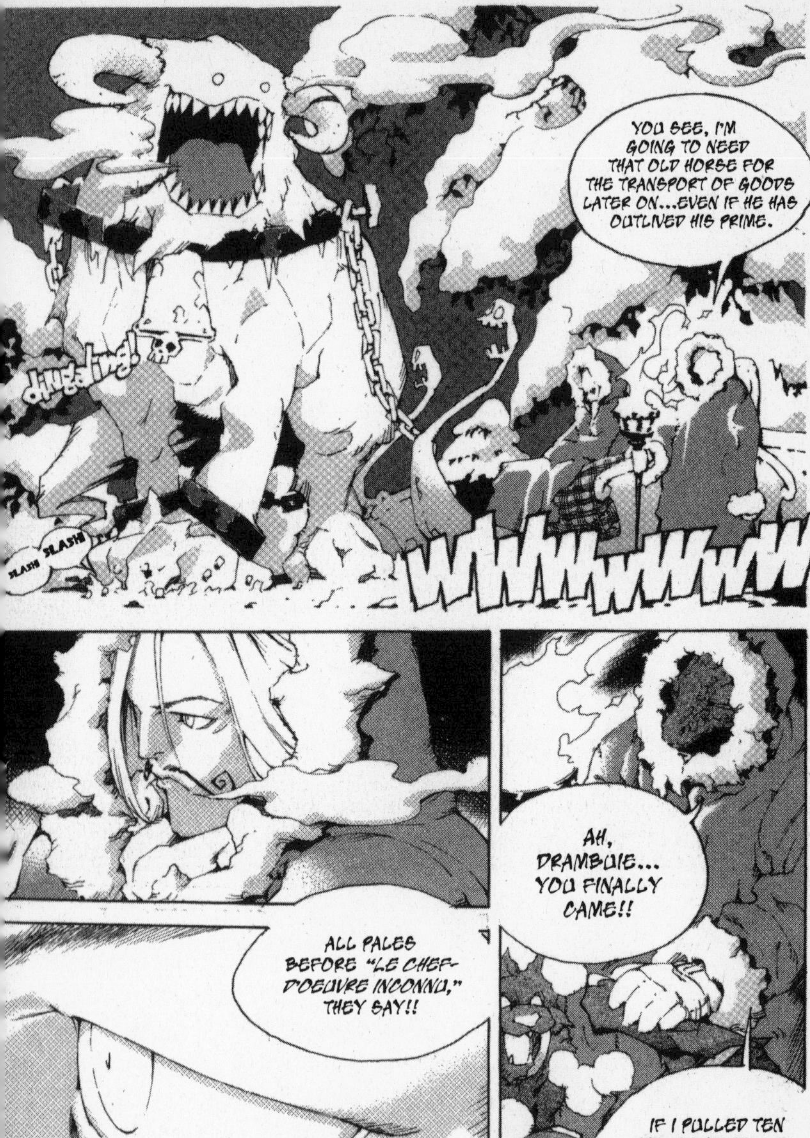
YOU SEE, I'M GOING TO NEED THAT OLD HORSE FOR THE TRANSPORT OF GOODS LATER ON...EVEN IF HE HAS OUTLIVED HIS PRIME.
WHWHWHWHWHW
dingaling!
SLASH SLASH
AH, DRAMBUIE... YOU FINALLY CAME!!
IF I PULLED TEN THOUSAND MOLARS, I DOUBT I'D COME CLOSE TO THE VALUE I'M ABOUT TO ENCOUNTER...
ALL PALES BEFORE "LE CHEF-D'OEUVRE INCONNU," THEY SAY!!

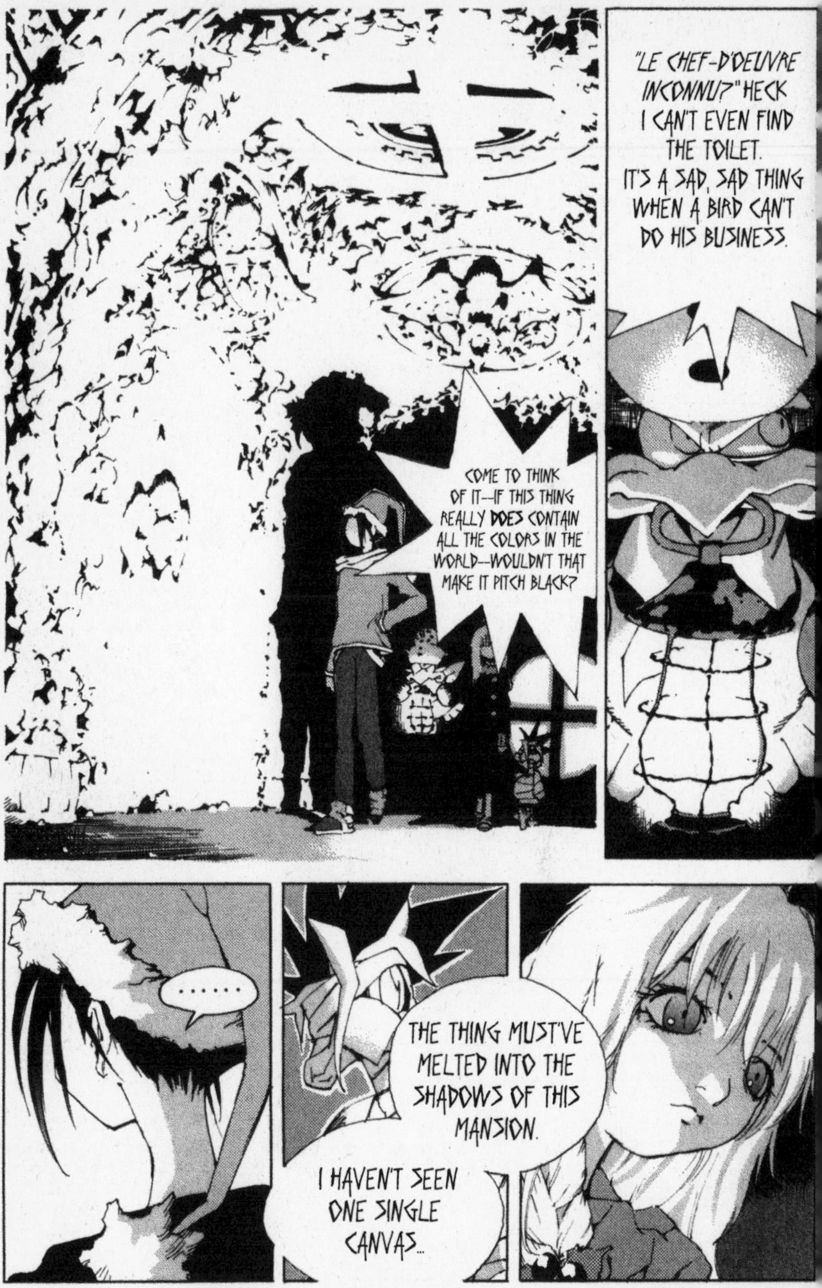
"LE CHEF-D'OEUVRE INCONNU?" HECK I CAN'T EVEN FIND THE TOILET. IT'S A SAD, SAD THING WHEN A BIRD CAN'T DO HIS BUSINESS.
COME TO THINK OF IT--IF THIS THING REALLY **DOES** CONTAIN ALL THE COLORS IN THE WORLD--WOULDN'T THAT MAKE IT PITCH BLACK?
I HAVEN'T SEEN ONE SINGLE CANVAS...
THE THING MUST'VE MELTED INTO THE SHADOWS OF THIS MANSION.
......

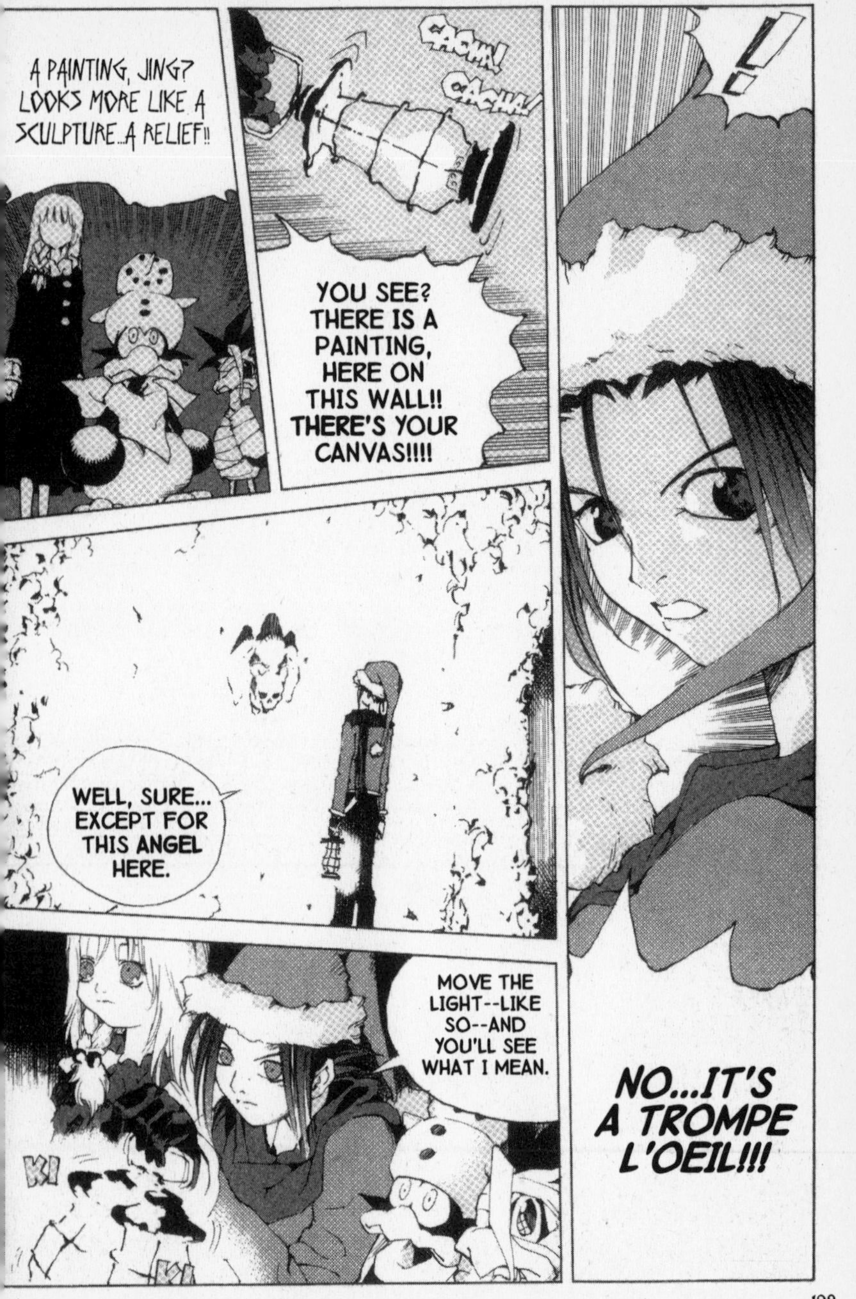
!
NO...IT'S A TROMPE L'OEIL!!!
CACHA!
CACHA!
YOU SEE? THERE IS A PAINTING, HERE ON THIS WALL!! THERE'S YOUR CANVAS!!!!
A PAINTING, JING? LOOKS MORE LIKE A SCULPTURE...A RELIEF!!
WELL, SURE... EXCEPT FOR THIS ANGEL HERE.
MOVE THE LIGHT--LIKE SO--AND YOU'LL SEE WHAT I MEAN.
KI
KI

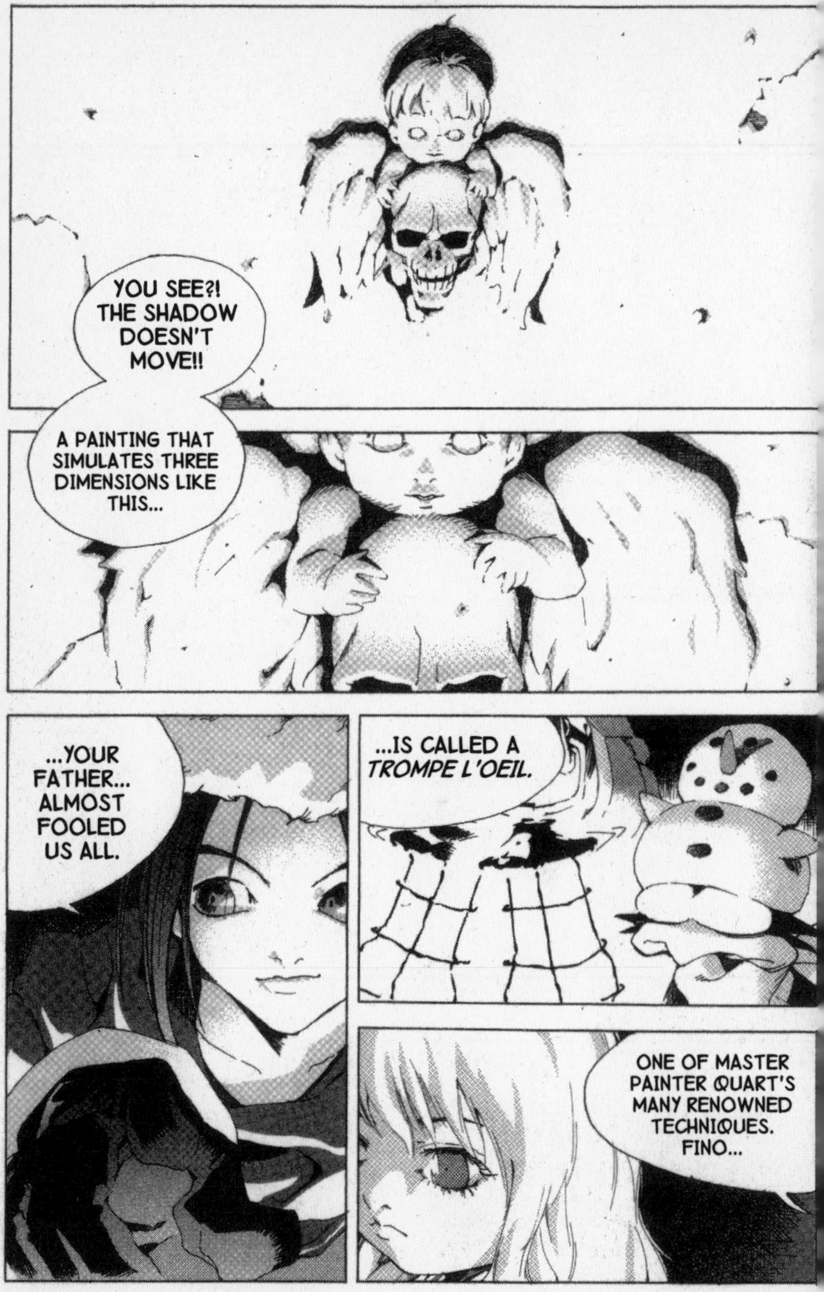
YOU SEE?! THE SHADOW DOESN'T MOVE!!
A PAINTING THAT SIMULATES THREE DIMENSIONS LIKE THIS...
...IS CALLED A *TROMPE L'OEIL.*
ONE OF MASTER PAINTER QUART'S MANY RENOWNED TECHNIQUES. FINO...
...YOUR FATHER... ALMOST FOOLED US ALL.

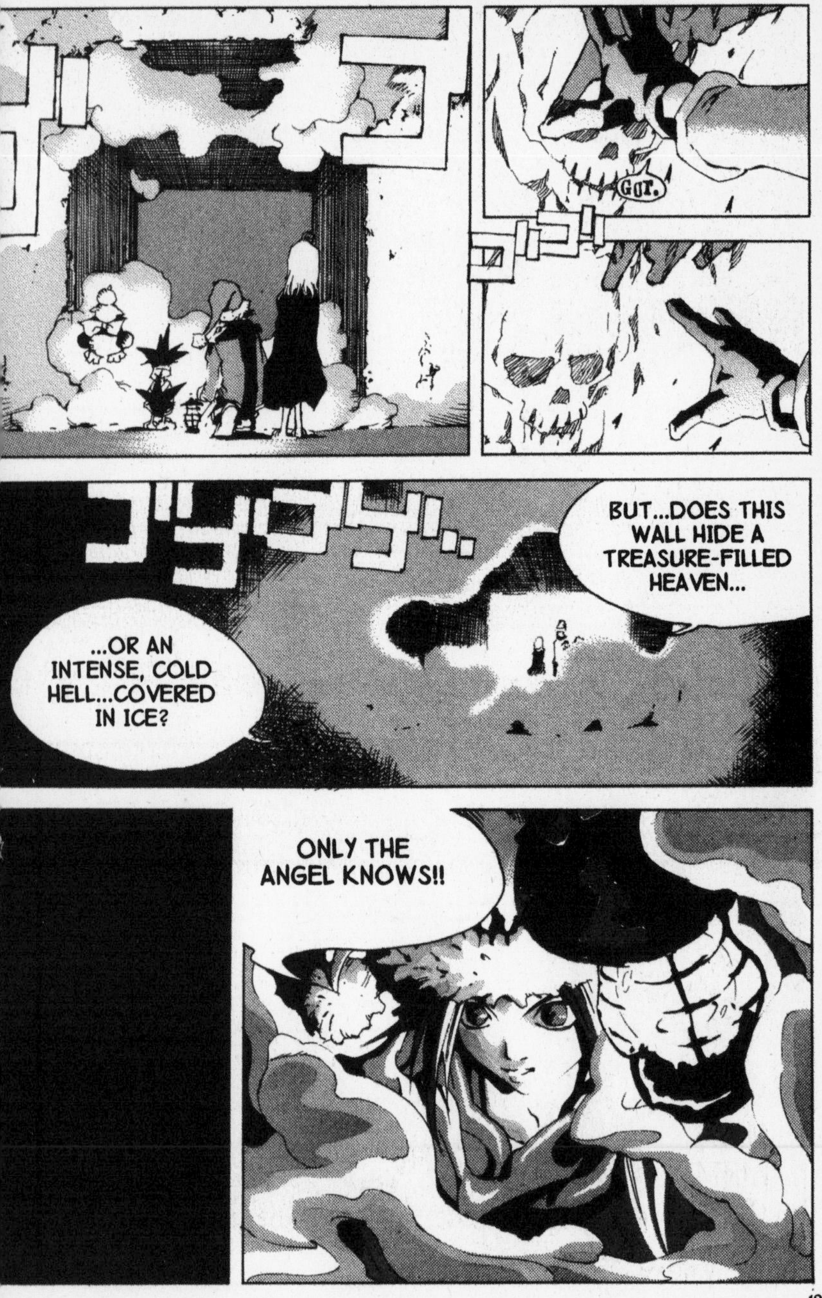
GOT.
BUT...DOES THIS WALL HIDE A TREASURE-FILLED HEAVEN...
...OR AN INTENSE, COLD HELL...COVERED IN ICE?
ONLY THE ANGEL KNOWS!!

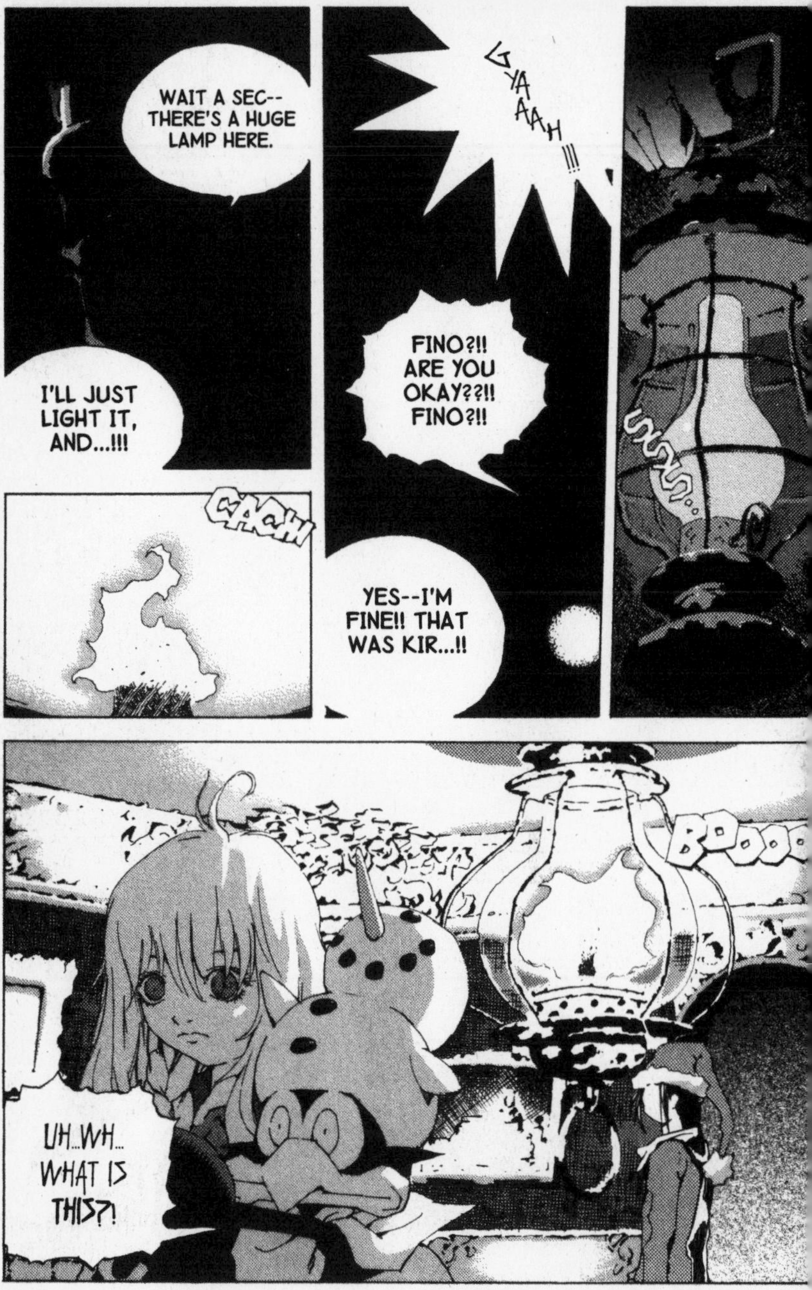
WAIT A SEC-- THERE'S A HUGE LAMP HERE.
I'LL JUST LIGHT IT, AND...!!!
CACHH
GYAAAH!!!
FINO?!! ARE YOU OKAY??!! FINO?!!
YES--I'M FINE!! THAT WAS KIR...!!
BOOOO
UH...WH... WHAT IS THIS?!

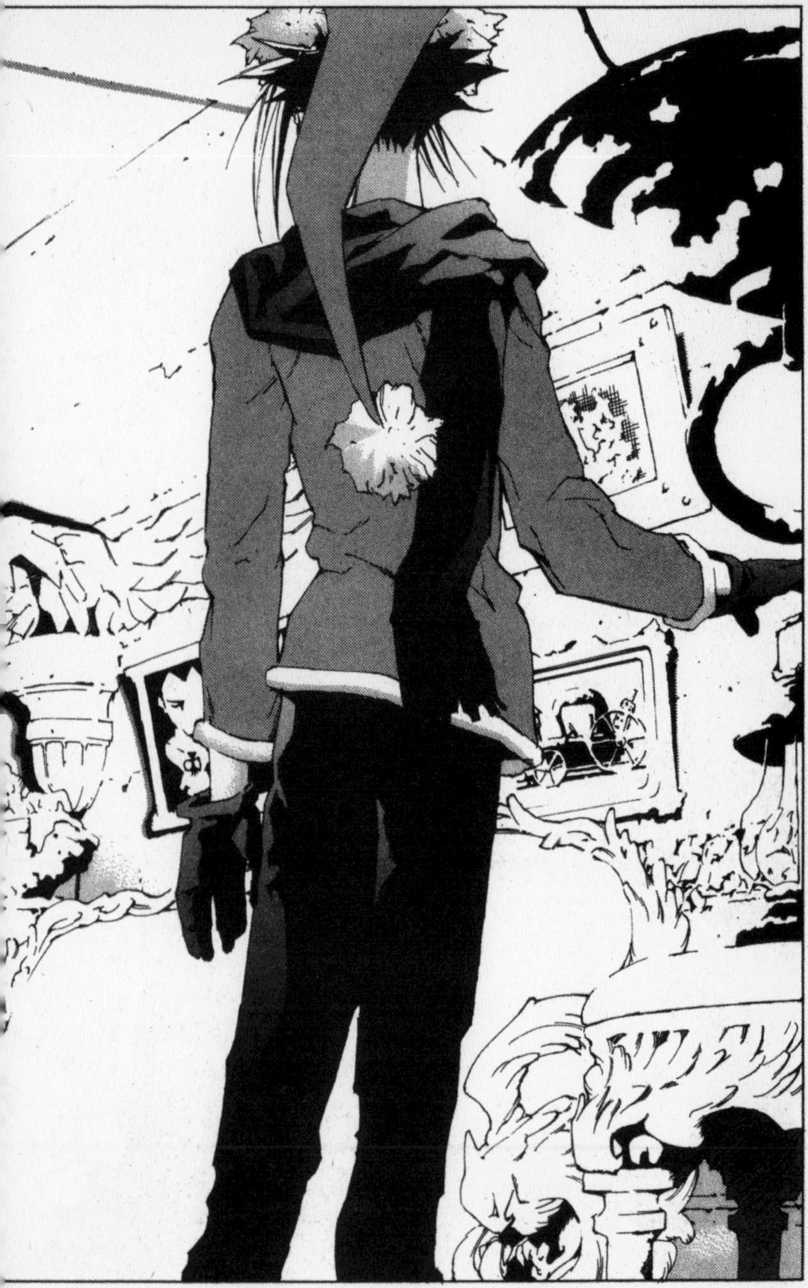

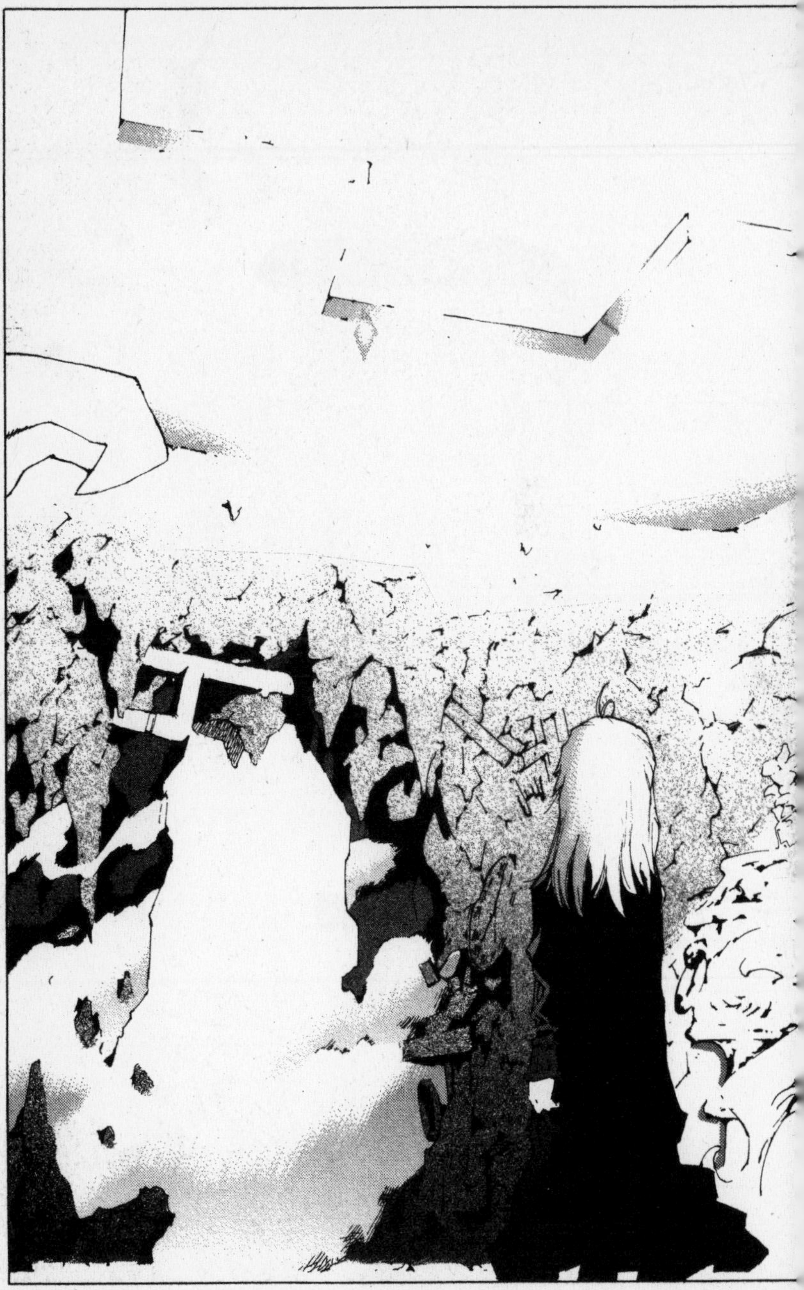

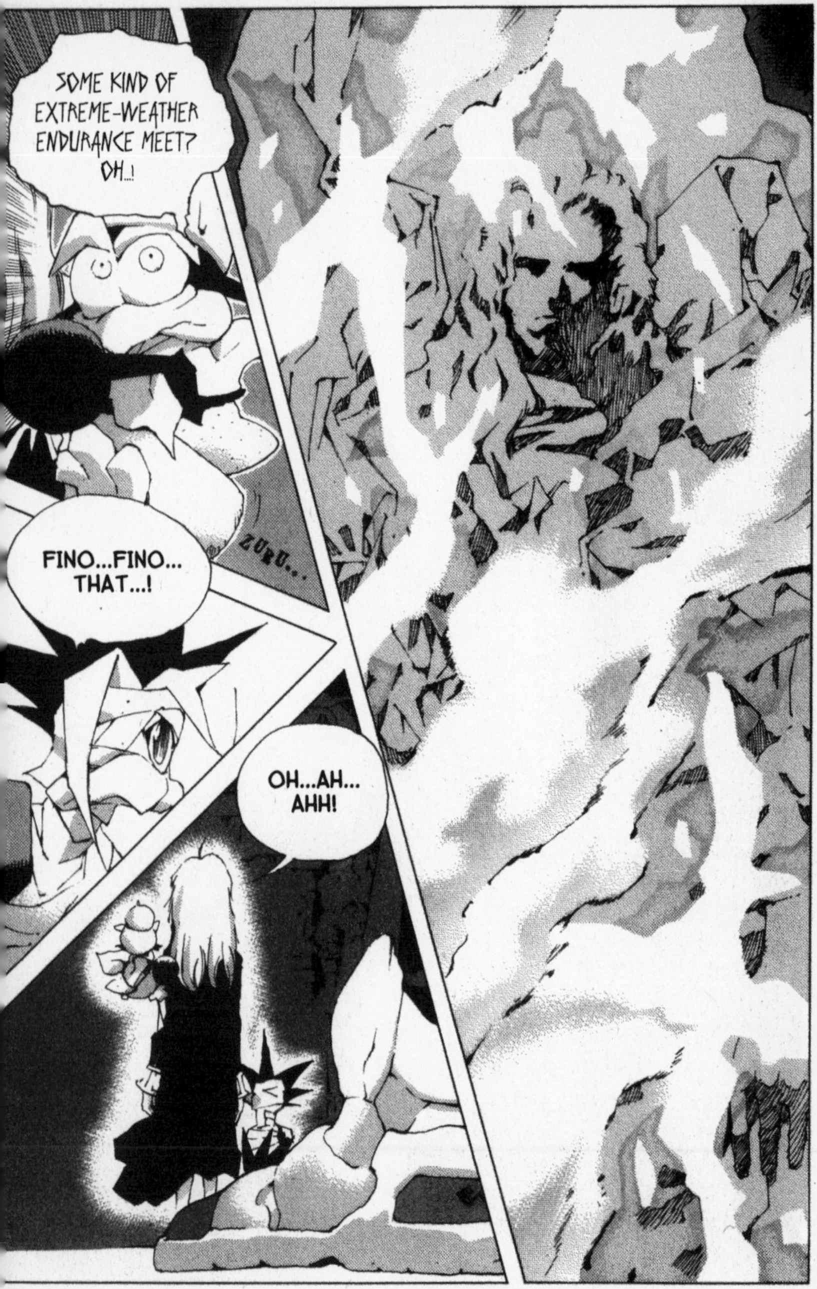
SOME KIND OF EXTREME-WEATHER ENDURANCE MEET? OH...!
ZURU...
FINO...FINO... THAT...!
OH...AH... AHH!

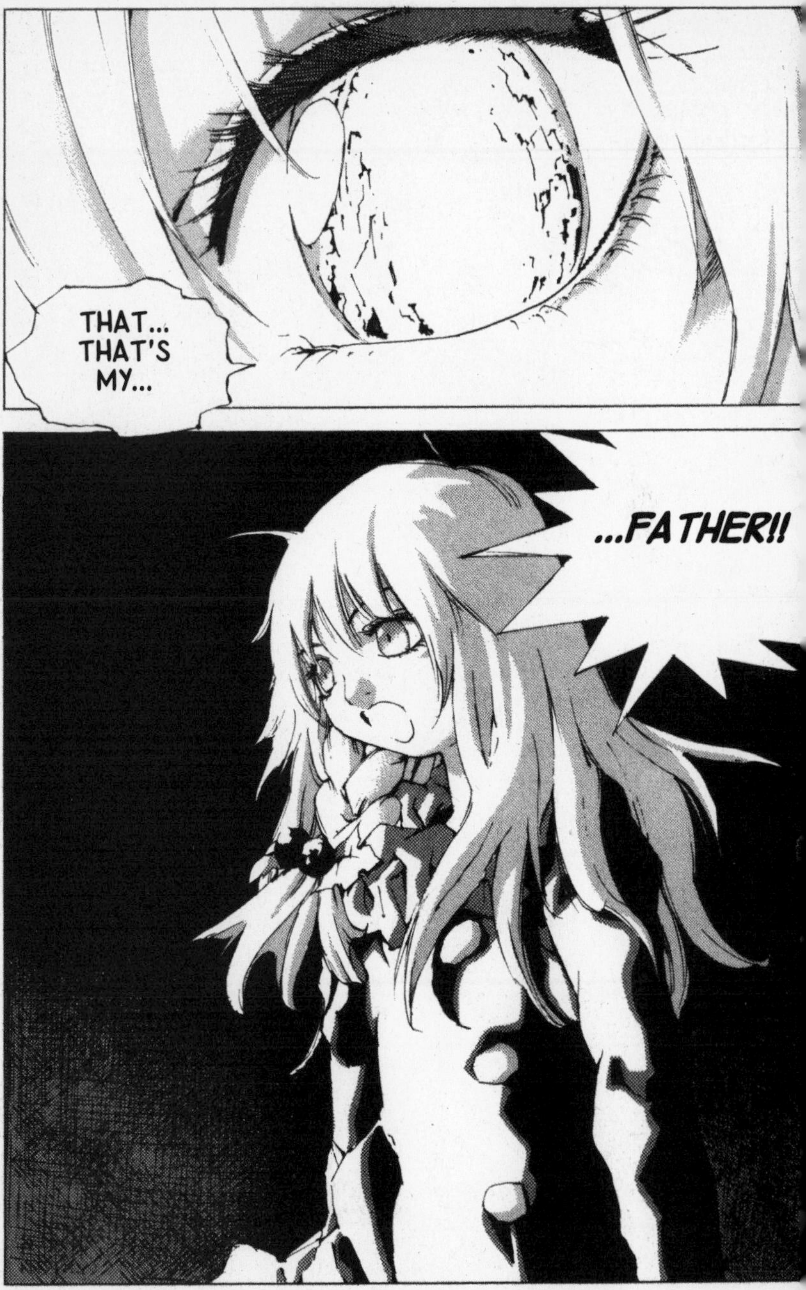
THAT... THAT'S MY...
...FATHER!!

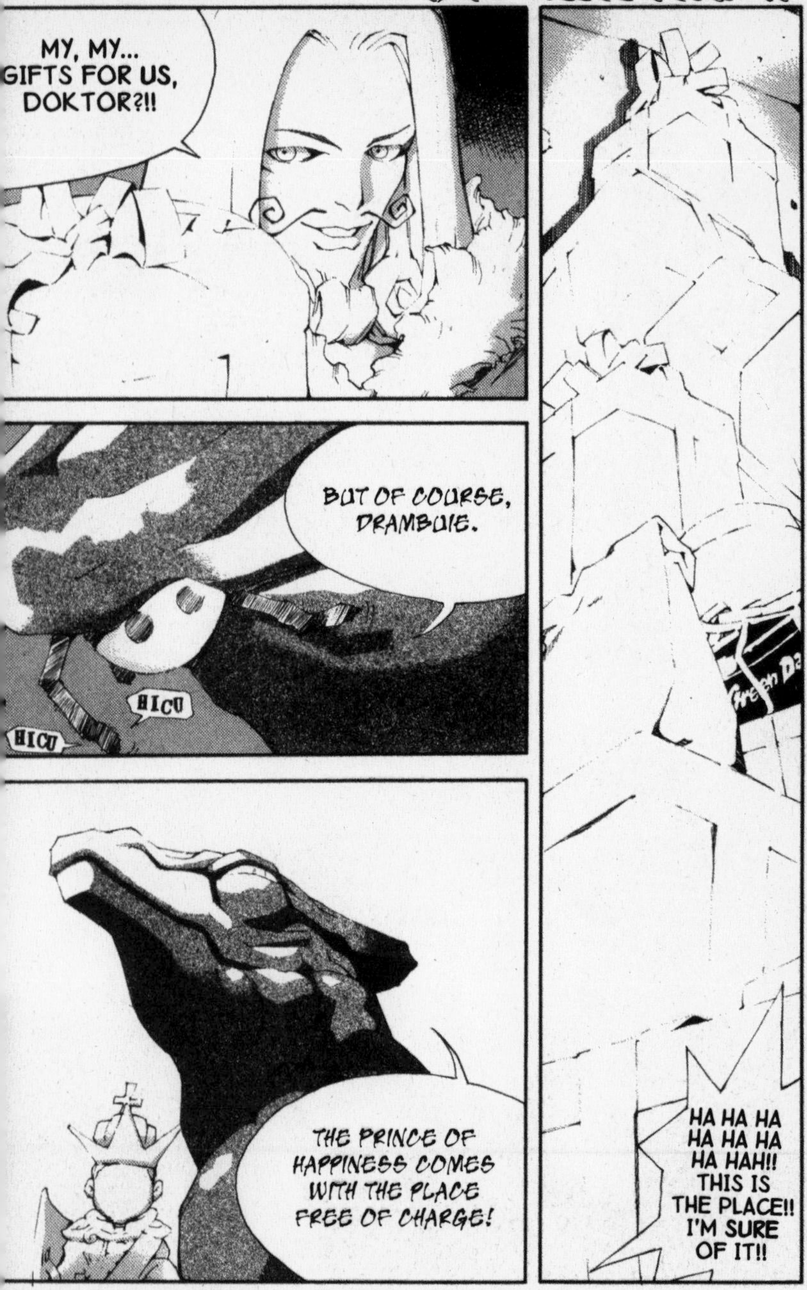
HA HA HA HA HA HA HA HAH!! THIS IS THE PLACE!! I'M SURE OF IT!!
MY, MY... GIFTS FOR US, DOKTOR?!!
BUT OF COURSE, DRAMBUIE.
HICU
HICU
THE PRINCE OF HAPPINESS COMES WITH THE PLACE FREE OF CHARGE!

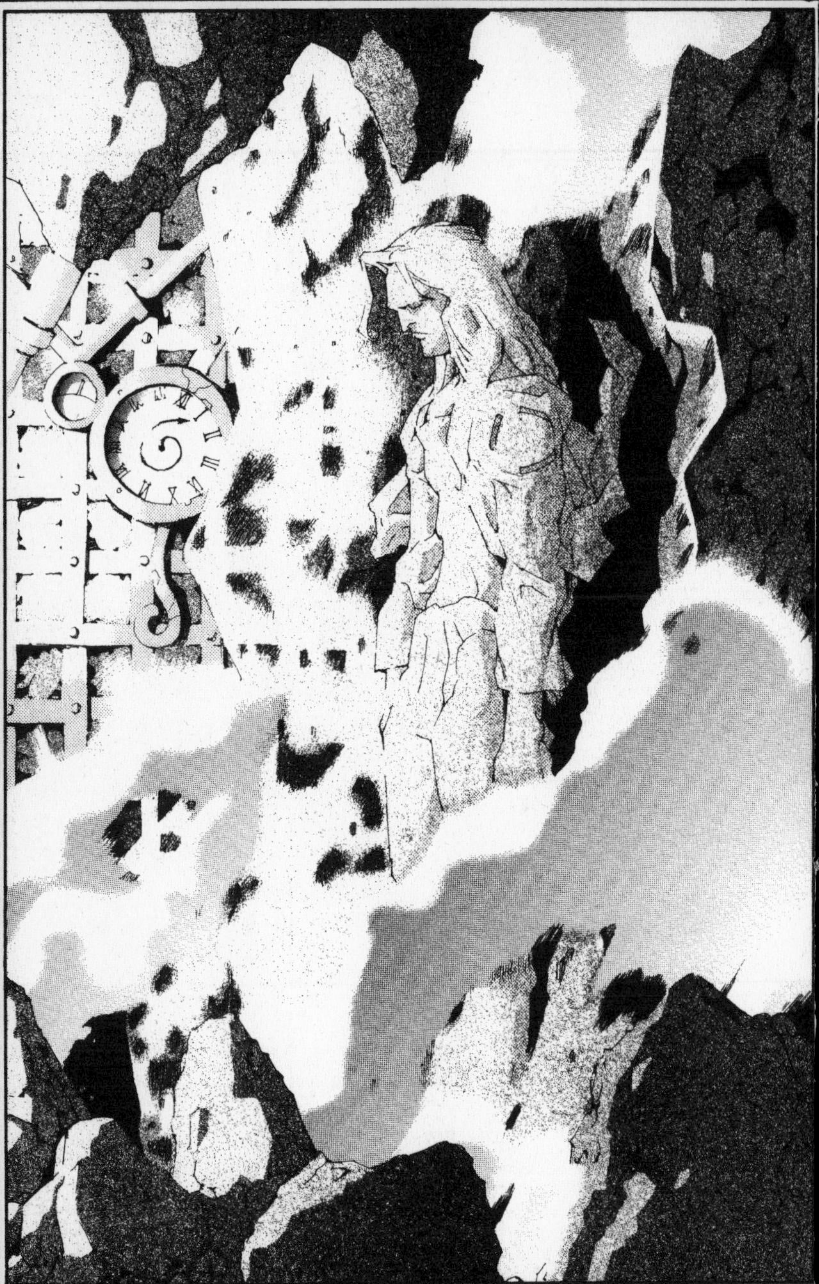

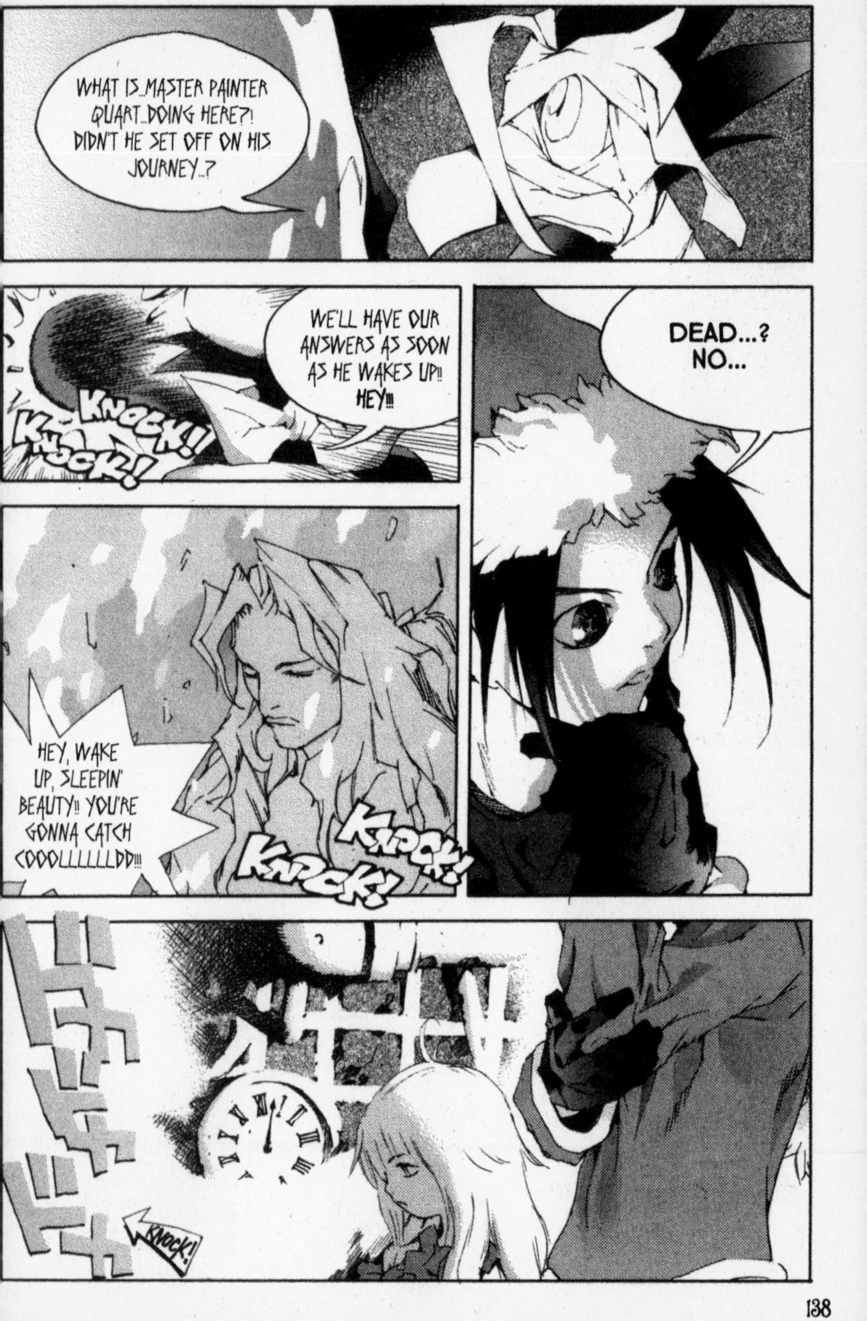

WHAT IS...MASTER PAINTER QUART...DOING HERE?! DIDN'T HE SET OFF ON HIS JOURNEY...?
DEAD...? NO...
WE'LL HAVE OUR ANSWERS AS SOON AS HE WAKES UP!! HEY!!!
KNOCK!! KNOCK!!
HEY, WAKE UP, SLEEPIN' BEAUTY!! YOU'RE GONNA CATCH COOOLLLLLLLDD!!!
KNOCK! KNOCK!
KNOCK!

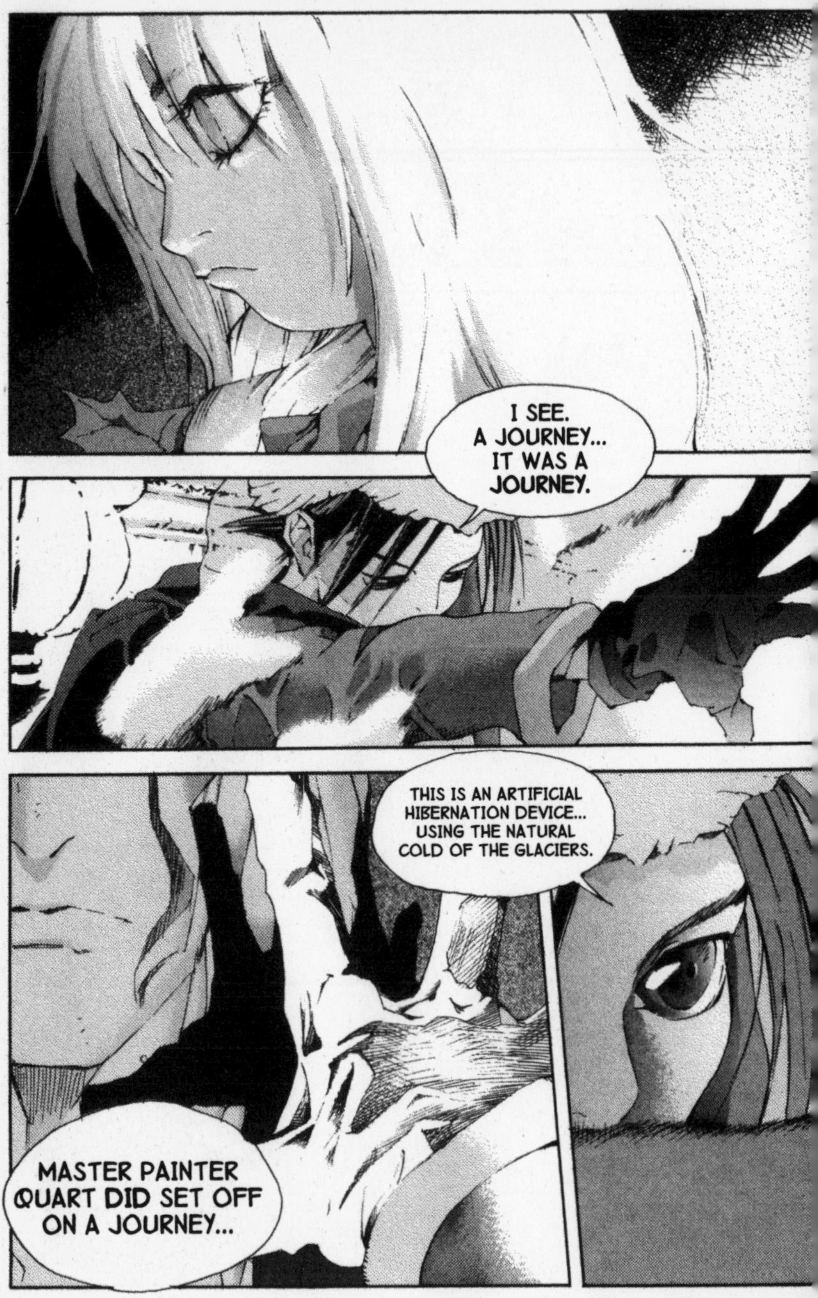
I SEE. A JOURNEY... IT WAS A JOURNEY.
THIS IS AN ARTIFICIAL HIBERNATION DEVICE... USING THE NATURAL COLD OF THE GLACIERS.
MASTER PAINTER QUART DID SET OFF ON A JOURNEY...

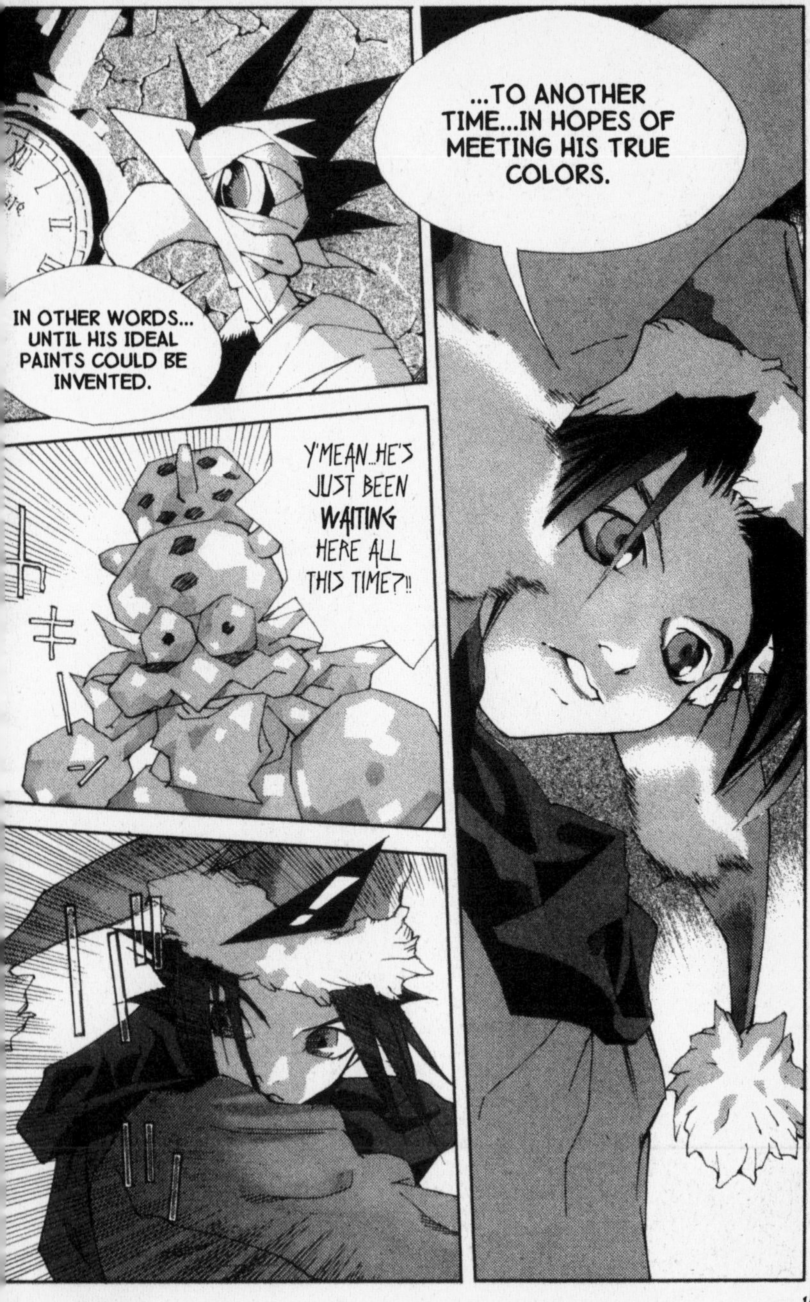
...TO ANOTHER TIME...IN HOPES OF MEETING HIS TRUE COLORS.
IN OTHER WORDS... UNTIL HIS IDEAL PAINTS COULD BE INVENTED.
Y'MEAN...HE'S JUST BEEN **WAITING** HERE ALL THIS TIME?!!

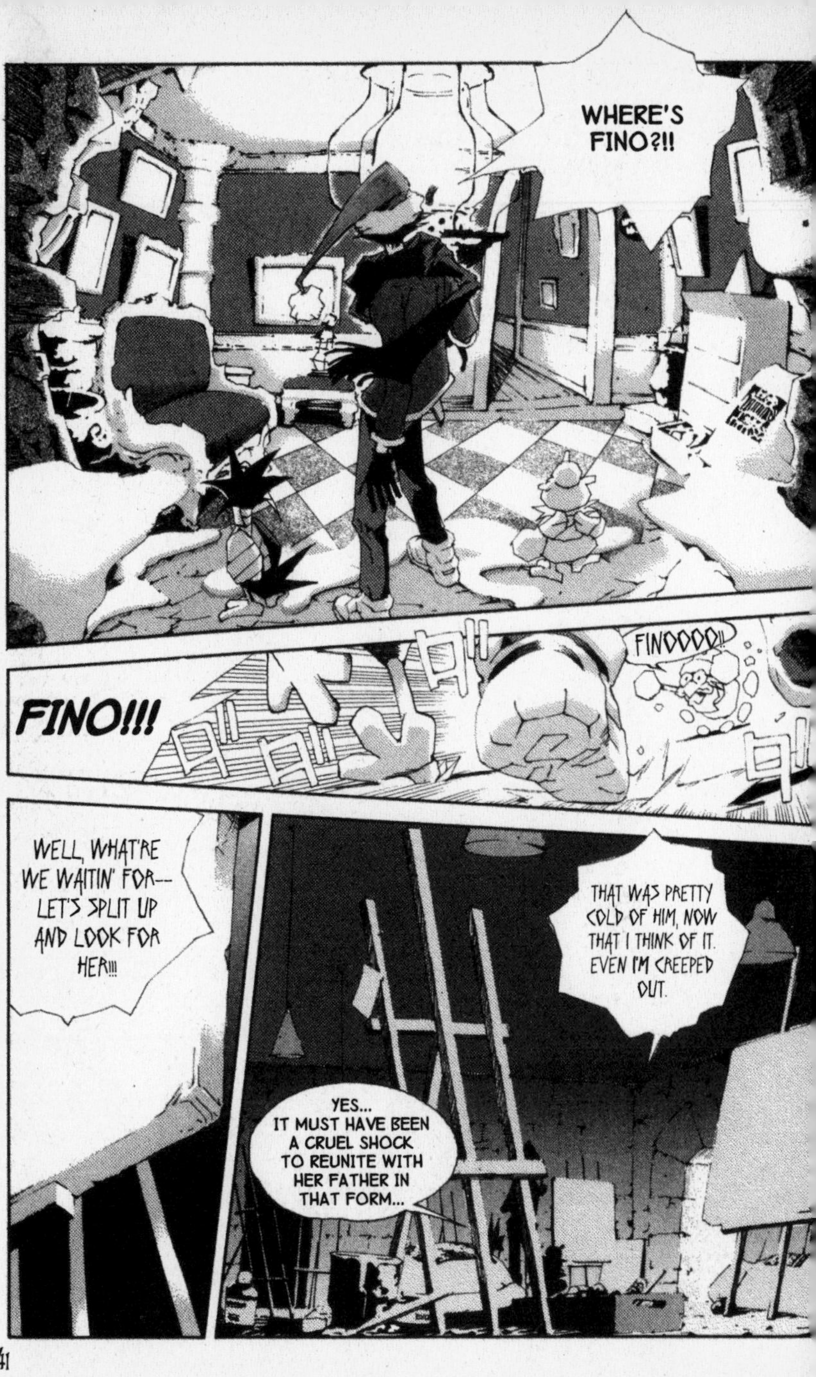
WHERE'S FINO?!!
FINOOOO!!
FINO!!!
THAT WAS PRETTY COLD OF HIM, NOW THAT I THINK OF IT. EVEN I'M CREEPED OUT.
YES... IT MUST HAVE BEEN A CRUEL SHOCK TO REUNITE WITH HER FATHER IN THAT FORM...
WELL, WHAT'RE WE WAITIN' FOR-- LET'S SPLIT UP AND LOOK FOR HER!!!

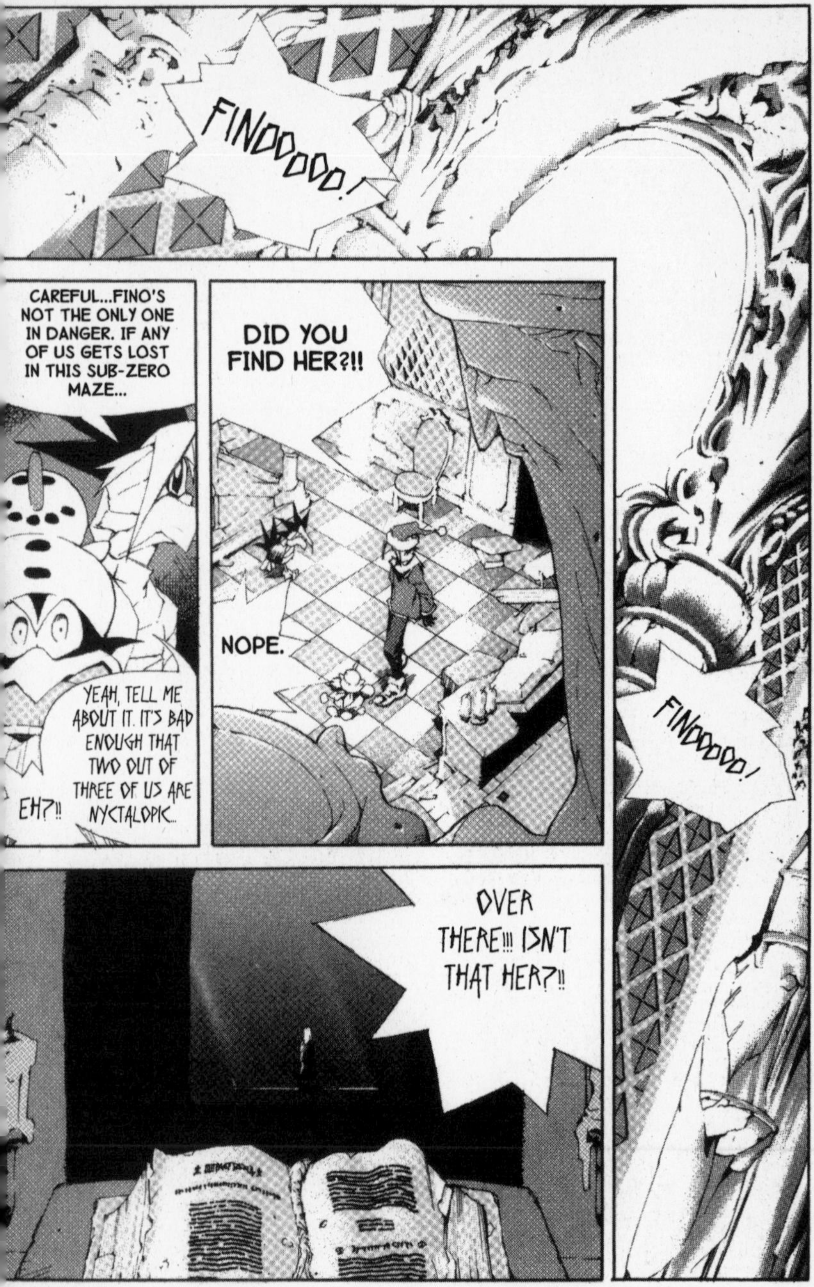
FINDOOOOO!
FINDOOOOO!
DID YOU FIND HER?!!
NOPE.
CAREFUL...FINO'S NOT THE ONLY ONE IN DANGER. IF ANY OF US GETS LOST IN THIS SUB-ZERO MAZE...
YEAH, TELL ME ABOUT IT. IT'S BAD ENOUGH THAT TWO OUT OF THREE OF US ARE NYCTALOPIC...
EH?!!
OVER THERE!!! ISN'T THAT HER?!!

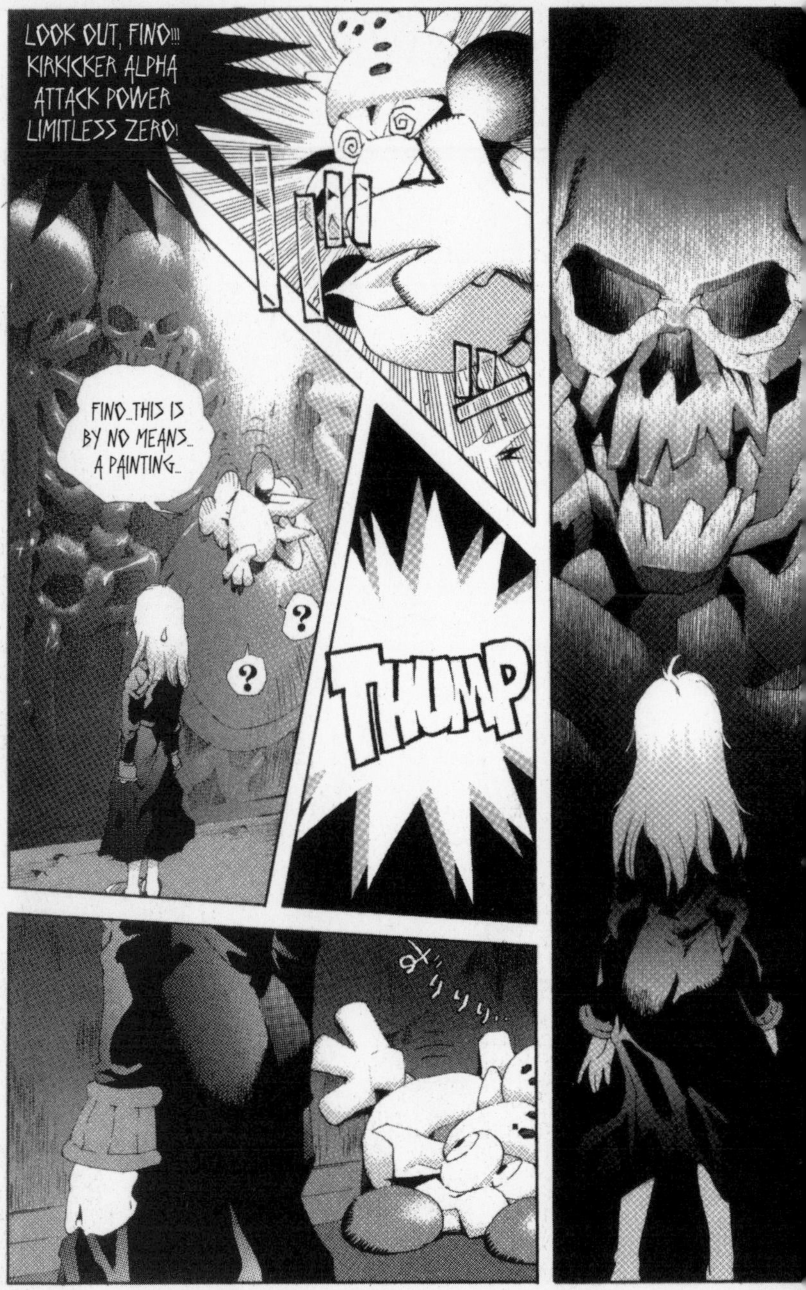
LOOK OUT, FINO!!! KIRKICKER ALPHA ATTACK POWER LIMITLESS ZERO!
THUMP
FINO...THIS IS BY NO MEANS... A PAINTING...
?
?

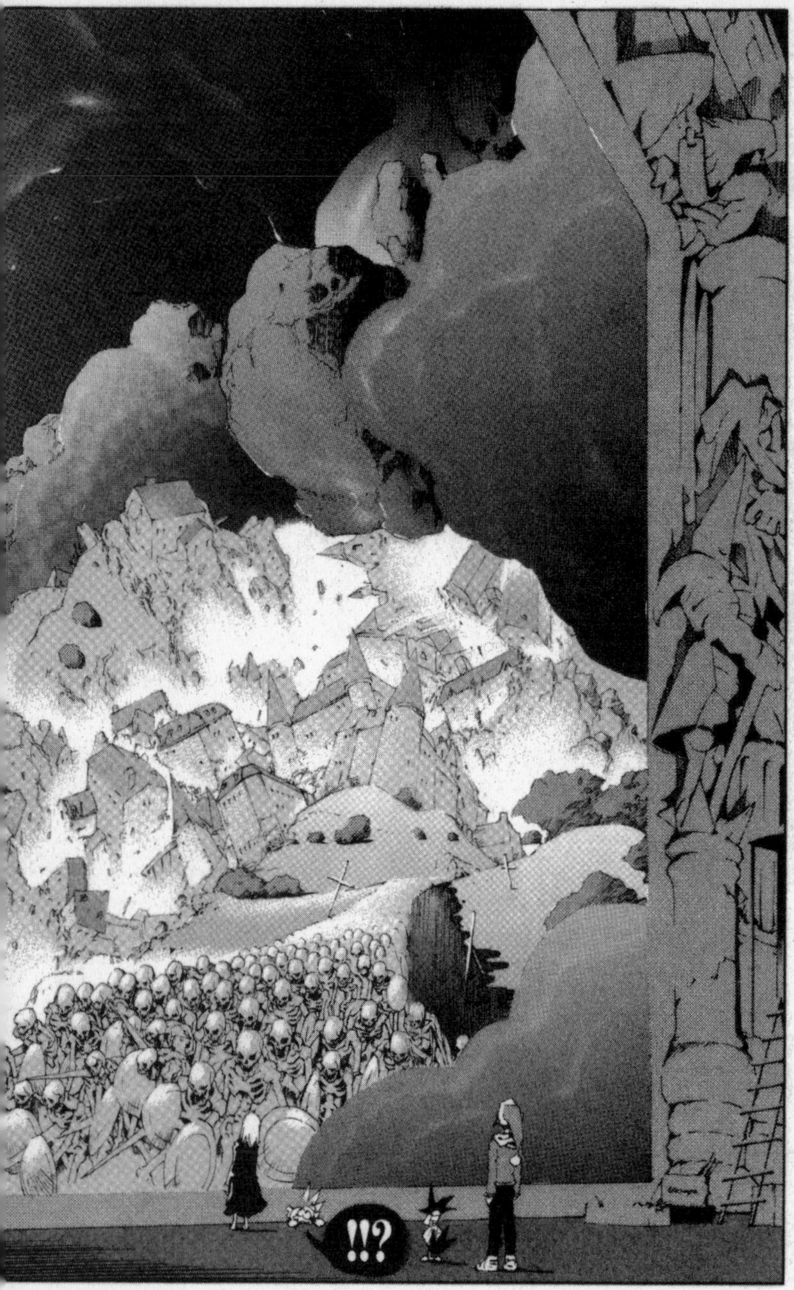
!!?

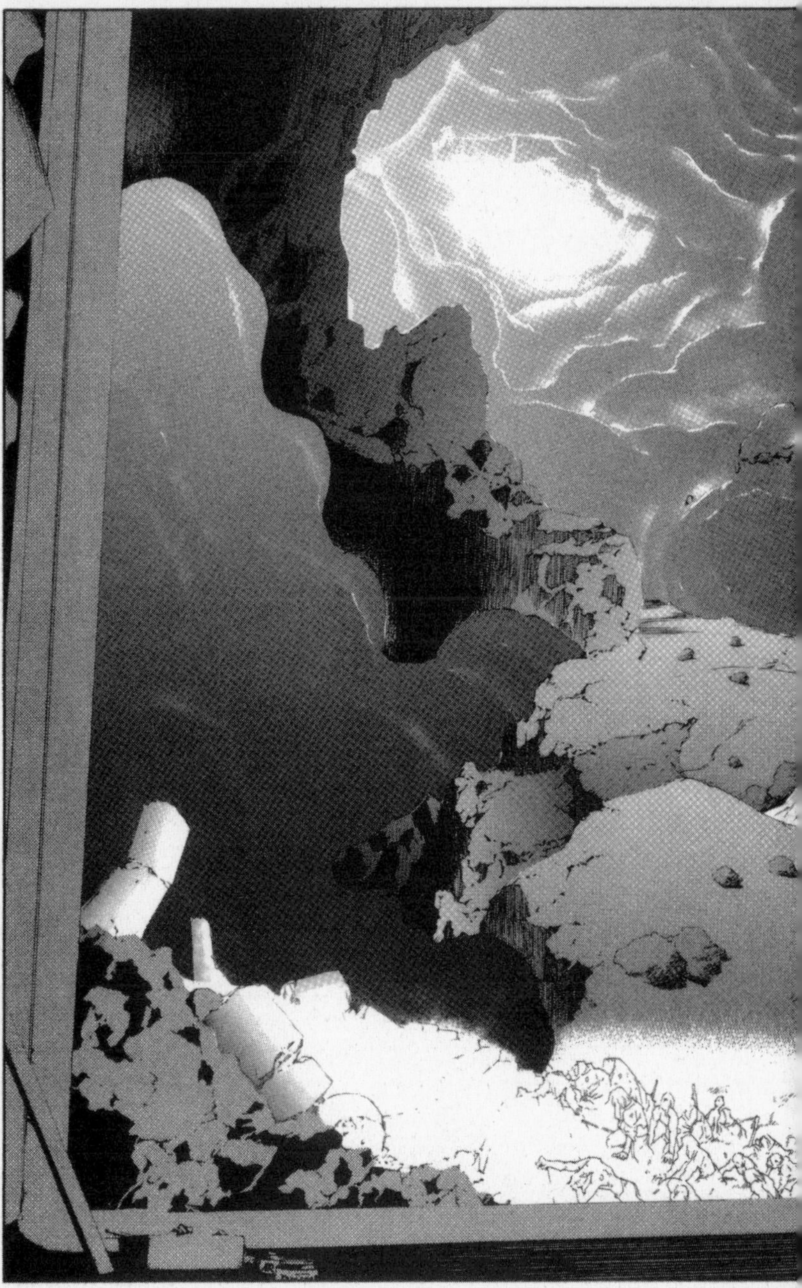

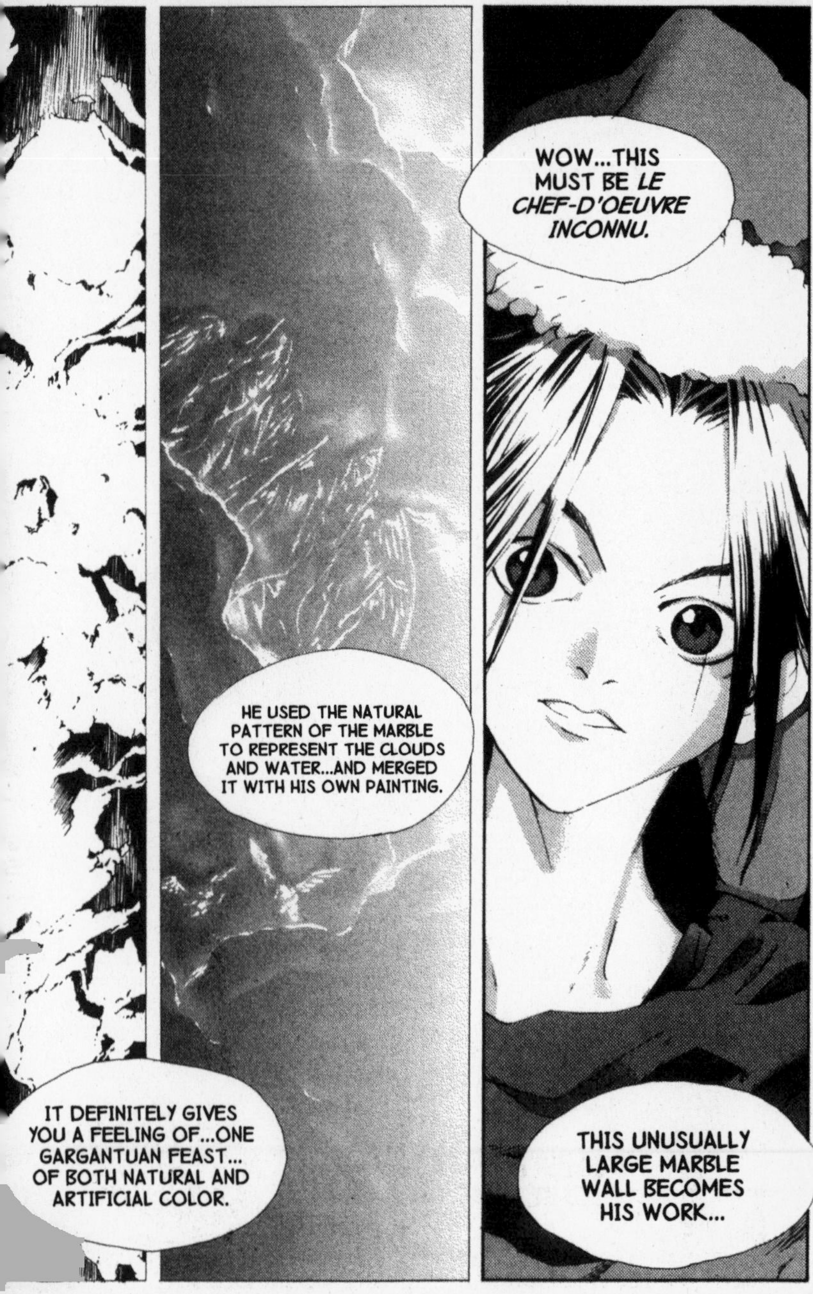
WOW...THIS MUST BE *LE CHEF-D'OEUVRE INCONNU.*
THIS UNUSUALLY LARGE MARBLE WALL BECOMES HIS WORK...
HE USED THE NATURAL PATTERN OF THE MARBLE TO REPRESENT THE CLOUDS AND WATER...AND MERGED IT WITH HIS OWN PAINTING.
IT DEFINITELY GIVES YOU A FEELING OF...ONE GARGANTUAN FEAST... OF BOTH NATURAL AND ARTIFICIAL COLOR.

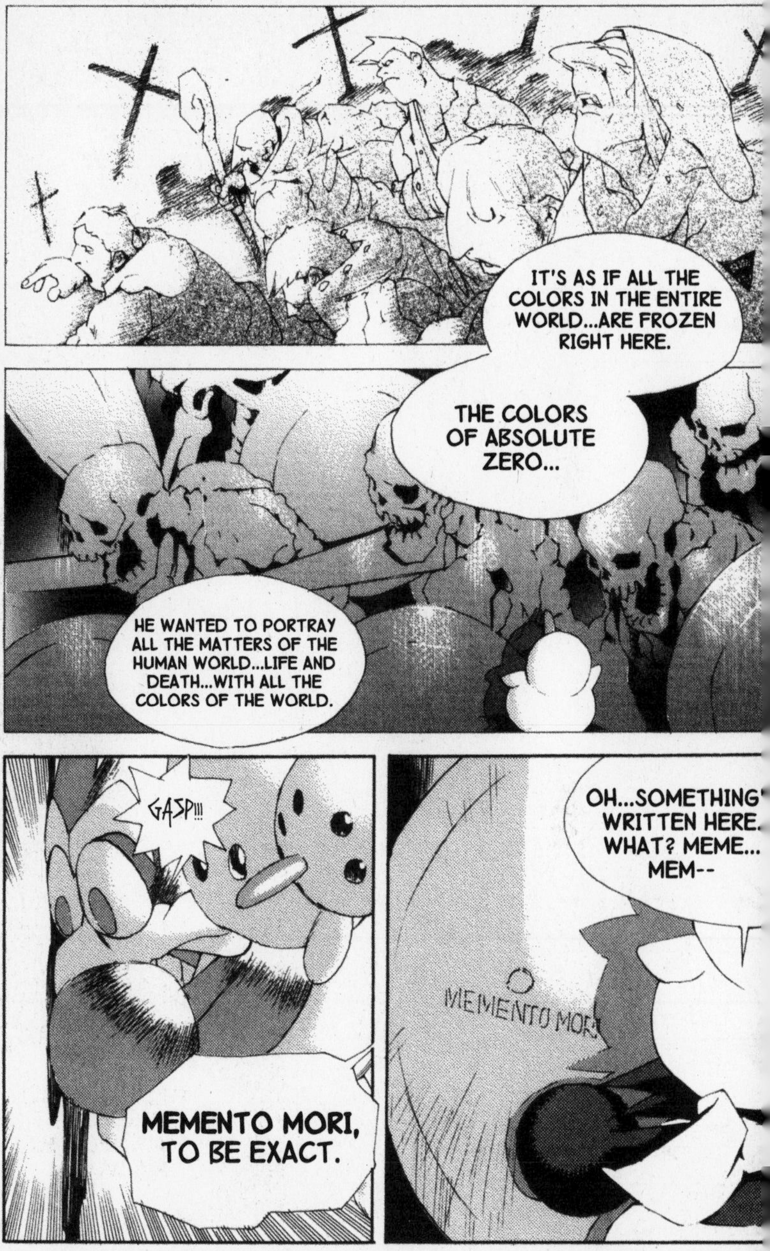
IT'S AS IF ALL THE COLORS IN THE ENTIRE WORLD...ARE FROZEN RIGHT HERE.
THE COLORS OF ABSOLUTE ZERO...
HE WANTED TO PORTRAY ALL THE MATTERS OF THE HUMAN WORLD...LIFE AND DEATH...WITH ALL THE COLORS OF THE WORLD.
OH...SOMETHING' WRITTEN HERE. WHAT? MEME... MEM--
MEMENTO MOR
GASP!!!
MEMENTO MORI, TO BE EXACT.

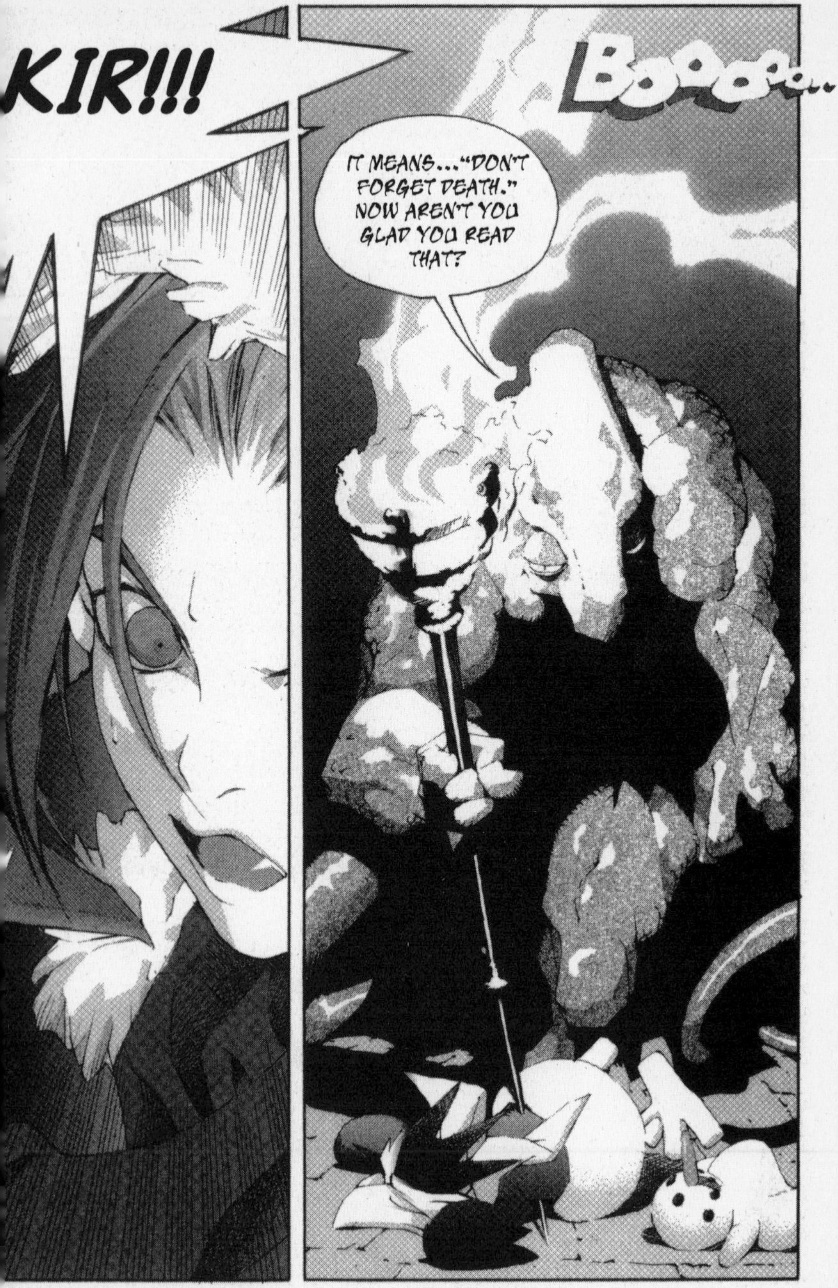
IT MEANS..."DON'T FORGET DEATH." NOW AREN'T YOU GLAD YOU READ THAT?
KIR!!!

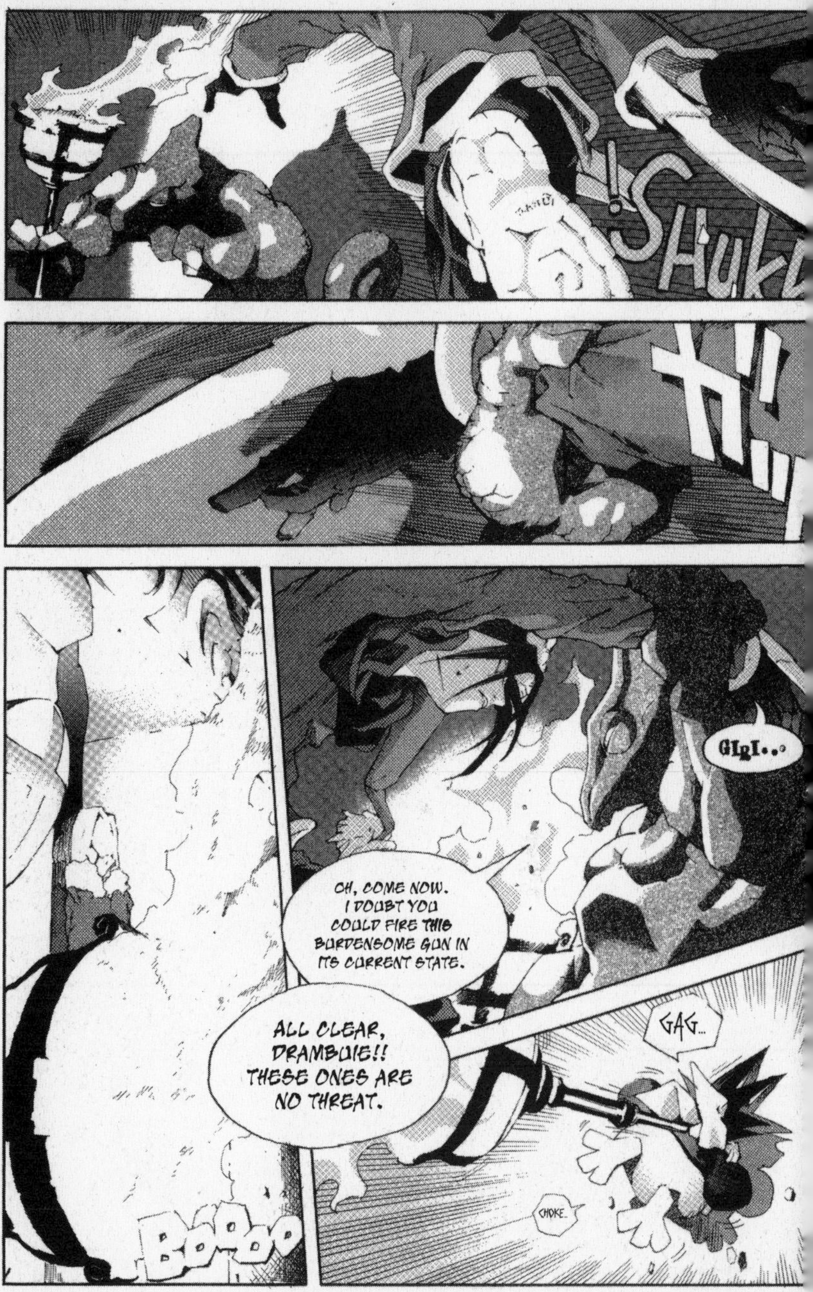
SHUKU
!
GIRI...
OH, COME NOW. I DOUBT YOU COULD FIRE THIS BURDENSOME GUN IN ITS CURRENT STATE.
ALL CLEAR, DRAMBUIE!! THESE ONES ARE NO THREAT.
GAG...
CHOKE..
BOBOO

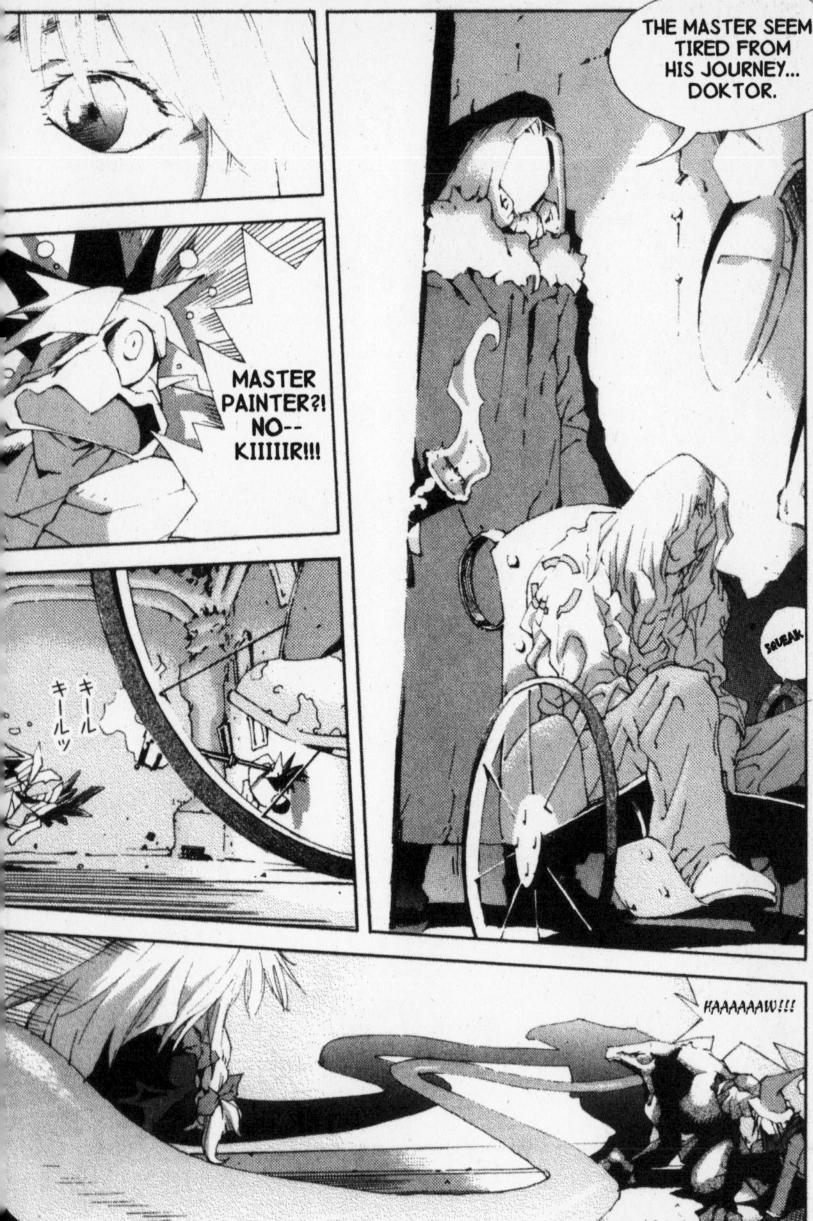
THE MASTER SEEMS TIRED FROM HIS JOURNEY... DOKTOR.
SQUEAK
MASTER PAINTER?! NO-- KIIIIIR!!!
キール
キールッ
HAAAAAAW!!!

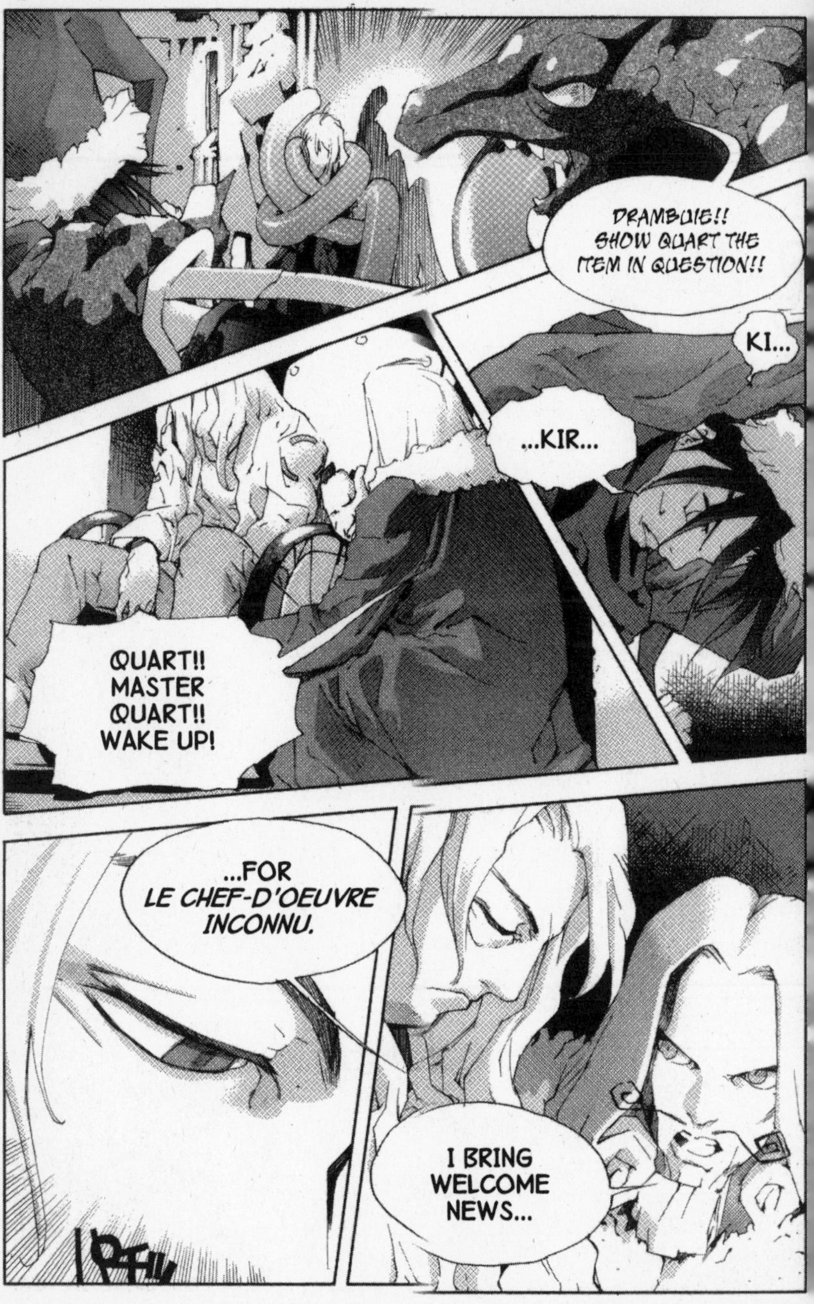
DRAMBUIE!! SHOW QUART THE ITEM IN QUESTION!!
KI...
...KIR...
QUART!! MASTER QUART!! WAKE UP!
I BRING WELCOME NEWS...
...FOR *LE CHEF-D'OEUVRE INCONNU.*

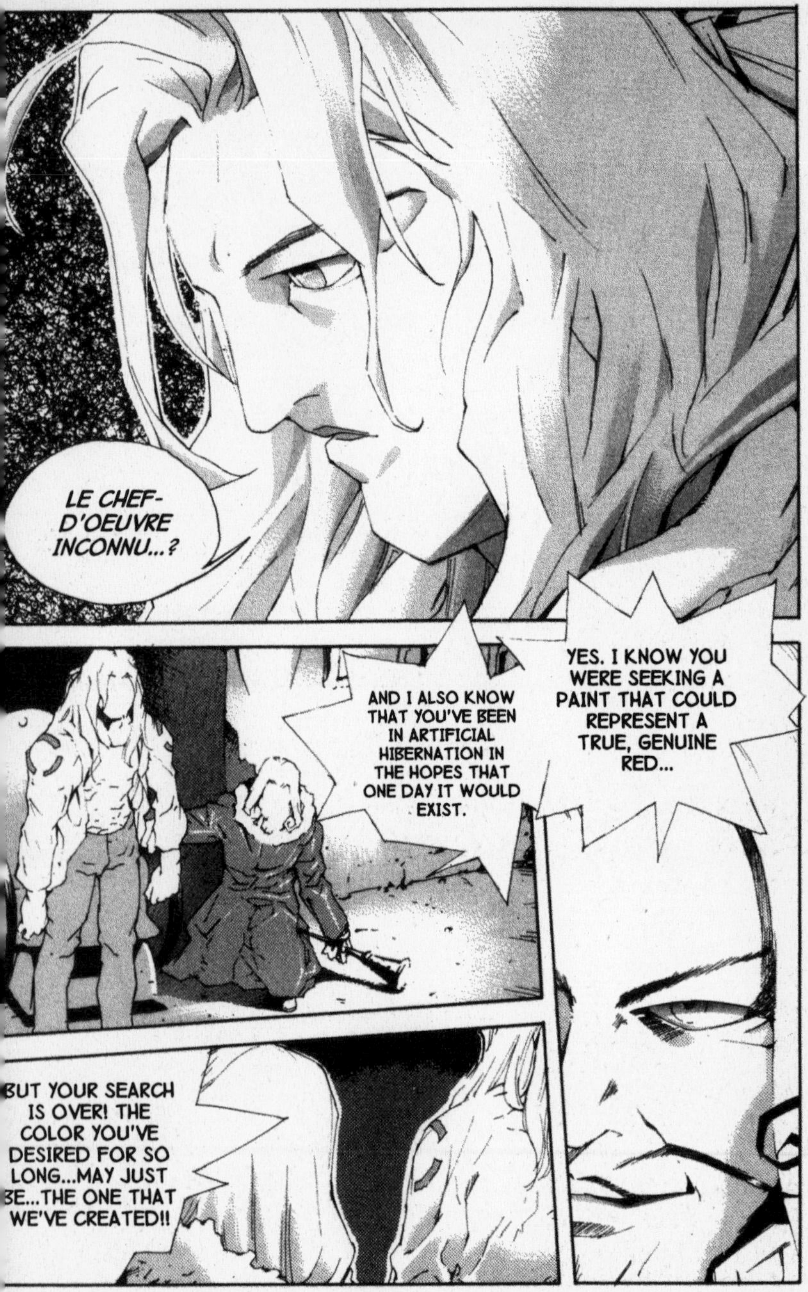
LE CHEF-D'OEUVRE INCONNU...?
YES. I KNOW YOU WERE SEEKING A PAINT THAT COULD REPRESENT A TRUE, GENUINE RED...
AND I ALSO KNOW THAT YOU'VE BEEN IN ARTIFICIAL HIBERNATION IN THE HOPES THAT ONE DAY IT WOULD EXIST.
BUT YOUR SEARCH IS OVER! THE COLOR YOU'VE DESIRED FOR SO LONG...MAY JUST BE...THE ONE THAT WE'VE CREATED!!

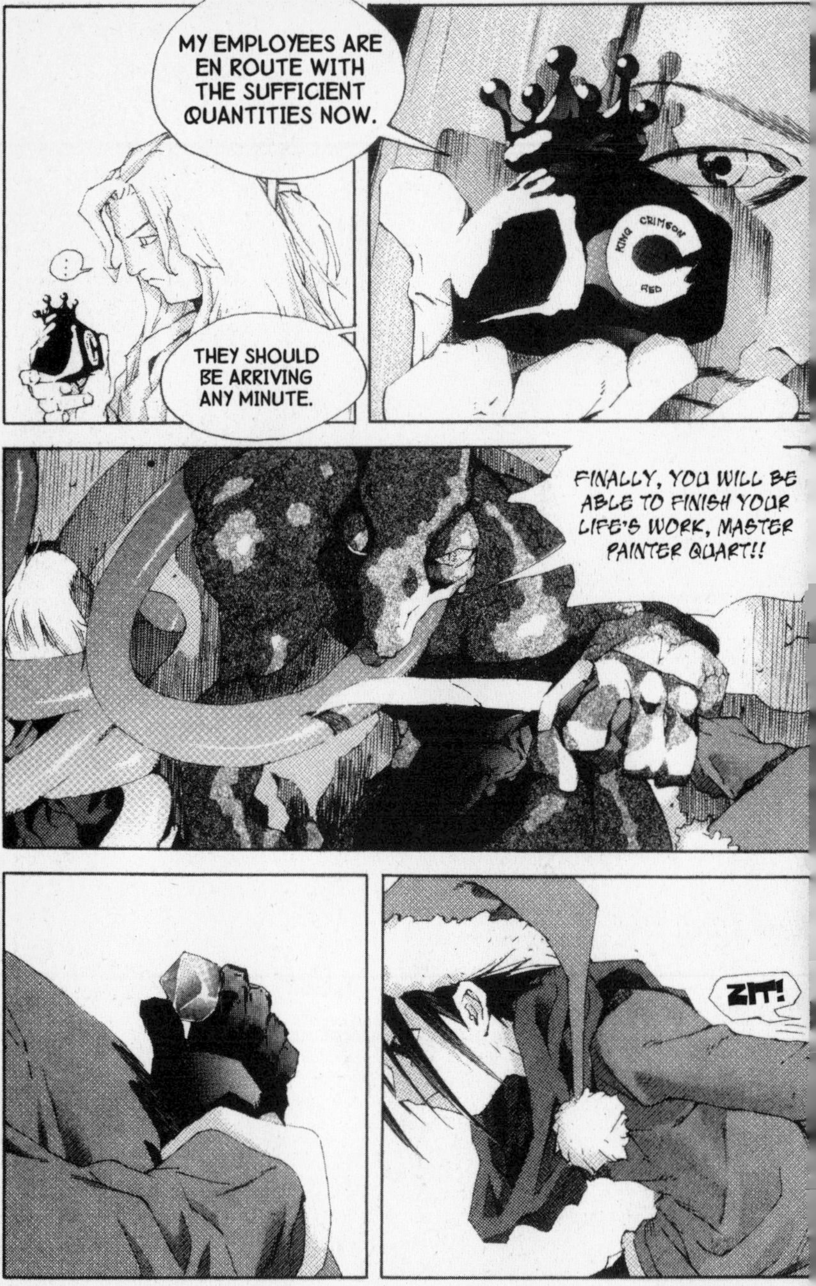
MY EMPLOYEES ARE EN ROUTE WITH THE SUFFICIENT QUANTITIES NOW.
THEY SHOULD BE ARRIVING ANY MINUTE.
...
KING CRIMSON RED
FINALLY, YOU WILL BE ABLE TO FINISH YOUR LIFE'S WORK, MASTER PAINTER QUART!!
ZIT!

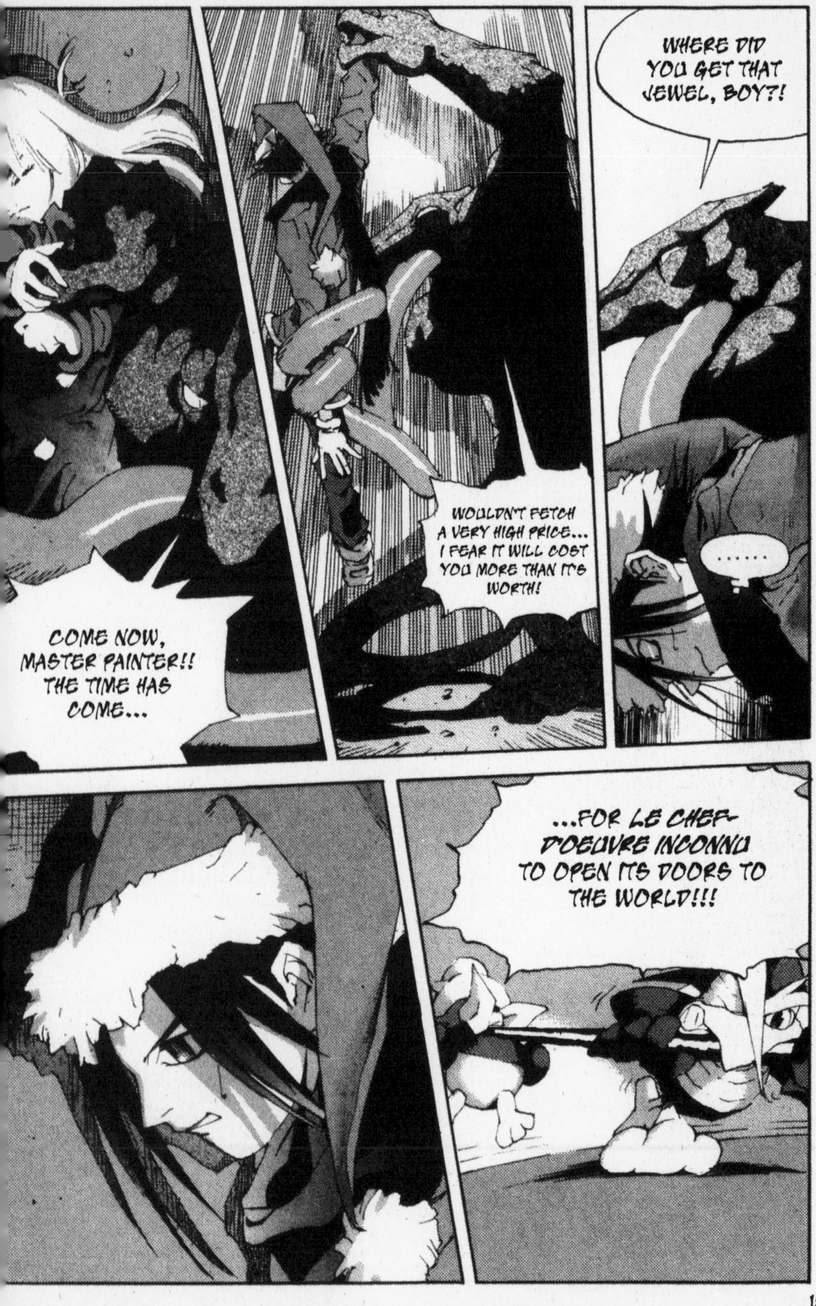
WHERE DID YOU GET THAT JEWEL, BOY?!
......
WOULDN'T FETCH A VERY HIGH PRICE... I FEAR IT WILL COST YOU MORE THAN IT'S WORTH!
COME NOW, MASTER PAINTER!! THE TIME HAS COME...
...FOR LE CHEF-D'OEUVRE INCONNU TO OPEN ITS DOORS TO THE WORLD!!!

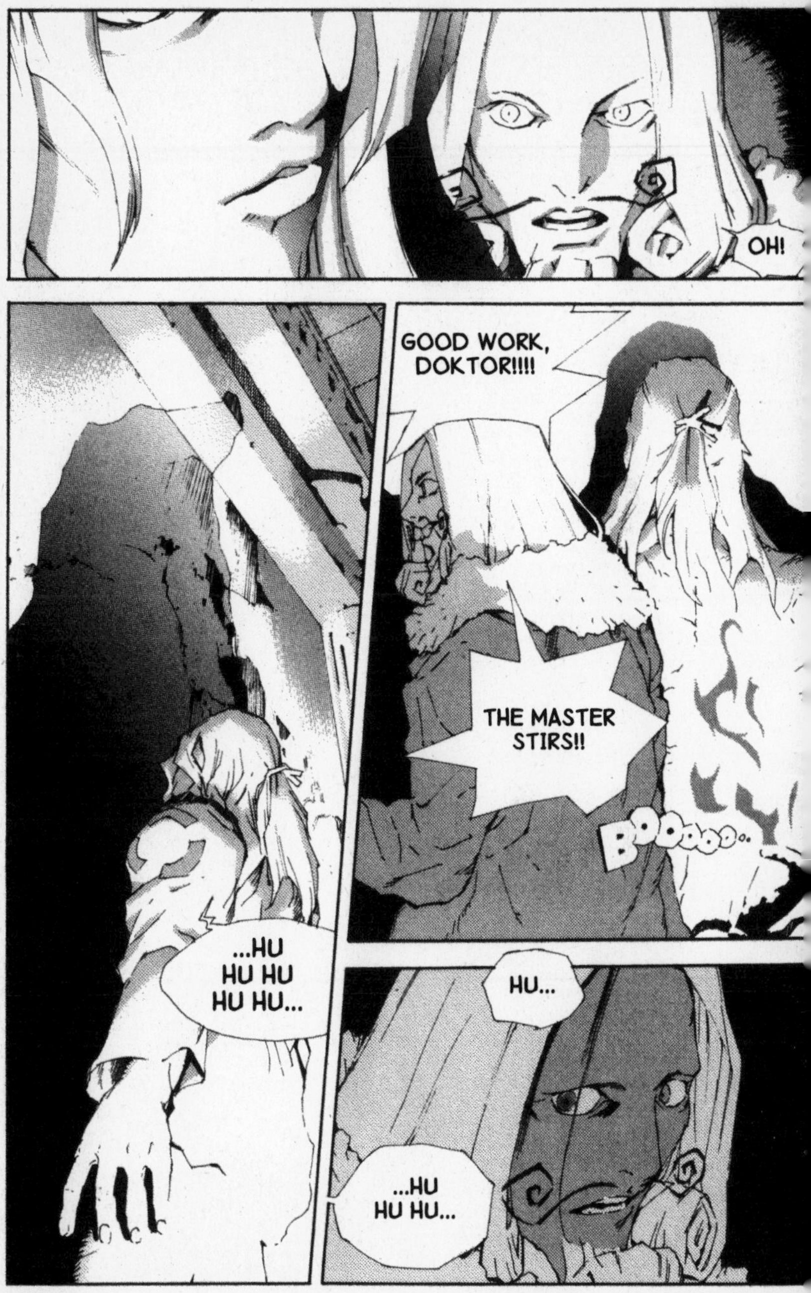
OH!
GOOD WORK, DOKTOR!!!!
THE MASTER STIRS!!
BOOOOOO.
HU...
...HU HU HU...
...HU HU HU HU HU...

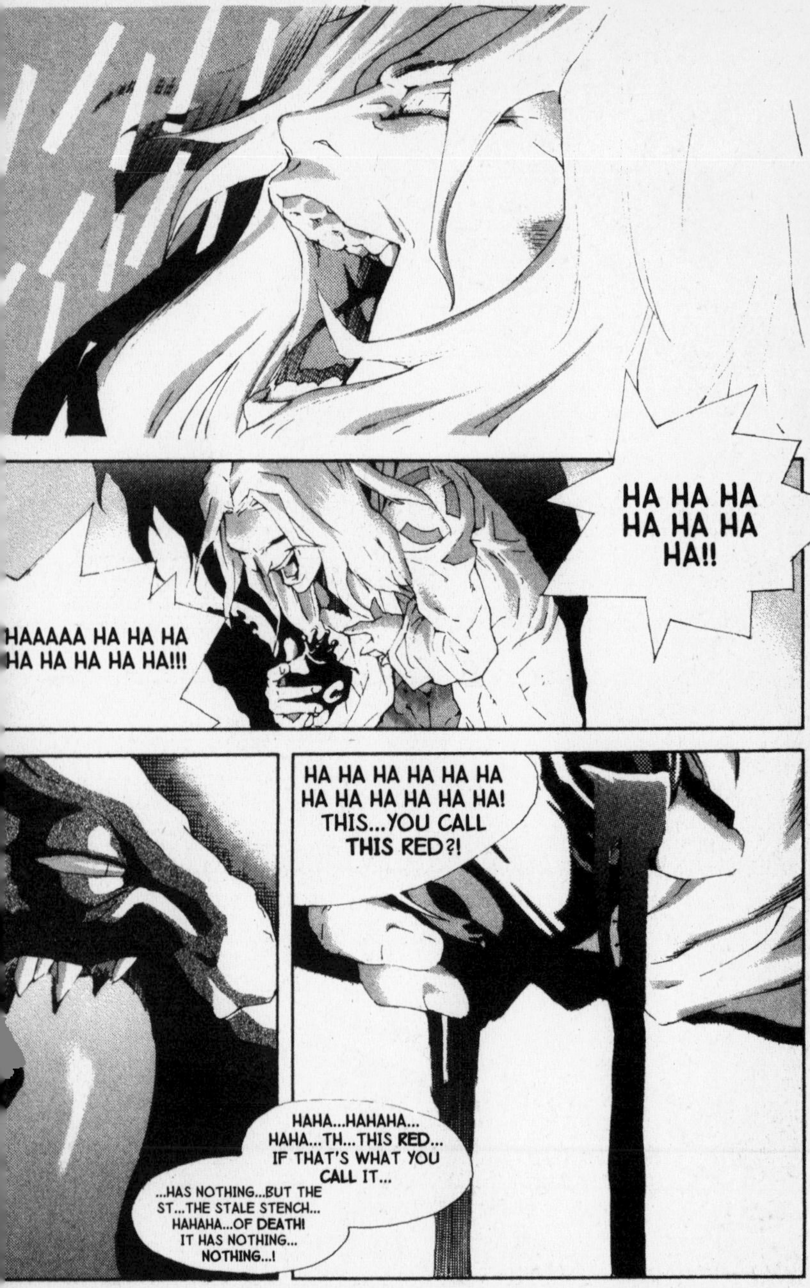
HA HA HA HA HA HA HA!!
HAAAAA HA HA HA HA HA HA HA HA!!!
HA HA HA HA HA HA HA HA HA HA HA HA! THIS...YOU CALL THIS RED?!
HAHA...HAHAHA... HAHA...TH...THIS RED... IF THAT'S WHAT YOU CALL IT...
...HAS NOTHING...BUT THE ST...THE STALE STENCH... HAHAHA...OF DEATH! IT HAS NOTHING... NOTHING...!

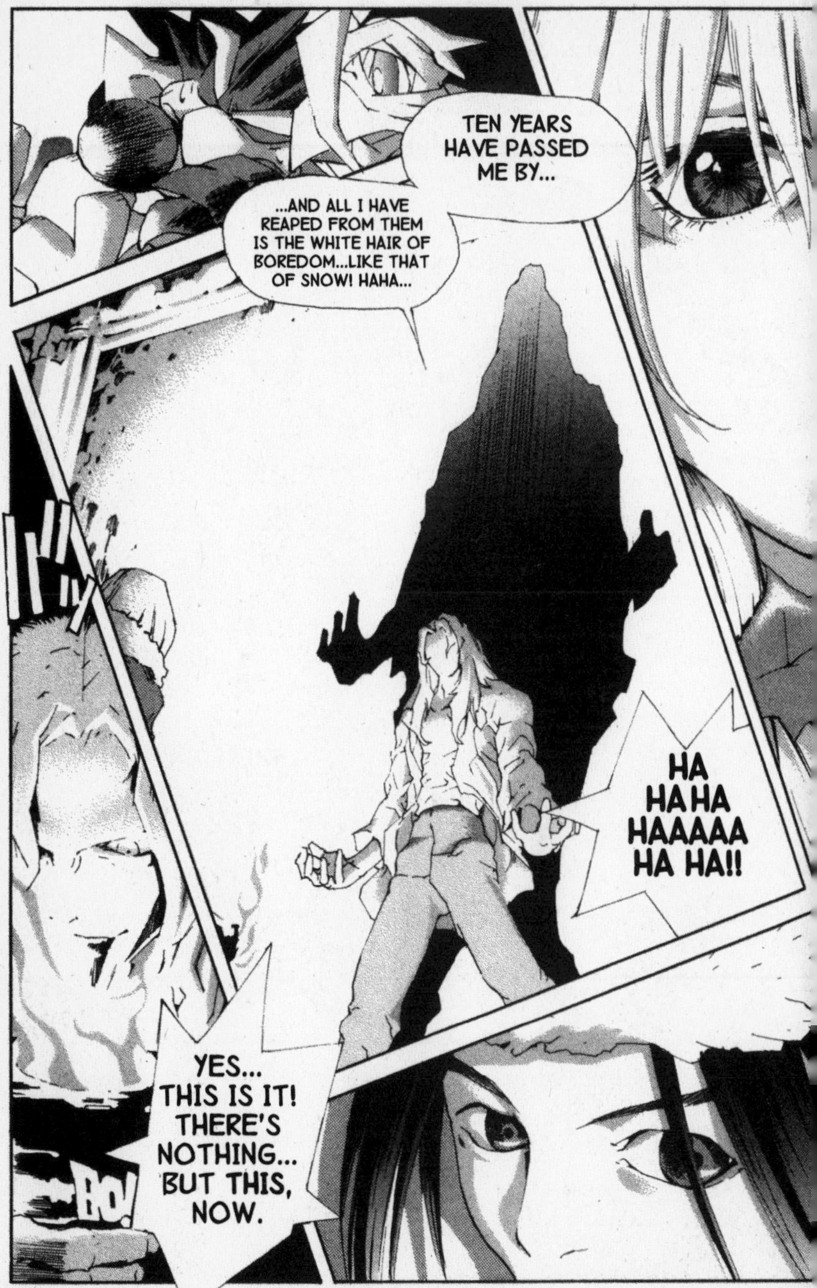
TEN YEARS HAVE PASSED ME BY...
...AND ALL I HAVE REAPED FROM THEM IS THE WHITE HAIR OF BOREDOM...LIKE THAT OF SNOW! HAHA...
HA HAHA HAAAAA HA HA!!
YES... THIS IS IT! THERE'S NOTHING... BUT THIS, NOW.
BO!

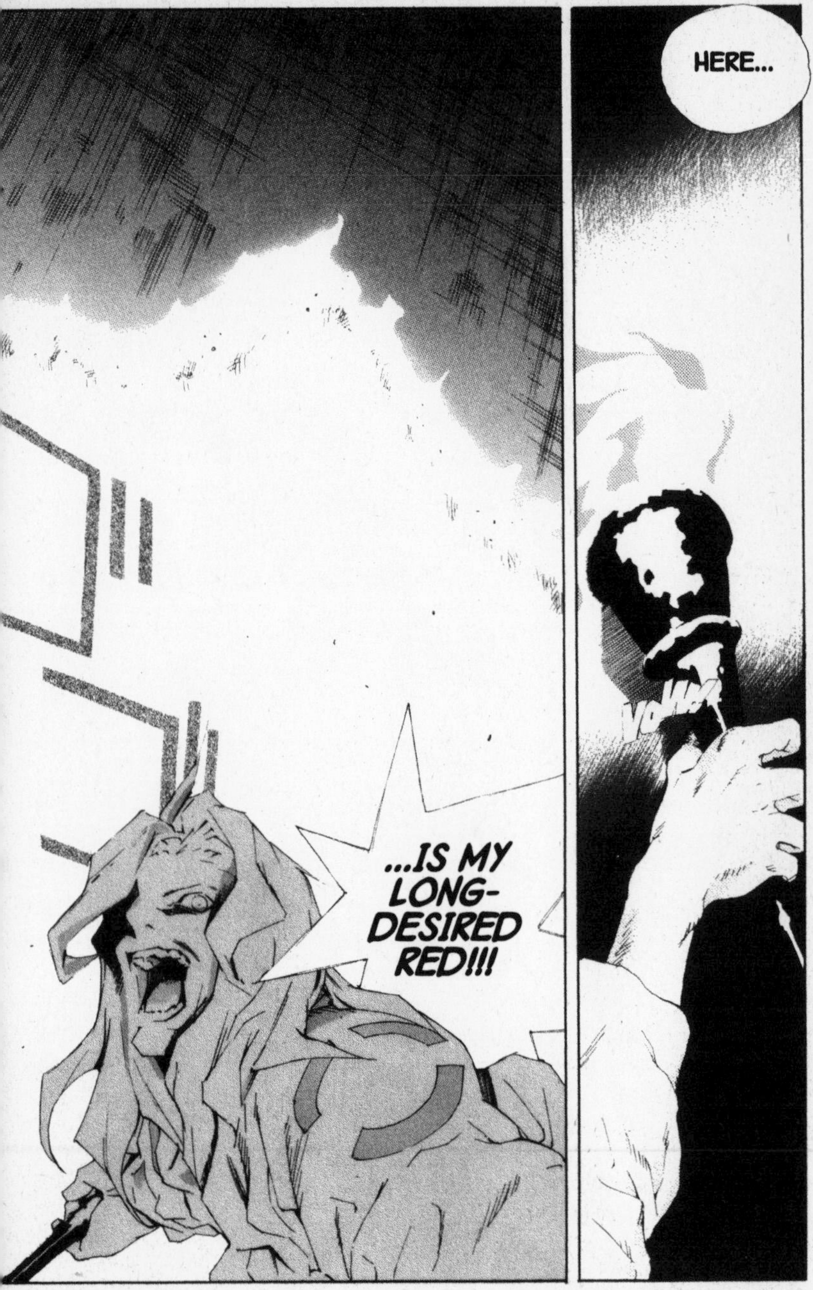
HERE...
...IS MY LONG-DESIRED RED!!!

37TH SHOT - WHITE TAPESTRY

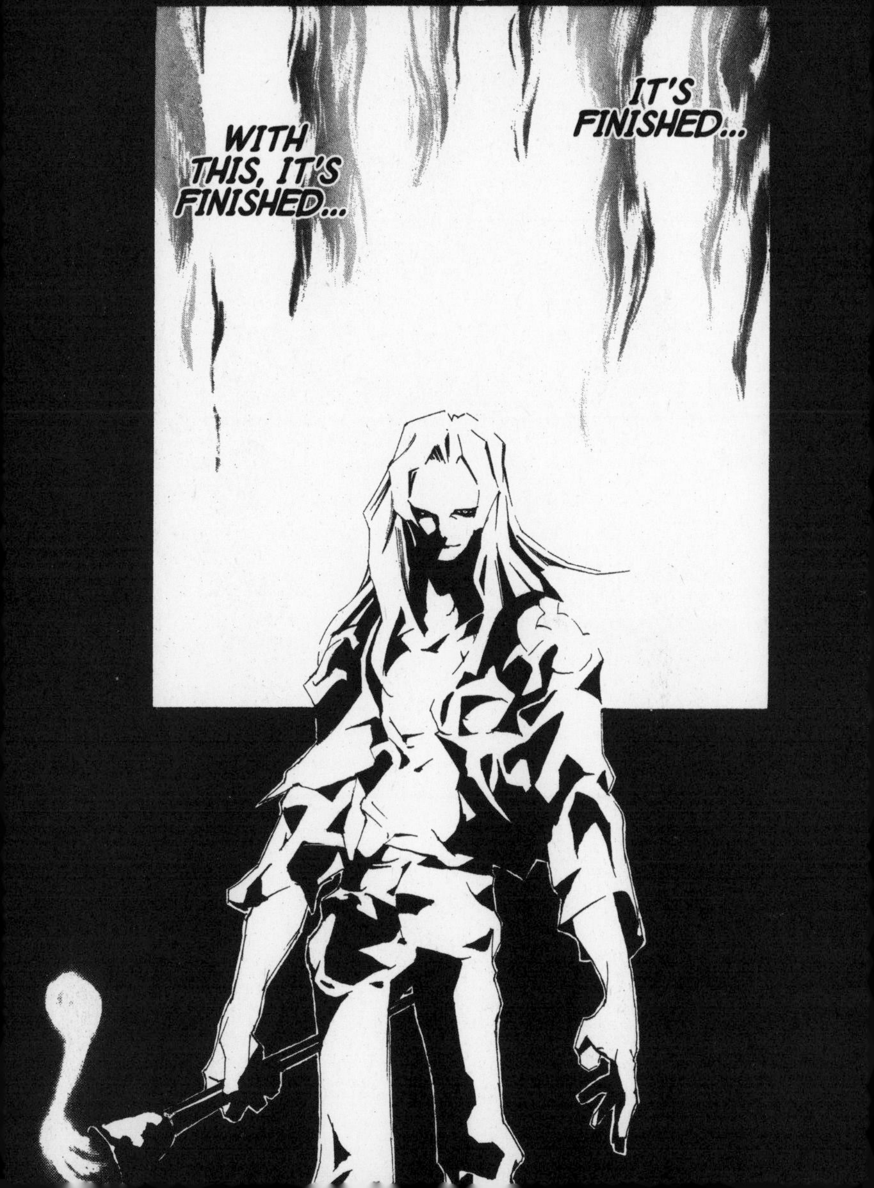
IT'S FINISHED...
WITH THIS, IT'S FINISHED...

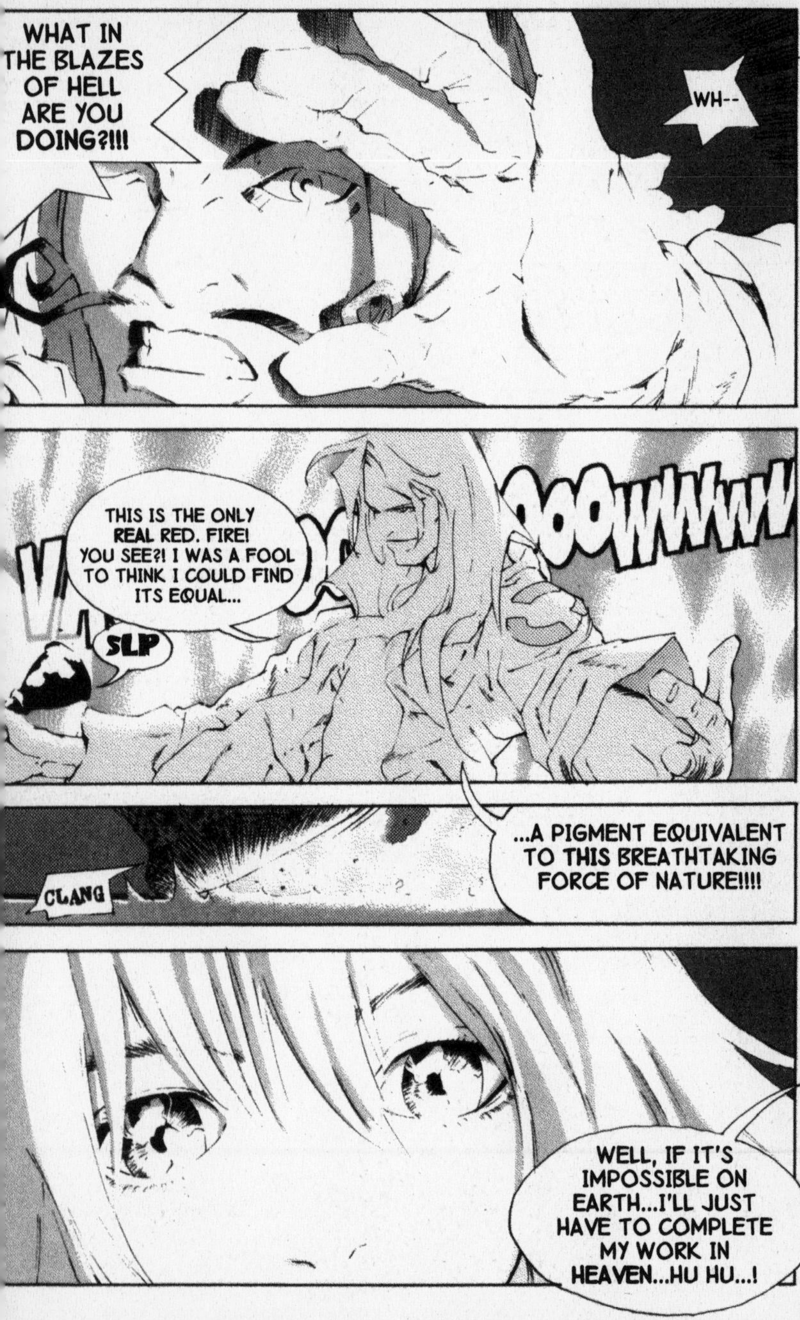
WH--
WHAT IN THE BLAZES OF HELL ARE YOU DOING?!!!
OOOWWWWW
THIS IS THE ONLY REAL RED. FIRE! YOU SEE?! I WAS A FOOL TO THINK I COULD FIND ITS EQUAL...
V
SLP
...A PIGMENT EQUIVALENT TO THIS BREATHTAKING FORCE OF NATURE!!!!
CLANG
WELL, IF IT'S IMPOSSIBLE ON EARTH...I'LL JUST HAVE TO COMPLETE MY WORK IN HEAVEN...HU HU...!

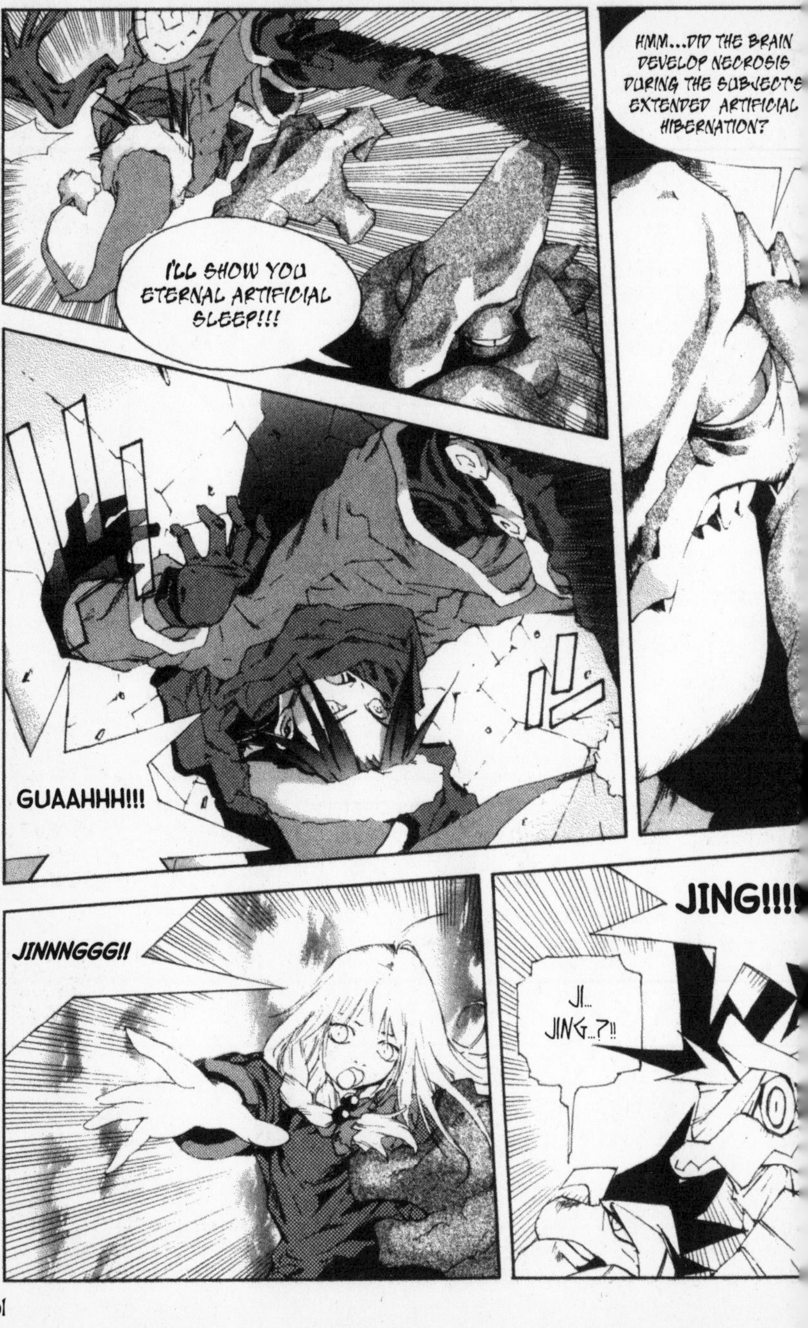
HMM...DID THE BRAIN DEVELOP NECROSIS DURING THE SUBJECT'S EXTENDED ARTIFICIAL HIBERNATION?
I'LL SHOW YOU ETERNAL ARTIFICIAL SLEEP!!!
GUAAHHH!!!
JING!!!!
JI... JING...?!!
JINNNGGG!!

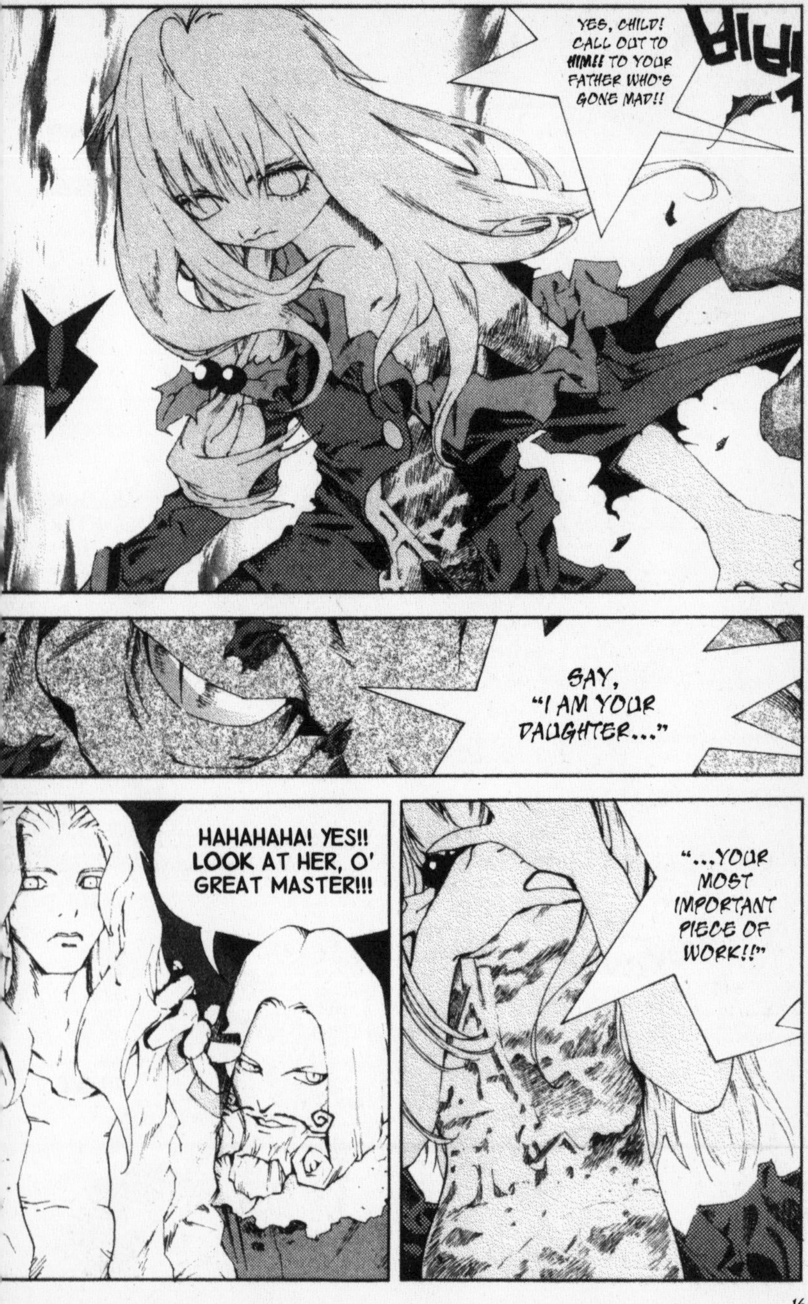
YES, CHILD! CALL OUT TO HIM!! TO YOUR FATHER WHO'S GONE MAD!!
SAY, "I AM YOUR DAUGHTER..."
"...YOUR MOST IMPORTANT PIECE OF WORK!!"
HAHAHAHA! YES!! LOOK AT HER, O' GREAT MASTER!!!

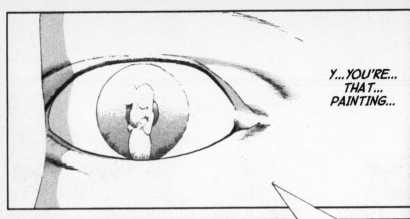

Y...YOU'RE... THAT... PAINTING...

YES... IT'S YOUR DAUGHTER, MASTER PAINTER.

LET US HELP CURE THE BRAIN THAT BECAME DEAD TO YOUR DAUGHTER.

H...HEY...

WHAT'RE YOU DOING?!!!

SLIDE

HEY!!!!!!!!........

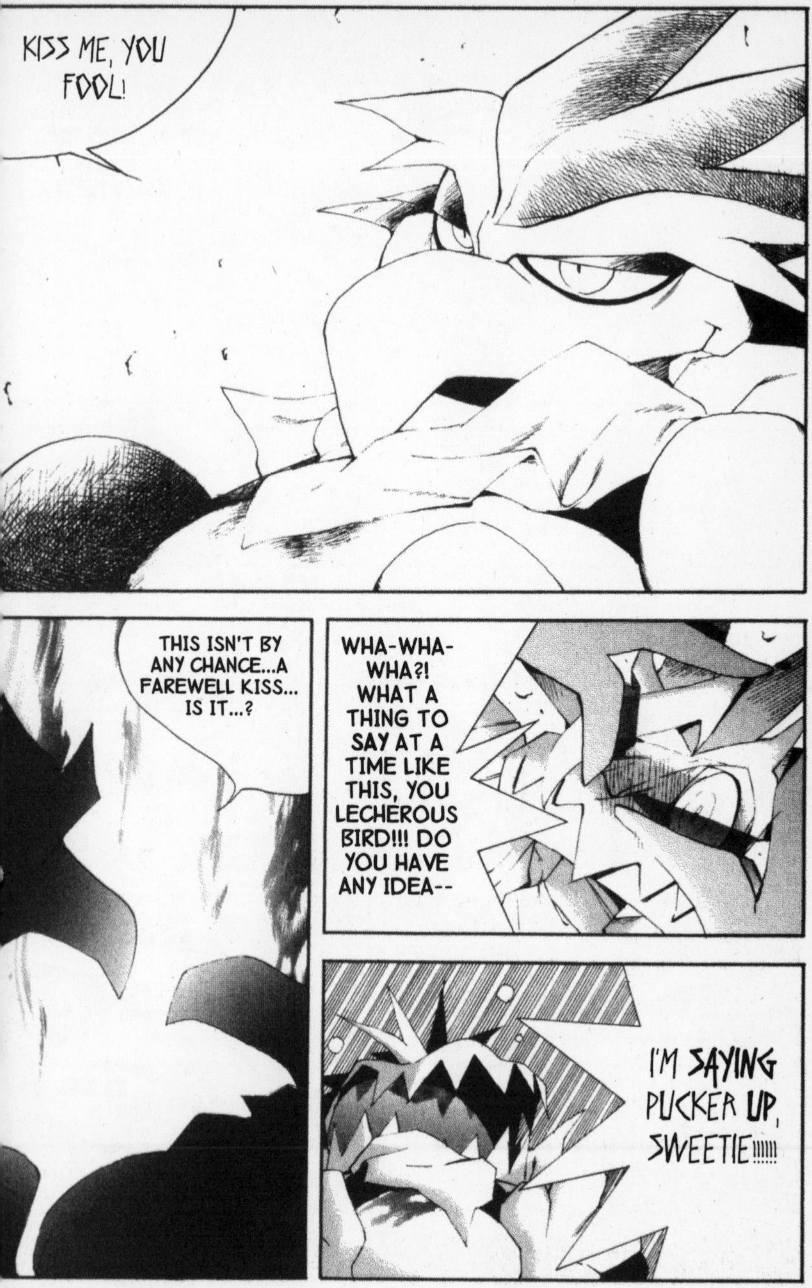
KISS ME, YOU FOOL!
WHA-WHA-WHA?! WHAT A THING TO SAY AT A TIME LIKE THIS, YOU LECHEROUS BIRD!!! DO YOU HAVE ANY IDEA--
I'M SAYING PUCKER UP, SWEETIE!!!!!!
THIS ISN'T BY ANY CHANCE...A FAREWELL KISS... IS IT...?

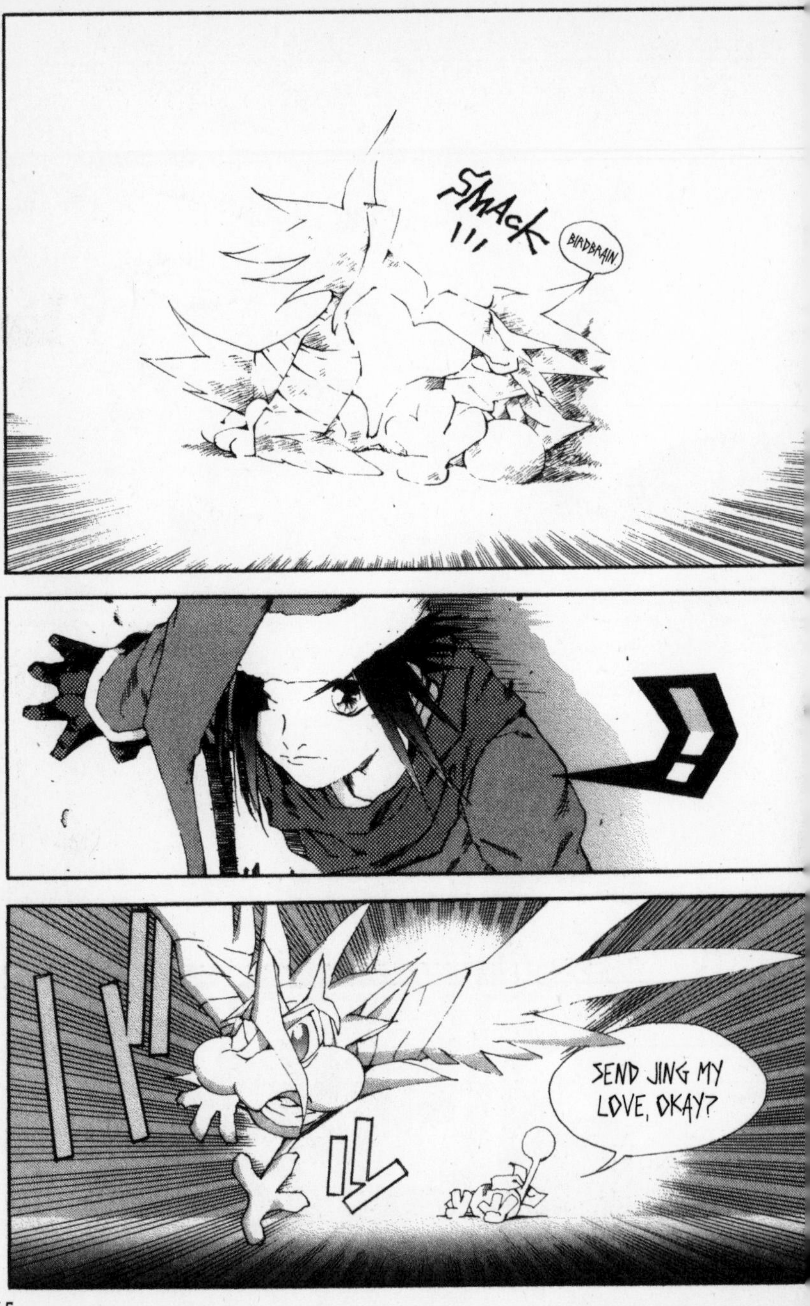
SMACK
BIRDBRAIN.
SEND JING MY LOVE, OKAY?

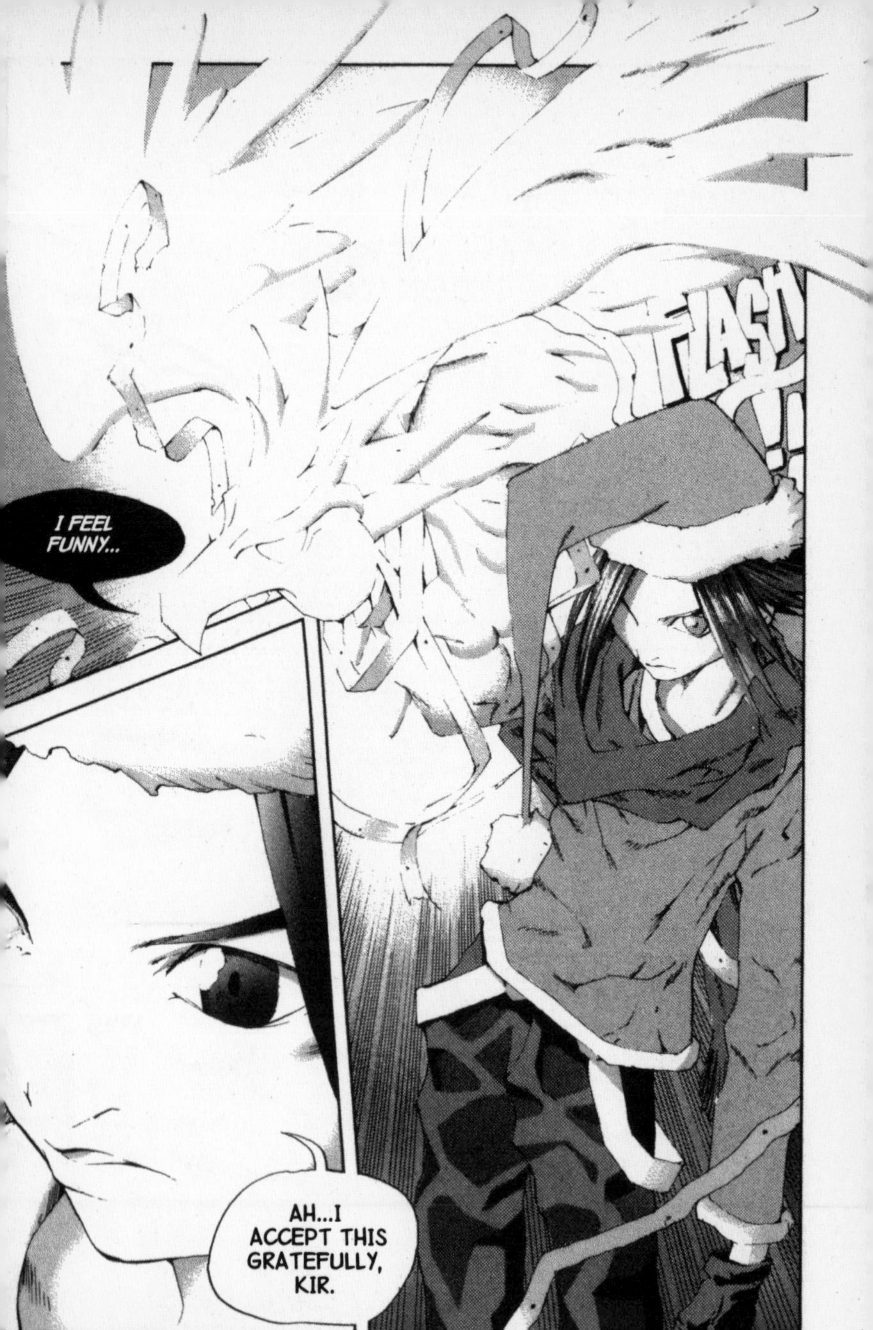
FLASH!!
I FEEL FUNNY...
AH...I ACCEPT THIS GRATEFULLY, KIR.

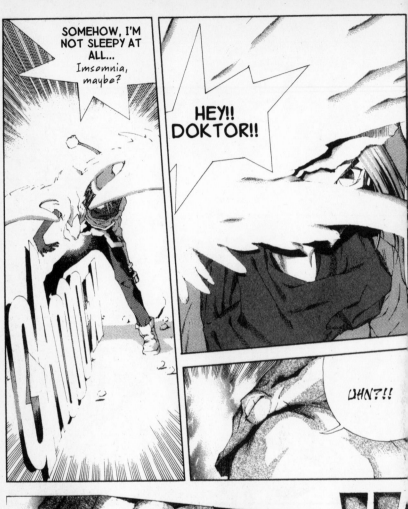

SOMEHOW, I'M NOT SLEEPY AT ALL... Imsomnia, maybe?

HEY!! DOKTOR!!

UHN?!!

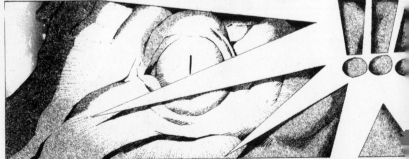

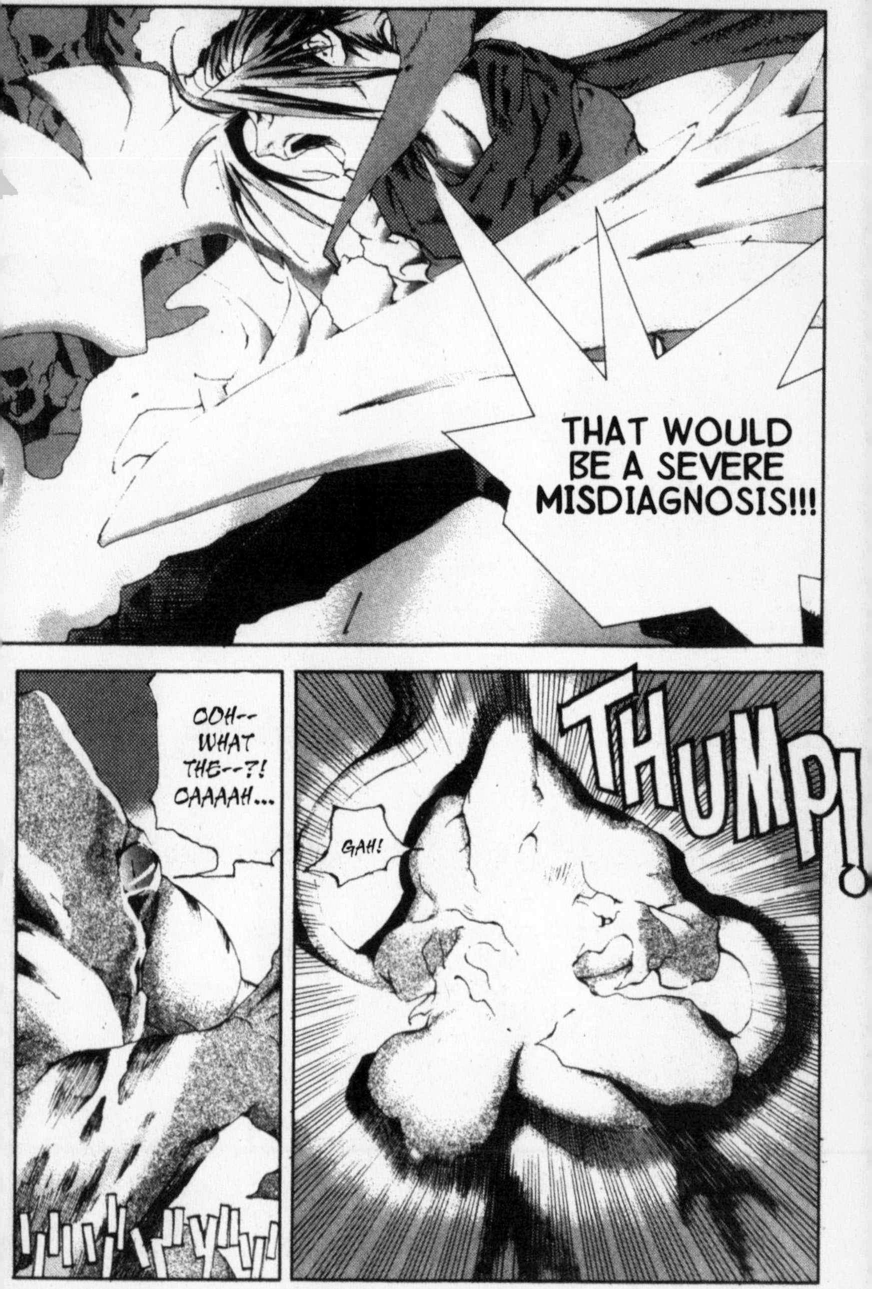
THAT WOULD BE A SEVERE MISDIAGNOSIS!!!
THUMP!
GAH!
OOH-- WHAT THE--?! OAAAAH...

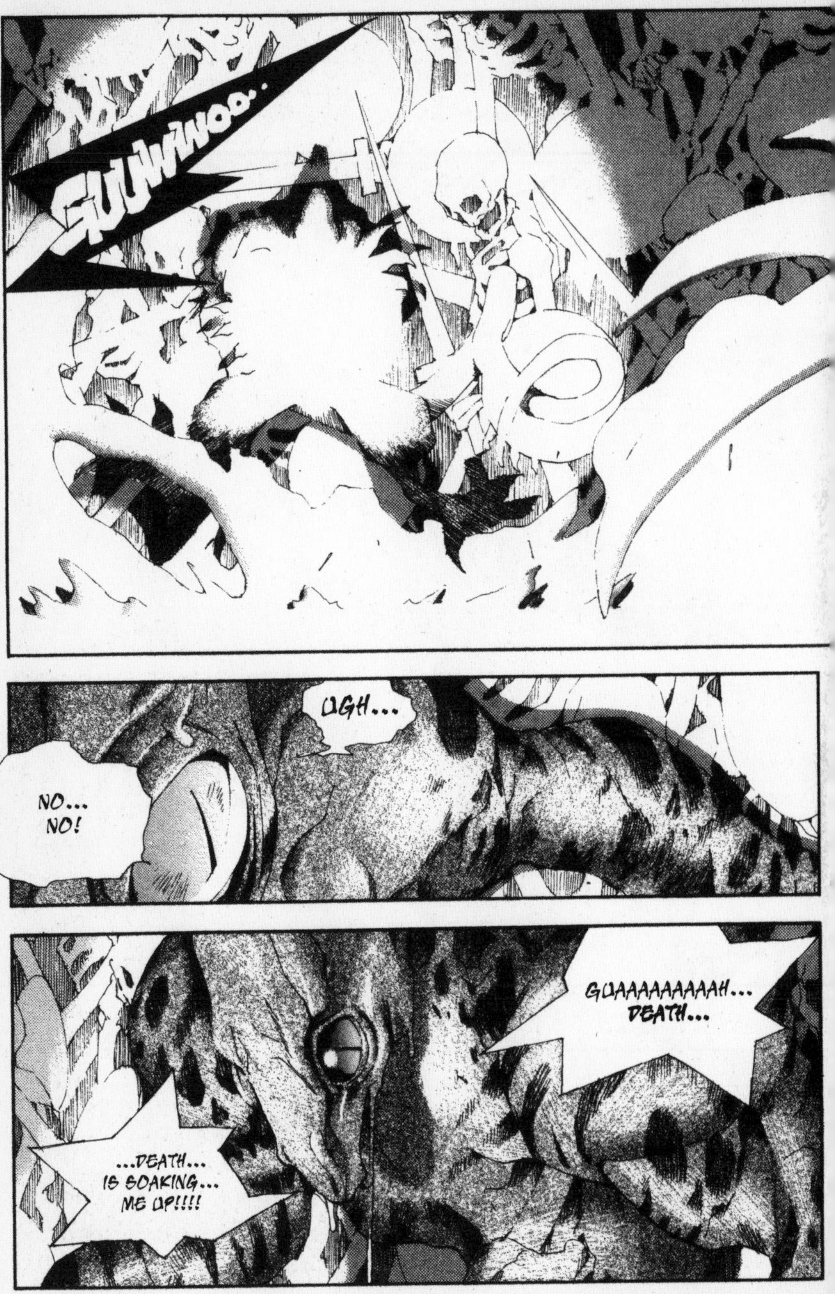
GUUWNOO..
UGH...
NO... NO!
GUAAAAAAAAAH... DEATH...
...DEATH... IS SOAKING... ME UP!!!!

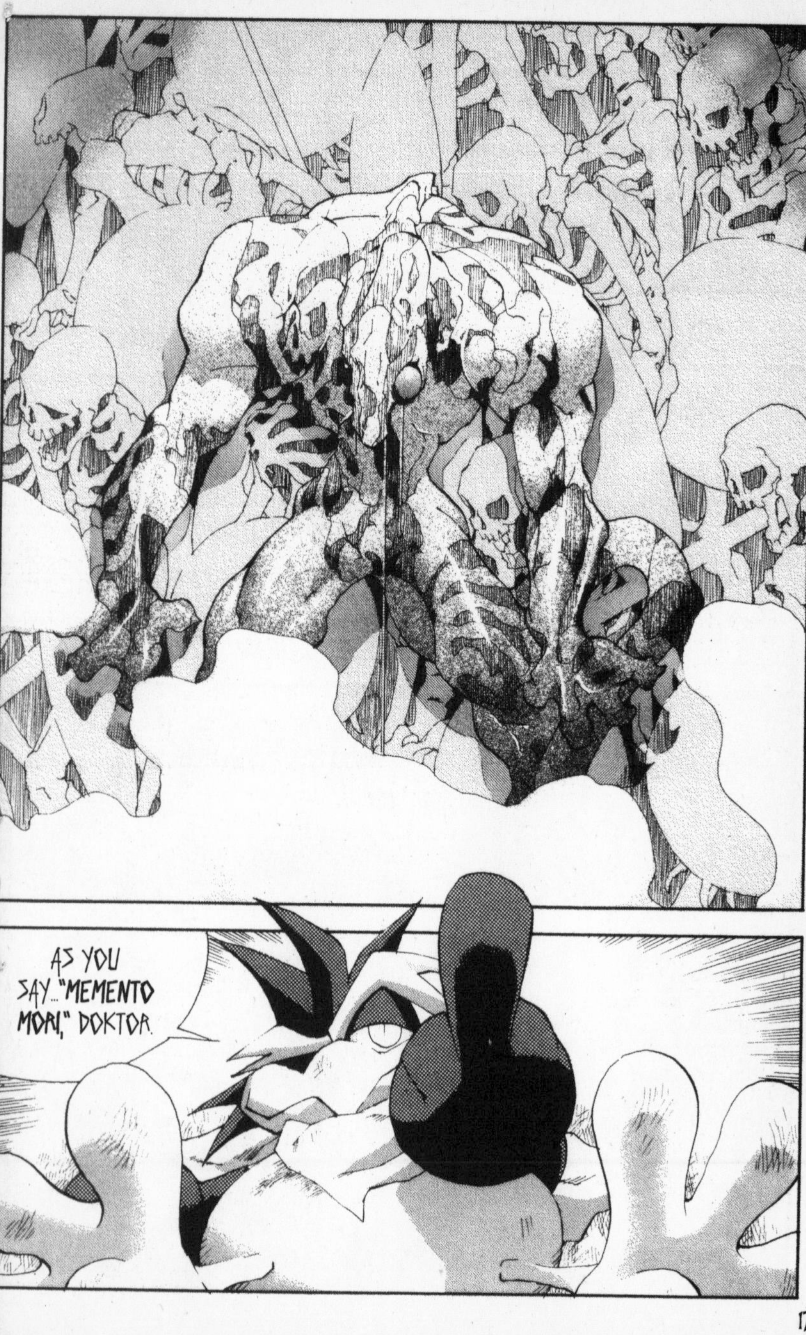
AS YOU SAY..."MEMENTO MORI," DOKTOR.

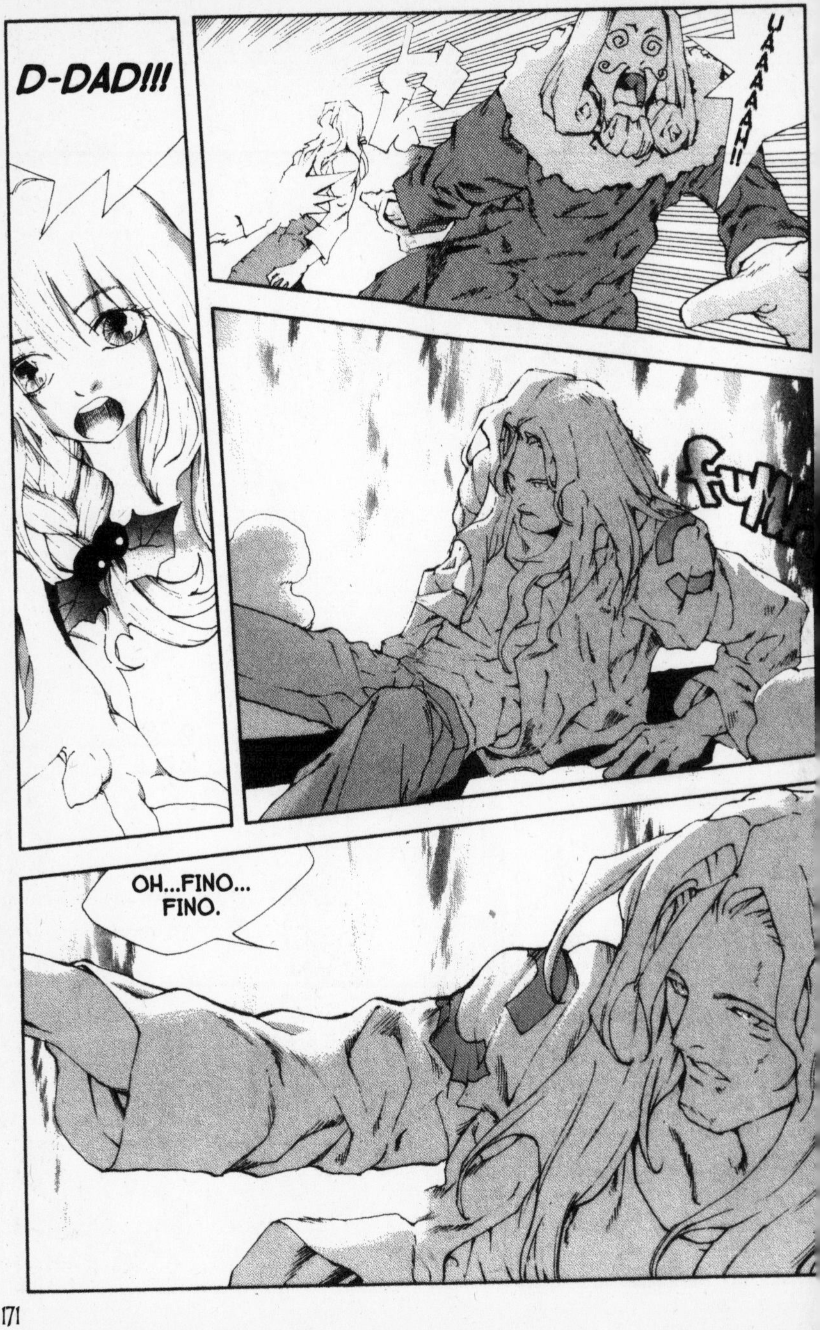
UAAAAAH!!
fuM
D-DAD!!!
OH...FINO...
FINO.

FINO!!!

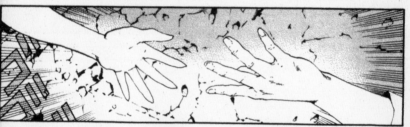

DAD!!!

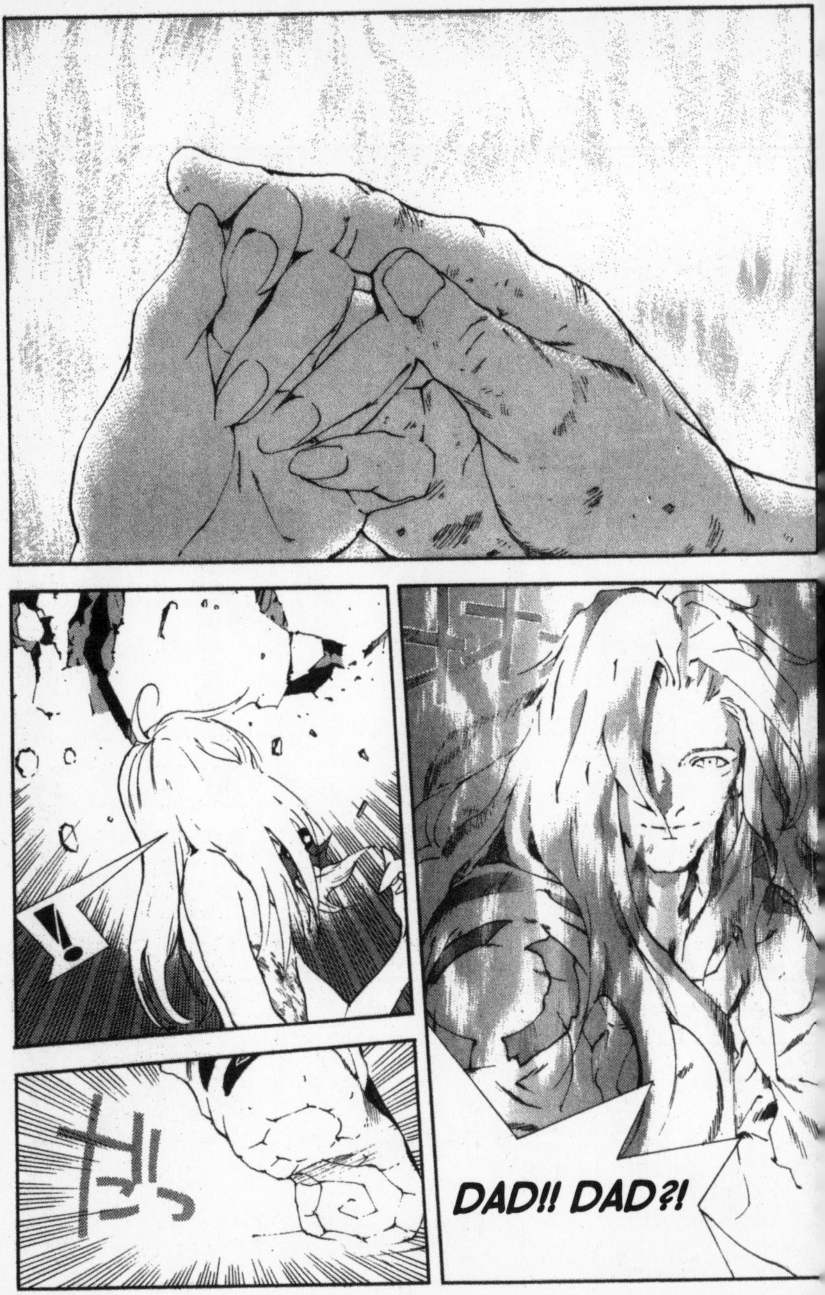
DAD!! DAD?!
!

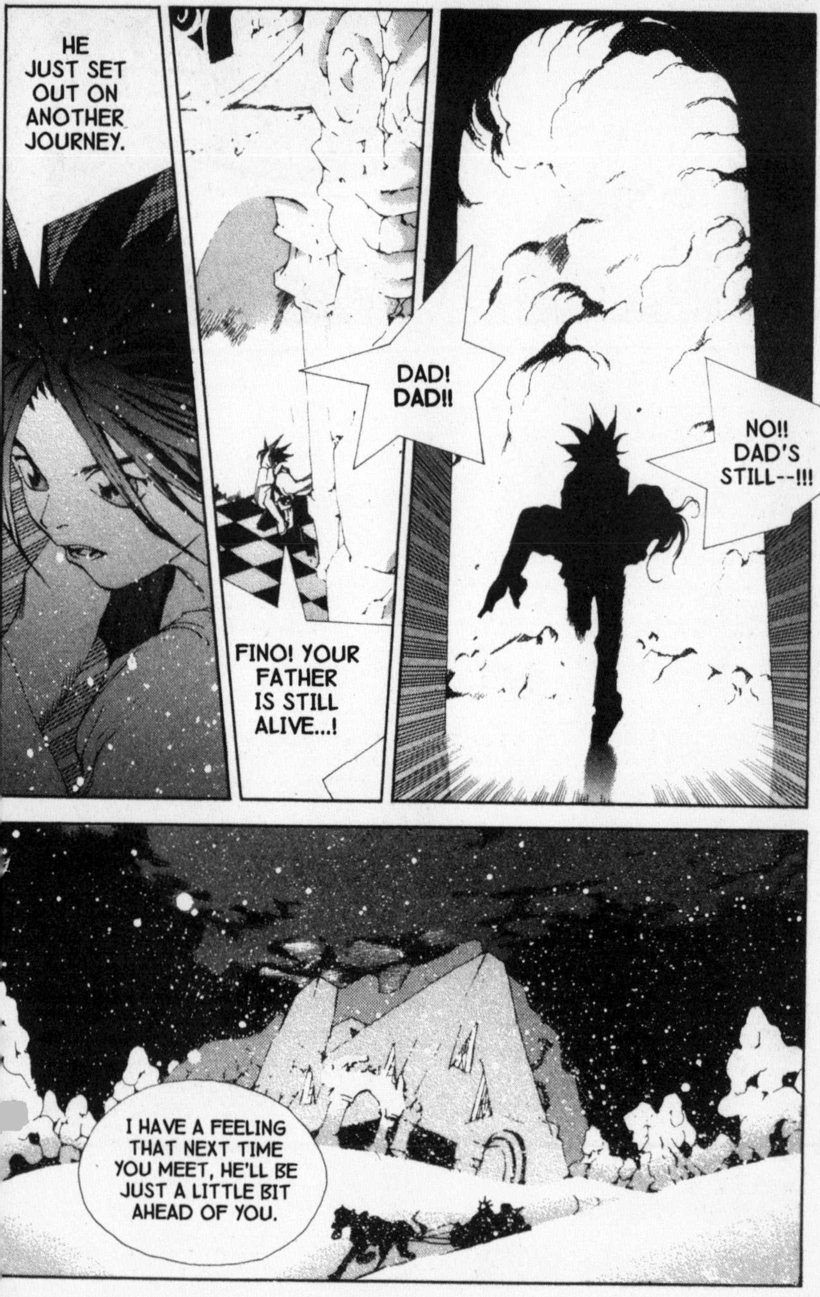
NO!! DAD'S STILL--!!!
DAD! DAD!!
FINO! YOUR FATHER IS STILL ALIVE...!
HE JUST SET OUT ON ANOTHER JOURNEY.
I HAVE A FEELING THAT NEXT TIME YOU MEET, HE'LL BE JUST A LITTLE BIT AHEAD OF YOU.

DAD JUST SET OUT ON ANOTHER JOURNEY... THAT'S WHAT JING SAID.

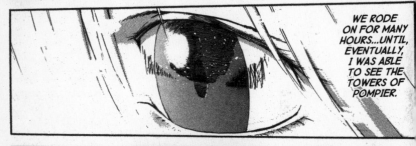

I DIGESTED THOSE WORDS MANY TIMES OVER...MANY, MANY TIMES...AS I ROCKED BACK AND FORTH IN THE SLEIGH.

WE RODE ON FOR MANY HOURS...UNTIL, EVENTUALLY, I WAS ABLE TO SEE THE TOWERS OF POMPIER.

BUT THEY WERE ALL COVERED IN SNOW...SNOW LIKE I'D NEVER SEEN BEFORE.

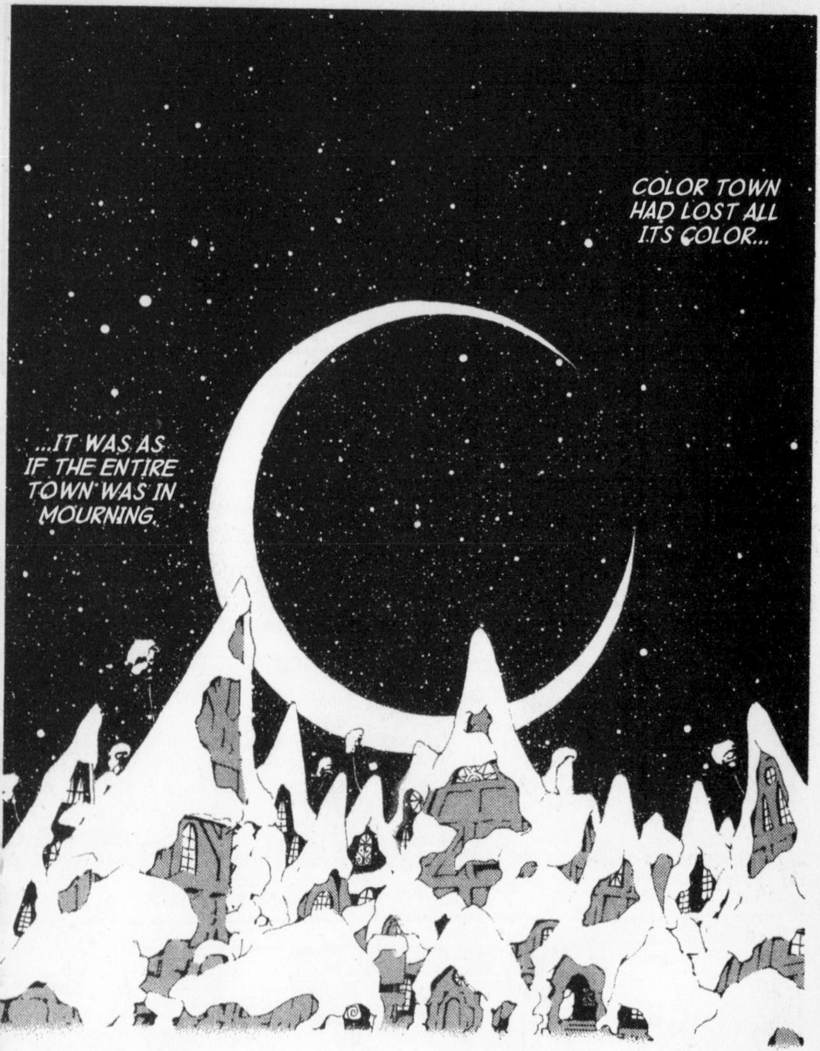
COLOR TOWN HAD LOST ALL ITS COLOR...
...IT WAS AS IF THE ENTIRE TOWN WAS IN MOURNING.

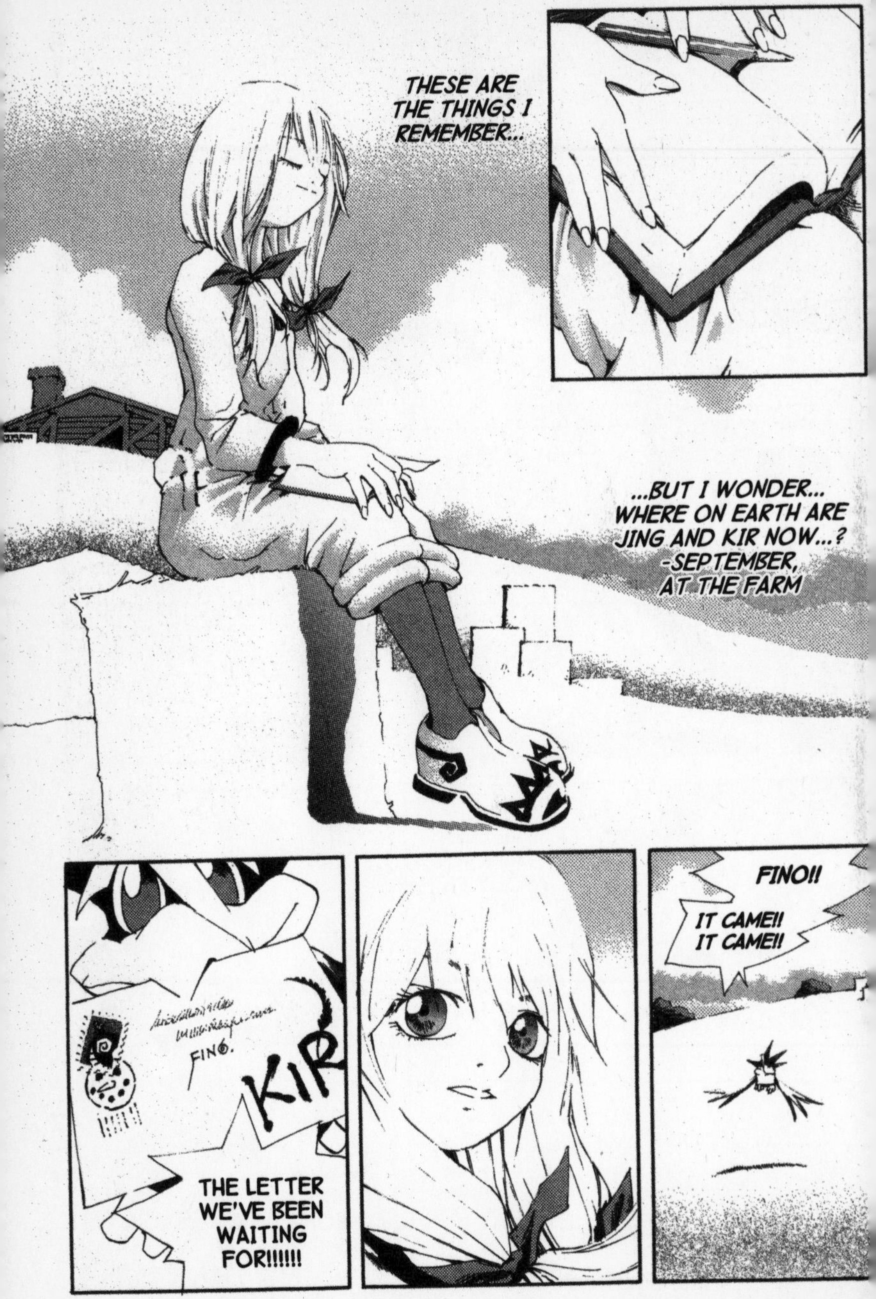
THESE ARE THE THINGS I REMEMBER...
...BUT I WONDER... WHERE ON EARTH ARE JING AND KIR NOW...? -SEPTEMBER, AT THE FARM
FINO!!
IT CAME!! IT CAME!!
FINO.
KIR
THE LETTER WE'VE BEEN WAITING FOR!!!!!!

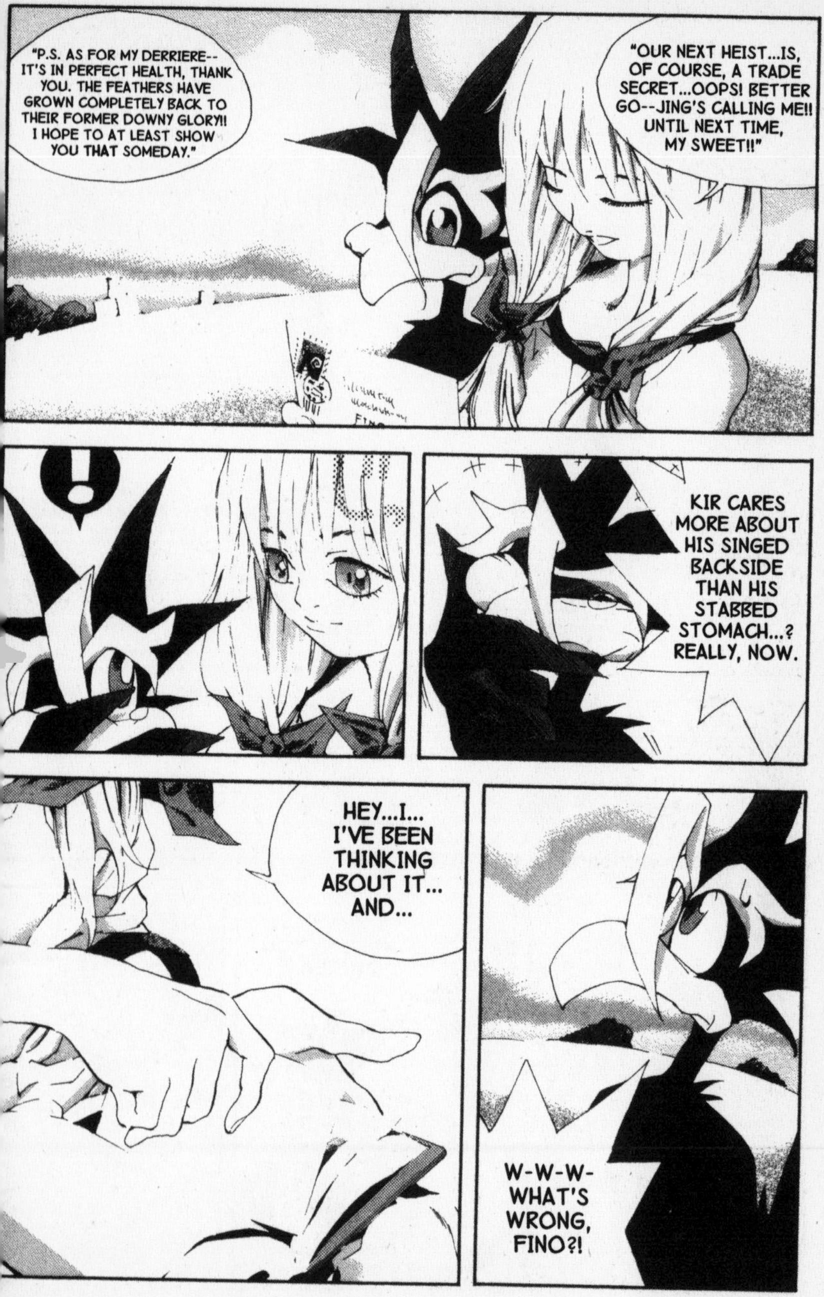
"OUR NEXT HEIST...IS, OF COURSE, A TRADE SECRET...OOPS! BETTER GO--JING'S CALLING ME!! UNTIL NEXT TIME, MY SWEET!!"
"P.S. AS FOR MY DERRIERE-- IT'S IN PERFECT HEALTH, THANK YOU. THE FEATHERS HAVE GROWN COMPLETELY BACK TO THEIR FORMER DOWNY GLORY!! I HOPE TO AT LEAST SHOW YOU THAT SOMEDAY."
KIR CARES MORE ABOUT HIS SINGED BACKSIDE THAN HIS STABBED STOMACH...? REALLY, NOW.
!
W-W-W-WHAT'S WRONG, FINO?!
HEY...I... I'VE BEEN THINKING ABOUT IT... AND...

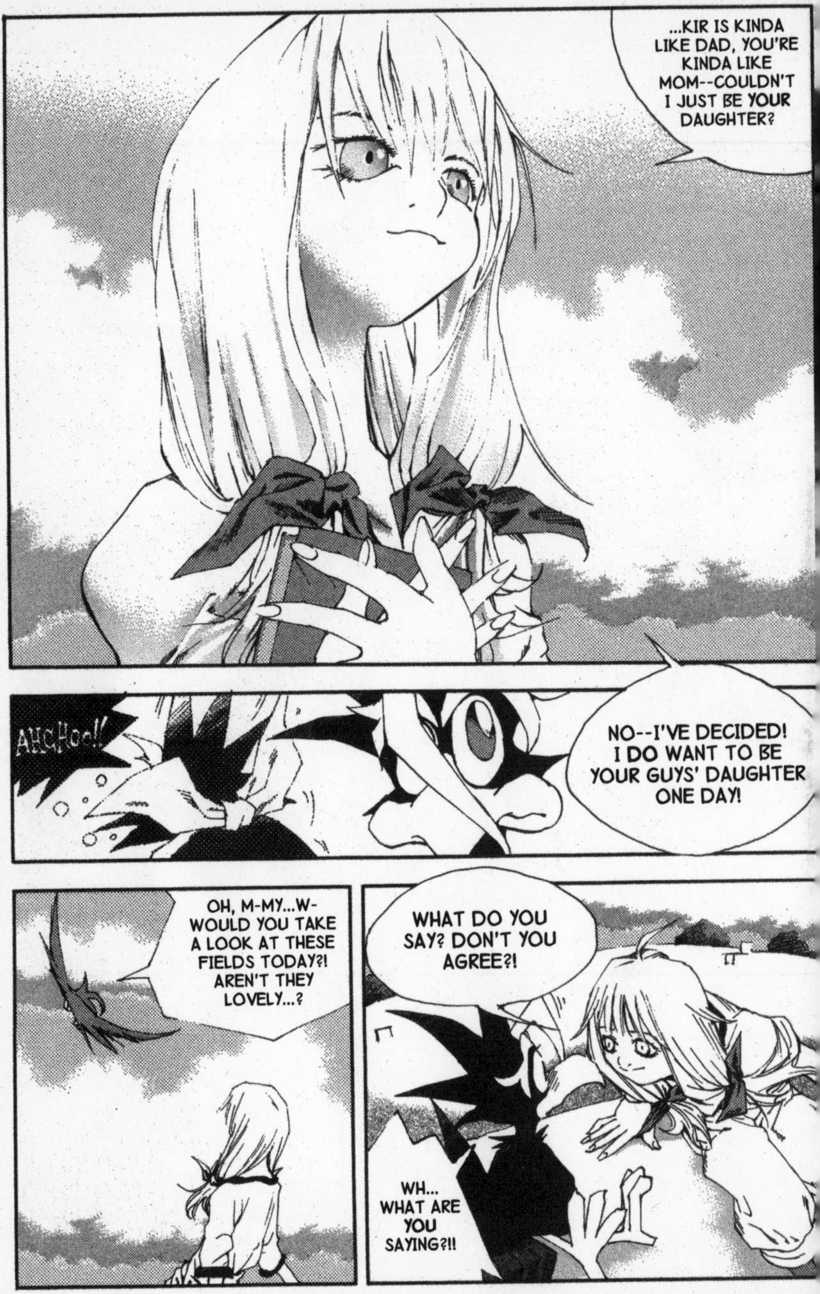
...KIR IS KINDA LIKE DAD, YOU'RE KINDA LIKE MOM--COULDN'T I JUST BE YOUR DAUGHTER?
NO--I'VE DECIDED! I DO WANT TO BE YOUR GUYS' DAUGHTER ONE DAY!
AHCHoo!!
WHAT DO YOU SAY? DON'T YOU AGREE?!
WH... WHAT ARE YOU SAYING?!!
OH, M-MY...W-WOULD YOU TAKE A LOOK AT THESE FIELDS TODAY?! AREN'T THEY LOVELY...?

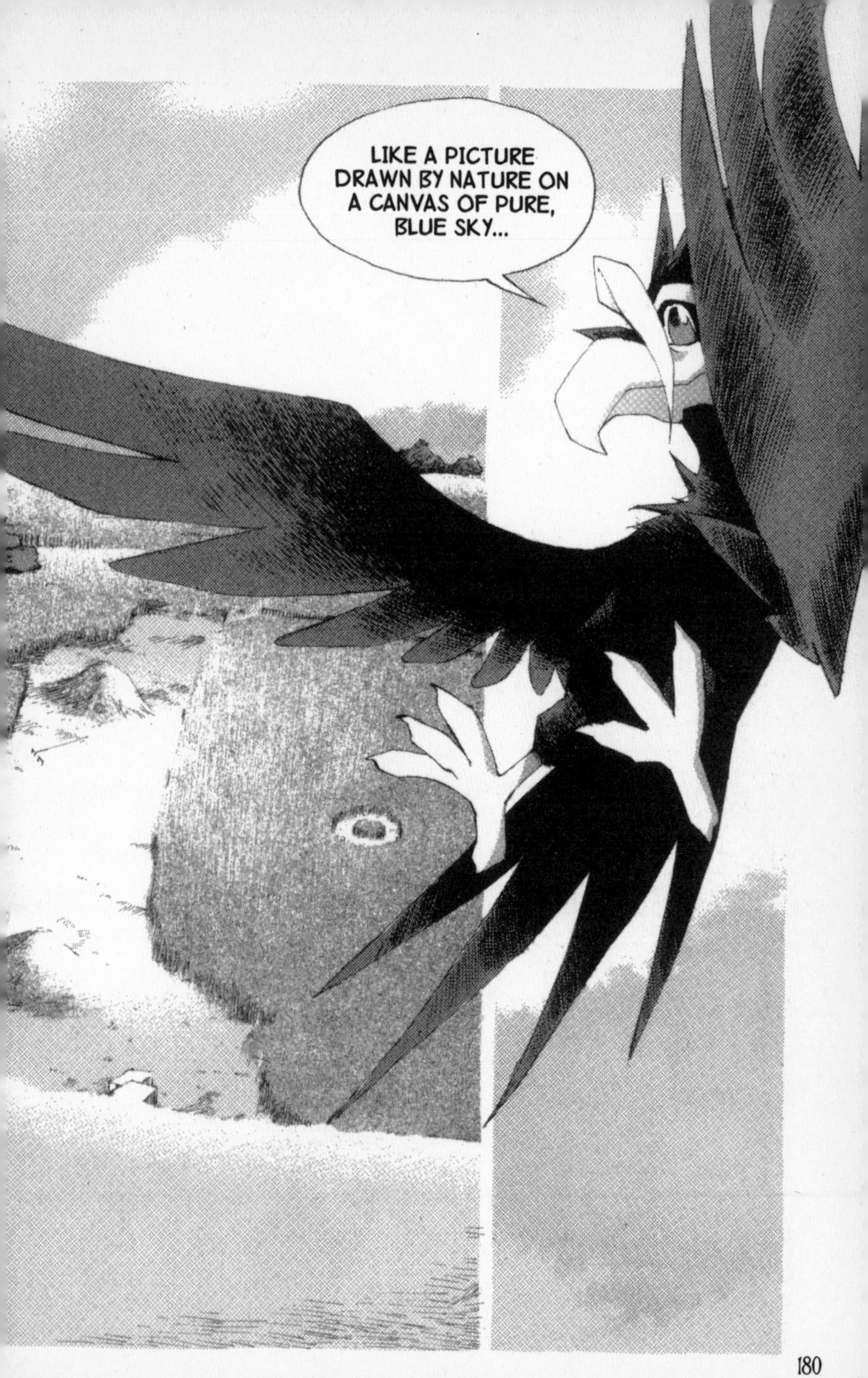
LIKE A PICTURE DRAWN BY NATURE ON A CANVAS OF PURE, BLUE SKY...

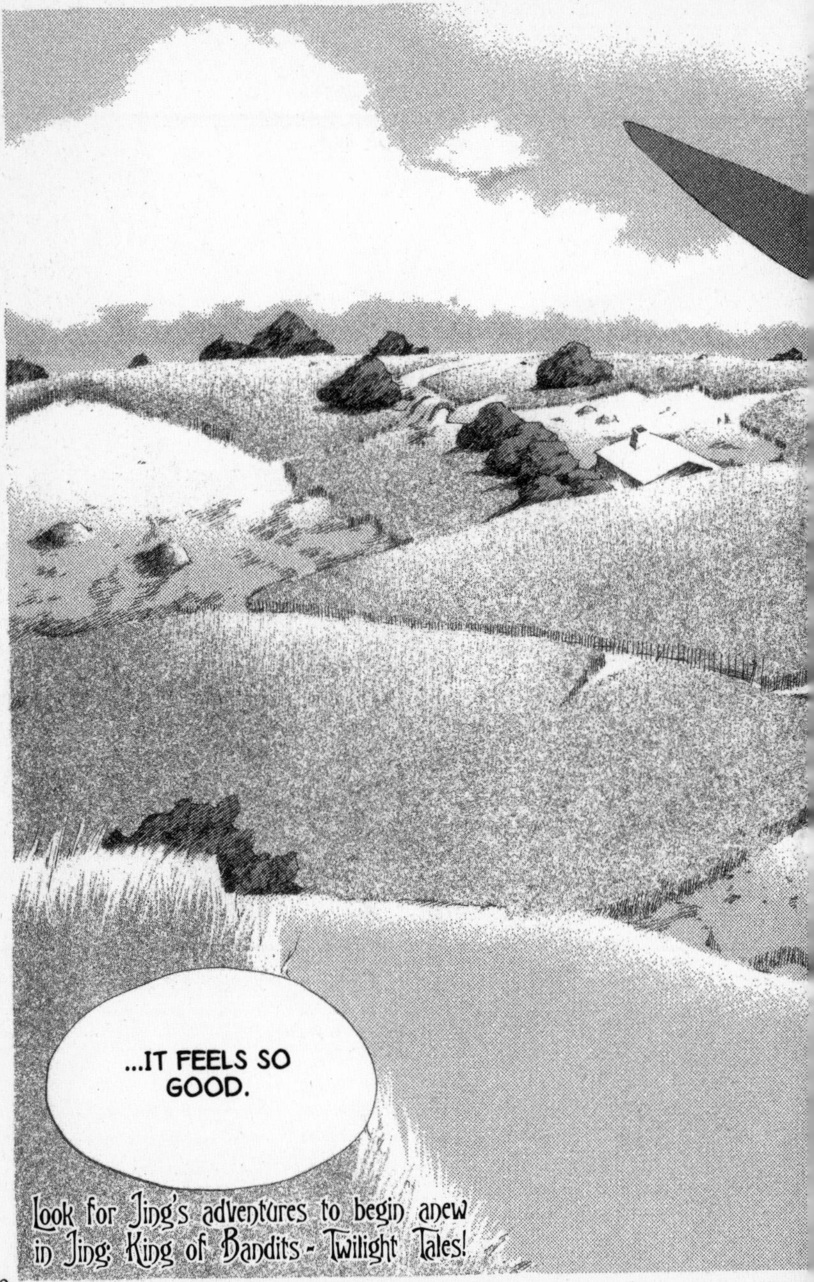
...IT FEELS SO GOOD.
Look for Jing's adventures to begin anew in Jing: King of Bandits - Twilight Tales!

熊倉裕一完全監修

who the hell is he !!?

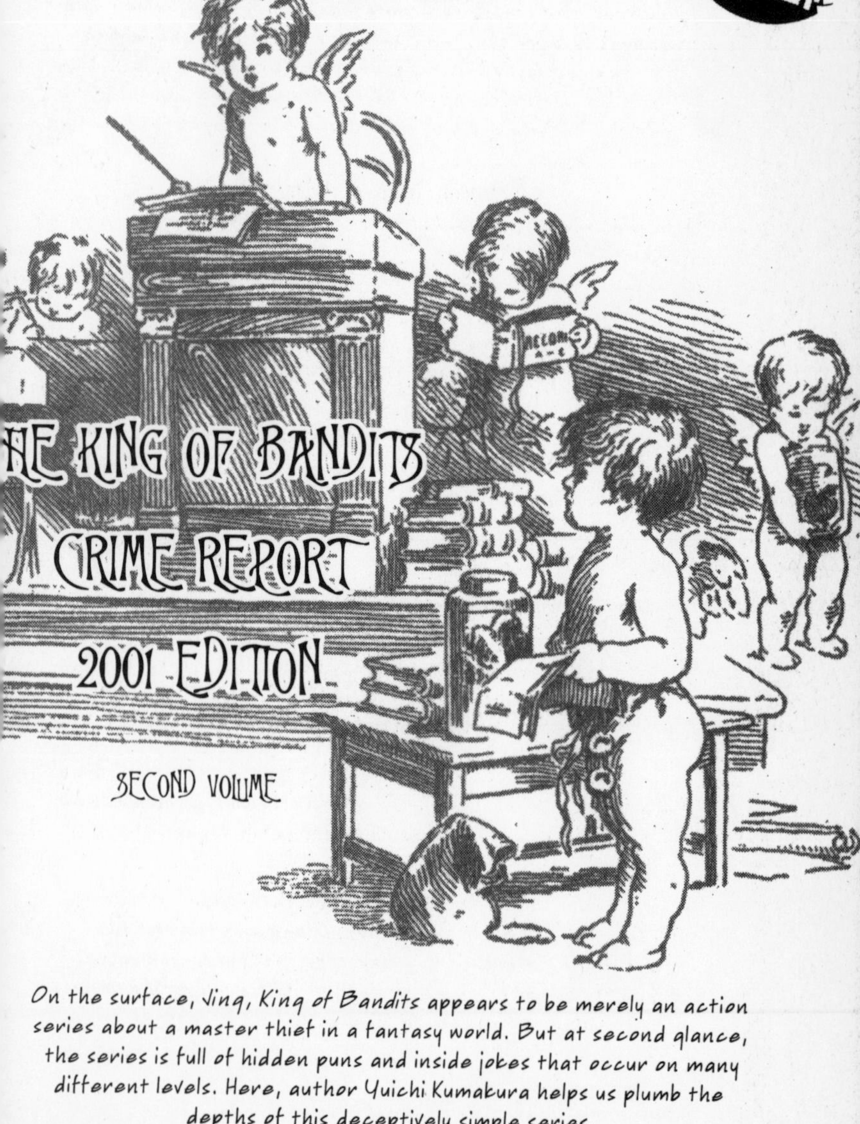

THE KING OF BANDITS CRIME REPORT 2001 EDITION

SECOND VOLUME

On the surface, Jing, King of Bandits appears to be merely an action series about a master thief in a fantasy world. But at second glance, the series is full of hidden puns and inside jokes that occur on many different levels. Here, author Yuichi Kumakura helps us plumb the depths of this deceptively simple series.

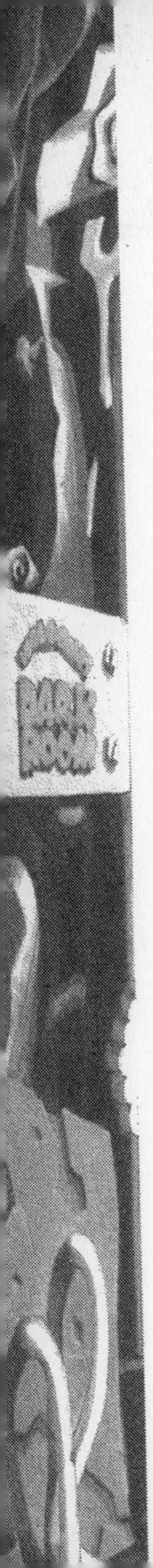

characters

Mara Suki-No [Mara Schino]

The boss of Seventh Heaven's name comes from a colorless liqueur reputedly made with rare Marasca cherries. When Jing escapes from prison, the figure of Maraschino, channeling the remains of his rage into complete insanity, is reminiscent of the aforementioned "La Vita di Benvenuto Cellini Fiorentino."

Medarudo Shishaku [Medardo]

Not the name of an alcholic beverage, but a reference to an Italo Calvino book called "Il Visconte Dimezzato," the main character of which is Medardo. It is expected that this story, which follows the life of a man mysteriously split in two by a shell during wartime, is currently being perused with great interest by Jing fans. (Akifumi Company Publications)

Bararaika [Balalaika]

Add white curacao and lemon to vodka, shake it, and voila, you have Balalaika. This stage for "Amarcord" is a charming town with rows of Russian-style minarets--appropriately enough, as balalaika is also the name of a typical Russian stringed instrument. You can see Russian words--as well as avant-garde design work from Russia--everywhere in the Kumakura world.

Pomu [Pomme]

"Apple" in French (can also mean "potato").

Minto [Mint]

Here, Mint can be interpreted as mint flavoring. This would be closest to peppermint (hakka) in Japan.

Kuyro-Bu [Clove]

A spice, called chouji in Japan. Along with the last two mentioned above, Clove completes the "three bad boys/ three strike-outs." Come to think of it, did you notice something of a baseball motif throughout this episode?

Kashisu [Cassis]

Cassis sounds better than "black gooseberry," doesn't it? This character from "Amarcord," along with the above-mentioned "strikeouts," is designated with the name of a raw material used in alcohol and cocktails. This is to imply that they are still children, and therefore underage [alcohol = adult].

Posuti-No [Postino]

It is not touched upon in this episode, but the oniisan who delivers the gun to Jing is popularly known as Postino (see JING, KING OF BANDITS--Twilight Tales, bottle 1). This is the Italian name for "postman." There was also a movie in 1995 called "Il Postino," in which a secluded poet wrote exchanges of the heart for the postman working on his island. Worth a look.

Pu-tao [Putao]

An ill-natured detective who bites Jing's head off with questioning. It is pronounced putaochuu, from the Chinese putaojiu. Speaking of which, his Chinese-style outfit, with the hairstyle, reminds me of a Qing dynasty pigtail. This man comes off as shrewd, even at the end of the Game Boy edition. If you are a fan, by all means, see for yourself.

Zaza [Zaza]

Add dubonnet and angostura bitters to dry gin, stir, and voila, you have Zaza. The panorama of Zaza that appears at the beginning of this story stemmed from a piece of work named "Venezia Senz'Acqua" by Clerici, a 20th-century Italian artist. Would you be satisfied to know that Zaza, assuming it is a city on the sea, is surrounded by desert? I wonder...

DuBone [DuBonnet]

A flavored wine prepared by garnishing wine plus distilled alcohol with Chinese tree bark, among other things. The mask that Countess Dubonnet wears was originally inspired by Japan's Noh masks, but it could be said that its true success lies in the fact that it matches the look of the houses and shops of Zaza, making you think more of Venice--a style entirely characteristic of Yuichi Kumakura.

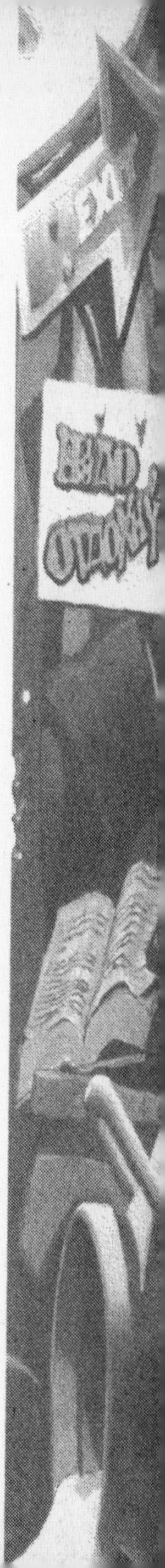

Sutea [Stir]

From the action "to stir" (blend with a bar spoon) that has appeared many times in previous recipes. It might be said that the name characterizes her wonderfully as someone who "stirs up" the town of Zaza. She embodies stout-heartedness and gallantry-- and is, appropriately, the most popular "Jinq girl."

Remon [Lemon]

Stir's younger brother. Since he died without ever having grown up, it looks like he was named for a fruit that never got to be an alcohol. Incidentally, Vodka's son, who appears in the Game Boy edition, is also named Lemon, but there is no special relation between the two. It is a name like "Tarou" for sure, you know.

Aisu Kyoudai [Ice Bros]

Three feared, cold-hearted brothers. Cube is cubed ice, Crush is crushed ice...but the very last one, Baffle, means, "to make bewildered/frustrated," so it is gibberish if you link it with ice. To that extent, you could interpret it as meaning the brothers' entire existence is incomprehensible, since their true nature is not actually human.

Angosuchura [Angostora]

Two men, young and old, with the same name-- Angostura, a bitter-tasting alcohol created in Venezuela, South America. This is something that happens a great deal in the West--the Young Angostura inherited his grandfather's name. In other words, it is like saying Louie the 13th or 14th. This family, for generations, has managed the protection of the Dubonnet family.

Ginjou [Ginjou]

Ginjou is a favorite fruity alcohol from Japan, made with more than 40% polished rice. The deadly technique of this vagabond warrior, who was aloof from the trivialities of the world, was called "wolf claw!!" If you translate it, it's "okuri ookami"--in other words, a man who commits evil by pretending to send a drunken girl home. What an insulting name!!!

Danda [Dunder]

Refers to the dregs that remain when rum alcohol is distilled. No wonder this bullfighter/lady-killer had such an unexpectedly dull name. His surname, Martinique, comes from the Martinique Islands of the Carribean Sea, an area that produces rum.

Abiesho [Aviation]

Aviation translates as "hikou" in Japanese. You could say the name of the town foreshadows the launch of Jing's adventure, when he solves the puzzle in the temple of light and soars into the sky on the legendary giant fish. Aviation is also a cocktail that adds lemon juice and other ingredients to a dry gin base.

Faji-Ne-buru [Fuzzy Navel]

Fuzzy Navel is a stirred drink that combines orange juice with peach liqueur. The "fuzz" in FUZZY refers to the fine, light hairs on the surface of peaches and similar fruits. But the word "fuzzy" also holds a big connotation in Japanese, as in "yuragi no aru." (Editor's note: long ago, the term "fuzzy" came to be a widely-used way to indicate electric products in Japan.) Although yuragu heso (= navel) is revealed as an untrodden plateau close to neither heaven nor earth, the name I gave it fits just right.

Kirushu [Kirsche]

Kirsche is a cherry liqueur made in Switzerland. It is a fairly strong alcohol, contrary to the image it evokes of a cute cherry...but I have a hunch that it strangely suits our strong-to-the-core kitty-chan character.

Araku [Arrack, Arak]

In a den of heathens, Arak is aware of the corruption within. His name comes from an alcohol, arrack, distilled from the dates that overwhelm the near and middle east. It has an appropriate ring for the person in charge of Fuzzy Navel, and contributes to an atmosphere that has no nationality of its own, but is roughly based on Asia.

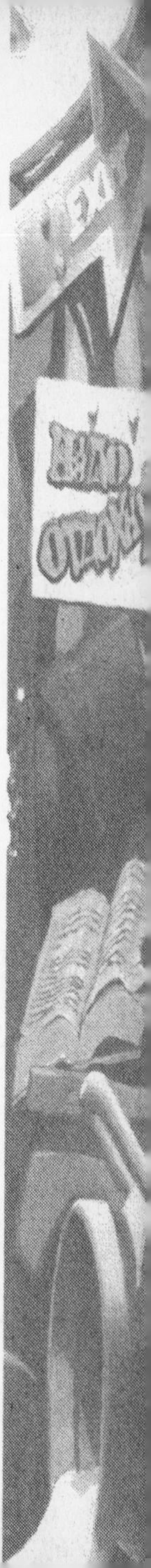

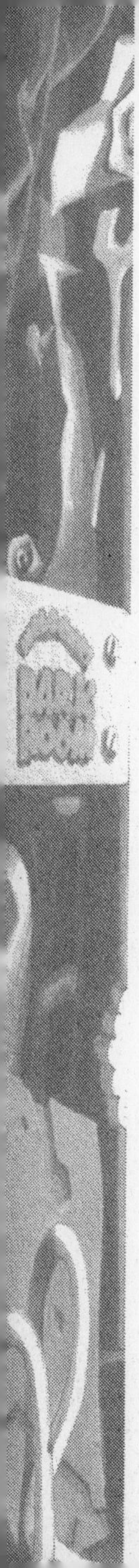

Pesuka [Pesca]

Pesca is Italian for "peach." It comes from the indispensable peach liqueur (momo no osake) used in a Fuzzy Navel. By the way, the "gigantessa" in the cloud sculpture, Pesca Gigantessa, means "gigantic." So if you translate the entire name into English, you get "giant peach"--just like the one in Tim Burton's animated masterpiece. Although this peach not only transports children to a new world...it takes them to Hell...

Ponpie [Pompier]

A cocktail that adds creme de cassis and soda water to vermouth. In French it means "fireman," and for that reason, the "painter's truck" that appears at the beginning of this story looks just like a fire truck. Also, this fire truck is used completely different from its original inspiration, which you may recognize from Francois Truffaut's Sci-Fi movie, "Fahrenheit 451."

Fino [Fino]

A variety of sherry whose light color is its chief characteristic. Fino's surname, Quart, is an indication of capacity based on the "ounce method" of weights and measures, which is different from the metric system. In America, 1 quart = 946 ml.

Doranbui [Drambuie]

The first English-produced liqueur. It combines herbs and other ingredients, using whiskey as it's base. Our character of the same name may look like a trump king, but he is in fact only the president-san of mere abacuses.

Shupe-tore-ze [Spätlese]

A sweet, strong German white wine that uses late-harvested, heated grapes. Although the chameleon doctor of our story might be better described as "rotting" than "ripened"...

Kurimuzonkingu [Crimson King]

Pompier's underground crimson lake. The name comes from the 1969 debut album of an English rock band. The record, "Crimson King's Palace," was a monumental work that opened up a new art form called progressive rock (short form, prog rock). Furthermore, the band's name, King Crimson, became the name of Color City's first enterprise, which Drambuie supervises.

Van [Vin]

"Vin," which means wine in extremely simple French, became the legendary painter's name. And "Le Chef-d'oeuvre Inconnu" was his posthumous work--but did you know that there is a short novel with the same name by France's literary master, Balzac? It is the story of a painter who ruined himself through his admiration of the arts, just like Fino's father!!!

Well, now. From here on out, we are not going to be concerned with character names, but will be searching every corner of every panel for meanings and homages hidden within the words and pictures.

- Volume 1 -

City of Thieves

As I touched on in the initial set-up collection of the first volume, the City of Thieves was drawn as an homage to the Tower of Babel. According to the Old Testament, there was only one universal language until the wrath of God came down on this tower. In other words, there were no barriers or national borders between the people before that. But it may also be said that the City of Thieves is a place where people from every conceivable race and country gather for one common purpose--crime is the only true equilizer...

Anchor Of The Phantom Ship

In the Game Boy edition, the anchor combination that attacks Jing and the others before they enter the casino has an actual name. The one who holds the chains on top is called Pantagruel, and the anchor's main body is called Gargantua. These names come from the works "Pantagruel" and "Gargantua," magnificently exaggerated stories by Francois Rabelais, a giant of the French Renaissance.

In The Nick Of Time?!!

A certain black-mustached man comes to pick a fight with Jing and the gang while they are making a killing in the casino. This man's outfit, if you look closely, is an homage to the barrels Mario jumped over in "Donkey Kong."

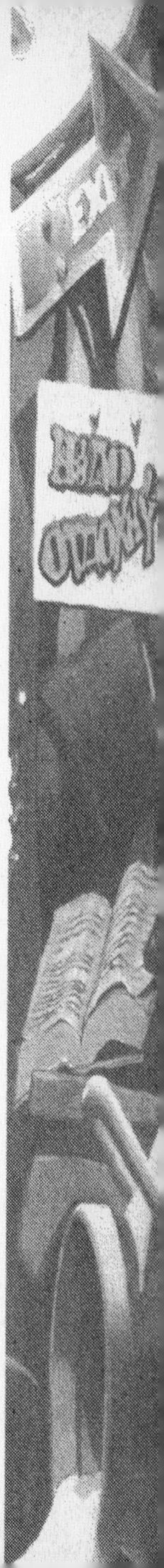

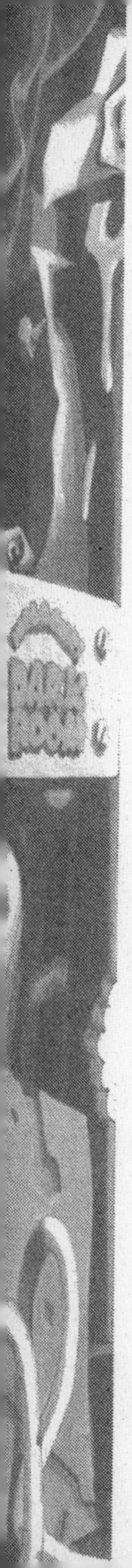

Clockwork Grape

What should come to your mind immediately is the aforementioned "Clockwork Orange." This masterpiece depicted, with cynical and stylish imagery, the "reverse rectification" of a young person who spent all his time on violence and sex.

Door That Tells Time

The entrance to the city of Adonis, guarded by the gear gate watchers. The source of the gigantic clock was the astrological clock of the city government office in Prague, the capital of the Czech Republic. It's a work of art by which people can enjoy the greeting of Christ's twelve disciples, along with a show of puppets that announce the time.

- Volume 2 -

A Big Mac is Fine, But...

The dream Kir had of the mustached old man, having barely escaped from Mastergear. A reference to that heroic fast food chain founder, the Colonel, judging from Kir's testimony that he would have been "fried" with potatoes!!!

Country of the World of the Dead=Neverland

The name of the country where the eternal child Peter Pan and his friends lived. The motif of James Barrie's original work, "Peter Pan," is inlaid everywhere in the "Time City" book. For example...

Captain

The "Captain" exchanged one hand, which was eaten by a crocodile (Clockodial), for a hook (key). A reference to Peter Pan's old enemy, Captain Hook himself. Furthermore...

Cock-A-Doodle Doooo

This war cry, in reference to Jing's seeing the morning sun when he enters the grapes tower, is also Peter Pan's favorite phrase.

"A Graveyard is the Most Economical Place to Stay"

This line, which the Captain says to Jing and the gang underground, is borrowed from Langston Hughes, an African-American black poet. Hughes crystallized the souls of black people, who went on living reassuringly even while suffering discrimination, in the form of his poems.

Sour Grapes...

Aesop's famous words, which everyone has heard at one time or another. It is the story of a fox who, when unable to eat some grapes growing in a high, unreachable place, made the excuse that, "Those grapes were sour anyway." Both the finest of grapes and the supremity of freedom were nothing but objects of intense jealousy to the cold-hearted female fox in our story!!!

Distortion

A popular name for the harvesters who flew around the big temple that produced the clockwork grapes. Distortion is a sound effect that warps the sound of an electric guitar on purpose. These harvesters probably got their name from the scythes that they held, which were shaped like electric guitars. (see Game Boy edition).

13th Hour

The spacious room where Jing and Vins Mousseux unfolded their final desperate struggle was furnished with carved statues representing the 12 constellations, in a shape that mirrored the 12 hours of a clock...but there was one extra figure. And so, Vin Mousseux related "not being part of this world" to the 13th Hour figure. Thirteen is a numeral that should be evaded, as far as most Christians are concerned. Its existence brings death to mind. The 13th figure, which held a heart-shaped lamp as if to symbolize human life, blocked Jing and the gang's escape route, tailing them even after Vins Mousseux was defeated!

Material from the "Animal Bombs, Porvoras" book:

Walt's Family?!

Much hidden art was concealed in the spread pages immediately after Jing set out on his trip with the Porvora. In the center of the picture was the "world's first famous mouse," and in the rocky mountain to the right were the spitting images of objects from "Le Voyage dan la lune," a work of Melies, a hero from the birth of cinema.

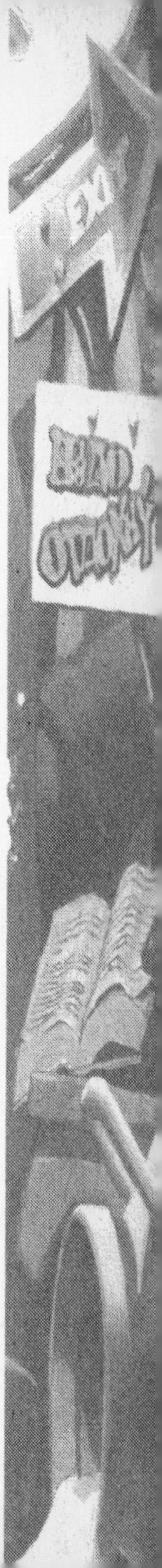

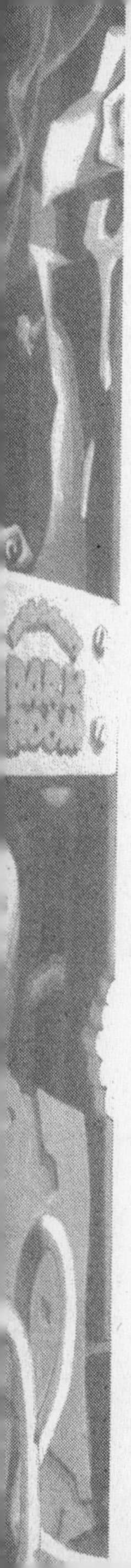

Why Spanish...

Necessary tools as seen in western movies can be seen in great numbers in the "Porvora" book, including a lot of Spanish vocabulary (since many western movies take place along the Mexican state border, Spanish expressions are often utilized). Even "Porvora" is Spanish. And "nino," used by Izarra to threaten Jing, means "baby." The "signore" of Signore Goblet is kind of like that, too.

- Volume 3 -

"Le Salaire de la Peur"

The final conception of this episode stemmed, no doubt, from the 1952 French movie masterpiece, Le Salaire de la Peur. The story of men who were unable to make a living, transporting great quantities of nitro-glycerin--only in preparation for their eventual deaths--was also a masterpiece of the famous Yves Montand, a chanson singer.

"Le Petit Prince"

We could also mention the motif of "Le Petit Prince," a masterpiece by French author Saint-Exupery, as another factor that made this episode rich and deep. Follow the reading carefully--in each episode different set-ups blend into the expressions, which invoke very deep impressions. For example, phrases like Goblet's "Baobab" mansion and "the most precious things aren't always visible to the naked eye" --there are too many to mention them all. But the most effective quote would be the last line of the "Porvora" book...

"The land of tears is strange country indeed...isn't it, Izarra...?"

While it came from the original text of Le Petit Prince, it is expected that many fans were deeply touched by this line, in which the nuance was subtly shifted.

By the way, the image of Izarra taking her shower in Sungria could almost double as the rose in the glass bin, which also appears in the original text.

Pale Rider

The scene of the Sungria mining location, where Kir's comrades are being worked so hard, looks a lot like the gold mine that appears in "Pale Rider," a 1985 film by director Clint Eastwood.

The Great Dictator

At one point, Goblet toys with a balloon that imitates the star gem. There is an identical scene in the 1940 Charlie Chaplin film "The Great Dictator."

Bateau Ivre

If we were to translate into Japanese the words of the boat's sail (with the miserable skeleton as its mast), it would be "yoidore fune." This is representative of the French poet Rimbaud. In this work, one extremely drunken ship goes forth to the middle of a dying world--similar to the tone of the "Reviver" book. Also in "Reviver," vestiges of the poems Verlaine wrote to his friend and lover, Rimbaud, peep out here and there.

Life And Death On Reverse Sides Of A Coin...

The town of Reviver, where Jing and the gang ended up. This island's story follows the archetype of "Die Toteninsel," or "The Island of Death," by Arnold Bocklin, a Swiss-born symbolic painter. An ironic reference, associating this town of eternal life with the island of death.

Odradek

Odradek, a "diminutive helper" who appears as a "flat, star-shaped spool of thread" at unexpected times and places and disappears quickly, first appeared in "Die Sorge des Hausvaters," a short story by Czech writer Franz Kafka. In the last part of that short story, a mysterious creature is mentioned...

"He does no harm to anyone that one can see; but the idea that he is likely to survive me I find almost painful."

Could it not be said that this might be the immortal king's feelings towards Vermouth...?

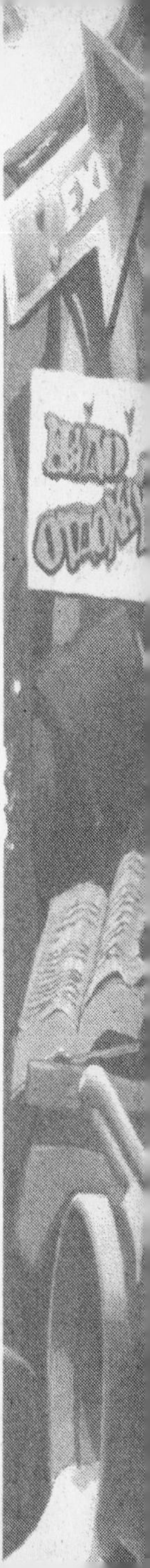

Church Of "The Second Puzzle"
It seems there is a church in Poland, one whose walls
is made entirely of human bones.

- Volume 4 -

Eternal Soup
Something called "Eternal Soup" appears in a famous episode of
"Der Zauberberg," a monumental work by a monumental German
author, Thomas Mann. He writes about how soup is served in the
sanitarium, as though stamped with a daily seal, isolated from
the normal flow of time--and, of course, it is not liquid and the
like within it.

Ants And Grasshoppers?!
The trembling violin player who makes excuse after excuse in the
convoy bus at the beginning of the "Seventh Heaven" book. It
looks like he committed a crime, thinking ill of someone who had
saved up some money, but...uhn? Wait--a guy who plays nothing
but music and a guy who is hoarding money, eh...? Somehow or
other, they remind me of an old parable...

This Mosquito Grade...
A rank in heavy and welter-weight boxing--but what Maraschino
refers to is a "mosquito coil," an insecticide that the above violin
player will ingest and die.

Le Cerveau Noir De Piranesi
The elegant, mazelike interior design of the prison is a huge
reference to the of a prison drawn by Piranesi, an 18th century
Italian engraver. He was a different yet capable artist who drew
from a unique perspective, excluding any emotional feelings.

Escape From Alcatraz
There is a 1979 Don Siegel-directed work, "Escape From Alca-
traz," starring Clint Eastwood. Speaking of which, the name of
the horned rat the old prisoner was feeding was something like
Clint...

A Straight Line to Hell

The bizarre aperture that announces "The only exit is here," right before the appearance of Benedictine, borrows the archetype of Prince Orsini's "Park of the Monsters" in Bomarzo, at the center of Italy. Somehow, this park has within it a reproduction of the gateway to Hell itself.

Dodo

Pulling the train that Jing's party boarded within the prison of dreams was an illusionary, flightless bird, the Dodo. If you're wondering why this rare bird, which went extinct from being preyed on by humans and animals because it could not fly, appears here, you should probably recall the fact that this prison of dreams was built from feelings, which would not necessarily rule out a lost race (ushinawareta shuzoku). After all, the Acacian tribe was also left to the mercy of fate, just like that helpless rare bird.

A Grieving Toy

Campari muttered these words, as though sneering at himself...

"I used a toy called a dream orb."

Speaking of sad toys, "Grieving Toy" is the title of a second anthology of poems by Ishikawa Takuboku, posthumously published in 1912. So many young poets die prematurely...is there some sort of epidemic that causes their hearts to choke?

Amarcord

"Amarcord" was a once-in-a-lifetime movie created in 1974 by Federico Fellini, a famous director who represented Italy. This work depicted dazzling images of Fellini's boyhood on stage in the town of Rimini, Italy, where he grew up. It is said that the title means "I remember" in Rimini dialect. That is why the story of young Jing's own indulgent memory carried that nostalgic word for its title.

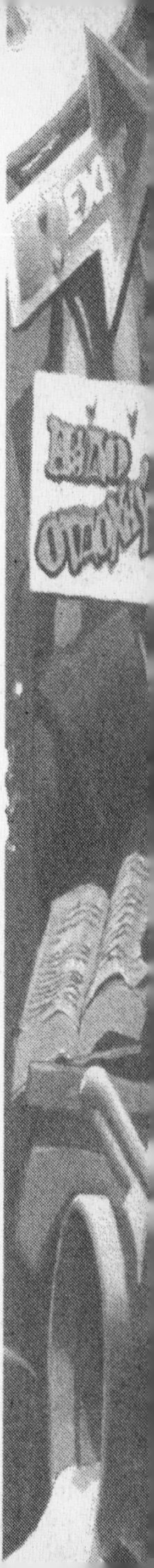

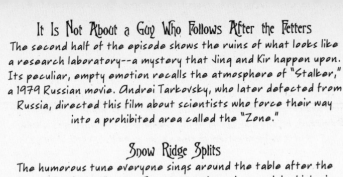

It Is Not About a Guy Who Follows After the Fetters

The second half of the episode shows the ruins of what looks like a research laboratory--a mystery that Jinq and Kir happen upon. Its peculiar, empty emotion recalls the atmosphere of "Stalker," a 1979 Russian movie. Andrei Tarkovsky, who later defected from Russia, directed this film about scientists who force their way into a prohibited area called the "Zone."

Snow Ridge Splits

The humorous tune everyone sings around the table after the first visit of the Kir-eqq. It appears there is an original joke in this somehow, but whose song it is is unclear. Even this editorial department is considering investigating it further.

- Volume 5 -

A Moveable Feast

This book, "A Moveable Feast Guide," is regarded as an official source of explanation from the outset. I have never heard of a feast that moved, but if you translate the existing work called "A Moveable Feast," the work of one Ernest Hemingway, a writer who represented the "lost generation" of America, it becomes "dou shukusaijitsu." In Hemingway's work, which documents the exciting lifestyles of 1920s Paris (in which he lived) he analyzes the city's festival-like atmosphere:

> "If you are lucky enough to have lived in
> Paris as a young man, then whenever
> you go for the rest of your life, it stays
> with you, for Paris is a moveable feast."

Would the book in our story that listed the town of Zaza, as though attempting to recall in us the same kind of deep emotion that Hemingway felt for Paris, be "A Moveable Feast Guide?"

Vintage Smile

"Vintage Smile" refers to the name of the timeframe in which grapes are harvested for wine. Since wine differs completely in quality of harvest from year to year, even if it is the same brand, wines from a year in which quality grapes are harvested are associated with the name of their harvest year and, as such, command a high price in the marketplace. Similarly, the word "vintage" is attached to this mask of utmost quality, which preserves the finest smile.

Warrior Of The Rising Sun

It is a well-known fact that "Hi Izurutokoro No Tenshi" is a masterpiece manga, in which Yamagishi Ryouko depicted Shoutoku Taishi in an unprecedented vision. One letter off that title is the name of this fighter, assumed to have come from the Far East, who becomes the center of the "mascorrida" storm. A newspaper caption turns the name into "Rising Son," but this is intentional. Although the original meaning refers to a sunrise, the other meaning connotes that the "son" candidate is rising quickly among the ranks...so, both are implied.

And Now, A Question For The Ages...

Often, in fan letters and the like, we come across questions like, "Does Tamori Wataru-sensei of 'Robotto Ponkottsu,' now appearing serialized (2001 to current) in the monthly publication comic Bonbon, have any relationship with Kumakura-sensei?" We will answer that question here. Yes, there is a relationship. Tamori-sensei was once Kumakura-sensei's assistant. But did you know that Tamori-sensei made a cameo appearance in the "Zaza" book? There was a cask-headed man among the townspeople, who were in an uproar about a sudden tremor under their feet during the confrontation with Baffle as our heroes left the mask cafe. That was him.

Even Stars Sparkle

You'll find that in a lot of Jing's stories, the sun and the moon play an important part. In this "Zaza" book, the Countess is liberated from her reverie of the past upon seeing the brilliance of the morning sun. It is probably not a mistake that this repeated motif brings out emotions of a similar scale in Jing.

- Volume 6 -

Could Be A World Legacy

Aviation's mysterious spectacle, where strange rocks protrude in countless numbers. It is not exactly clear where they begin, but it brings to mind that land of mystery, Cappadocia--a large, picturesque place in Turkey somewhere. It is said that young Christian monks settled there in secret and cultivated their own personal culture on one side of the wastelands, where many strange rocks like these stand close together.

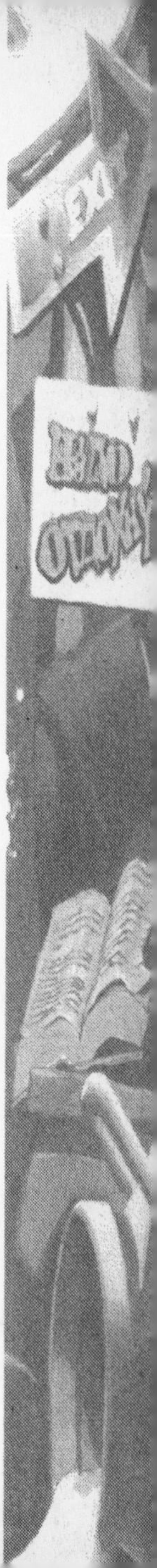

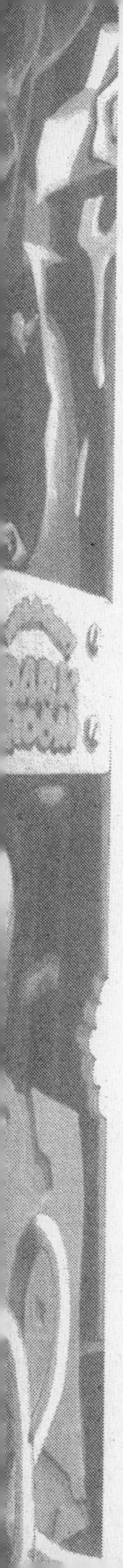

High Praise For Takahata Isao

A giant fish that flew in the sky and was attracted by the light from the temple. However, although Jing saw it, the giant fish took him by force, and one of the kittens looked up into the vexing sky. This image had a source in "Tale of Tales," a work of Russian animation artist Yuri Norstein. In it, a fish, that is being chased escapes to the sky, as a cat looks up and gives a sorrowful cry.

Stray Cats

"Noraneko" in English means STRAY CATS, but it is in close conjunction with an expression frequently used in Christianity, STRAY SHEEP (mayoeru kohitsuji). This name, which has a double meaning, was created for the kittens Kirsche leads, likening them to devout sisters who serve God.

Electricity Killed The Cat

These words were written throughout the town, a parody of a saying in English, "CURIOSITY KILLED THE CAT" (koukishin, neko wo korosu). Roughly, it means that nothing goes right when you stick your nose into things that aren't your business. But with the change from CURIOSITY to ELECTRICITY, it has come to be a slogan of another kind that expresses the Stray Cats' sense of respect towards electricity.

Let There Be Light

These are famous words from the Old Testament, which tells of the time when God created the world, but the religion that appears within this work has no direct relationship whatsoever with Christianity. Rather, regarding these words as an ignition point, it would be better to think about a new religion that accomplished an original evolution. The Cahier sect is a different denomination from that of Kirsche and the gang--that is, while showing respect to the same thing [God=light], one side assumes light should be distributed to everyone, and the other assumes it should be monopolized.

"Two Powers Dominate Space, Light And Gravity"

These words were spoken like an incantation by the two Cahier sect believers who targeted the lives of Jing and the gang as they arrived in Fuzzy Navel. In fact, these are the words of an actual philosopher, Simone Weil, a female thinker from France. There is one passage within her masterpiece, "La Pesanteur et la Grace," which collected these words. Perhaps the believers of the Cahier sect chose to bend and interpret these words, which originally held a similar sentiment to the above-mentioned "Let There Be Light," as an excuse to toy with the lives of heretics.

Solid Gold Batteries

I have never heard of any actual instances of mercury batteries turning into solid gold batteries. However, in the Jing world, it is as if a technique of producing electricity from gold really does exist. It certainly gives the impression of being the highest grade dry cell battery, but it appears that peoples' chief interest is in the value of the gold itself, and that they are being exchanged solely as gambling chips.

Jing on Air

ON AIR is an expression used in radio and television broadcasts, but this story, borrowing only the nuance of the words, tried to leave the impression of Jing actually riding an electro-magnetic wave and dancing into the air.

- Volume 7 -

Tattooed Heart

One could say that this episode's subtitle, "Tattooed Heart," was an outstanding title that splendidly expressed the work's theme, but it originally came from an album title of Aaron Neville, an African-American musician. Rather, it may be said that this subtitle existed before the contents of the story were established. Sources for the idea were, in fact, various.

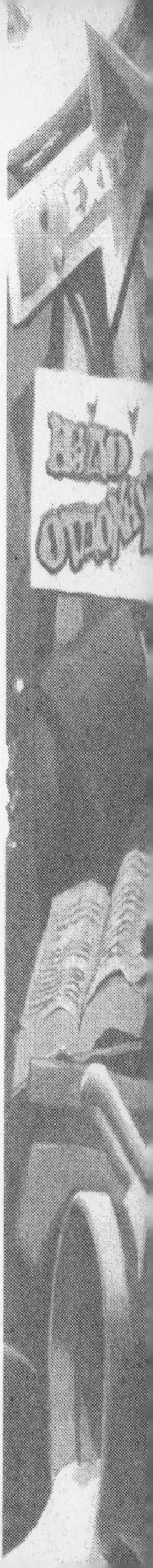

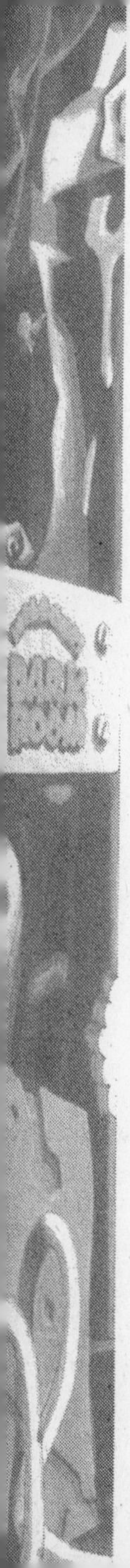

Conceal the Head...

There is a work of reportage called "The Island of Sakhalin" by Anton Chekhov, a Russian author. Within it is a passage telling of a bird on death's door that had its feathers plucked before taking its flight from life. It is as though Kir's desperate infiltration campaign was somehow or another inspired by this anecdote.

Color City

There is a song with the name "Color City" on Oonuki Taeko's album, Cliche. Its pop music gave the impression of regarding colorful images as having a rhythmical melody all their own.

Burning House Of Ice River

The image of a burning house is sometimes used as a Buddhist symbol for setting ablaze the world of worldly desire and suffering. But to the house's owner, Quart, whose personal ideals could not be achieved in this world, it symbolized that the living world was equivalent to his own personal "Hell."

Gobanme No Youso=Fifth Element

Obviously, director Luc Besson's super epic sci-fi film.

It's Like Having Drawn the Picture Completely...

All sorts of artist's supplies were incorporated into the backgrounds and props, which was appropriate for the subject matter in the "Color City" book. The factory where Jing & Fino took refuge used paintbrushes as smokestacks. And the armed group that chased after Fino carried compass-type machine guns.

Director David Lean's Work

There is a beautiful sequence from "Doctor Zhivago," a 1965 English film, in which two lovers are living in a deserted house that appears to be decorated in snow and ice. Whether or not it was a direct reference is unknown...but does this image not give an impression similar to the Quart mansion, where the ice river was hidden?

Memento Mori

It is assumed that humans instinctively avoid death, and form all kinds of theories about it with the secret wish of concealing its deeper meaning. It can probably be said, then, that the words memento mori have always managed to shake up mankind's concealed handiwork, while continuing to provide it an opportunity to look its inevitable fate in the face. In Latin, the words mean, "Do not forget death." This expression gave a voice to humanity's sense of powerlessness long before the affluence of plague and war that followed the Middle Ages. It not only addressed the age-old question, "Can death and humanity be reconciled?" but also raised the important question, "Must we go?"

It goes without saying that the "Town of Eternal Life, Reviver" book took a cold, hard look at death. Jing himself is somewhat based in death, since his mother, whom he regards as his heart's guide, is already dead. Perhaps this unspeakable grief has defined him more than anyone knows.

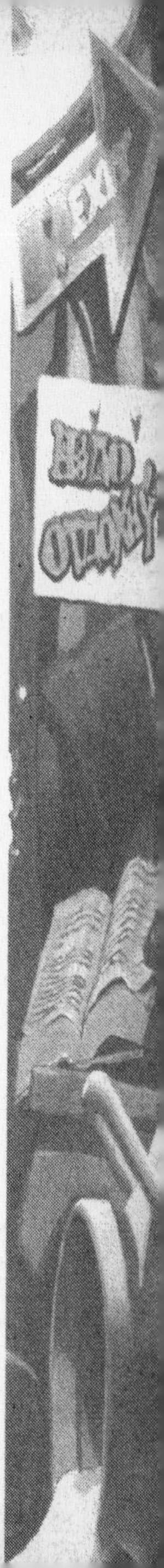

TWILIGHT TALES

KING OF BANDITS

王ドロボウJING

The last chapter has closed on **Jing: King of Bandits**, but don't feel blue–Jing and Kir will return in **Jing: Twilight Tales**, a new series coming soon that is already leaving fans green with envy! Get ready to take fresh, fantastical, and far-out journeys with Jing and his feisty, feathered friend Kir! **Twilight Tales** is an awesome new series with a darker, more sophisticated take on our heroes!

When Jing sets his sights on a valuable jewel in the coffin of a notorious mafia boss, is he really playing with fire? Will Jing get away with it all, or does **la cosa nostra's** reach extend beyond the grave?

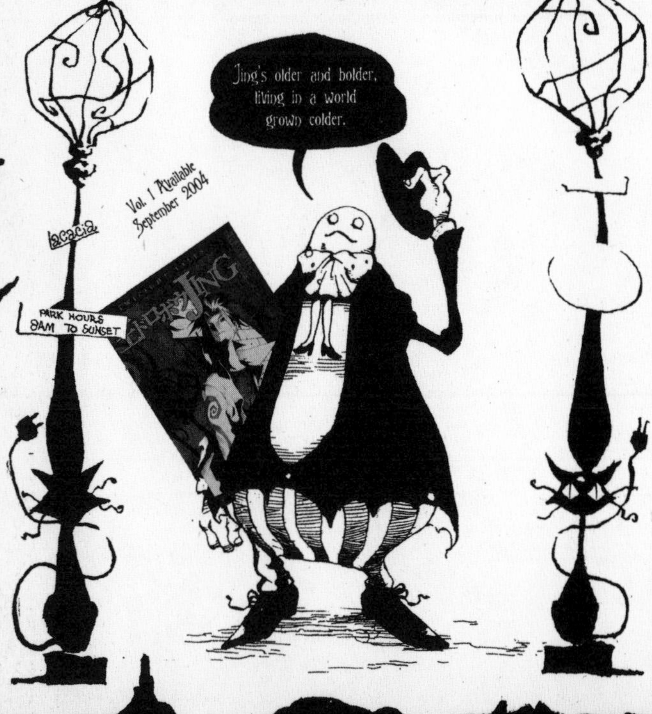
Jing's older and bolder, living in a world grown colder.
Vol. 1 Available September 2004
PARK HOURS 9AM TO SUNSET

Princess

A Diva torn from Chaos...
A Savior doomed to Love

Created by
Courtney Love
and **D.J. Milky**

TEEN
AGE 13+

www.TOKYOPOP.com

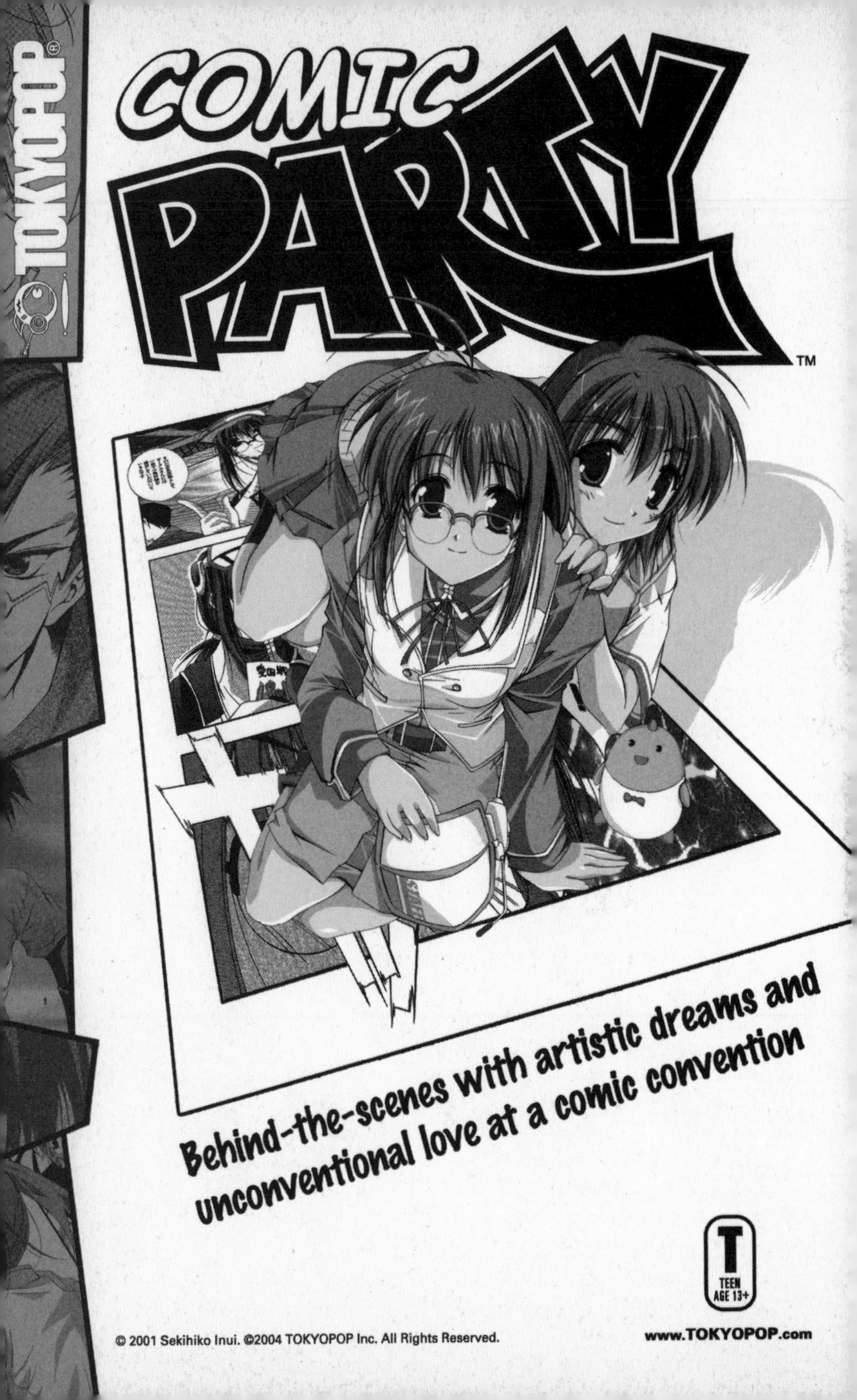
TOKYOPOP®
COMIC PARTY™
Behind-the-scenes with artistic dreams and unconventional love at a comic convention
T TEEN AGE 13+
© 2001 Sekihiko Inui. ©2004 TOKYOPOP Inc. All Rights Reserved.
www.TOKYOPOP.com

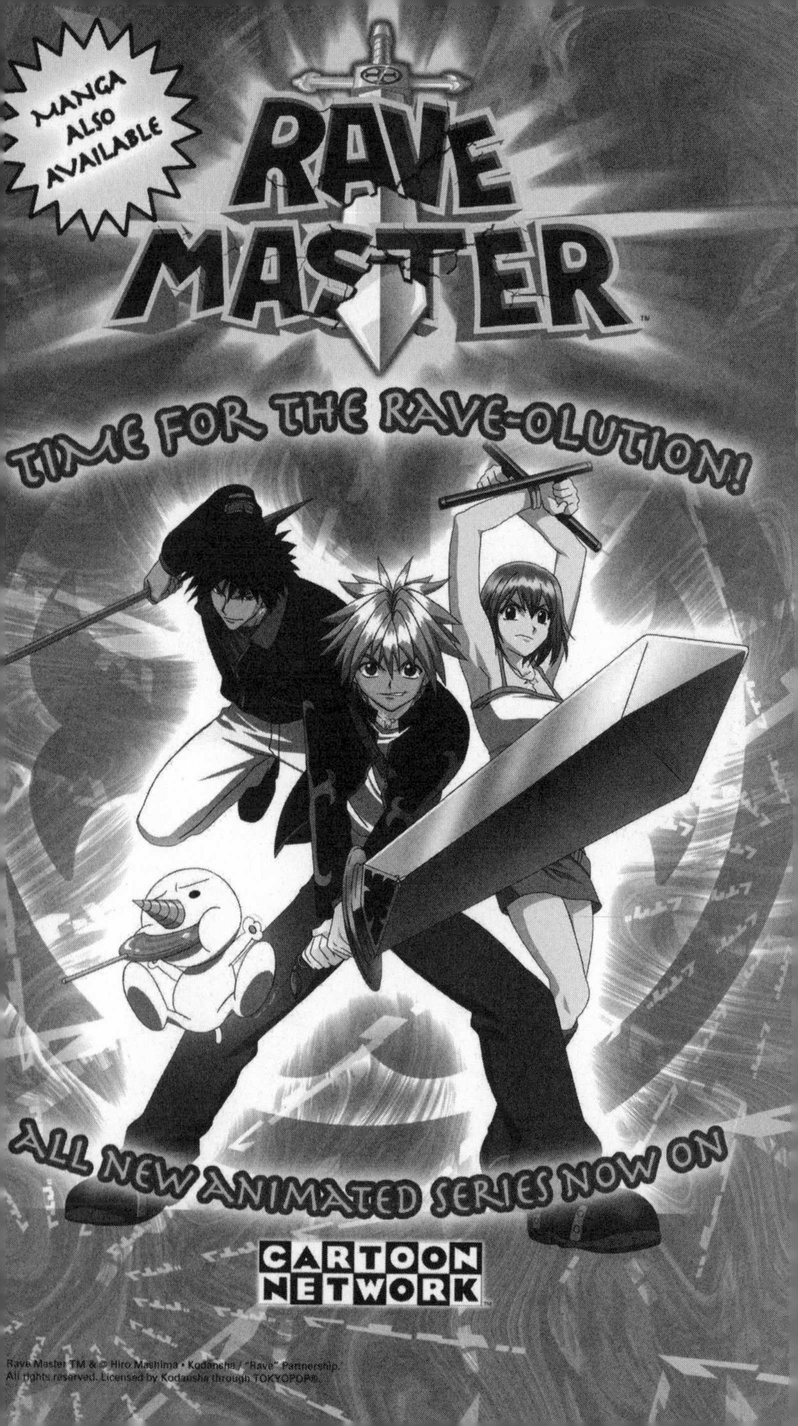
MANGA ALSO AVAILABLE
RAVE MASTER™
TIME FOR THE RAVE-OLUTION!
ALL NEW ANIMATED SERIES NOW ON
CARTOON NETWORK

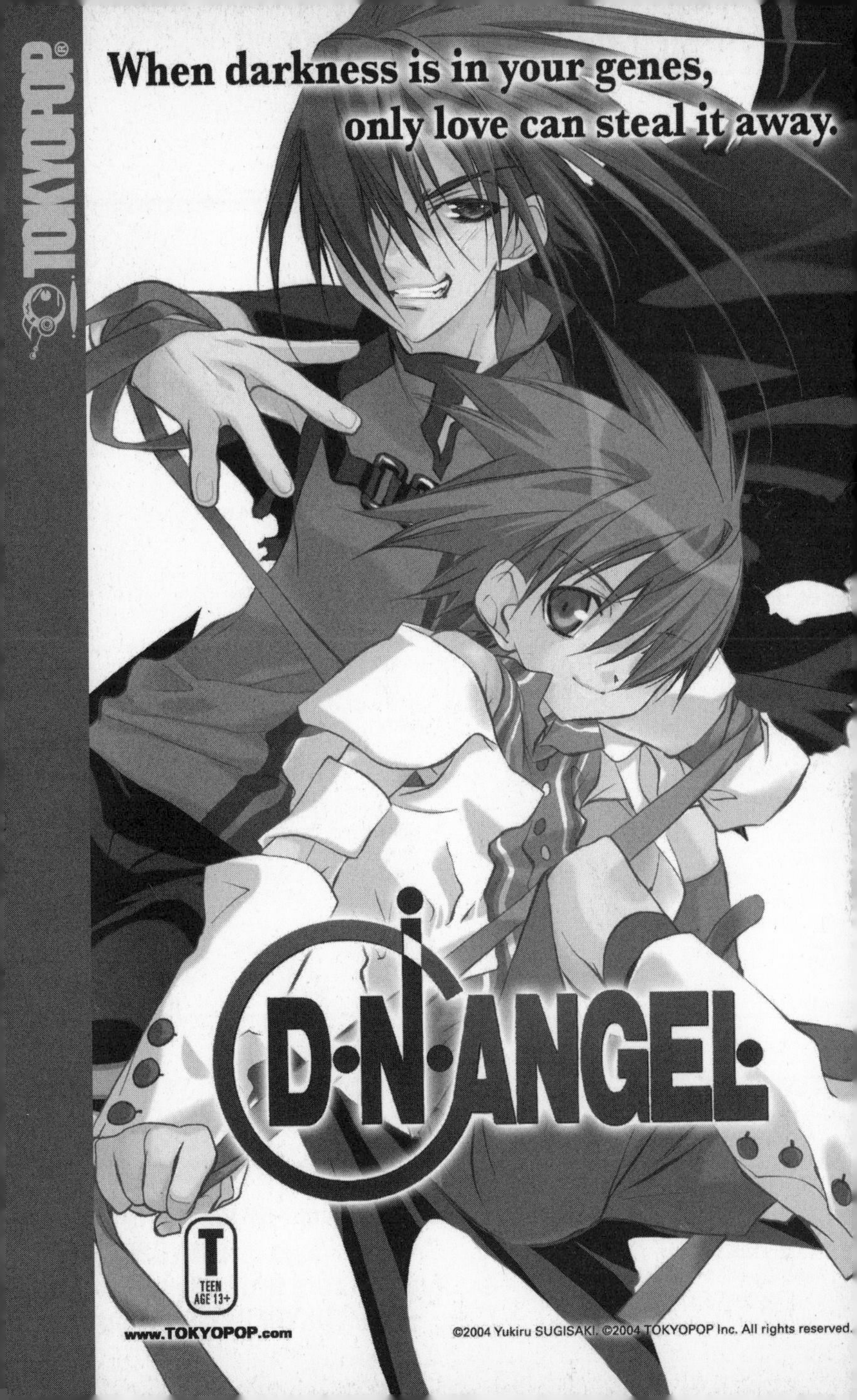
TOKYOPOP
When darkness is in your genes,
only love can steal it away.
D·N·ANGEL
T
TEEN
AGE 13+
www.TOKYOPOP.com
©2004 Yukiru SUGISAKI. ©2004 TOKYOPOP Inc. All rights reserved.

ALSO AVAILABLE FROM TOKYOPOP®

'LANET LADDER
'LANETES
PRIEST
'RINCESS AI
PSYCHIC ACADEMY
QUEEN'S KNIGHT, THE
RAGNAROK
RAVE MASTER
REALITY CHECK
REBIRTH
REBOUND
REMOTE
RISING STARS OF MANGA
SABER MARIONETTE J
SAILOR MOON
SAINT TAIL
SAIYUKI
SAMURAI DEEPER KYO
SAMURAI GIRL REAL BOUT HIGH SCHOOL
SCRYED
SEIKAI TRILOGY, THE
SGT. FROG
HAOLIN SISTERS
HIRAHIME-SYO: SNOW GODDESS TALES
HUTTERBOX
KULL MAN, THE
NOW DROP
ORCERER HUNTERS
TONE
UIKODEN III
UKI
HREADS OF TIME
OKYO BABYLON
OKYO MEW MEW
OKYO TRIBES
RAMPS LIKE US
NDER THE GLASS MOON
AMPIRE GAME
ISION OF ESCAFLOWNE, THE
VARRIORS OF TAO
VILD ACT
VISH
VORLD OF HARTZ
-DAY
ODIAC P.I.

NOVELS

LAMP SCHOOL PARANORMAL INVESTIGATORS
ARMA CLUB
AILOR MOON
LAYERS

RT BOOKS

RT OF CARDCAPTOR SAKURA
RT OF MAGIC KNIGHT RAYEARTH, THE
EACH: MIWA UEDA ILLUSTRATIONS

ANIME GUIDES

COWBOY BEBOP
GUNDAM TECHNICAL MANUALS
SAILOR MOON SCOUT GUIDES

TOKYOPOP KIDS

STRAY SHEEP

CINE-MANGA™

ALADDIN
CARDCAPTORS
DUEL MASTERS
FAIRLY ODDPARENTS, THE
FAMILY GUY
FINDING NEMO
G.I. JOE SPY TROOPS
GREATEST STARS OF THE NBA
JACKIE CHAN ADVENTURES
JIMMY NEUTRON: BOY GENIUS, THE ADVENTURES OF
KIM POSSIBLE
LILO & STITCH: THE SERIES
LIZZIE MCGUIRE
LIZZIE MCGUIRE MOVIE, THE
MALCOLM IN THE MIDDLE
POWER RANGERS: DINO THUNDER
POWER RANGERS: NINJA STORM
PRINCESS DIARIES 2
RAVE MASTER
SHREK 2
SIMPLE LIFE, THE
SPONGEBOB SQUAREPANTS
SPY KIDS 2
SPY KIDS 3-D: GAME OVER
THAT'S SO RAVEN
TOTALLY SPIES
TRANSFORMERS: ARMADA
TRANSFORMERS: ENERGON
VAN HELSING

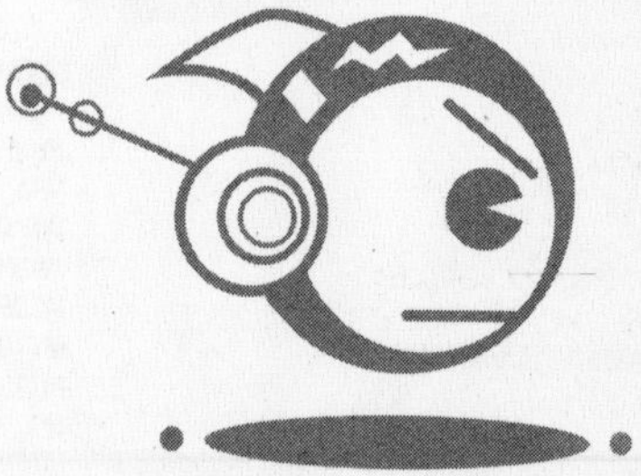

You want it? We got it!
A full range of TOKYOPOP products are available now at:
www.TOKYOPOP.com/shop

04.23.04T

ALSO AVAILABLE FROM 🐢 TOKYOPOP®

MANGA

.HACK//LEGEND OF THE TWILIGHT
@LARGE
ABENOBASHI: MAGICAL SHOPPING ARCADE
A.I. LOVE YOU
AI YORI AOSHI
ANGELIC LAYER
ARM OF KANNON
BABY BIRTH
BATTLE ROYALE
BATTLE VIXENS
BRAIN POWERED
BRIGADOON
B'TX
CANDIDATE FOR GODDESS, THE
CARDCAPTOR SAKURA
CARDCAPTOR SAKURA - MASTER OF THE CLOW
CHOBITS
CHRONICLES OF THE CURSED SWORD
CLAMP SCHOOL DETECTIVES
CLOVER
COMIC PARTY
CONFIDENTIAL CONFESSIONS
CORRECTOR YUI
COWBOY BEBOP
COWBOY BEBOP: SHOOTING STAR
CRAZY LOVE STORY
CRESCENT MOON
CROSS
CULDCEPT
CYBORG 009
D•N•ANGEL
DEMON DIARY
DEMON ORORON, THE
DEUS VITAE
DIABOLO
DIGIMON
DIGIMON TAMERS
DIGIMON ZERO TWO
DOLL
DRAGON HUNTER
DRAGON KNIGHTS
DRAGON VOICE
DREAM SAGA
DUKLYON: CLAMP SCHOOL DEFENDERS
EERIE QUEERIE!
ERICA SAKURAZAWA: COLLECTED WORKS
ET CETERA
ETERNITY
EVIL'S RETURN
FAERIES' LANDING
FAKE
FLCL
FLOWER OF THE DEEP SLEEP
FORBIDDEN DANCE
FRUITS BASKET
G GUNDAM

GATEKEEPERS
GETBACKERS
GIRL GOT GAME
GIRLS' EDUCATIONAL CHARTER
GRAVITATION
GTO
GUNDAM BLUE DESTINY
GUNDAM SEED ASTRAY
GUNDAM WING
GUNDAM WING: BATTLEFIELD OF PACIFISTS
GUNDAM WING: ENDLESS WALTZ
GUNDAM WING: THE LAST OUTPOST (G-UNIT)
GUYS' GUIDE TO GIRLS
HANDS OFF!
HAPPY MANIA
HARLEM BEAT
I.N.V.U.
IMMORTAL RAIN
INITIAL D
INSTANT TEEN: JUST ADD NUTS
ISLAND
JING: KING OF BANDITS
JING: KING OF BANDITS - TWILIGHT TALES
JULINE
KARE KANO
KILL ME, KISS ME
KINDAICHI CASE FILES, THE
KING OF HELL
KODOCHA: SANA'S STAGE
LAMENT OF THE LAMB
LEGAL DRUG
LEGEND OF CHUN HYANG, THE
LES BIJOUX
LOVE HINA
LUPIN III
LUPIN III: WORLD'S MOST WANTED
MAGIC KNIGHT RAYEARTH I
MAGIC KNIGHT RAYEARTH II
MAHOROMATIC: AUTOMATIC MAIDEN
MAN OF MANY FACES
MARMALADE BOY
MARS
MARS: HORSE WITH NO NAME
MINK
MIRACLE GIRLS
MIYUKI-CHAN IN WONDERLAND
MODEL
MY LOVE
NECK AND NECK
ONE
ONE I LOVE, THE
PARADISE KISS
PARASYTE
PASSION FRUIT
PEACH GIRL
PEACH GIRL: CHANGE OF HEART
PET SHOP OF HORRORS
PITA-TEN

04.23.04T

STOP!

This is the back of the book.
You wouldn't want to spoil a great ending!

This book is printed "manga-style," in the authentic Japanese right-to-left format. Since none of the artwork has been flipped or altered, readers get to experience the story just as the creator intended. You've been asking for it, so TOKYOPOP® delivered: authentic, hot-off-the-press, and far more fun!

DIRECTIONS

If this is your first time reading manga-style, here's a quick guide to help you understand how it works.

It's easy… just start in the top right panel and follow the numbers. Have fun, and look for more 100% authentic manga from TOKYOPOP®!